D1569909

DATE DUE			

WEST CAMPUS

If We Must Die

If We Must Die

African American Voices on War and Peace

Edited by
Karin L. Stanford

ROWMAN & LITTLEFIELD PUBLISHERS, INC.
Lanham • Boulder • New York • Toronto • Plymouth, UK

ROWMAN & LITTLEFIELD PUBLISHERS, INC.

Published in the United States of America
by Rowman & Littlefield Publishers, Inc.
A wholly owned subsidiary of The Rowman & Littlefield Publishing Group, Inc.
4501 Forbes Boulevard, Suite 200, Lanham, Maryland 20706
www.rowmanlittlefield.com

Estover Road
Plymouth PL6 7PY
United Kingdom

British Library Cataloguing in Publication Information Available

Library of Congress Cataloging-in-Publication Data

If we must die : African American voices on war and peace / edited by Karin L.
    Stanford.
        p. cm.
    Includes bibliographical references and index.
    ISBN-13: 978-0-7425-4113-9 (cloth : alk. paper)
    ISBN-10: 0-7425-4113-4 (cloth : alk. paper)
    ISBN-13: 978-0-7425-4114-6 (pbk. : alk. paper)
    ISBN-10: 0-7425-4114-2 (pbk. : alk. paper)
    1. United States—History, Military. 2. African Americans—History. 3. United
States—Armed Forces—African Americans—History. 4. African Americans—Social
conditions. 5. Patriotism—United States—History. 6. Black nationalism—United
States—History. 7. War and society—United States—History. 8. Peace—History.
I. Stanford, Karin L., 1961–
E181.I26 2008
355.00973—dc22   2007046310

Printed in the United States of America

♾™ The paper used in this publication meets the minimum requirements of
American National Standard for Information Sciences—Permanence of Paper
for Printed Library Materials, ANSI/NISO Z39.48-1992.

To the Spirit and convictions of African Americans
who fought in America's wars and
to those who conscientiously objected

If this is a white man's government, and we grant that it is, let him take care of it. The Negro has no flag to defend.

—Bishop Henry McNeal Turner, May 1899

We have never betrayed or deceived you. You know that as it has been, so it will be. Whether in war or in peace, whether in slavery or in freedom, we have always been loyal to the Stars and Stripes.

—Booker T. Washington, October 1898

~

Contents

Acknowledgments

Several individuals provided invaluable assistance to the development and production of this work. Julianne Malveaux and Ronald W. Walters both encouraged me to write on African American perspectives on America's wars. Malveaux provided the impetus to write on this topic by including my article in her anthology *The Paradox of Loyalty: An African American Response to the War on Terrorism*. As usual, Ronald Walters gave me the confidence and support to move forward.

I am especially grateful to those who took the time to engage me in discussions about the direction of this project. Scot Brown shared his research on African Americans in the Philippines and directed me to wonderful sources for the book. The "Georgia State crew," specifically Charles Jones, Mukungu Akinyele and Akinyele Umoja also responded enthusiastically to my request for information, ideas and resources. I owe an enormous debt of gratitude to the late Damu Smith, my comrade and hero, who gave me critical suggestions and provided serious analysis about African American internationalism for the narrative. I hope by some small measure that this work is a reflection of his spirit and commitment. I must also give a "shout out" to Maurice Carney, who helped me reconsider the ideological framework and contributed his thoughts to the introduction.

I am also indebted to Rafiki Cai and Jim Barmier, who both helped to shape the entire manuscript. Their research, analysis and enthusiasm for this project were indispensable. A special shout out to Garfield Bright, my friend and colleague who took time out from his busy schedule to edit and lend his creativity to this manuscript. The respect that I have for Bright's intellectual gifts cannot be measured in words. Deep thanks also to Meri Danquah, Eric Burrell, James Simmons and Isaac Gordon for your inspiration, insights and for continuing to cheer me on.

It would not have been possible to complete this manuscript without my Northridge family. I relied on the continual support of my good friends Vicki White, Erica Pace and Ivie O'Brian, who made it possible for me to write by providing a safe and loving enviroment for my daughter, Ashley. I am also grateful to Stella Theodoulou, the Dean of the College of Social and Behavioral Sciences for funding the entire manuscript, and Pan African Studies Professors Tom Spencer Walters and Johnie Scott who both edited and commented on the work. Several students assisted in this project: Season Barnette, Rebecca Fenderson, Patrice Ferguson, Antoinette Griffin, Phallon Phyffer and Jasmin Young. These students selected important documents, engaged in research, prepared biographical profiles and found other important historical data that ultimately enriched this manuscript. Phallon and Jasmin both took on the arduous task of securing permissions so that we could use the commentaries in this volume. Jasmin, I can't say enough about how much your commitment to this project meant to me. Not only did you directly support this work, but you supported my daughter—helping her to adjust to my long hours of editing. I am also thankful to Lynn Lampert, a reference librarian at CSUN who went above and beyond her job requirements to help secure permissions for this project.

And finally, thanks to my editors at Rowman & Littlefield for turning this book idea into a reality. Jennifer Knerr, my first editor, believed in this project, while Renee Leggett provided administrative support and encouragement. Thanks also to my new editorial team, Niels Aaboe and Asa Johnson, for shepherding the book through. And finally, to those who granted us permission to use their commentaries for this book, I am eternally grateful.

~

Introduction

The first casualty when war comes is truth.

—Hiram Johnson

From the Revolutionary War to the current hostilities in Iraq, warfare has been used by U.S. officials as an instrument to preserve or to destroy the status quo. Thus, the United States and war have been constant bedfellows. Even still, U.S. citizens have been sharply divided about the value and usefulness of war. This conundrum about supporting the nation's wars has been especially true for African Americans. Considering their subjection to forced servitude; blatant denial of equal social, political, economic and cultural rights; and rampant discrimination under the guise of Jim Crowism, African Americans have long questioned the goals and objectives of U.S. wars. The lingering question has been, should African Americans, who have suffered under a system of discrimination merely because of their skin color, be concerned with preserving the broader idea of nationality when the nation is at war, or should they deny their support until the race problem at home is resolved? If African Americans support the nation, even while being denied basic civil and human rights, would they then be supporting hypocritical values?

From every angle of the prism, African Americans have juxtaposed their country's wars with their domestic experiences, acutely aware that non–African Americans have initiated every one of the nation's violent conflicts since the Revolutionary War: white Americans hold the primary positions of power;

1

influence the power structure that sets in motion the military's wars; own the companies that make the weapons of war; determine how wars are financed; hold the key decision-making positions in the U.S. armed forces; create the rules of military engagement; and ultimately direct wars as commanders-in-chief. For the most part, what has been left for African Americans is to purchase war bonds and serve as soldiers.

Even so, despite the apparent contradictions between the stated war objectives of the U.S. and the reality of their lives, African American attitudes toward the military and U.S. wars have not always been monolithic. Some African Americans have supported the various war efforts by joining the military, even if it was simply to gain greater economic opportunities or to escape a haunting life of poverty and stagnation. Others have endorsed the nation's military actions because they detested the enemy or believed that their involvement might relieve the suffering of African or other oppressed people in various parts of the world. Still others have identified with the United States—not necessarily because they have felt fully accepted as equal citizens but rather because they consider it their country and are therefore willing to fight to protect their homeland and loved ones. The most optimistic African Americans believe that their country has made important and fundamental changes in racial and social relations, despite its imperfections. Clearly, there is evidence that African Americans have improved their lives and gained respect during the last century, and certainly those improvements can be linked to the loyalty demonstrated by fighting in America's wars.

On the opposite end of the spectrum are those African Americans who generally oppose U.S. war endeavors and sometimes even express particular disdain for the U.S. military. Having no proof that inequality and discrimination would ever end, given the capitalistic and racist superstructure, they object to African Americans dying on the battlefield for a country that has consistently treated them as subhuman. Even integrationists, such as Frederick Douglass, mocked the patriotism that government officials asked of them during times of war. In a speech during the U.S.-Mexican War, after having returned to the U.S. from exile in England, Douglass said:

> Ours is a glorious land, and from across the Atlantic we welcome those who are stricken by the storms of despotism. Yet the damning fact remains, there is not a rood of earth under the stars and the eagle on your flag, where a man of my complexion can stand free. There is no mountain so high, no plain so extensive, no spot so sacred, that it can secure to me the right of liberty . . .
>
> No, I make no pretension to patriotism. So long as my voice can be heard on this or the other side of the Atlantic, I will hold up America to the light-

ning scorn of moral indignation. In doing this, I shall feel myself discharging the duty of a true patriot; for he is a lover of his country who rebukes and does not excuse its sins.[1]

In 1963, more than one hundred years later, Malcolm X, national spokesman for the Nation of Islam, also addressed the issue of patriotism while making a direct connection to the issue of war. In an interview with Gordon Parks published in *Life* magazine in 1963, the Black leader questioned why African Americans would show respect for the U.S. flag:

The black man has died under the flag. His women have been raped under it. He has been oppressed, and beaten under it—and still . . . they'll ask him to fight their enemies under it. I'll do my fighting right here at home, where the enemy looks me in the eye every day of my life. I'm not talking against the flag. I'm talking about it![2]

At each stage in their sociocultural evolution, including slavery and government-mandated segregation, African Americans have vociferously articulated their perspectives on issues of war and peace. Even as the country matured and African Americans began to play more central roles in national decision making, the question of supporting U.S. war policy has continued to provoke loud and piercing debate within the African American community.

African American Perspectives on War and Peace

African American perspectives on America's wars can be categorized into two types. The first is the integrationist/patriotic perspective. Those who advocate this point of view believe that supporting U.S. foreign policy objectives and fighting in America's wars is the duty of African Americans—simply because, granted by the 14th Amendment, they are Americans. Inherent in the ideology of integrationism is the belief that racial problems within the U.S. can be resolved. Furthermore, African Americans can prove they deserve fair treatment by demonstrating a willingness to defend the U.S. and make the ultimate sacrifice for their country. An excellent example of this view was set forth by Booker T. Washington during the Spanish-American War, when he praised African Americans for choosing to side with their country. Washington said, "When a few months ago, the safety and honor of the Republic were threatened by a foreign foe, when the wail and anguish of the oppressed from a distant isle reached his ears, we find the

Negro forgetting the laws and customs that discriminate against him in his own country, and again we find our black citizen choosing the better part."[3]

The second perspective is embedded in the ideology of Black nationalism, which advocates Black pride, unity and group self-reliance. Black nationalists believe that racism is the primary cause of African American subordination and that there can be no peace with white Americans until systemic racial discrimination and subordination is abolished. Inherent in Black nationalism is a Pan African consciousness that obligates Africans to support each other everywhere.[4] Proponents of this approach stress that U.S. foreign policy is not divorced from the domestic experiences of African Americans: on the contrary, it is often intertwined. Accordingly, the experiences of African Americans are viewed as an authentic barometer for assessing U.S. motives abroad. Contradictions of U.S. foreign policy on issues of liberty and equality are emphasized by those who embrace a nationalist perspective. They argue ultimately that if the U.S. government is serious about adhering to the principles of democracy and liberty for all of its citizens, then it would first promote true equality inside the United States. Consequently, support for U.S. foreign policy objectives should only occur if the result is a tangible benefit for their community.

Although the Black nationalist approach can be considered isolationist, that is not always the case. Black nationalists are isolationist in their contention that the U.S. should work to reslove its racial and domestic discord at home before becoming embroiled in avoidable international conflicts. However, because nationalism embodies a Pan African perspective and supports the liberation of African people everywhere, it accepts intervention in the interest of uplifting or defending African nations, those in the African diaspora and other oppressed people. Integrationists, on the other hand, are more likely to accept the idea that the "darker races" or Third World nations should be supported by Western countries —but only to the extent that they accept Western-style democracy or other "civilizing" principles.

In general, African Americans show an affinity for anti-imperialism and anti-interventionism unless human life is at stake. Expansionism, if it occurs at all, should benefit or support underdeveloped or oppressed nations, and primarily fortify that nation. However, one should note that in the Black ideological and political tradition, it is not uncommon for African Americans to switch perspectives as circumstances change. A. Philip Randolph, for instance, argued against World War I, but economic interests prompted his support for African American integration into the defense industries during World War II.

At the same time, categorizing African American international perspectives into the realist or idealist conceptual models that are traditionally used to explain U.S. foreign affairs can be difficult. Realism or Realpolitik supports policies that are rooted in reality or see the world as it really is. This approach argues that U.S. foreign affairs must be based on practical concerns and therefore promoting its national interests in policy development and implementation is only natural and also required. Realists are philosophically opposed to idealists, who see the world as it ought to be and therefore seek to develop policies that will produce humanitarian, moral and collective outcomes that can benefit the international community at large.[5] Secretary of State Henry Kissinger was well known for advocating a realist approach in his dealings with the Soviet Union during the Cold War era, and therefore arguing for military build-up as protection against Soviet expansionism.

On the opposite end of the realist/idealist continuum was President Woodrow Wilson who, in 1918, enunciated "Fourteen Points" during the First World War as a philosophy to help maintain peace. The Fourteen Points were based on idealistic principles that included open diplomacy, the creation of the League of Nations, removal of economic trade barriers, international supervision of colonies and disarmament. Although there is certainly a degree of realism in African American war perspectives, its leadership and public tend to support idealism.

Clearly, history demonstrates that African American opinions on U.S. wars are impacted by the existence of racism, oppression and inequality. Similar to the views expressed by Third World leaders who supported the "Non-Aligned Movement," a group of nation-states who rebuffed an alignment with the major power blocs during the Cold War, African Americans look forward in hope that the international community will reject the exploitation of indigenous people for territorial or monetary gain. That perspective is reflected in a large number of the commentaries in this book.

Outlook and Organization

The title *If We Must Die: African American Voices on War and Peace* is drawn from the poem "If We Must Die" written by Claude McKay at the end of World War I, during the Red Summer of 1919. This was a time when African Americans were subjected to random racial violence and lynchings. McKay's defiant poem reflected the resolve of African Americans to defend themselves and fight back against violence and oppression. In this context, *If We Must Die* reflects that same sentiment—but moreover, it indicates the will to fight for honor, liberty and democracy, even if the cost is death. For African Americans aligned with the U.S. during wartime, *If We Must Die* is an expression of loyalty, patriotism and concurrence with U.S. actions. Those

African Americans have been willing to sacrifice their lives as evidence of their support to the nation. On the opposite side are those African Americans who were also willing to risk their lives, not to support the U.S. war effort, but to advance the cause of their community, by speaking out, even at the risk of harassment, persecution, or death administered by their own government.

If We Must Die is organized by America's major wars. Each chapter begins with an introduction that describes the war, its causes, important foreign policy issues, the African American condition during the time of the war and the context for the African American response. Following each introduction the book also contains the first-person commentary of African American leaders, intellectuals, noted figures and average citizens—to allow the voices to speak themselves.

The African American voices that make up this collection come from a myriad of locales. Some are deep in the trenches, next to the velocity of war, while others are far away, standing on some political or social platform. Although this book does not emphasize the role of military figures, they are examined because of their important contributions to a particular war. Moreover, the treatment of soldiers often provides the stimulus for discussion by African Americans on war.

Although historically war is considered to be a masculine endeavor, African American women commented on America's wars as well. Certainly, their commentary supported the views of their male counterparts, but also highlighted the distinct concerns of women during wartime. Their observations added to the richness of views in the book.

Given the challenge of presenting a cross section of African American opinions on America's wars in one volume, limiting the scope was essential. Space limitations and repetitiveness also required that this work spotlight the larger wars and those that potentially had greater opportunity to touch the lives of African Americans, either as participants, beneficiaries or observers. Accordingly, smaller wars—such as the Mexican-American war— were excluded.

The commentaries selected for inclusion were based on their significance to the war, the era and/or which best represented a particular point of view. Not all of the commentaries are directly related to a war, but if the remarks helped to illuminate the context of African American wartime expression, then it was incorporated in this volume. All things considered, the documents included were based both on the availability of African American expression and the uniqueness of the perspective. Of course, a principal limitation is that not all African American expressions are written or have been recorded. Who knows what insights have been lost either out of illiteracy or because the expression was never preserved?

The intent of this work was to provide a balance of perspectives and a diversity of opinions, both to highlight the richness of African American expression and to avoid any unintentional slanting. However, considering that African American views are rooted in the experiences of slavery, exploitation and racism, commentary critical of U.S. wars constitutes a greater portion of this book. Even so, although much is critical, little is typical: instead each voice reflects experience dictated by unique perspectives filtered through an African American consciousness. If that voice is negative, that is their perception of the truth.

African Americans have lived in a country founded on democratic principles, while constantly being denied the benefits that should theoretically result from such egalitarian notions—including the opportunity to pursue life, liberty and happiness. How they responded to that contradiction during times of war determines the tone, slant and pitch of their voice.

Notes

1. Frederick Douglass, speech made in Syracuse, New York, in 1847. Reprinted in *A Patriot's Handbook*, ed. Caroline Kennedy (New York: Hyperion, 2003), 202–3.

2. Gordon Parks, interview with Malcolm X in "What Their Cry Means to Me," *Life Magazine*, May 31, 1963, 3.

3. Booker T. Washington, "An Address in the National Peace Jubilee," October 16, 1898. *The Booker T. Washington Papers*, ed. Louis R. Harlan and Raymond W. Smock (Urbana: University of Illinois Press, 1975), 4:490–92.

4. For a detailed discussion on Black ideology and the tenets of Black integrationism and Black nationalism, see Robert C. Smith, "Ideology as an Enduring Dilemma of Black Politics," in *Dilemmas of Black Politics*, ed. Georgia Persons (New York: HarperCollins, 1993).

5. Jack C. Plano and Roy Olton, *The International Relations Dictionary* (Kalamazoo, Mich.: New Issues Press, 1969), 133–34.

CHAPTER ONE

~

Revolutionary War:
My Liberation, Your Freedom

1775–1783

More than 500,000 enslaved people of African descent lived in America in 1776, the year the 13 colonies declared their independence from England.[1] Crucial to the economy and social structure, slave labor produced the key export crops of the South, including tobacco, rice and indigo. Although the system of chattel slavery was highly profitable for many Europeans, for the slave, life was untenable at best. After suffering through 5 to 12 weeks of the "Middle Passage," which brought African people to America in chains, they were dehumanized and sold as property to European colonists, royalists and others. The African slaves had no legal rights, voting rights, civil rights or family rights.

The colonial governments adopted laws and restrictive codes to control their slaves. The codes limited their movements, set forth rules for selling slaves and required them to carry a pass when traveling away from their owner's plantation. The laws also allowed for harsh punishment for those who attempted to escape, including whipping, branding, mutilation or even castration. Supplementing the formal laws were informal rules. Women were not allowed to decline their owners' sexual advances, and slaves had to suffer even more indignation when speaking to their owner, whom they were required to refer to as "master."

African slaves, however, were not docile candidates for exploitation. Many slaves pressed for the abolition of slavery in many ways. In 1773, slaves living in Boston and other towns in Massachusetts signed and presented a "Petition of Slaves in Boston" to the governor of Massachusetts, his council, and the

House of Representatives. The petition requested government officials to "take [the slaves'] unhappy state and condition under your wise and just consideration" and grant "such relief as is consistent with your wisdom, justice and goodness."[2] Others rose up against slavery using more violent methods. Herbert Aptheker documented 250 slave revolts between 1700 and 1860.[3] Slave owners were aware of the desire for freedom among the enslaved, and many lived in fear of the Africans under their control.

The most viable opportunity for freedom arose from the growing tension between the British Royals and the American colonies. For more than a decade, colonists endured the proclamations of King George III and the English Parliament, which levied taxes against them through such devices as the Sugar Act of 1764 and the Stamp Act of 1765.[4] Other decrees that limited their right to self-governance included the Currency Act (1766), which prohibited the colonists from issuing any legal tender paper money, and the Quartering Act (1765), which required colonists to house British troops and supply them with food.

The colonists attempted to wrest their freedom from tyrannical British rule by using a variety of tactics. In February 1768, Samuel Adams, a colonial legislator of Massachusetts, wrote a circular letter opposing taxation without representation and called on the colonists to unite in their actions against the British government. In 1769, merchants from Philadelphia and New Jersey were the first to formally boycott British goods. Perhaps the most well-known rebellious act occurred in 1773, when colonial activists disguised as Mohawk Indians boarded British ships and dumped 342 containers of tea into the harbor. This event, later labeled the "Boston Tea Party," was a response to the three-penny-per-pound import tax on tea arriving in the colonies. The virtual tea monopoly given to British East India Company allowed it to sell directly to colonial agents, bypassing any middlemen and thus underselling American merchants.

The conflict between the colonists and the British government was further exacerbated in 1774, when representatives from the 13 English colonies met in Congress to formally oppose the British government's "coercive acts." Soon thereafter, military skirmishes occurred between British soldiers and Massachusetts militiamen. On April 18, 1775, an unordered "shot heard around the world" led to the beginning of the American Revolution. Believing that they were about to become engaged in a very bloody battle against the British for independence, the colonists, led by John Hancock, held the Second Continental Congress in Philadelphia in May 1775. During this tense meeting the Congress placed the colonies in a state of defense. Then, on June 15, Congress unanimously voted to appoint George Washington general and commander-in-chief of the new Continental Army.

The colonial patriots were indeed spirited in their indignation of England's infringement upon their liberty—so spirited that many actually framed themselves as "slaves." John Dickinson, the largest slaveholder in Philadelphia, wrote in 1768: "Those who are taxed without their own consent, expressed by themselves or their representatives, are slaves. We are therefore—SLAVES."[5] During a meeting of the Second Continental Congress the delegates issued a "Declaration on the Causes and Necessity of Taking Up Arms," detailing the colonists' reasons for fighting the British, which stated that the Americans were "resolved to die free men rather than live as slaves."[6]

Of course, contradicting the colonists' eloquent articulation of their support for freedom, liberty and independence was the reality that many of them benefited from slavery. African thinkers, such as Olaudah Equiano, the former slave who wrote of his experiences during the Middle Passage, vigorously criticized the Christians for their treatment of Blacks.[7] White colonists also pointed to the contradiction of the slaveholders. Thomas Paine, noted author of *Common Sense,* who openly challenged the British for independence, stated, "With what consistency, or decency, [colonists] complain so loudly of attempts to enslave them, while they hold so many hundred thousand in slavery."[8] This open critique of American slaveholders was also made by many Quakers, and the likes of one 21-year-old Benjamin Franklin, a printer who published several anti-slavery tracts.

The British governor of Virginia, Lord Dunmore, saw the contradictions and vulnerability of the South's slaveholders. In particular, he noted that Africans bound in servitude vastly outnumbered the Continental Army's 18,000 men. Lord Dunmore believed that by persuading slaves and free Blacks to fight on the side of the British that the colonists might well be defeated. In November 1775, Dunmore issued a proclamation promising freedom to any slave of a rebel who could make it to the British lines.

For those enslaved, freedom offered from any hand, even the British, was a welcome blessing. Thousands of slaves responded. Thomas Jefferson calculated that in 1778, 30,000 slaves fled Virginia. In addition, from 1775 to 1783, 25,000 slaves fled South Carolina. Dunmore was able to organize an "Ethiopian" brigade of about 300 former slaves who saw action at the Battle of Great Bridge, which took place seven months before the Declaration of Independence. The battle resulted in the capture of Norfolk by the Americans and led to the expulsion of Dunmore and the British from Virginia.[9]

Eventually, the British decision to include Africans in their ranks paid dividends. A Charleston slave named Duncan supplied field intelligence to the British that gave them considerable advantage during the siege of Charleston in May of 1780. During this battle, 6,000 American soldiers surrendered along with five ships and 300 cannons, marking one of the greatest British victories of the war. Other escaped slaves who fought for the British included Colonel Tye, a Black soldier who led a Black brigade that wreaked havoc upon the colonists in New Jersey and New York, and Boston King, a runaway slave from South Carolina who survived smallpox, escaped from capture by slave-hunters and later emigrated to Sierra Leone where he became a schoolmaster.[10]

Despite the large number of slaves that fled the Southern states and their potential to swell the ranks of the British army, the Southern colonists were very hesitant to arm their slaves to fight in the War for Independence. They feared slave revolts more than their lack of manpower to face the British. Their fear was so great that the majority of Southern representatives to the Continental Congress supported efforts to expel freed slaves who had already enlisted in the Continental Army. Committees of Safety, organized throughout the colonies, constantly met to express their fears about revolts from armed slaves.[11] As a slaveholder himself, George Washington was well aware of the sentiment of Southern slaveholders, and at the beginning of the war he issued a proclamation forbidding even freed Blacks from joining the Continental Army.[12] He later experienced a change of heart, reversing his mandate as the manpower needs of the Continental Army became greater and greater.

Many others, particularly in the New England states, believed that Black enlistment was necessary to defeat the British. In a letter to John Jay, Alexander Hamilton declared that enlisting Blacks as soldiers "promises very important advantages . . . I have not the least doubt that the Negroes will make very excellent soldiers, with proper management."[13]

Thus colonial Americans found themselves split over the question of arming Africans to support their war for independence. On one hand, the Continental Army needed all the soldiers it could recruit against the British. On the other, Southerners feared that their own slaves would become emboldened to liberate themselves through armed rebellion.

In the Northern states, the solution was to sparingly allow freed Blacks to enlist. Noted men like Prince Hall, who would become the legendary leader of Black Masons in America, and Lemuel Hayes, a noted minister, took up the call.

Other free Blacks and former slaves contributed greatly to the War for Independence. Crispus Attucks was the first person killed during the Boston Massacre of 1770. Salem Poor fought for Washington's army at White Plains, New York, and at Valley Forge. Peter Salem, who was a slave, became a member of the famous Massachusetts Minutemen. He served in the Battles of Lexington, Bunker Hill, Concord and Saratoga—the first American victory of the war. The Virginia slave James Armistead served as a spy for the French nobleman Marquis de Lafayette. He provided vital information to the Continental Army after he infiltrated the British lines at Yorktown posing as a runaway slave. Prince Whipple crossed the Delaware with General Washington, and Washington's slave, William Lee, served with him throughout the War for Independence.

Black women also distinguished themselves. Deborah Gannett (aka Molly Pitcher) enlisted and served as a soldier in the Revolutionary Army for over a year. Originating from Massachusetts, Gannett disguised herself as a man and used the name Robert Shurtliff. Gannett was later granted a pension for her service.[14]

The first Black regiment was from Rhode Island. The 132-man regiment was formed in 1778 when the state announced that slaves volunteering for battle would be "absolutely free" and would receive the same wages and benefits as all other soldiers. The Rhode Island regiment was crucial to the only Revolutionary military engagement in their state. The regiment held the line for four hours against British assaults and helped the American army escape battle. Although the Battle of Rhode Island was lost, heavy casualties were inflicted upon the British.[15]

The Revolutionary War came to a close on April 19, 1783, after the British surrender at Yorktown. The actual peace treaty was signed in September of that year in Paris, France. After the Revolutionary War ended, the colonists began the task of building a new nation. Fifty-five delegates met in convention to draft a constitution that would govern the homeland. Black people living in America had hoped that the ideas represented in the Declaration of Independence and their contribution to the war would influence the delegates at the convention to endorse the principles of freedom and liberty for all. However, the delegates ratified a constitution in 1787 that not only extended the slave trade until 1808, but counted Blacks as three-fifths human in order to boost the representation of the slave states in Congress. Perhaps even more discouraging was the inclusion of a fugitive slave clause, which allowed slave owners to recapture their runaway slaves.[16]

The commentary in this section reflects the views and experiences of Black people during the Revolutionary War. Philliss Wheatley wrote a poem to George Washington urging him to proceed against the English in the cause of liberty. Wheatley believed that the War for Independence would lead to freedom and equality. Slaves wrote several petitions to state legislatures pleading for freedom. One such petition, signed by Freemason Prince Hall, expressed "astonishment that it has never been considered, that every principle from which America has acted, in the course of her unhappy difficulties with Great Britain, bears stronger than a thousand arguments in favor of your humble petitioners."[17] Another petition, signed by Ned Griffin asserted that he should be freed because he served the military on behalf of his master.

Benjamin Banneker, the first African American inventor, mathematician and astronomer, used the Revolutionary War as a springboard for conversations with Secretary of State Thomas Jefferson on how to maintain peace in America, which included the absolute abolishment of slavery and equal treatment of all men. Although huge numbers of Black people pursued freedom during the revolutionary era, very few actually found it. Data shows that as a result of the Revolutionary War, the population of free Blacks increased from about 25,000 in 1776 to nearly 60,000 when the first census was conducted in 1790.[18] Those who did not become free were befallen to a myriad of unfortunate circumstances. Although the number is indeterminable, certainly scores of Blacks were killed in battle. Others were felled by fatal sickness, imprisoned or recaptured and sold back into slavery. Attempts at drawing pensions for their service became an ordeal for Black soldiers.

Blacks who aided the British were in double indemnity. The British did take some Black loyalists to Europe as they retreated from America, and a particular group of 3,000 initially settled in Nova Scotia.[19] Eleven years later a third of them emigrated to Freetown, Sierra Leone, West Africa, because of the harsh conditions and the British government's refusal to provide them with the necessary resources for survival.[20] Boston King's commentary provides insight into the experiences of Black people who fought on the side of the British.

Ultimately, Black involvement in the Revolutionary War validated their cries for freedom. They proved a willingness to fight for their freedom and the freedom of the U.S. Although that freedom was not granted, their poetic genius, wartime public commentary and political and military activism expanded the notions of liberty. Consequently, anti-slavery activism became more prevalent and intense.

PHILLIS WHEATLEY
(1753–1797)

Wheatley was the first African American to publish a book and earn the status of a great African American writer and poet. Born in 1753 in Africa, Phillis Wheatley was kidnapped and sold as a slave at age seven to a prosperous Boston family who educated her. Although she never attended formal school, Wheatley not only learned English, but Greek and Latin as well. In addition to her literary work, she was also a well-known abolitionist. Wheatley wrote a poem of praise to General George Washington for his leadership during the Revolutionary War. The letter and poem moved him to comment on her genius and extraordinary talent. He invited her to visit him in Cambridge and she accepted his invitation the following year.

"To His Excellency General Washington"
October 26, 1775

Sir,

I have taken the freedom to address your Excellency in the enclosed poem, and entreat your acceptance, though I am not insensible of its inaccuracies. Your being appointed by the Grand Continental Congress to be Generalissimo of the armies of North America, together with the fame of your virtues, excite sensations not easy to suppress. Your generosity, therefore, I presume, will pardon the attempt. Wishing your Excellency all possible success in the great cause you are so generously engaged in. I am,

Your Excellency's most obedient humble servant,

Phillis Wheatley

To His Excellency General Washington

Celestial choir! enthron'd in realms of light,
Columbia's scenes of glorious toils I write.
While freedom's cause her anxious breast alarms,
She flashes dreadful in refulgent arms.
See mother earth her offspring's fate bemoan,
And nations gaze at scenes before unknown!
See the bright beams of heaven's revolving light
Involved in sorrows and veil of night!

The goddess comes, she moves divinely fair,
Olive and laurel bind her golden hair:
Wherever shines this native of the skies,
Unnumber'd charms and recent rise.

Muse! bow propitious while my pen relates
How pour her armies through a thousand gates,
As when Eolus heaven's fair face deforms,
Enwrapp'd in tempest and night of storm;
Astonish'd ocean feels the wild uproar,
The refluent surges beat the sounding shore;
Or thick as leaves in Autumn's golden reign,
Such, and so many, moves the warrior's train.
In bright array they seek the work of war,
Where high unfurl'd the ensign waves in the air.
Shall I to Washington their praise recite?
Enough thou know'st them in the fields of fight.
Thee, first in peace and honours,—we demand
The grace and glory of thy marital band.
Fam'd for thy valour, for thy virtues more,
Hear every tongue thy guardian aid implore!
One century scarce perform'd its destined round,
When Gallic powers Columbia's fury found;

And so may you, whoever dares disgrace
The land of freedom's heaven-defended race!
Fix'd are the eyes of nations on the scales,
For in their hopes Columbia's arm prevails.
Anon Britannia droops the pensive head,
While round increase the rising hills of dead,
Ah! cruel blindness to Columbia's state!
Lament they thirst of boundless power to late.

Proceed, great chief, with virtue on thy side,
Thy ev'ry action let the goddess guide.
A crown, a mansion, and a throne that shine,
With gold unfading, WASHINGTON! be thine.

George Washington's Response
February 28, 1776

Miss Phillis:—Your favour of the 26th of October did not reach my hands 'till the middle of December. Time enough, you will say, to have given an answer ere this. Granted. But a variety of important occurences, continually interposing to distract the mind and withdraw the attention, I hope will apologize for the delay, and plead my excuse for the seeming, but not real neglect.

I thank you most sincerely for your polite notice of me, in the elegant Lines you enclosed; and however undeserving I may be of such encomium and panegyrick, the style and manner exhibit a striking proof of your poetical Talents. In honour of which, and as a tribute justly due to you, I would have published the Poem, had I not been apprehensive, that, while I only meant to give the World this new instance of your genius, I might have incurred the imputation of Vanity. This and nothing else, determined me not to give it place in the public Prints.

If you should ever come to Cambridge, or near Head Quarters, I shall be happy to see a person so favoured by the Muses, and to whom Nature has been so liberal and beneficent in her dispensations.

I am, with great Respect, your obedient, humble servant.

NED GRIFFIN
(N.D.)

African people who served in the Revolutionary War hoped they would receive their freedom. There were instances in which white slave masters required their slaves to serve or purchased others to serve in their place. Ned Griffin was sold by his former owner to William Kitchen for such a purpose. In return for his service, Griffin was promised his freedom, but instead, he was forced back into servitude and later sold to Abner Roberson. Below is a petition for freedom by Ned Griffin, who wrote to the General Assembly of North Carolina to plead for his freedom.

Petition to the General Assembly of the State of North Carolina
1784

Ned Griffin

To the General Assembly of the State of North Carolina

The Petitioner of Ned Griffin a Man of mixed Blood Humbley Saieth that a Small space of Time before the Battle of Gilford a certain William Kitchen then in the Service of his Countrey as a Soldier Deserted from his line for which he was Turned in to the Continental Service to serve as the Law Directs—Your Petitioner was then a Servant to William Griffin and was purchased by the said Kitchen for the purpose of Serving in His place, with a Solom Assurance that if he your petitioner would faithfully serve the Term of Time that the said Kitchen was Returned for he should be a free Man—Upon which said Promise and Assurance your Petitioner Consented to enter in to the Continental Service in said Kitchens Behalf and was Received by Colo: James Armstrong at Martinborough as a free Man. Your Petitioner further saieth that at that Time no Person could have been hired to have served in said Kitchens behalf for so small a sum as what I was purchased for and that at the Time that I was Received into Service by said Colo: Armstrong said Kitchen Openly Declaired me to be free Man—

The Faithfull purformance of the above agreement will appear from my Discharge,—some Time after your Petitioners Return he was Seized upon by said Kitchen and Sold to a Certain Abner Roberson who now holds me as Servant—Your Petitioner therefore thinks that by Contract and merit he is Intitled to his Freedom.

I therefore submit my case to your Honourable Body hoping that I shall have that Justice done me as you in your Wisdom shall think I am Intitled to and Deserving of & Your Petitioner as in duty bound Will Pray.[22]

N Carolina

Edgecomb County

April 4th 1784

his

Ned X Griffin

mark

LANCASTER HILL ET AL.
(N.D.)

Massachusetts Slaves Petition for Freedom
n.d.

Resulting from the actions preceding and following the Revolutionary War, Blacks living in the American colonies petitioned various state governments for freedom. The letter printed below is one of the most well-known examples of such petitions and signed by such noted figures as Prince Hall, the founder of Black Masonry in the United States. Although this example was reprinted from William C. Nell's early collection of Black thought during the Revolutionary War era, many other petitions were submitted to states that asserted the belief that Blacks were entitled to the same freedoms that whites achieved as a result of the war against Great Britain.

The petition of a great number of Negroes, who are detained in a state of slavery in the very bowels of a free and Christian country, humbly showing,—

That your petitioners apprehend that they have, in common with all other men, a natural and inalienable right to that freedom, which the great Parent of the universe hath bestowed equally on all mankind, and which they have never forfeited by any compact or agreement whatever. But they were unjustly dragged by the cruel hand of power from their dearest friends, and some of them even torn from the embraces of their tender parents,—from a populous, pleasant and plentiful country, and in violation of the laws of nature and of nations, and in defiance of all the tender feelings of humanity, brought hither to be sold like beasts of burthen, and, like them, condemned to slavery for life—among a people possessing the mild religion of Jesus—a people not insensible of the sweets of national freedom, nor without a spirit to resent the unjust endeavors of others to reduce them to a state of bondage and subjection.

Your Honors need not to be informed that a life of slavery like that of your petitioners, deprived of every social privilege, of every thing requisite to render life even tolerable, is far worse than non-existence.

In imitation of the laudable example of the good people of these States, your petitioners have long and patiently waited the event of petition after petition, by them presented to the legislative body of this State, and cannot but with grief reflect that their success has been but too similar.

They cannot but express their astonishment that it has never been considered, that every principle from which America has acted, in the course of her unhappy difficulties with Great Britain, bears stronger than a thousand arguments in favor of your humble petitioners. They therefore humbly beseech Your Honors to give their petition its due weight and consideration, and cause an act of the legislature to be passed, whereby they may be restored to the enjoyment of that freedom, which is the natural right of all men, and their children (who were born in this land of liberty) may not be held as slaves after they arrive at the age of twenty-one years. So may the inhabitants of this State (no longer chargeable with the inconsistency of acting themselves the part which they condemn and oppose in others) be prospered in their glorious struggles for liberty, and have those blessings secured to them by Heaven, of which benevolent minds cannot wish to deprive their fellow-men.

Any your petitioners, as in duty bound, shall ever pray:—

LANCASTER HILL,
PETER BESS,
BRISTER SLENFEN,
PRINCE HALL,
JACK PIERPONT, [his X mark]
NERO FUNELO, [his X mark]
NEWPORT SUMNER [his X mark]

BOSTON KING
(1760–1802)

Boston King was born a slave near Charleston, South Carolina. At the age of sixteen King was apprenticed to a carpenter. His life was unbearable, as he was often beaten and abused by his master. During the Revolutionary War, King escaped to the British lines after another servant stole a horse he had borrowed. King was one of many slaves who risked their lives in hopes of gaining freedom by fighting for the British. At the war's end King left the United States for England, then Nova Scotia. He later became a schoolteacher and settled in Sierra Leone.

Memoirs of the Life of Boston King: A Black Preacher
1798

My master being apprehensive that Charles-Town was in danger on account of the war, removed into the country, about 38 miles off. Here we built a large house for Mr. Waters, during which time the English took Charles-Town. Having obtained leave one day to see my parents, who lived about 12 miles off, and it being late before I could go, I was obliged to borrow one of Mr. Waters, horses; but a servant of my master's, took the horse from me to go a little journey, and stayed two or three days longer than he ought. This involved me in the greatest perplexity, and I expected the severest punishment, because the gentleman to whom the horse belonged was a very bad man, and knew not how to shew mercy. To escape his cruelty, I determined to go to Charles-Town, and throw myself into the hands of the English. They received me readily, and I began to feel the happiness of liberty, of which I knew nothing before, altho' I was much grieved at first, to be obliged to leave my friends, and reside among strangers. In this situation I was seized with the small-pox, and suffered great hardships; for all the Blacks affected with that disease, were ordered to be carried a mile from the camp, lest the soldiers should be infected, and disabled from marching. This was a grievous circumstance to me and many others. We lay sometimes a whole day without any thing to eat or drink; but Providence sent a man, who belonged to York volunteers whom I was acquainted with, to my relief. He brought me such things as I stood in need of; and by the blessing of the Lord I began to recover.

. . . Being recovered, I marched with the army to Chamblem. When we came to the head-quarters our regiment was 35 miles off. I stayed at the head-quarters three weeks, during which time our regiment had an engagement with the Americans, and the man who relieved me when I was ill of the small-pox, was wounded in the battle, and brought to the hospital. As soon as I heard of his misfortune, I went to see him, and tarried with him in the hospital six weeks, till he recovered; rejoicing that it was in my power to return him the kindness he had shewed me.

From thence I went to a place about 35 miles off, where we stayed two months: at the expiration of which, an express came to the Colonel to decamp in fifteen minutes. When these orders arrived I was at a distance from the camp, catching some fish for the captain that I waited upon; upon returning to the camp, to my great astonishment, I found all the English were gone, and had left only a few militia. I felt my mind greatly alarmed, but Captain Lewes, who commanded the militia, said, "You need not be uneasy, for you will see your regiment before 7 o'clock tonight." This satisfied me for the present, and in two hours we set off.

As were on the march, the Captain asked, "How will you like me to be your master?"

I answered, that I was Captain Grey's servant. "Yes," said he; "but I expect that they are all taken prisoners before now; and I have been long enough in the English service, and am determined to leave them." These words roused my indignation, and I spoke some sharp words to him. But he calmly replied, "If you do not behave well, I will put you in irons, and give you a dozen stripes every morning." I now perceived that my case was desperate, and that I had nothing to trust to, but to wait the first opportunity for making my escape. The next morning, I was sent with a little boy over the river to an island to fetch the Captain some horses. When we came to the Island we found about fifty of the English horses, that Captain Lewes had stolen from them at different times while they were at Rockmount. Upon our return to the Captain with the horses we were sent for, he immediately set off by himself . . .

I tarried with Captain Grey about a year, and then left him, and came to Nelson's-ferry. Here I entered into the service of the commanding officer of that place. But our situation was very precarious, and we expected to be made prisoners every day; for the Americans had 1600 men, not far off; whereas our whole number amounted only to 250: But there were 1200 English about 30 miles off; only we knew not how to inform them of our danger, as the Americans were in possession of the country. Our commander at length determined to send me with a letter, promising me great rewards, if I was successful in the business. I refused going on horse-back, and set off on foot about 3 o'clock in the afternoon; I expected every moment to fall in with the enemy, whom I well knew would shew me no mercy . . .

Soon after I went to Charles-Town, and entered on board a man of war. As we were going to Chesapeak-bay, we were at the taking of a rich prize. We stayed in the bay two days, and then sailed for New-York, where we went on shore. Here I endeavored to follow my trade, but for want of tools was obliged to relinquish it, and enter into service. But the wages were so low that I was not able to keep myself in clothes, so I stayed with him four months, but he never paid me, and I was obliged to leave him also, and work about the town until I was married. A year after I was taken very ill, but the Lord raised me up again in about five weeks. I then went out in a pilot-boat. We were at sea eight days, and had only provisions for five, so that we were in danger of starving. On the 9th day we were taken by an American whale-boat. I went on board them with a cheerful countenance, and asked for bread and water, and made very free with them. They carried me to Brunswick [New York], and used me well. Notwithstanding which, my mind was sorely distressed at the thought of being again reduced to slavery, and separated from my wife and family; and at the same time it was exceeding difficult to escape from my bondage, because the river at Amboy was above a mile over, and likewise another to cross at Staten-Island. I called to remembrance the many great deliverances the Lord had wrought for me, and besought him save me this once, and I would serve him all the days of my life . . .

I traveled till about five in the morning, and then concealed myself till seven o'clock at night, when I proceeded forward, thro' bushes and marshes, near the road, for fear of being discovered. When I came to the river, opposite Staten-Island, I found a boat; and altho' it was very near a whale-boat, yet I ventured into it, and cutting the rope, got safe over. The commanding officer, when informed of my case, gave me a passport, and I proceeded to New-York.

When I arrived at New-York, my friends rejoiced to see me once more restored to liberty, and joined me in praising the Lord for his mercy and goodness. But not withstanding this great deliverance, and the promises I had made to serve GOD, yet my good resolutions soon vanished away like the morning dew: The love of this world extinguished my good desires, and stole away my heart from GOD, so that I rested in a mere form of religion for near three years. About which time, [in 1783] the horrors and devastation of war happily terminated, and peace was restored between America and Great Britain, which diffused universal joy among all parties, except us, who had escaped from slavery, and taken refuge in the English army; for a report prevailed at New-York, that all the slaves, in number 2000, were to be delivered up to their masters, altho' some of them had been three or four years among the English. This dreadful rumour filled us all with inexpressible anguish and terror, especially when we saw our old masters coming from Virginia, North-Carolina, and other parts, and seizing upon their slaves in the streets of New-York, or even dragging them out of their beds. Many of the slaves had very cruel masters, so that the thought of returning home with them embittered life to us. For some days we lost our appetite for food, and sleep departed from our eyes. The English had compassion upon us in the day of distress, and issued out the Proclamation, importing, That all slaves should be free, who had taken refuge in the British lines, and claimed the sanction and privileges of the Proclamations respecting the security and protections of Negroes in consequence of this, each of us received a certificate from the commanding officer at New-York, which dispelled all our fears, and filled us with joy and gratitude. Soon after, ships were fitted out, and furnished with every necessary for conveying us to Nova Scotia.

BENJAMIN BANNEKER
(1731–1806)

Banneker, the first known African American inventor, mathematician and as-
tronomer, was also the surveyor of the District of Columbia. He is perhaps most
famous for being the inventor of the Almanac. Although he was a free man, Ban-
neker felt the plight of his African brethren. He wrote this peace plan appealing to
two significant principles: the federal government's responsibility to service its citi-
zens, and most importantly the idea that the country should adhere to the principles
of Christianity and equal treatment of all men.

Letter to the Secretary of State:
A Plan of Peace Office for the United States
August 19, 1791

Among the many defects which have been pointed out in the federal constitution by its antifederal enemies, it is much to be lamented that no person has
taken notice of its total silence upon the subject of an office of the utmost importance to the welfare of the United States, that is, an office for promoting and
preserving perpetual peace in our country.

It is to be hoped that no objection will be made to the establishment of such
an office, while we are engaged in a war with Indians, for as the War-Office of
the United States was established in time of peace, it is equally reasonable that
a Peace-Office should be established in time of war.

The plan of this office is as follows:

I. Let a Secretary of Peace be appointed to preside in this office, who shall be
perfectly free from all present absurd and vulgar European prejudices upon the
subject of government; let him be a genuine republican and sincere Christian,
for the principles of republicanism and Christianity are no less friendly to universal and perpetual peace, than they are to universal and equal liberty.

II. Let a power be given to this Secretary to establish and maintain free
schools in every city, village, and township of the United States; and let him be
made responsible for the talents, principles, and morals of all his schoolmasters.
Let the youth of our country be carefully instructed in reading, writing, and
arithmetic, and in the doctrines of a religion of some kind; the Christian religion
should be preferred to all others; for it belongs to this religion exclusively to
teach us not only to cultivate peace with all men, but to forgive, nay more—to
love our very enemies. It belongs to it further to teach us that the Supreme Being alone possesses a power to take away human life, and that we rebel against
his laws whenever we undertake to execute death in any way whatever upon
any of his creatures.

III. Let every family in the United States be furnished at the public expense, by the Secretary of this office, with a copy of an American edition of the Bible. This measure has become the more necessary in our country, since the banishment of the Bible, as a school-book, from most of the schools in the United States. Unless the price of this book be paid for by the public, there is reason to fear that in a few years it will be met with only in courts of justice or in magistrates' offices; and should the absurd mode of establishing truth by kissing this sacred book fall into disuse, it may probably, in the course of the next generation, be seen only as a curiosity on a shelf in Mr. Peale's museum.

IV. Let the following sentence be inscribed in letters of gold over the door of every home in the United States:

THE SON OF MAN CAME INTO THE WORLD, NOT TO DESTROY MEN'S LIVES, BUT TO SAVE THEM.

V. To inspire a veneration for human life, and an horror at the shedding of human blood, let all those laws be repealed which authorize juries, judges, sheriffs, or hangmen to assume the resentments of individuals, and to commit murder in cold blood in any case whatever. Until this reformation in our code of penal jurisprudence takes place, it will be in vain to attempt to introduce universal and perpetual peace in our country.

VI. To subdue that passion for war which education added to human depravity, has made universal, familiarity with the instruments of death, as well as all military shows, should be carefully avoided. For which reason, militia laws should everywhere be repealed and military dresses and military titles should be laid aside: reviews tend to lessen the horrors of a battle by connecting them with the charms of order; militia laws generate idleness and vice, and thereby produce the wars they are said to prevent; military dresses fascinate the mind of young men, and lead them from serious and useful professions; were there no uniforms, there would probably be no armies; lastly, military titles feed vanity, and keep up ideas in the mind which lessen a sense of the folly and miseries of war.

In the seventh and last place, let a large room, adjoining the federal hall, be appointed for transacting the business and preserving all the records of this office. Over the door of this room let there be a sign, on which the figures of a lamb, a dove, and an olive-branch should be painted, together with the following inscriptions in letters of gold:

PEACE ON EARTH—GOOD-WILL TO MAN.

AH! WHY SHOULD MEN FORGET THAT THEY ARE BRETHREN?

Within this apartment let there be a collection of plough-shares and pruning-hooks made out of swords and spears; and on each of the walls of the apartment the following pictures as large as life:

1. A lion eating straw with an ox, and an adder playing upon the lips of a child.

2. An Indian boiling his venison in the same pot with a citizen of Kentucky.
3. Lord Cornwallis and Tippo Saib, under the shade of a sycamore tree in the East Indies, drinking Madeira wine out of the same decanter.
4. A group of French and Austrian soldiers dancing, arm in arm, under a bower erected in the neighborhood of Mons.
5. A St. Domingo planter, a man of color, and a native of Africa, legislating together in the same colonial assembly.

To complete the entertainment of this delightful apartment, let a group of young ladies, clad in white robes, assemble every day at a certain hour, in a gallery to be erected for the purpose, and sing odes, and hymns, and anthems in praise of the blessings of peace.

One of these songs should consist of the following beautiful lines of Mr. Pope:

> Peace o'er the world her olive wand extends,
> And white-rob'd innocence from heaven descends;
> All crimes shall cease, and ancient frauds shall fail,
> Returning justice lifts aloft her scale.

Notes

1. See Peter M. Bergman, *The Chronological History of the Negro in America* (New York: Harper & Row, 1929), 49–52, for the census of the Black population, including a state-by-state breakdown.

2. William C. Nell, *The Colored Patriots of the American Revolution* (New York: Arno Press and the *New York Times*, 1968), 40–41. Reprinted from a copy at the Moorland Spingarn Collection, Howard University, Washington, D.C.

3. Herbert Aptheker, *American Negro Slave Revolts* (1943; New York: International Publishers, 1983).

4. For a general discussion of colonial history and the Revolutionary era, see John Hope Franklin and Alfred A. Moss Jr., *From Slavery to Freedom: A History of African Americans*, 7th ed. (New York: McGraw-Hill, 1994); Samuel Eliot Morison, *Oxford History of the American People* (New York: Oxford University Press, 1965); and Samuel Eliot Morison, *Growth of the American Republic*, 7th ed., vol. 1 (New York: Oxford University Press, 1980).

5. Letter VII, 1776–1778, in *Empire and Nation: John Dickinson, Letters from a Farmer in Pennsylvania and Richard Henry Lee, Letters from the Federal Farmer*, ed. Forrest McDonald, 2nd ed. (1962; Indianapolis: Liberty Fund, 1999).

6. House Document no. 398, in *Documents Illustrative of the Formation of the Union of the American States*, ed. Charles C. Tansill (Washington, D.C.: Government Printing Office, 1927).

7. Olaudah Equiano, *The Interesting Narrative of the Life of Olaudah Equiano, or Gustavus Vassa, The African*. (1789; New York: St. Martin's, 2000).

8. Eric Foner, *Tom Paine and the American Revolution* (New York: Oxford University Press, 1976), 73.

9. For sources on the contributions of African Americans to the Revolutionary War, see Benjamin Quarles, *The Negro in the American Revolution* (Chapel Hill: University of North Carolina, 1961); Franklin and Moss, *From Slavery to Freedom*, 64–78; Nell, *Colored Patriots*; Gail Buckley, *American Patriots: The Story of Blacks in the Military from the Revolution to Desert Storm* (New York: Random House, 2001), 1–39; and Sylvia R. Frey, *Water from the Rock: Black Resistance in a Revolutionary Age* (Princeton, N.J.: Princeton University Press, 1999).

10. Vincent Carretta, ed., *Unchained Voices: An Anthology of Black Authors in the English-Speaking World of the Eighteenth Century* (Lexington: University of Kentucky Press, 1996), 351–66. Originally published as "Memoirs of the Life of Boston King, a Black Preacher. Written by Himself, during his Residence at Kingswood-School," *The Methodist Magazine (London)*, March 1798. Also see Phyllis R. Blakely, "Boston King: A Negro Loyalist Who Sought Refuge in Nova Scotia," *Dalhousie Review* 48 (Autumn 1968): 347–56.

11. See "Proceedings of the Safety Committee in Pitt County, July 8, 1775," *Colonial Records of North Carolina*, vol. 10 (1890; New York: AMS Press, 1968), 87. Also see Franklin and Moss, *From Slavery to Freedom*, 68; Buckley, *American Patriots*, 14; and Aptheker, *American Negro Slave Revolts*, 22.

12. Buckley, *American Patriots*, 14.

13. Reprinted in Henry Cabot Lodge, ed., *The Works of Alexander Hamilton*, vol. 7 (New York and London, 1886), 564–67; and Louis Ruchames, ed., *Racial Thought in America: From the Puritans to Abraham Lincoln* (New York: Grosset & Dunlap, 1969), 157–59.

14. NAACP, *Black Heroes of the American Revolution, 1775–1783* (New York: NAACP, n.d.), 23–24.

15. The account of events told by a white military officer only identified as Dr. Harris is located in Nell, *Colored Patriots*, 130; additional information on the Rhode Island regiment can be found on pages 50–51 and 126–27. For further details on the battle in Rhode Island, see Ray Raphael, *A People's History of the American Revolution* (New York: New Press, 2001), 287, and Buckley, *American Patriots*, 25.

16. For a brief analysis of slavery and the Constitution, see John Hope Franklin, "Race and the Constitution in the Nineteenth Century," in *African Americans and the Living Constitution*, ed. John Hope Franklin and Genna Rae McNeil (Washington, D.C.: Smithsonian, 1995), 21–31.

17. Nell, *Colored Patriots*, 47–48.

18. See Bergman, *Chronological History*, 68–70.

19. Buckley, *American Patriots*, 35.

20. Sidney Kaplan and Emma Nogrady Kaplan, *The Black Presence in the Era of the American Revolution* (Amherst: University of Massachusetts Press, 1989), 87–88; and Ray Raphael, *A People's History of the American Revolution: How Common People Shaped the Fight for Independence* (New York: New Press, 2001), 179–80.

CHAPTER TWO

∿

War of 1812:
From the Plantation
to the Battlefield

1 8 1 2 - 1 8 1 5

The War of 1812 was a continuation of the conflict between America and Britain over the British right to impose its will upon the new nation. Involved in a continuing dispute with France, which included the management of commodities in and out of Europe, Britain set forth a series of regulations that forced American ships to enter through Britain into Europe. It was not uncommon for the British to board an American ship, capture U.S. sailors and impress them into service. In fact, the frequent impressing of soldiers supplied the fuel that would push the two nations into a second, but limited war.

In the years leading up to the war, the U.S. officially ended its participation in the slave trade in 1808, as was decreed in the U.S. Constitution. However, violations of the law were numerous as shipmasters and merchants continued trafficking in humans. The slave trade had been driven underground and slavery remained a legal institution in full effect in the states.[1] Hardly any changes occurred for Black people in the U.S. until the Emancipation Proclamation of 1863.

As was the case in the Revolutionary War, the priority for most African people was how to gain some semblance of freedom. Many volunteered to serve in the military in hopes of becoming emancipated in return. Martin Delany, a Black physician and emigrationist, who served in the Civil War, described the temper of Blacks at the time as "ready and willing to volunteer in your service as any other" and "not compelled to go; they were not draghted [drafted]. They were volunteers."[2]

Others were enticed by Britain's offer of absolute liberty in return for fighting on their side. Betrayed by the results of their loyal efforts in the Revolutionary War, it was not uncommon for many Blacks to align themselves with the British. "Before the War ended, 3,000 to 5,000 slaves of the Upper South, nearly one-third of them women, fled to the British side."[3]

Black people living in the U.S. played a crucial role in the war at its onset. In 1808, the British ship *Leopard* ordered the American *Chesapeake* to allow the boat to be inspected for British dissidents. When Captain James Barron refused, the British opened fire on the *Chesapeake* and apprehended four sailors. One of those men was in fact a British deserter, but the other three were Black men: David Martin, John Strachan and William Ware. The men remained in British custody until 1811. It was this incident that began the rancorous dialogue that culminated in the War of 1812.[4]

By 1811, President James Madison had ended all trade with Britain. On June 1st of the following year, he asked Congress for a declaration of war. On June 16th the British announced that they would rescind their shipping laws. In spite of this, Congress still declared war on Britain in June of 1812.

Prior to the war, Congress passed a bill calling for the creation of a "uniform militia" for national defense.[5] Initially, the land forces were primarily composed of 6,000[6] white men. Free Blacks volunteered, but were oftentimes refused the opportunity to serve despite their willingness. Some communities used free and enslaved Blacks to build defense fortifications, but they were afraid to arm them.

However, prohibitions against arming Blacks changed when the British forces, which included a significant number of Black marines, seized and burned Washington, D.C. Surrounding states, threatened by the arson and violence, took immediate action and opened their ranks to Blacks; the first were New York and Pennsylvania. Despite Congress's ban on the use of Black soldiers, the ongoing shortage of labor and fear of rebellion compelled many other forces to welcome and recruit both the free and the bonded. It has been estimated that at least one-tenth of the troops of the triumphant Great Lakes were Black. Philadelphia and New York were among the states that formed all-Black regiments.

The fear caused by the ambush of Washington, D.C., was preceded by the violent uprising that had occurred in Saint Dominique, now known as Haiti.[7] In the 18th century, Saint Dominique became France's wealthiest producing colony, based on a plantation system similar to that of the U.S., which exploited the free labor of Africans. The enslaved Africans and free Blacks, who outnumbered their masters 15 to 1, began to rebel en masse. Inspired by the French Revolution of 1789 and the "Declaration of the Rights of Man," which had been decreed by the National Assembly of France, the rebels claimed the same "rights of man" which the French revolutionaries demanded from the aristocracy and monarchy of France. Led by the former slave Toussaint L'Ouverture, who worked with the French to defeat the Spanish and British forces previously, Blacks were organized into armies. By 1801, Santo Domingo had been conquered and slavery eradicated. In 1801, Napoleon Bonaparte dispatched more forces to capture Toussaint, reinstate slavery and restore French rule. Although Toussaint was eventually captured and imprisoned in France, Jean-Jacques Dessalines, one of Toussaint's generals, led the final battle that defeated Napoleon's forces. On January 1, 1804, Dessalines declared the nation independent, under its indigenous name of Haiti, thus making it the first independent nation in Latin America.[8]

Initially, many Americans supported the upheaval on the island, until the French began migrating to the United States, often bringing their slaves with them. Afraid that the influx of slaves would inspire those held in bondage in the states with the possibility of liberty through rebellion, fear enveloped the atmosphere of the U.S. throughout the War of 1812. Ironically, these same Haitian slaves had played an enormous part in defending the Southern states from the British during the Revolutionary War.

The Haitian Revolution played an enormous part in shaping the minds of both Blacks and whites regarding slavery and the future of Africans in the Americas. In a pamphlet entitled *A Narrative of the Proceedings of the Black People During the Late Calamity in Philadelphia*, Richard Allen and Absalom Jones wrote, "The dreadful insurrections they [the French slaves] have made . . . is enough to convince a reasonable man, that great uneasiness and not contentment, is the inhabitant of their [the slaves'] heart."[9]

White fear of Blacks was expressed by a South Carolina resident in the summer of 1812, who identified the danger arising from the growth of the Black population in a letter stating, "Consider, I beseech you, that the coast of S. Carolina and Georgia is principally inhabited by a black population, which it is not to be denied, the whites are not able to control . . . A regiment of militia has been sent us from the interior for our protection, but they have mutinied . . . tho' the mutiny is arrested for the moment, the spirit of it is by no means quelled."[10]

By 1813, Congress passed an act officially opening the naval ranks to people of color. In fact, more Black Americans served on sea than on land throughout the war.[11] During the early nineteenth century, African Americans constituted 20 percent of the entire naval forces.[12] Apparently, the tightly cramped environment of the ship was not conducive to segregation or partition and therefore forced interracial association. Commodore Oliver

Perry, who led a crew in the Battle of Lake Erie, praised the bravery of his Black American crew members by referring to them as "absolutely insensible to danger."[13] In addition to the Black battalion who served under Commodore Perry, two other battalions of Black Americans were with General Andrew Jackson at the Battle of New Orleans. The soldiers who fought with Jackson were noted for their fighting skills and for erecting cotton bag defenses against British attacks.

In the fall of 1814, General Andrew Jackson issued a call for Black troops. He promised Blacks the same wages white troops received, along with their freedom after service. It has been recorded that General Jackson often went directly to the plantations to personally select his recruits. He would say, "Had you not as soon go into battle and fight, as to stay here in the cotton-field, dying and never die? If you will go, and the battle is fought and the victory gained on Israel's side, you shall be free."[14] Jackson never followed through with his promise of freedom for his enslaved soldiers.

One consequence of the War of 1812 was the disruption of plans by some Blacks to emigrate to Africa. Although many whites desired the emigration of Blacks back to Africa, many Blacks in the U.S. advocated a similar strategy, albeit for different reasons. Martin Delany, Henry Highland Garnet and others saw Africa and even some Western countries as an opportunity for Blacks to determine their own destiny. Paul Cuffe, a ship captain and merchant, had plans to emigrate along with other willing Blacks to Sierra Leone. However, as a result of the war, all trade with Britain and its colonies was forbidden. Therefore, Cuffe's petition to Congress to trade in contravention of the embargo was unsuccessful. The basic issue was soon submerged in larger sectional and political concerns, with the bulk of support for Cuffe coming from states where the war was most unpopular. Eventually his petition passed in the Senate but failed in the House of Representatives. Even the directors of the African Institution in England had applied for a license on Cuffe's behalf, but they had been informed that none could be granted until the war was over.

Throughout the war, James Forten managed Cuffe's business concerns in Philadelphia. Forten and others were concerned about the potential financial loss to Cuffe and to others as a result of the war. Certainly Cuffe's mission had the capacity to bring wealth to many Blacks. When one of Cuffe's ships was threatened with seizure for debt, Forten wrote him warning of the problem. For a city that relied on international trade, the embargo and the attacks on merchant shipping had proved to be devastating.

By February of 1815, Forten and Cuffe had reason to be hopeful. The Senate had ratified the Treaty of Ghent (ending the war) and commercial life in the city was again coming to life. The African Institution of Philadelphia had survived the war as well. Forten wrote to Cuffe: "I approve very highly of your proposition of building a ship for the African trade by the men of Colour and shall lay it before the Society when next we meet."[15] Evidently, for Forten, the commercial potential of Sierra Leone took priority over emigration. However, he and his colleagues did what they could to assist Cuffe in finding suitable colonists. In 1815, Cuffe sailed for the colony of Sierra Leone in Africa with 38 free Blacks aboard. There he created a successful homestead for them, a project he personally financed.

The commentaries in this section reflect the environment for Blacks during the War of 1812. A Virginia slave insurgent confessed the details of a conspiracy to rebel saying, "The Negroes in the neighborhood said that these British people was about to rise against this Country, and that they intended to rise sometime in next May . . . That they said they were not made to work for white people, but they (the white people), made to work for themselves; and that they (the Negroes), would have it so."[16] Also in this section is an excerpt from Martin Delany, who wrote of the bravery of colored troops.

James Roberts, a slave who fought bravely under Jackson in New Orleans, expressed anger at being denied his freedom after the war's end. He lamented the fact that after saving the U.S. from the onslaught of the British, U.S. officials had the audacity to declare that he would be "shot simply for contending for my freedom which both my master and Jackson had solemnly before high heaven had promised before I left home."[17]

Finally, a letter from Paul Cuffe expresses his disappointment that the War of 1812 interfered with his attempts to help more Blacks emigrate back to Africa. He stated, "As here appears to be an open declaration of war of the United States of America against Great Britain, I see not how I am to get the *Traveller* to Sierra Leone in Africa, as there seems to be several families that have made up their minds to go to Sierra Leone in order to render Africa some assistance."[18]

TOM
(N.D.)

Considering it an opportune time to join other attacks against the U.S., violent rebellions against slavery were prompted by the War of 1812. In Virginia on April 2, 1812, a slave called Tom, property of John Smith of the County of Henry, confessed to the murder of his master and other conspiracies to cause the end of slavery. Tom's confession was made in a letter that was delivered to the governor of Virginia, who was thereafter secretary of war in President James Buchanan's cabinet. In the letter, delivered by John Floyd and Henry Edmondson, justices of the peace for the County of Montgomery, Tom declared that he murdered his master on Monday, the 23rd day of March. He further stated that his crime had been instigated by a woman, the property of said Smith, by the name of Celia.

Confession of a Virginia Rebel
1812

Question: Have you any knowledge of other Negroes other than the woman before mentioned who are disposed to rise in order to kill their masters?

Answer of Tom: I know of a great many—thirty or forty who appear to be instigated to kill their masters by a Negro man in the County of Rockingham, N. Carolina, by the name of Goomer, who is called by the Negroes a conjurer. A Negro man Jack, the property of the widow Wit, told me to kill my master; that I could not be hurt for it, and that Goomer would conjure me clear, and that when they got fixed they intended to rise and kill the white people. That George Harsten of Henry was to be poisoned by himself (Jack), the poison to be furnished by Goomer. That W. Hill was to be waylaid and shot by Tom, boy, the property of (master not known to him), and one of Goomer's men; and he was to be paid 200lbs. of Hemp for it by W. Hill's Hannah. Major Redd of Henry was to be poisoned by Jack, the poison to be furnished by Goomer.

Celia told me that the widow Penn's Jim of P.C., who has a wife at Mr. Staples in Henry, that if he was in my place he would not serve my master any longer, but wait till he could meet him coming home drunk and kill him, but that he must not kill him in the plantation. The Negroes in the neighborhood said that these British people was about to rise against this Country, and that they intended to rise sometime in next May. That they were buying up guns for the purpose. That they said they were not made to work for the white people, but they (the white people), made to work for themselves; and that they (the Negroes), would have it so. That the plan in the neighborhood was first to break open Ned Staples' store in order to get the Guns, Powder, &c out of it—that they would then raise an army, Goomer was to be one of their head men, and George Powell's Harry another. Mrs. Wit's Jack said he would make haste and learn all he could (being at the time nearly equal to Goomer in conjuration), and get as high as he could. The Negroes in the neighborhood said they were glad that the people were burnt in Richmond, and wished that all the white people had been burnt with them. That God Almighty had sent them a little Hell for the white people, and that in a little time they would get a greater. That the Negroes in his neighborhood had sent word by——, a Negro waggoner for Mr. Staples, of their plans to the Negroes at Lynchburg and received for answer to be ready in May next. The plan was to rise about the middle of May in the night and do all the mischief they could before they were found out. That I said when he was in Lynchburg the white people were draughting and exercising, but what was that—it would do no good, and that when the Negroes rose they would put a stop to it. That there were ten Negroes for one white man.

Question: Did you ever hear them say whether they intended to murder the white women and children, or not?

Answer of Tom: I never heard them say.

Question: How did you hear that the British were about to rise against this country[?]

Answer: It was heard from the poor people in the neighborhood, and by hearing the newspapers read.

He further stated that he was to have killed his master some time before. That on Saturday he was to kill him, and that he and his master passed two or three miles together, but he could not. That he and the Negro woman (Celia) had a further conversation about it on Sunday night, and the next day about 1 o'clock he killed him. That when he returned to the house on the evening, the Negro woman (Celia) asked him if he had killed his master. He told her he had. She told him to take a horse and clear himself. He told her he did not wish to go then, that they would think he had killed his master. She told him he must not stay there, that if he did she would be brought in with him; on which he started, and that he met with a Negro woman of a Mr. Hall's in Franklin. That he told her he was a runaway, and that he had killed his master. Also that the Negroes were shortly to rise against the white people. She said they could not rise too soon for her, as she had rather be in hell than where she was.

PAUL CUFFE
(1759–1818)

Paul Cuffe was born free on Chuttyhunk Island, Massachusetts. His father was a slave and his mother was Indian. As a teenager he sued the Massachusetts courts for the right to vote, stating taxation without representation was illegal. Paul Cuffe and his brother built a boat and began a trading business, manned entirely by a Black staff. Their business gradually grew into a large fleet of merchant vessels. Cuffe also owned a shipyard, thus making him one of the wealthiest men in America. Despite his upper-class financial status, Cuffe was treated as a second-class citizen. He came to believe that only emigrating to Africa would ensure the Black race's humanity. As a result, Cuffe embarked on a "Back to Africa" crusade. Cuffe also traveled to many other countries to gather support for his mission, including London, where the British had a program to send unwanted Blacks to Sierra Leone. There he met William Allen, a British chemist, Quaker and abolitionist, who endorsed his voyage to Africa. Cuffe's trade and emigration plans were interrupted and delayed by the War of 1812. Yet after a substantial amount of research and investments he set sail on December 10, 1815, for Sierra Leone, Africa, with a group of nine freed Black families. In this letter to Allen, Cuffe provides an update on his emigration plans.

Letter to William Allen
Late August, 1812

Dear Friend William Allen

Having obtained all the information that I can at present, I shall at this time write to thee and hope it may reach thee in safety. As here appears to be an open declaration of war of the United States of America against Great Britain, I see not how I am to get the *Traveller* to Sierra Leone in Africa, as there appears to be several families that have made up their minds to go to Sierra Leone in order to render Africa some assistance.

When I was at the seat of government they then told me that they would render me every assistance that they could consistent with the laws of the United States. I believe if there could be a license obtained from the British government, it [might also] be obtained from this government, if thee can intercede with the English government to grant a license for the brig *Traveller*, a cargo, crew and passengers, names not altogether ascertained.

If the above liberties can be granted, I shall endeavor to send the *Traveller* to Africa this fall. As here appears many minds much influenced to see Sierra Leone, I should wish for the way to be kept open.

Notwithstanding the declaration of war between these countries, I hope that that chain of brotherly union in the true church is not shortened. I can truly say that I feel all near and dear unto that belongs unto this church of peace and harmony. Beloved friends may we all unite in observing on earth peace and towards men good will, and glory to God on high, amen.

NB The ship *Alpha* sunk me on my half 3500 dollars last voyage, and my bark ship that has gone round Cape Horn on a whale voyage has not yet returned, but is looked for everyday. But I do not see any chance for her to escape the British cruiser and I have no insurance on her; and the *Traveller*'s voyage to Africa thou art sensible was not a profitable one as to property.

And many of these people that might, and I dare say would, be serviceable if they could get to Sierra Leone, I am willing to do all that I can do. There is few that has property to assist themselves, etc. Again, can grants of lands, houses, or some small aid or privilege be granted to those who may leave their land for the promotion of Africa?

Any error or omission in my statement, please to excuse and correct. The above, I believe, is a true statement of facts. In love, I am thy well-wishing friend.

Paul Cuffe

P.S. Still think that a sawmill is much needed in Sierra Leone, and I shall endeavor to send materials for one and a man who understands of tending one. The most that stands in the way will be a millwright to erect her. I have it on my mind to send out a plow and a wagon to assist in carrying loads through the streets instead of being carried on men's heads.

MARTIN ROBINSON DELANY
(1812–1885)

Martin Delany was best known as an abolitionist, nationalist and emigrationist. He was born free in Charleston, Virginia, although his father Samuel was a slave. Delany became a physician and an officer in the army during the Civil War. In 1852, Delany published the famous book The Condition, Elevation, Emigration, and Destiny of the Colored People of the United States, Politically Considered. *He argued that Black people in America should settle outside the United States, possibly in Africa, but more likely in Canada or Latin America, and for a time Delaney lived in Ontario. In this excerpt from his book, Delany comments on the bravery of Black people during the War of 1812. He specifically clarifies the Black soldiers' role in the famous battle for New Orleans which took place on December 23, 1814. In that battle, the British advance on the Americans was stopped by the protection of cotton bales. Although the successful plan has often been attributed to the genius of General Andrew Jackson, Delaney argues that Black soldiers should be given the credit. According to Delaney, Black soldiers "wrought havoc" among the British General Edward Pakenham's army as they advanced across the open ground in front of the American lines. In less than a half hour the attack was repulsed. British casualties were in the thousands and scores were taken as prisoners. General Pakenham was killed, while American losses were minimal.*

Excerpt from *The Condition, Elevation, Emigration, and Destiny of the Colored People:* Colored American Warriors (1852)

A circumstance that reflects as well upon the devisor, as upon the commander, or the engineer of the army, is not generally known to the American people. The redoubt of cotton bales, has ever been attributed to the judgment, skill, quick perception, and superior tact of Major General Andrew Jackson; than whom, a braver heart, never beat in the breast of man. But this is a mistake. The suggestion of the cotton bales was made by a colored man, at the instant, when the city of New Orleans was put under martial law. The colored troops were gathering, and their recruiting officers (being colored) were scouring the city in every direction, and particularly on the Levee, where the people throng for news—to hear, see, and be seen. As such times in particular, the blacks are found in great numbers. The cotton shipped down the Mississippi in large quantities to the city, is landed and piled in regular terrace walls, several thousand feet long, sometimes double rows—and fifteen or twenty feet high. When the sun shines in winter, the days become warm and pleasant after the morning passes off, and at such times, there may be found many of the idle blacks, lying up on the top, and in comfortable positions between or behind those walls of cotton bales. On the approach of the recruiting officer, a number of persons were found stretched out upon the bales, lying scattered upon the ground. On addressing them, they were found to be slaves, which the pride of the recently promoted free colored soldiers, nor the policy of the proclamation, then justified them in enrolling. On questioning them respecting their fears of the approaching contest—they expressed themselves as perfectly satisfied and *safe*, while permitted to lie *behind* the bales. The idea was at once impressed—Chalmet Plain, the battle field, being entirely barren without trees, brush, or stone, and the ingenuity of the General-in-chief and engineer of the army, having been for several days taxed, without successful device; the officer determined that he would muster courage, and hazard the consequences of an approach to the General, and suggest the idea suggested to him, by the observation of a slave, who was indifferent to the safety of others, so that he was secure—and perhaps justly so—whether conscious or not of the importance of its bearing. General Jackson, whatever may be said to the contrary, though firm and determined, was pleasant, affable, and easily approached, and always set equal estimate upon the manhood of a colored man; believing every thing of him, that he expressed in his proclamation to the colored freeman of Louisiana. He did not pretend to justify the holding of slaves, especially on the assumed unjust plea of their incapacity for self-government—he always hooted at the idea; never would become a member of the Colonization Society, always saying "Let the colored people be—they were quiet now, in comparative satisfaction—let them be." But he held them as a policy, by which to make money—and would just as readily have held a white man, had it been the policy of the country, as a black one in slavery. The General was approached—the suggestion made—slaves set to work—the bales conveyed down—the breast-works raised—the Americans protected, as the musketry and artillery proved powerless against the elastic cushion-wall of cotton bales; the battle fought—the British vanquished—the Americans victorious, and Major General Andrew Jackson "all covered with glory," as the most distinguished and skillful captain of the age. It has always been thought by colored men familiar with this circumstance, that the reference of the General is directed to this, when he expresses himself in his last proclamation to them: "*You have done more than I expected.*" Doubtless this was the case. Whatever valor and capacity to endure hardships, the General knew colored men to possess, it *was* more than he expected of them, to bring skill to his aid, and assist in counseling plans for the defence of the army

. . . In speaking of the war of 1812, a colored veteran of Philadelphia, the late James Forten, who had himself enlisted and was imprisoned on board of a

British man-of-war, the "Old Jersey Prison Ship," affirms: "The vessels of war of that period were all, to greater or less extent, manned with colored men." The father-in-law of the writer, has often related to him that he saw the three hundred and sixty colored marines, in military pomp and naval array, when passing through Pittsburg in 1812 on their way to the frigate Constitution, then on lake Erie under command of the gallant Commodore Perry.

JAMES ROBERTS
(1753–UNKNOWN)

Roberts was born a slave in 1753 on the eastern shore of Maryland. He belonged to Francis De Shields, a colonel in George Washington's army. As a servant he faced combat in a number of wars and battles. At the end of the war, Roberts hoped that he would be freed for his allegiance and patriotism to his country. However, instead of setting him free, General Andrew Jackson, the future president of the U.S., allowed the soldier to remain in bondage. Later, Roberts petitioned for his pension, which was denied. Roberts wrote of his experiences in an autobiography published in 1858. He bitterly advised Black people living in America to refuse any opportunities to fight in America's wars.

The Narrative of James Roberts:
The Battle of New Orleans
(1858)

General Jackson, in order to prepare to meet Packenham, the British General, in the contest at New Orleans, came into our section of the country, enlisting soldiers. He came to Calvin Smith's, and made a bargain with him to enlist five hundred negroes. Jackson came into the field, chose out the ones he wanted, and then addressed us thus: "Had you not as soon go into the battle and fight, as to stay here in the cotton-field, dying and never die? If you will go, and the battle is fought and the victory gained on Israel's side, you shall be free." This short speech seemed to us like divine revelation, and it filled our souls with buoyant expectations. Hardships, of whatever kind or however severe, vanished into vapor at the sound of freedom, and I made Jackson this reply: that, in hope of freedom we would "run through a troop and leap over a wall;" that I had as well go there and die for an old sheep as for a lamb. We were taken to Washington, in Louisiana, and drilled. Jackson again told us that we should be free after the battle.

Captain Brown mustered and drilled us, taking us through the evolutions: how to wheel to the right and left, from a single file to a double platoon; to march and wheel with the left foot foremost; to charge, cock and fire, ease arms, &c. Being satisfied as to our proficiency in military tactics, we prepared to start to New Orleans.

We took up our march from Natchez, and traveled the whole distance, three hundred miles by land, on foot. Every man had a sack and musket. When we came to the swamps in Louisiana, the water in some places was knee deep, with thick green scum over it, which we had to remove before we could get to the stinking water. At night we made little piles of brush, wood and grass for our beds. Here the musquitos, gallinippers and the red-belly snakes, at night when we laid down, contested with one another, over our bodies, which should get the greatest share of blood before morning. We had to sleep with one eye, keep awake with the other, in order to keep off the snakes, which we would thrust away a dozen times a night, when they would be crawling over us.

A number of the white Kentuckians died in the swamps from drinking the poisonous water. Jackson addressed them to this effect: It is a pity that you white devils did not stay at your homes. The negroes are no trouble at all. It would have been far better for us to have had no whites, for there is not a day or night passes that we do not have to dig a hole and bury five or six of you. It will be better for us to discharge you all and take you no farther.

In one week after leaving Natchez, we arrived in sight of New Orleans. We marched forward till we came in sight of the British army, and the first view of it was very impressive indeed. The British soldiers wore large, brilliant steel breast-plates, steel caps and steel covers on their arms up to the shoulders. The sun shining on these plates, and on their bright swords and spears, gave an appearance that inspired in me a dread and fear that is not easily described. Jackson said to us: "Don't be discouraged. Take the second look at them; they are but men like yourselves. Courage will overcome your fears and dread." We then marched next to the marsh and formed a single file. Then Jackson and Packenham the British general met and held a consultation. Then each general counted the number of the other's army. Packenham had ten to Jackson's one. Packenham asked Jackson if he was ready for operations. Jackson replied, he had not consulted his mind. Packenham said, I will give you two days to make up your mind.

Now Jackson consulted what was best to be done. In the mean-time Packenham drew up his army along the water side, and remained there two days. There was in Jackson's army a colored soldier named Pompey, who gave Jackson the first idea about the *cotton-bag fort*, and superintended the construction of it. We engaged in making it, and it was completed in the latter part of the second day. The cotton-bags were so placed as to leave port holes for three muskets to point through each.

On the third day, Packenham, buoyant with hope and flush with ambition, came towards our camp and demanded an interview with Jackson. The two generals met, in full view of the two armies, and held a consultation again. Packenham asked Jackson if he was ready for operations now, who replied that he was, and then asked Packenham how he liked his wooly-headed boys. Packenham said he had rather fight ten white men to their one, for, when they begin, there is no rule with them to stop but death. Then, said Jackson, say the word, and the wool flies. This day, said the exulting Packenham, I will either eat my dinner in the city of New Orleans, or in h—l! Poor, ill-fated man! Little did he know that, within two hours from that moment, he was to fall by the hand of one of the wooly-headed boys.

Each general returned to his respective army, and in twenty minutes the British fired. They fired three rounds; and the fourth we opened upon them. Here they began to throw shells into our fort, and had they continued to do so for some time, there is no doubt but victory would have been easy to them. But Packenham, who headed his army, impatient to carry everything by main force, doubting nothing as to his ability to take the fort in a short period, rushed forward in quick evolutions; and, as they came, we felled them like grass before the scythe. Platoon after platoon lay like scattered hail upon the ground. Packenham seeing this, and observing the rapid loss of his men, marched them single file up to our fort. He himself mounted the wall, encouraging his men in the most energetic manner. And here, at this point of the battle he might have succeeded, had he exercised some discretion. Instead of ordering the bags to be pushed inside next to us, he ordered them to be pulled outside, which entangled his men, and while in that entanglement we slew them by scores, and piled them by hundreds upon the bags as they endeavored to climb over them. While this was going on in the main body of our fort, the left wing of the fort gave way, which brought us and the British in immediate contact, with the broad-sword, and they fell before us like grass before the scythe. At this point I lost the fore finger of my left hand, and received a deep wound on my head from a British sword. After that I took the fellow's head off, and five more of his fellow soldiers'. Packenham at that moment was shot from the wall, and in two minutes the red flag was hauled down and the white one hoisted, the battle ceased and victory declared on our side. Jackson, who, during the battle, had taken a stand at some distance, ordering his men by an aid-decamp, came up to the line and gave us three cheers, and observing me to be all over bloody, asked me what was the matter with me. I told him not anything, for I had not yet discovered the loss of my finger, nor the wound upon my head. He said, "you have lost one of your fingers and received a deep wound upon your head; go to the hospital and have your wounds dressed." I did so, and returned to him, and asked him to let me go on the side of the British and see the slain. He said, "go where you please; the ground is free to you all, and all yours." I went and saw the slain lying, for one quarter of a mile, as thick as they could lie upon the ground, and I walked shoe deep in blood that distance and back. Some of the poor fellows were dead, some dying, some half dead, some cut in half and still living, and, as I passed by them, they grated their teeth at me, and made efforts to come at me. We were ordered to bury the slain of the British. We dug trenches and pulled them in with our grab-hooks, whether they were dead or still breathing. We were ordered to cover up the devils whether dead or alive, which we did, and tramped them down with our feet, into the blood and water knee deep. We then buried our own dead, putting them into coffins and burying them in the city.

In that battle some sixty or seventy or more of the colored men were killed, of whom no account whatever was ever taken in the details of the war, although they were, without doubt, as Jackson himself acknowledged, the instrumental cause of the victory. Such black ingratitude deserves the deepest reprehension. A savage would have been more grateful. Had we thus fought in the army of the cruel Turks, we should have received that applause which such merit deserved. But this inhuman neglect was left for Jackson's reprehensible duplicity.

Having buried our dead, we returned back to the fort. The British had by this time got a pipe of rum from the city, to preserve the body of Packenham, into which the body was put and headed up.

We formed a line, took our arms, and serenaded the battle-ground. Gabriel Winton, with his two colored boys, conducted the music. One played the fife, and the other the base drum. One was named Spot, and the other Wot. These boys excelled, in this department of necessary warfare, any that were upon that battle-ground. The battle was now fully closed. Next day morning, we put all our guns away in the ammunition house, and Jackson ordered them to be unloaded, to serve a wicked end he had in view, which I shall presently notice. The next day morning, being the second day after the battle, we came to get our guns, to march. We had power to put our guns away, but none to take them out of the ammunition house. A white man handed them out to us. We formed a line and marched down Fourth street, up Porass street, where the ladies through the windows waved their handkerchiefs and complimented Jackson on his success and victory. Here we formed a line in the presence of thousands. Jackson came riding along and said, "Well done, my brave boys, I will give you the praise; you have fought like bull-dogs, and wallowed in your blood;" then, addressing the crowd, he said, "if you ever want a battle fought, get the negro's Ebenezer up, he will run through a troop and leap over a wall. They are the best nation to fight in existence." Again turning to his colored soldiers, he said, "Now, behave yourselves well, and go home to your masters." I then said, A word to you, General, if you please: have you time to speak a word to me? "What is the word you wish to speak to me?" I asked him if he did not promise me my freedom, if that battle was fought and victory gained? He replied, "I did, but I took your master's word, as he told me. You are not my property, and I cannot take another man's property and set it free." My answer was, You can use your influence with our master, and have us set free. He replied thus: "If I were to hire you my horse, could you sell it without my leave? You are another man's property, and I have not money sufficient to buy all of you, and set you free." At that moment I cocked my gun; but there being no priming in it, I bit off a piece of cartridge, and, going to prime it, I for the first time discovered it was not loaded. Had my gun been loaded, doubtless Jackson would have been a dead man in a moment. There was no fear in my soul, at that time, of anything, neither man, death, nor mortal. The war-blood was up. I had just two days before cut off the heads of six brave Englishmen, and Jackson's life, at that moment, appeared no more to me than theirs. It was well for him that he took the precaution to have our guns unloaded when in the ammunition house. His guilty conscience smote him, and told him he was doing us a great piece of injustice, in promising us, by the most solemn protestation, that we should be free if the victory were gained. I would then have shot him dead a thousand times, if that could have been done. My soul was stirred in me, and maddened to desperation, to think that we had placed our lives in such imminent peril, through the persuasions of such false-heartedness, and now told to go back home to our masters!

Jackson asked me if I contended for freedom. I said I did. He said, "I think you are very presumptuous." I told him, the time had come for us to claim our rights. He said, "You promised me that you would fight manfully." I did, sir, and now is the time for me to claim the benefit of the promise you made me. I did fight manfully and gained the victory, now where is my freedom? He replied, as he had nothing else to reply, "You are a day too late; and if you are not willing to go home, I will put you in confinement, and send for your master; he will take you home; you seem to be the hardest among the whole crew." Some of the whites standing round said, "He ought to be shot." Now, just think of that! Two days before, I had, with my fellow soldiers, saved their city from fire and massacre, and their wives and children from blood and burning; now, "he ought to be shot!" simply for contending for my freedom, which, both my master and Jackson had solemnly before high heaven promised, before I left home.

Captain Brown, however, who knew something at least of the value of our services, or in some degree appreciated them, said, "No, he shall not be shot. You should not have promised him his liberty," addressing Jackson, "if you did not intend to fulfil your word. All negroes are not fools," said he; "some of them have as good sense as you or I."

I said, as for my part, I have sense enough to know there has been great falsehood practiced in this whole transaction; and had I had the least anticipation of it, I would never have come here to put my life in peril for such a cause.

. . . In concluding this brief history of my life, I think I cannot do it better than by giving some advice to my race of people, since it is right that the young should profit by the experience of their aged fathers.

Never be led into such hurtful errors as your fathers have been before you. Now then take counsel from me, one who has fought in the revolutionary war, and thereby caused the chains of slavery to be bound tighter around the necks of my people than they were before; and not being satisfied at that, by fighting in Jackson's war at New Orleans, riveted the chains closer, ten times, than they would have been had we colored men never fought in that battle; for it was by the indomitable bravery of the colored men that the battle was fought and victory gained. Had there been less bravery with us, the British would have gained the victory, and in that event they would have set the slaves free; so that I now can see how we, in that war, contributed to fasten our chains tighter. Therefore, my earnest and departing request is, that should this country ever again engage in war with any nation, have nothing whatever to do with the war, although the fairest promises should be made to you. Do not forget the promise Jackson made us in the New Orleans war—"If the battle is fought and victory gained on Israel's side, you shall all be free," when at the same time he had made a bargain with our masters to return home again all that were not killed. Never will a better promise be made to our race on a similar occasion. But for our faithfulness and manly courage, we should all be free men and women this day. Avoid being duped by the white man—he wants nothing to do with our race further than to subserve his own interest, in any thing under the sun.

It is not for me to foretell the end of oppression in this country, but one thing is certain, virtue, sobriety, industry, temperance, economy, education and religion, will fit you for any emergency whatever, and are the best qualifications for free men. That their attainment may be your constant pursuit and most earnest endeavor, is the prayer of one now ready to depart.

Notes

1. John Hope Franklin and Alfred A. Moss Jr., *From Slavery to Freedom: A History of African Americans*, 7th ed. (New York: McGraw-Hill, 1994), 90–92.

2. Martin Delany, *The Condition, Elevation, Emigration, and Destiny of the Colored People of the United States* (New York: Arno Press, 1969), 73.

3. Clayborne Carson, *African American Lives: The Struggle for Freedom* (New York: Pearson Longman, 2005).

4. Kai Wright, *Soldiers of Freedom: An Illustrated History of African Americans in the Armed Forces* (New York: Black Dog & Leventhal, 2002), 42.

5. Wright, Soldiers of Freedom, 42.

6. James Oliver Horton and Lois E. Horton, *Slavery and the Making of America* (New York: Oxford University Press, 2005), 80.

7. Saint Dominique was the name of the island while it was a colony of France. The name was later changed to Haiti after the traditional Arawak name for the island.

8. T. G. Steward, *The Haitian Revolution: 1791–1804* (New York: Russell & Russell, 1971), 235–38.

9. Carson, *African American Lives*, 143.

10. Herbert Aptheker, *American Negro Slave Revolts* (1943; New York: International Publishers, 1983), 23.

11. Horton and Horton, *Slavery and the Making of America*, 80.

12. Horton and Horton, *Slavery and the Making of America*, 80.

13. Horton and Horton, *Slavery and the Making of America*, 80.

14. Horton and Horton, *Slavery and the Making of America*, 81.

15. Forten to Cuffe, February 15, 1815. Cuffe Letterbook, Paul Cuffe Papers, Free Public Library, New Bedford, Mass. Letter further discussed in Julie Winch, *Philadelphia's Black Elite: Activism, Accommodation and the Struggle for Autonomy, 1787–1848* (Philadelphia: Temple University Press, 1988), 33.

16. Herbert Aptheker, *A Documentary History of the Negro People in the United States*, vol. 1, *From the Colonial Times through the Civil War* (Secaucus, N.J.: Citadel Press, 1979).

17. In Roberts, *The Narrative of James Roberts, A Soldier under Gen. Washington in the Revolutionary War and under Gen. Jackson at the Battle of New Orleans, in the War of 1812: "A Battle Which Cost Me a Limb, Some Blood and Almost My Life."* (Chicago: printed for the author, 1858), 13.

18. Sheldon H. Harris, *Paul Cuffe: Black America and the African Return* (New York: Simon & Schuster, 1972).

CHAPTER THREE

~

Civil War:
One Shot Away from
Emancipation
1 8 6 1 - 1 8 6 5

The Civil War engendered the first opportunity for Black people in America to openly bear arms in their own defense. Even so, Black involvement in the Civil War has been a controversial subject. Questions related to the importance of slavery as the central reason for the Civil War, to assertions that Blacks were not even key participants, have colored the discussion of their wartime participation.[1] Southern resistance to the national government's economic policy has been cited by many as the primary cause of the war. However, as noted by John Hope Franklin, "It was the question of slavery that sundered the sections and forced them to settle the question by a bloody war."[2] The issue of slavery led to increased hostilities between Southerners and the U.S. government and ultimately provoked the Civil War.

By 1860, a year before the Civil War began, the Black population in the U.S. was 4,441,830, or 14 percent of the total U.S. population. Approximately 11 percent of Blacks were free while the rest were slaves.[3] To combat the injustices of slavery, a strong abolitionist movement emerged in the North. Perhaps the best known was the American Anti-Slavery Society, led by noted members James Forten, a former solider of the Revolutionary War; Robert Purvis, a wealthy businessman and Forten's son-in-law; and William Lloyd Garrison, a noted white abolitionist and publisher of the anti-slavery organ the *Liberator*. First published in 1831, the *Liberator* soon amassed a large readership, which increased the visibility of the Anti-Slavery Society. The popular organization provided an early platform for Frederick Douglass, who told of his experiences as a slave to the Society's audiences. In 1847,

Douglass left the Anti-Slavery Society and began publishing the *North Star*, a newspaper dedicated to abolition and justice for free Blacks. Because of his great oratory skills, charisma and vast knowledge, Douglass eventually became the voice of Black America and the most politically powerful Black person during his time. Using tactics which included moral persuasion, petitions and education, Douglass, Garrison and Forten alike worked tirelessly to end slavery.

On the opposite end of the spectrum were those who advocated self-defense and violence to defend the rights and dignities of African Americans. In 1831, Nat Turner led a slave rebellion which resulted in the massacre of some 50 whites in Southampton, Virginia. More than 3,000 armed men responded to the call to capture Turner and his cohorts, who were eventually apprehended and hanged. David Walker, owner of a secondhand clothing store in Cambridge, Massachusetts, published an "Appeal to the Coloured Citizens of the World," in which he called on Black people to respond to slavery and other injustices with violence.[4] Another noted abolitionist, Henry Highland Garnet, also supported violent rebellion, if necessary, to defeat slavery. During a meeting of the Negro Convention Movement in Buffalo, New York, in 1843, Garnet implored Blacks to let their "motto be resistance" by any means to free themselves. Garnet published his "Call to Rebellion," along with David Walker's "Appeal" in 1848; Walker had been found dead in 1830, three months after the publication of the third edition of the "Appeal."[5]

Within the context of the abolition movement emerged the Underground Railroad. Formally organized in 1838 to help Blacks escape slavery in the South by fleeing to the North, the Underground Railroad was a response to increasing Southern white violence against slave families and the further entrenchment of slavery. The Underground Railroad consisted of "stations" in several cities that provided fugitive slaves with transportation, food, clothing and other resources as they journeyed to the North. By the early 1850s Harriet Tubman, also a fugitive slave, became one of the most active workers on the eastern branch of the Railroad. Born in 1820, Tubman escaped from her master's abuse in 1849. She eventually led more than 300 slaves to freedom.

Inevitably, the slavery debate took place within the context of political campaigns and was fueled by the political parties. The Free Soil Party, composed of mainly white people, was formed in 1848 with the agenda to stop slavery's expansion. The American Party, also known as the Know-Nothing Party, was formed to halt the onslaught of European immigrants to the United States. In the 1850s, the Know-Nothings won significant victories in Congress and on the local level in the North, but lost their political strength over factionalism brought on by infighting over slavery. The Whig Party, which promoted business and property interests, was not opposed to slavery, but against its expansion.

The Free Soil Party and the Whig Party were both supported by Black and white abolitionists as a way to organize against slavery within the electoral system. After both organizations disbanded, the Republican Party was founded in 1854. Made up of former Free Soil, Know-Nothing and Whig Party members, the Republicans also included Northern industrialists and free white workers. Many Republicans opposed the spread of slavery because it interfered with labor opportunities for whites who lived in the territories opening in the West. Hence, many white Republicans were not particularly friendly to Blacks, slave or free. The Republican Party was purely a sectional party in that they did not attempt to run candidates in the slave states. Their plan was to gain political control in the North in order to harness enough electoral strength to elect their own presidential candidate.

The Democratic Party on the other hand advocated the perpetuation and expansion of slavery. It was led by some of the most ardent slavery supporters, including President James Buchanan (1857–1861), who endorsed a pro-slavery constitution for the new states entering the Union. However, the party, already weakened over sectionalism and the slavery issue, soon splintered when fellow Democrat Senator Stephen A. Douglas of Illinois demanded a legitimate popular vote on the question of slavery in Kansas. To demonstrate their disdain for Douglass, Southern Democrats walked out of the Democratic National Convention of 1860, after he was nominated on a popular sovereignty platform. Southern Democrats named John C. Breckenridge as their own candidate who would run for the presidency on a slave code ticket. The split opened the opportunity for Abraham Lincoln, a relatively unknown railroad lawyer and former Whig congressman from the fairly young Republican Party, to win the White House. The election of a Northerner who had clearly opposed the expansion of slavery alarmed the South even further.

There were other important occurrences throughout the 1860s that led to the onset of actual hostilities between the North and South. In 1850, Congress passed a Fugitive Slave Law, which strengthened previous laws that mandated the extradition of runaway slaves to their masters. The law guaranteed that virtually every Black person charged with running away was almost certain to be sent back into slavery. Among other tenets,

> The law required U.S. marshals, their deputies and ordinary citizens to help seize suspected runaways. Those who refused to help apprehend fugitives or who helped a runaway could be fined and imprisoned. The law made it nearly

impossible for Black people to prove that they were free because slave owners only had to provide legal documentation of ownership from their home state or the testimony of white witnesses before a federal commissioner. The federal commissioners were given extra incentives to apprehend Blacks as a result of the payment they received for their services—$10 for captives returned to bondage and $5 for those declared free.[6]

Anti-slavery forces became even more alarmed after the Supreme Court ruling in the Dred Scott decision of 1857. Scott, who was born in Virginia, was taken to free areas to live with his master, Dr. John Emerson, including Illinois, Wisconsin and parts of the Louisiana Purchase. Dr. Emerson died in 1843 and John F. A. Sanford, Mrs. Emerson's brother, became executor of the estate. Scott sued for his freedom based on the Missouri Doctrine, "once free—always free." After several earlier decisions, Scott's case was appealed to the Supreme Court, in which the court ruled that Blacks were not citizens of the U.S. and therefore had no standing to sue in Court. That decision further divided the nation. Meetings and rallies were held throughout the North condemning the decision.[7]

The disagreement over slavery became violent as a result of the proposed Kansas-Nebraska Act. After Democratic Senator Stephan Douglass introduced a bill in 1854 that would permit local residents of Kansas to decide for themselves whether to allow slavery, both pro-slavery and anti-slavery forces sprang into action. Abolitionists feared that whites would vote to expand slavery into areas where it had been prohibited by the Missouri Compromise of 1850. Pro-slavery forces sought to expand their agrarian system westward and vowed to maintain their source of free labor. Violent skirmishes occurred between the factions. In fact, the battles became so bloody that Kansas was nicknamed "bleeding Kansas." Anti-slavery forces were led by the white abolitionist John Brown and his sons, while the Border Ruffians, pro-slavery poor whites that lived in Missouri, stuffed ballot boxes and violently attacked free-soilers. Although the acts of the Border Ruffians were applauded by the South, Kansas entered the Union as a free state in January 1861.

John Brown's raid of the federal arsenal at Harpers Ferry, Virginia, provided further stress on the already fractious Union. Brown and his posse of 21 men hoped to secure sufficient ammunition to carry on a large-scale operation against the Virginia slaveholders. They reasoned that attacking the arsenal was in effect attacking the federal government. On October 16, Brown set out for Harpers Ferry with 16 white men and 5 Blacks, including Dangerfield Newby, who hoped to rescue his wife who was still a slave. They first cut the telegraph lines, then captured the federal armory and arsenal and Hall's Rifle Works, a supplier of weapons to the government. After rounding up 60 prominent citizens of the town, the local militia pinned Brown and his men down. News of the insurrection, relayed by the conductor of an express train heading to Baltimore, reached President James Buchanan. Federal troops were alerted and eventually John Brown and his men were arrested and hanged under the leadership of Confederate Colonel Robert E. Lee. Although the raid failed, Brown and his men helped to intensify the debate around slavery and proved that whites were also willing to commit violence and die for their anti-slavery beliefs.[8] Abolitionists became even more emboldened after Brown's raid, while Southerners were outraged that Brown had become a hero to so many in the nation. Brown's raid further propelled the South to move toward succession from the Union.

For the South, the final assault on their quest for home rule was the election of Republican Abraham Lincoln as president. The Republican Party officially opposed the expansion of slavery to the western territories. Even so, in his quest to preserve the Union, Lincoln sought to calm the fears of whites by affirming states' rights to control their own local institutions.

Blacks were not sure that they could trust Lincoln. During the campaign debates with his Democratic opponent Stephen A. Douglas, Lincoln made it clear that he saw no need to abolish the Fugitive Slave Law, and during his inaugural speech in March 1861, he promised not to interfere with slavery where it already existed.[9] H. Ford Douglass from Illinois set forth Black suspicion about Lincoln when he said at the annual Fourth of July picnic in Framingham, Massachusetts:

> I do not believe in the anti-slavery of Abraham Lincoln . . . What does he propose to do? Simply to let the people and the Territories regulate their domestic institutions in their own way . . . ? What did he say in Freeport? Why, that the South was entitled to a Fugitive Slave Law; and although he thought the law could be modified a little, yet, he said, if he was in Congress, he would have it done in such a way as not to lessen its efficiency![10]

Frederick Douglass also had mixed reactions to Lincoln's win. He stated that although Lincoln was not an "abolitionist president," that his election remained important because it had broken the power of the South. "More important still, it has demonstrated the possibility of electing, if not an Abolitionist, at least an anti-slavery reputation to the Presidency."[11]

Despite Lincoln's pro-slavery rhetoric, Southerners remained convinced that he intended to eradicate slavery. Unable to accept the possibility of losing access to the free labor that planted and harvested their crops and cotton, South Carolina voted to withdraw from the Union on December 20, 1860. By February 1861, one month before Lincoln was to take office,

Florida, Alabama, Georgia, Texas, Mississippi and Louisiana also left the Union. The newly independent states established a congress and elected Jefferson Davis of Mississippi as their president. They also wrote a new constitution for the Confederacy that protected slavery and regulated the relationship between the slaves, other states and foreign governments. Shortly thereafter, on April 12, South Carolina troops fired upon the federal troops stationed at Fort Sumter in Charleston, South Carolina, until the federal troops surrendered. In response to the Battle of Fort Sumter, Lincoln called for all remaining states in the Union to send troops to recapture Sumter and other forts, defend the capital, and preserve the Union. But, instead of supporting the Union, the four states of Virginia, Arkansas, Tennessee and North Carolina joined the Confederacy, for a total of 11. Richmond, Virginia, became the capital of the Confederacy. The remaining slave states of Delaware, Maryland, Kentucky and Missouri, which were not major cotton producers but grew tobacco and other crops, did not secede. They joined the Union forces by sending troops and other resources to protect the federal government and end the secession.

For many abolitionists, the secession of Southern states was not entirely problematic. William Garrison had advocated for the separation of the North from the South for more than twenty years. Frederick Douglass said before an audience at Joy Street Church in Boston:

> If we could have such a government that would force the South to behave herself, under those circumstances I would be for the continuance of the Union. If, on the contrary—no if about it—We have what we have, I shall be glad of the news, come when it will, that the slave states are an independent government, and that you are no longer called upon to deliver fugitive slaves to their masters, and that you are no longer called to shoulder your arms and guard with your swords those States—no longer called to go into them to put down John Brown, or anybody else who may strike for liberation.[12]

Others were even more enthusiastic. Equating a northern win with southern subjugation and ultimately an end to slavery, thousands of Blacks responded to Lincoln's call for soldiers to sign up for three months' duty. John Mercer Langston, a Black attorney who served on Ohio's board of education, offered to raise 1,000 troops for the war, "upon the sole condition that they be received duly organized, officered and employed as regular soldiers in the national service."[13] However, Langston's patriotic zeal was not shared by all Blacks. Opposed to Langston were those who reasoned that Blacks should not fight for the Republican government until it proved that it supported emancipation and justice. In the *Anglo-African*, a Black man, who was only known by his signed initials, R. H. V., argued that:

> No regiments of black troops should leave their bodies to rot upon the battle-field beneath a Southern sun, to conquer a peace based upon the perpetuity of human bondage. I claim that the raising of black regiments for the war would be highly impolitic and uncalled for under the present state of affairs, knowing as we do, the policy of the Government in relation to colored men . . . Our policy must be neutral, ever praying for the success of that party determined to initiate first the policy of justice and equal rights.[14]

The U.S. War Department agreed that Blacks were not needed to win this war. The War Department not only refused to recruit Black soldiers, but even denied entry to the thousands who showed up to enlist. The response by Ohio governor David Tod to Langston's offer to recruit Black troops was, in substance, " . . . Do you know, Mr. Langston, that this is a white man's government and that white men are able to defend and protect it, and that to enlist a Negro Soldier would be to drive every white man out of the service?"[15] Later Tod reversed his decision and employed Langston to organize the 5th U.S. Colored Troops from Ohio.

President Lincoln's reasoning for refusing to accept Blacks as soldiers was that arming Blacks, especially slaves, might further antagonize the South and weaken his chances of convincing the slave states to come back into the Union. Moreover, Lincoln had little faith that Blacks would make good fighters. In September 1862, the president told a delegation of Chicago Christians who advocated emancipation and arming Blacks for the war, that "if we were to arm the Negroes, I fear that in a few weeks the arms would be in the hands of the rebels."[16] It was not until after the disastrous battle of Bull Run in July 1861, in which the Union army lost 4,700 casualties, that President Lincoln issued a call for Blacks to join the Union force.

But even before Lincoln had agreed to accept Black servicemen, Black fugitive slaves had begun serving at General Benjamin Butler's camp at Fort Monroe in Virginia. Having nowhere to go and viewing military service as an opportunity to defeat slavery and their former slave masters, the fugitives were ripe for duty. Butler labeled fugitive slaves contraband—enemy property seized at war—and put them to work.[17]

In Butler's opinion there was no reason to send these people back to their former slave masters who might use them against the Union. Going one step further, General John C. Fremont, previously a Free Soil presidential candidate and abolitionist from Missouri, declared that any former slave who took up arms on behalf of the Union would be made free. President Lincoln ordered a reversal of Fremont's declaration and later removed him from command, stating that Fremont's proclamation gave him "some anxiety."[18]

Annoyed by Lincoln's reiteration that his goal was to hold the nation together at the expense of the slaves, as well as his refusal to wholeheartedly accept Blacks as troops, Frederick Douglass and other Black leaders met with the president at the White House on August 14, 1862, for an interview. During the meeting, Lincoln told his guests that based on broad racial differences, Negroes and Caucasians would not be able to live together. He also presented his colonization plan for slaves and willing free Blacks. The tenets of Lincoln's proposal included compensating slave owners for the loss of their slaves, and the slaves in turn would be freed but forced to settle in Central America or West Africa. Free Blacks who desired emigration would receive federal assistance.[19] For Lincoln, this was not a new idea. In his earlier message to Congress on December 3, 1861, Lincoln recommended colonization of the slaves who had crossed over into Union lines, plus willing free Blacks. As part of an early emancipation experiment, Lincoln also recommended that Congress liberate the slaves of Washington, D.C., and appropriated funds to pay owners for the newly emancipated. "He urged Congress to appropriate money for the acquisition of territory for this purpose." Congress acted on Lincoln's suggestion and appropriated funds to help finance voluntary emigration of those Blacks who were free.[20]

While Lincoln continued to search for ways to appease the South, the war impacted Black life greatly. Contraband camps sprang up throughout the North to support the Union efforts. Northern abolitionists began to travel to the South to help organize and educate the slaves who had been deserted by their masters after the Union defeat of their towns. Charlotte Forten, a teacher and granddaughter of James Forten, was the first Northern African American schoolteacher to go South to teach former slaves. She taught children on St. Helena Island for two years before succumbing to ill health, which sent her back to the North. She later wrote of her experiences in the Sea Islands right after emancipation.[21]

Black women and children suffered greatly during the war. While the army offered sanctuary to men willing to fight, they frequently refused to aid the wives and children of those men. Some wives were able to live in a tent with their husbands, while others sometimes worked alongside the men, engaging in hard and heavy labor. Although some women received scant help from Southern relief agencies, a large percentage took care of themselves. Still others became entrepreneurs and received payment for their services as nurses, laundresses and cooks.

In addition to the foregoing, Black women were directly involved in military work, serving as soldiers and spies. For three years, Harriet Tubman served as a nurse, scout and spy for the Union army. One of the most heroic feats of Tubman occurred in June 1863, when she helped 756 enslaved Africans on the Combahee River flee to the Union lines in South Carolina. In addition to destroying bridges and cutting off supply routes, during the Combahee River expedition Tubman's squad also discovered and destroyed thousands of dollars' worth of Confederate supplies, including torpedoes. After the war, the United States government denied her a military pension because she had no formal position. However, Tubman received full military honors during her funeral in 1913.[22]

Harriet Tubman was not the only Black woman noted for her direct involvement in the military. Maria Lewis of Virginia served as a soldier with the Eighth New York Cavalry. She disguised herself as a man and saw combat in several battles. As a soldier, she accompanied the New York Cavalry to Washington, D.C., to present 17 captured rebel flags to the War Department. Maria Elizabeth Bowser, a free Black woman, also served as a spy for the Union. She served undercover as an illiterate in the Richmond home of Jefferson Davis. She reported important military information to Union soldiers. "When she came under suspicion, Bowser fled to Union lines after attempting to burn the Confederate White House in January 1864."[23]

Gradually, Lincoln began to warm up to the idea that the Union needed the manpower, enthusiasm and skills of Black soldiers. The examples of patriotism demonstrated by Black individuals such as Robert Smalls were well known. Smalls became a Union hero after he stole the Confederate ship *Planter* from its dock in the Charleston Harbor with the white crew still on board in May 1862. After Smalls hijacked the steamer he delivered it to the Union squadron that was blocking the harbor by waving a white flag.[24]

The events that occurred at Antietam, considered a major turning point in the war, prompted Lincoln to move toward the Emancipation Proclamation. In that battle, General Robert E. Lee sought to push the war into the North and disrupt the railroad lines that supplied Washington, D.C. On September 17, 1862, Lee's troops met Union troops at Sharpsburg on Antietam Creek in Maryland to pursue his strategy. The result was one of the bloodiest one-day battles of the war. More than 22,000 soldiers died or suffered casualties.[25] Lee's advance was stopped and he retreated. The battle was seen as a major defeat for the South by the Union and other countries, including England and France, who had previously supported the South. Recognizing the value of Black fighters, five days after the triumph at Antietam, Lincoln issued a preliminary proclamation that promised freedom to slaves living in the Confederate states, scheduled to take effect January 1, 1863.

Soon thereafter, the efforts to organize Blacks to fight for the Union were stepped up tremendously. More Black regiments joined the ranks of the Corps d'Afrique, the first all-Black regiment. Black troops were now permitted to officially enlist. More soldiers were recruited for service, fought in major battles and were noted for their service and valor. Martin Delaney, a physician and noted emigrationist, became the first Black U.S. army major.

Along with the increase of Black soldiers came increased discrimination within the military. Black soldiers often received the most difficult tasks and were similarly relegated to manual and arduous labor. Black troops served in separate all-Black units headed predominately by white officers. The Massachusetts 54th, primarily staffed by free Blacks, was the first Northern Black volunteer regiment. Led by their young white colonel, Robert Gould Shaw, this battalion withstood relentless assaults and was highly touted for its courage and skill. Frederick Douglass's sons Lewis and Charles both marched with the Massachusetts 54th.

Black soldiers also had to engage in a fierce battle with the military for equal pay. The Massachusetts 54th actually refused to accept any pay until their earnings equaled those of white soldiers for four months. After more than two years of pressure from Northern abolitionists and soldiers, Congress passed legislation equalizing pay in June 1864. Even still, the legislation was made retroactive only to January 1, 1864, exempting Black men who had never been slaves from that rule. Consequently, those who had not been slaves and had joined the military before January 1 would not receive equal pay for the entire period of their service.

In addition to the harsh and discriminatory treatment Blacks suffered as Union troops, they were not recognized as legitimate soldiers by the Confederates, and therefore would not be entitled to the normal rules of engagement when captured. Confederate Secretary of War James A. Seddon ordered that captured Black soldiers be executed, based on the notion that Confederate soldiers should not be inconvenienced with such prisoners.[26] One well-known atrocity committed against Black troops occurred on April 12, 1864, at Fort Pillow in Tennessee. Fort Pillow was manned by a force of approximately 600 troops, made up of the 11th U.S. Colored Troops and the White Unionists of the 13th Tennessee Cavalry. They were stormed by the Confederate cavalry under the command of Bedford Forrest. After Union forces surrendered, the Confederate commander ordered the slaughter of Black troops. Two hundred and thirty-one Union troops, most of them Black, were murdered. "Blacks were set on fire and the bodies mutilated. The wounded and the black children inside the fort were massacred along with the soldiers."[27] In addition to the killings, 100 Black soldiers were seriously wounded and 168 whites and 58 Blacks were captured. During an interrogation of events at Fort Pillow, Eli Carlton, (colored) private, company B, 6th United States heavy artillery, recounted that after being shot with a musket:

> I was hit once on the battle-field before we surrendered. They took me down to a little hospital under the hill. I was in the hospital when they shot me a second time. Some of our privates commenced talking. They said, "Do you fight with these God damned niggers?" they said, "Yes." Then they said, "God damn you, then, we will shoot you," and they shot one of them right down. They said, "I would not kill you, but, God damn you, you fight with these damned niggers and we will kill you;" and they blew his brains out of his head . . . [28]

Even though the official reports from Fort Pillow documented the atrocities, Lincoln's administration never retaliated for the murders. No one was apprehended and Bedford Forrest later established a violent, racist organization, the Ku Klux Klan (KKK).

Black soldiers not only served on the Union side of the conflict, there were Black Confederate soldiers as well. Those who supported the Confederacy were likely to receive financial rewards, or were pressured by local officials to serve. Confederate states such as Virginia passed impressment laws that forced free Blacks to serve in the war as laborers. Many Black Confederate soldiers were slaves, still beholden to their owners, whom they accompanied in camps and sometimes in battle. Although some slaves used the opportunity away from the plantation to run away, others fought in the hope that their masters might set them free after the war.[29] In New Orleans, free Black men of mixed-race bloodlines that formed the "Native Guards" decided that they should support the new Confederate government and volunteer for military service. However, because of the fear of arming Blacks, in addition to the charges that Blacks were natural cowards, the Native Guards were never used by the Confederacy. Notwithstanding Confederate refusal to accept them, the Native Guards still resolved to fight in the Civil War. Thus, when Union forces captured New Orleans in the spring of 1862, the Black regiment refused to desert the city, as the rest of the Confederate Army had. Instead they met with Union forces and eventually declared their allegiance to the Union.[30] In September 1862, the Native Guards became the first officially sanctioned regiment of Black soldiers in the U.S. army. The regiment served under the leadership of General Benjamin Butler.

By 1864, the embattled Confederates began to openly debate the value of enlisting Blacks as soldiers for their side. Recognizing that part of the

Northern advantage in the war was the added manpower of enthusiastic Black troops, the Confederates began to soften their previous views on Black service. They reasoned that giving Blacks their freedom in return for service was an attractive incentive for slaves. General Lee first sanctioned the policy of arming slaves in a letter to a Confederate senator written January 11, 1864, in which he said, "we must decide whether slavery shall be extinguished by our enemies and the slave be used against us, or use them ourselves at the risk of the effects which may be produced upon our social institutions . . . "[31] Adhering to the viewpoint of Lee and others, President Jefferson Davis signed a Negro's Soldier Law on March 13, which authorized the enlistment of Black soldiers.

The tide of the war turned after the Union army defeated the Confederates at the Battle of Gettysburg in Virginia, during summer 1963. Considered the bloodiest battle of the war, more than 23,000 Union soldiers and 28,000 Confederate soldiers were killed or sustained severe casualties. In the three-day clash, more than half of the Confederate troops were shot down. African Americans were essential to this battle, serving as troops and other support to the Union army.

Soon thereafter, Blacks marched with General William T. Sherman in May 1864, as he took Georgia. While in Savannah, Georgia, Sherman met with a group of Black ministers who petitioned for land. The "general responded by issuing Special Field Order No. 15, granting thousands of acres of confiscated land along the Florida, Georgia and South Carolina coast to Black families in 40 acre plots."[32]

On April 9, 1865, General Lee surrendered at Virginia's Appomattox Court House. Six days later, President Lincoln was assassinated by actor and Confederate sympathizer John Wilkes Booth, as he watched a play at Ford's Theatre in Washington, D.C.

Despite their tumultuous past, Blacks had finally made peace with Lincoln. The Black troops of the 22nd USCT led Lincoln's funeral procession. At the war's end, Black Americans made up approximately 10 to 12 percent of the Union army. These men fought in 449 battles and approximately 20 percent of them suffered casualties.[33]

The commentary in this section reflects the Black experience during the Civil War. It includes such documents as Frederick Douglass's passionate plea for Black involvement to support the Union army in his famous speech, "Men of Color, To Arms!" Abolitionists William Wells Brown and Martin R. Delany both lament the exclusion of Blacks from the war effort. Martin R. Delany, also an ardent emigrationist, felt so strongly about the potential for ending slavery as a result of the war that he became a recruiting agent of Black troops and a major in the Union army.

In a dictated letter to Franklin Sanborn, editor of *Commonwealth*, an antislavery newspaper, Harriet Tubman elucidates the difficult issues that women had to face during the war. Tubman, who was a nurse, scout and a spy for the Union, addressed the nature of the dress code for women in battle, which she saw as an added burden for women in war. She eventually gave up skirts for "bloomers" and became active in the temperance and women's rights movements. Corporal James Henry Gooding, who served with the all-Black 54th Massachusetts Colored Regiment, sent an open letter to President Abraham Lincoln protesting the uneven pay scale between Blacks and whites.

The voices of Black people presented in this section clarify their perspectives on the Civil War. What is observable in the timbre of the distinct voices is their eagerness to use arms to win their freedom, and their willingness to fight alongside Union forces, even when they were being treated unfairly. These documents also set the stage for African American involvement in subsequent American war efforts.

WILLIAM WELLS BROWN
(1814–1884)

Conductor on the Underground Railroad and long-time activist with the American Anti-Slavery Society, William Wells Brown wrote a novel on Thomas Jefferson's affair with the slave Sally Hemings. This passage is a speech by Brown, delivered May 6, 1862, at the annual meeting in New York of the American Anti-Slavery Society. In the letter Brown argues against President Lincoln's policy to exclude Blacks from service in the Union army. Brown also acknowledges the contribution of the "contraband" to the Union.

A Demand for the Black Man
May 6, 1862

. . . All I demand for the black man is, that the white people shall take their heels off his neck, and let him have a chance to rise by his own efforts. One of the first things that I heard when I arrived in the free States—and it was the strangest thing to me that I heard—was, that the slaves cannot take care of themselves. I came off without any education. Society did not take me up; I took myself up. I did not ask society to take me up. All I asked of the white people was, to get out of the way, and give me a chance to come from the South to the North. That was all I asked, and I went to work with my own hands. And that is all I demand for my brethren of the South today—that they shall have an opportunity to exercise their own physical and mental abilities. Give me them that, and I will leave the slaves to take care of themselves, and be satisfied with the result.

Now, Mr. President, I think that the present contest has shown clearly that the fidelity of the black people of this country to the cause of freedom is enough to put to shame every white man in the land who would think of driving us out of the country, provided freedom shall be proclaimed. I remember well, when Mr. Lincoln's proclamation went forth, calling for the first 75,000 men, that among the first to respond to that call were the colored men. A meeting was held in Boston, crowded as I never saw a meeting before; meetings were held in Rhode Island and Connecticut, in New York and Philadelphia, and throughout the West, responding to the President's call. Although the colored men in many of the free States were disenfranchised, abused, taxed without representation, their children turned out of the schools, nevertheless, they went on, determined to try to discharge their duty to the country, and to save it from the tyrannical power of the slaveholders of the South. But the cry went forth—"We won't have the Negroes; we won't have anything to do with them; we won't fight with them; we won't have them in the army, nor about us." Yet scarcely had you got into conflict with the South, when you were glad to receive the news that contrabands brought. The first telegram announcing any news from the disaffected district commences with—"A contraband just in from Maryland tells us" so much. The last telegram, in today's paper, announces that a contraband tells us so much about Jefferson Davis and Mrs. Davis and the little Davises. The nation is glad to receive the news from the contraband. We have an old law with regard to the mails, that a Negro shall not touch the mails at all; and for fifty years the black has not had the privilege of touching the mails of the United States with his little finger; but we are glad enough now to have the Negro bring the mail in his pocket! The first thing asked of a contraband is "Have you got a newspaper?— what's the news?" And the news is greedily taken in from the lowest officer or soldier in the army, up to the Secretary of War. They have tried to keep the Negro out of war, but they could not keep him out, and now they drag him in, with his news, and are glad to do so. General Wool says the contrabands have brought the most reliable news. Other Generals say their information can be relied upon. The Negro is taken as a pilot to guide the fleet of General Burnside through the inlets of the South. The black man welcomes your armies and your fleets, takes care of your sick, is ready to do anything, from cooking up to shouldering a musket; and yet these would-be patriots and professed lovers of the land talk about driving the Negro out!

FREDERICK DOUGLASS
(1818–1895)

Douglass was born to a slave woman and a white man in Maryland. At the age of eight Douglass was sent to Baltimore to live with a ship carpenter. He escaped from slavery on September 3, 1838, and later moved to Massachusetts. It was there that Douglass became renowned as an eloquent orator, leading abolitionist, and publisher of the anti-slavery newspaper, the North Star. *During the Civil War, Douglass served as a recruiter for the Union army and advisor to Abraham Lincoln. The following passage is an editorial urging African Americans to fight in the Civil War. It was published only three days after Douglass was appointed to the position of recruiter.*

Men of Color, To Arms!
March 2, 1863

When first the rebel cannon shattered the walls of Sumter and drove away its starving garrison, I predicted that the war then and there inaugurated would not be fought out entirely by white men. Every month's experience during these weary years has confirmed that opinion. A war undertaken and brazenly carried on for the perpetual enslavement of colored men, calls logically and loudly for colored men to help suppress it. Only a moderate share of sagacity was needed to see that the arm of the slave was the best defense against the arm of the slaveholder. Hence with every reverse to the national arms, with every exulting shout of victory raised by slaveholding rebels, I have implored the imperiled nation to unchain against her foes, her powerful black hand.

Slowly and reluctantly that appeal is beginning to be heeded. Stop not now to complain that it was not heeded sooner. That it should not, may or it may not have been best. This is not the time to discuss that question. Leave it to the future. When the war is over, the country is saved, peace is established, and the black man's rights are secured, as they will be, history with an impartial hand will dispose of that and sundry other questions. Action! Action! Not criticism is the plain duty of this hour. Words are now useful only as they stimulate to blows. The office of speech now is only to point out when, where, and how to strike to the best advantage.

There is no time to delay. The tide is at its flood that leads on to future. From East and West, from North to South, the sky is written all over, "Now or never." "Liberty won by white men would lose half its luster." "Who would be free themselves must strike the blow." "Better even die free, than to live slaves." This is the sentiment of every brave colored man amongst us.

There are weak cowardly men in all nations. We have them amongst us. They tell you this is the "white man's war"; that you will be no "better off after than before the war"; that the getting of you into the army is to "sacrifice you on the first opportunity." Believe them not; cowards themselves, they do not wish to have cowardice shamed by your brave example. Leave them to their timidity, or to whatever motive may hold them back.

I have not thought lightly of the words I am now addressing you. The counsel I give comes of close observation of the great struggle now in progress, and of the deep conviction that this is your hour and mine. In good earnest then, and after the best deliberation, I now for the first time during this war feel at liberty to call and counsel you to arms.

By every consideration which binds you to your enslaved fellow-countrymen, and the peace and welfare of your country; by every aspiration which you cherish for the freedom and equality of yourselves and your children; by all the ties of blood and identity which make us one with the brave black men now fighting our battles in Louisiana and in South Carolina, I urge you to fly to arms, and smite with death the power that would bury the government and your liberty in the same hopeless grave.

I wish I could tell you that the State of New York calls you to this high honor. For the moment her constituted authorities are silent on the subject. They will speak by and by, and doubtless on the right side; but we are not compelled to wait for her. We can get at the throat of treason and slavery through the State of Massachusetts. She was first in the War of Independence; first to break the chains of her slaves; first to make the black man equal before the law; first to admit colored children to her common schools, and she was to answer with her blood the alarm cry of the nation, when its capital was menaced by rebels. You know her patriotic governor, and you know Charles Sumner. I need not add more.

Massachusetts now welcomes you to arms as soldiers. She has but a small colored population from which to recruit. She has full leave of the general government to send one regiment to the war, and she has undertaken to do it. Go quickly and help fill up the first colored regiment from the North. I am authorized to assure you that you will receive the same wages, the same rations, the same equipments, the same protection, the same treatment, and the same bounty officers, men who will take especial pride in your efficiency and success. They will be quick to accord to you all the honor you shall merit by your valor, and see that your rights and feelings are respected by other soldiers. I have assured myself on these points, and can speak with authority.

More than twenty years of unswerving devotion to our common cause may give me some humble claim to be trusted at this momentous crisis. I will not argue. To do so implies hesitation and doubt, and you do not hesitate. You do not doubt. The day dawns; the morning star is bright upon the horizon! The iron gate of our prison stands open. One gallant rush from the North will fling it wide open, while four millions of our brothers and sisters shall march out into liberty. The chance is now given you to end in a day the bondage of centuries, and rise in one bound from social degradation to the plan of common equality with all other varieties of men.

Remember Denmark Vesey of Charleston; remember Nathanial Turner of Southampton; remember Shields Green of Copeland, who followed noble John Brown, and fell as glorious martyrs for the cause of the slave. Remember that in a contest with oppression, the Almighty has no attribute which can take sides with oppressors.

The case is before you. This is our golden opportunity. Let us accept it, and forever wipe out the dark reproaches unsparingly hurled against us by our enemies. Let us win for ourselves the gratitude of our country, and the best blessings of our posterity through all time. The nucleus of this first regiment is now in camp at Readville, a short distance from Boston. I will undertake to forward to Boston all persons adjudged fit to be mustered into the regiment, who shall apply to me at any time within the next two weeks.

MARTIN ROBINSON DELANY
(1812–1883)

A graduate of Harvard Medical School, Delany played an important role in enlisting Black people in the Union army. He published an anti-slavery paper "The Mystery," and worked with Frederick Douglass on the North Star. *In 1859, Delany visited the country of the Yorubas (now part of Nigeria) to negotiate with local kings a place for the settlement of Black people willing to emigrate from America. He summarized his findings in* The Official Report of the Niger Valley Exploring Party *(1861). Upon his return to the United States, Delany encountered the Civil War, which led him to abandon his earlier emigrationist ideas to fight for Black liberty with the U.S. President Abraham Lincoln appointed Delany as a major in charge of recruiting all-Black Union units. After the war Delany worked for the Freedmen's Bureau and became a Republican politician. He was later awarded a judgeship in Charleston. The following letter from Delany is to Secretary of War Edwin Stanton requesting permission to recruit colored troops from the "seceded states."*

Recruiting Black Troops for the Civil War
December 15, 1863

The subject and policy of black troops have become of much interest in our country, and the effective means and method of raising them is a matter of much importance. In consideration of this, sir, I embrace the earliest opportunity of asking the privilege of calling the attention of your department of the fact, that as a policy in perfect harmony with the course of the President, and your own enlightened views, that the agency of intelligent, competent, black men adapted to the work must be the most effective means of obtaining black troops; because knowing and being of that people as a race, they can command such influences as is required to accomplish the object. I have been successfully engaged as recruiting agent of black troops, first as a recruiting agent for Massachusetts, 54th Regiment, and the commencement as the managing agent in the West and Southwest, for Rhode Island Heavy Artillery, which is now nearly full; and now have contract from the State authorities of Connecticut, for the entire West and South-West, in raising colored troops to fill her quota. During these engagements, I have had associated with me, Mr. John Jones, a very respectable and responsible business colored man of this city, and we have associated ourselves permanently together in an agency for raising black troops for all parts of the country. We are able sir, to command all the effective black men, as agents, in the United States, and in the event of an order from your department, giving us the authority to recruit colored troops in any of the southern or seceded States, we will be ready and able to raise a regiment, or brigade, if required, in a shorter time than can be otherwise effected. With the belief sir, that this is one of the measures in which the claims of the black man may be officially recognized, without seemingly infringing upon those of other citizens, I confidently ask sir, that this humble request may engage your early notice. All satisfactory references will be given by both of us.

HARRIET TUBMAN
(1820–1913)

Legendary for her fearless shepherding of over 300 slaves to freedom, Tubman also served as an intelligence agent for the Union army. She led many raids against the Confederates, one of the most famous being the Combahee River Raid, in which her contacts in the South Carolina coastal region warned of floating land mines set on the Combahee River as a trap for the Union army. The following is a letter written to Tubman's friend, Franklin B. Sanborn, editor of the anti-slavery newspaper Commonwealth. *In the letter, Tubman complains of the impractical clothes she wore during her expeditions. She vowed to never wear long dresses again during her exploits.*

Letter to Franklin Sanborn
June 30, 1863

Last fall, when the people here became very much alarmed for fear of an invasion from the rebels, all my clothes were packed and sent with others to Hilton Head, and lost; and I have never been able to get any trace of them since. I was sick at the time, and unable to look after them myself. I want, among the rest, a bloomer dress, made of some coarse, strong material, to wear on expeditions. In our late expedition up the Combahee River, in coming on board the boat, I was carrying two pigs for a poor sick woman, who had a child to carry, and the order "double quick" was given and I started to run, stepped on my dress, it being rather long, and fell and tore it almost off, so that when I got on board the boat, there was hardly anything left of it but shreds. I made up my mind then I would never wear a long dress again on another expedition of the kind, but would have a bloomer as soon as I could get it . . . You have, without doubt, seen a full account of the expedition I refer to. Don't you think we colored people are entitled to some credit for that exploit, under the lead of the brave Colonel Montgomery? We weakened the rebels by bringing away seven hundred and fifty-six of their most valuable live stock, known up in your region as "contrabands," and this, too, without the loss of a single life on our part . . . Nearly or quite all the able-bodied men have joined the colored regiments here.

CORPORAL JAMES HENRY GOODING
(1837–1864)

Corporal James Henry Gooding was a freeborn man of African descent. In 1856, when Gooding was 19 years old, he signed on as a seaman on a whaler in New Bedford, Massachusetts. He later joined the 54th Massachusetts Infantry of the Union army. Based upon Gooding's letters it is clear that he was well educated. In this editorial, Gooding discusses Black reaction to the Militia Act of 1862, which legally permitted the discriminatory act of paying Black soldiers less in wages than white soldiers.

A Black Soldier's Civil War Letters from the Front
August 9, 1863

Messrs Editors: Since my last weekly mélange, the situation remains about the same in this department. The 55th regiment, Col. N. P. Hallowell commanding, arrived here from Newbern last Monday, and on Tuesday the regiment was introduced to Messrs. Shovel and Spade, a firm largely interested in building rifle pits, breastworks and batteries. The men appear to be in splendid physical condition, and taking the two regiments in the aggregate, I think the 55th is superior in material to the 54th. But the hardships incident to a soldier's life may equalize them in a month or two.

Last Wednesday night, as a party of men on a fatigue expedition were approaching Fort Johnson, a little too near, they narrowly escaped being captured. The party were in boats containing lumber, for the purpose of building a bridge across a creek which divides this island from James Island. The tide falling, near morning they were discovered by the rebel pickets, who commenced firing on them. Had not our own sharpshooters been near, the rebels would no doubt have captured some of our men; as it was, however, the fatigue party scrambled out of the boats, and made tracks through the mud and mire for camp. The rebels did succeed in capturing a captain and five men, but they escaped.

The sickly season has now about commenced; daily we hear muffled drum, accompanied by shrill, shrieking tones of the fife, which tells us that the "fell destroyer, Death" is near. Three times yesterday the plaintive notes of Bonaparte crossing the Alps were played passing our camp, followed by some noble son of New England in each instance. Our own regiment, too, lost one yesterday. His name was John Pieere, of Philadelphia; his complaint was fever.

About noon yesterday there was sudden cessation of firing; the cause of it was the rebels sent out a flag of truce, and after that some of the general officers rode to the front and met those bearing it. What the result was is not known; but there were many rumors afloat during the afternoon in regard to it; some even hinting that Fort Wagner's defenders wished to sue for conditional terms; others to the effect that the "populace" of Charleston, not unlike their confreres in New York, were becoming clamorous for peace, threatening Jeff, Beauregard & Co. with violence if they persisted in holding on to Charleston, in view of the vast preparations the "Yankees" were making for their destruction; and that Beauregard came to make some treaty for the surrender of the city. But the news manufacturers didn't hit the nail on the head, I guess, for by 6 o'clock they were blazing away at each other nicely, with every prospect of—"to be continued."

Last Wednesday afternoon the companies were all formed in line in their respective streets, when Col. Littlefield addressed each company separately to this effect: "I have been requested by the paymaster to say that if the men are ready to receive TEN dollars per month as part pay, he will come over and pay the men off; you need not be afraid though that you won't get your THIRTEEN dollars per month, for you surely will." He then went on explaining how this little financial hitch was brought about, by telling us of some old record on file in relation to paying laborers or contrabands employed on public works, which the War Department had construed as applying to colored soldiers, urging us to take the TEN NOW and wait for some action of the Government for the other three. He then said, "all who wish to take the ten dollars per month, raise your right hand," and I am glad to say not one man in the whole regiment lifted a hand. He then said, we might not receive any money till after the convening of Congress. We replied that we had been over five months waiting, and we would wait till the Government could frame some *special* law, for the payment of part of its troops. The 2d South Carolina regiment was paid the ten dollars per month; but we were enlisted under different circumstances. Too many of our comrades' bones lie bleaching near the walls of Fort Wagner to subtract even one cent from our hard earned pay. If the nation can ill afford to pay us, we are men and will do our duty while we are here without a murmur, as we have done always, before and since that day we were offered to sell our manhood for thirteen dollars per month.

J.H.G

P.S.—I have just learned on "undoubted authority" that the flag of truce was for the purpose of returning the letters, valuables and money found on our dead and wounded in the assault of the 18th July. This may seem wonderful, that the rebels should act so honorably, but it is fact. May be they are putting in practice what Hon. A. H. Stephens undertook to negotiate, thinking we will be magnanimous when we enter Charleston.

J.H.G

SOJOURNER TRUTH
(1797–1883)

Born with the slave name Isabella Van Baumfree in 1797, the fierce activist Sojourner Truth spent her entire adult life fighting for the liberation of Black people and women. Truth's determined spirit was exemplified by her daring escape to freedom in 1827 to Canada with the youngest of her five children. In 1829, she returned to the U.S. after the state of New York abolished slavery. An active participant and leader of the abolitionist and women's rights movements, Sojourner Truth became a well-publicized speaker on both struggles, specifically with the famous poem "Ain't I a Woman?" In 1850, Truth and friend Olive Gilbert composed her biography, The Narrative of Sojourner Truth. This song was written by Truth for the first Michigan Regiment of Colored Soldiers and was composed during the war. The song was a testament to the fighting spirit of Black soldiers and her hopes for the freedom of those enslaved. Truth also applauds the passage of the Emancipation Proclamation.

The Valiant Soldiers
Narrative 126, n.d.

We are the valiant soldiers who've 'listed for the war;
We are fighting for the union, we are fighting for the law;
We can shoot a rebel farther than a white man ever saw;
As we go marching on.
Chorus.—
Glory, glory, hallelujah! Glory, glory, hallelujah!
Glory, glory, hallelujah, as we go marching on.
Look there above the center, where the flag is waving bright;
We are going out of slavery, we are bound for freedom's light;
We mean to show Jeff Davis how the Africans can fight,
As we go marching on.—Cho.
We are done with hoeing cotton, we are done with hoeing corn;
We are colored Yankee soldiers as sure as you are born.
When massa hears us shouting, he will think 'tis Gabriel's horn,
As we go marching on.—Cho.
They will have to pay us wages, the wages of their sin;
They will have to bow their foreheads to their colored kith and kin;
They will have to give us house-room, or the roof will tumble in,
As we go marching on.—Cho.
We hear the proclamation, massa, hush it as you will;
The birds will sing it to us, hopping on the cotton hill;

The possum up the gum tree could n't keep it still,
As we go marching on.—Cho
Father Abraham has spoken, and the message has been sent;
The prison doors have opened, and out the prisoners went
To join the sable army of African descent
As we go marching on.—Cho

Notes

1. In a biography of General Ulysses S. Grant published in 1928, W. E. Woodward stated, "The American Negroes are the only people in the history of the world, so far as I know, that ever became free without any effort of their own." W. E. Woodward, *Meet General Grant* (New York: Liveright, 1928).

2. John Hope Franklin and Alfred A. Moss Jr., *From Slavery to Freedom: A History of African Americans* (New York: McGraw Hill, 1994), 180.

3. Peter M. Bergman, *The Chronological History of the Negro in America* (New York: Harper & Row, 1969), 221.

4. David Walker, *David Walker's Appeal to the Coloured Citizens of the World, but in Particular and Very Expressly to Those of the United States of America*, rev. ed. (New York: Hill & Wang, 1995).

5. David Walker and Henry Highland Garnet, *Walker's Appeal and Garnet's Address to the Slaves of the United States of America* (1848; Nashville, Tenn.: James C. Winston, 1994).

6. For additional information on the Fugitive Slave Law of 1850, see Darlene Clark Hine et al., *The African-American Odyssey* (Upper Saddle River, N.J.: Prentice Hall, 2003), 212.

7. For a brief synopsis of the Dred Scott case, see Paul C. Bartholomew and Joseph F. Menez, *Summaries of Leading Cases on the Constitution* (Lanham, Md.: Rowman & Littlefield, 1989), 268–70. Also see Clark Hine, *African-American Odyssey*, 219–21, for further discussion.

8. Benjamin Quarles, *Allies for Freedom & Blacks on John Brown* (New York: Oxford University Press, 1974).

9. Paul M. Arohe, ed., *The Complete Lincoln and Douglas Debates of 1858* (Chicago: University of Chicago Press, 1991), 141; and Roy Basler, *Abraham Lincoln: His Speeches and Writings* (New York: Plenum, 1990), 580.

10. John Rock, *The Liberator*, February 3, 1860; H. Ford Douglass speech in *The Liberator*, July 13, 1860; both reprinted in James McPherson, *The Negro's Civil War: How American Blacks Felt and Acted during the War for the Union* (New York: Random House, 1993), 5–7.

11. *Douglass Monthly* 3 (December 1860): 370; excerpted in McPherson, *Negro's Civil War*, 11.

12. *Douglass Monthly* 3 (January 1861): 392.

13. John Mercer Langston, *From the Virginia Plantation to the National Capital* (Hartford, Conn.: American, 1894), 205–21; and McPherson, *Negro's Civil War*, 182.

14. *Anglo-African*, September 28, 1861.

15. Langston, *Virginia Plantation*, 205–7.

16. Roy Basler, ed., *The Collected Works of Abraham Lincoln* (New Brunswick, N.J.: Rutgers University Press, 1953), 5:419–25.

17. McPherson, *Negro's Civil War*, 28. Also see Samuel Eliot Morison, *The Growth of the American Republic* (New York: Oxford University Press, 1980), 663.

18. Basler, *Collected Works of Lincoln*, 4:506, 517–18.

19. "Address on Colonization to a Deputation of Negros" in Basler, *Collected Works of Lincoln*, 5:370–74.

20. "Message to Congress," in Basler, *Collected Works of Lincoln*, 5:48.

21. Charlotte Forten, "Life on the Sea Islands," *Atlantic Monthly* 13 and 14 (May and June 1864).

22. Jean M. Humez, *Harriet Tubman: The Life and the Life Stories* (Madison: University of Wisconsin Press, 2004); Ella Forbes, *African American Women during the Civil War* (New York: Garland Publishing, 1998); and C. Peter Ripley, ed., *The Black Abolitionist Papers*, vol. 5, *The United States, 1859–1865* (Chapel Hill: University of North Carolina Press, 1992), 220–21.

23. For information on Maria Lewis and Mary Elizabeth Bowser, see Forbes, *African American Women*, 41; Michael Lee Lanning, *The African American Soldier: From Crispus Attucks to Colin Powell* (Secaucus, N.J.: Birch Lane Press, 1997).

24. After the Civil War, Robert Smalls served five terms in the U.S. House of Representatives from South Carolina. For more information about Robert Smalls, see Edward A. Miller, *Gullah Statesman: Robert Smalls from Slavery to Congress, 1839–1915* (Columbia: University of South Carolina Press, 1995); and William J. Simmons, *Men of Mark: Eminent, Progressive and Rising* (Chicago: Johnson Publishing, 1970).

25. James M. McPherson, *Crossroads of Freedom: Antietam* (New York: Oxford University Press, 2002), 129.

26. For more on Seddon's views, see "Let Us All Be Grateful That We Have Colored Troops That Will Fight," in *Black Soldiers in Blue: African American Troops in the Civil War Era*, ed. John David Smith (Chapel Hill: University of North Carolina Press, 2002), 74, and notes, 77–78.

27. Gail Buckley, *American Patriots: The Story of Blacks in the Military from the Revolution to Desert Storm* (New York: Random House, 2001), 103.

28. House Committee on the Conduct of the War, Report #65, *Fort Pillow Massacre*, 38th Cong., 1st sess., 1864, Report #65, 17, 25–28. Testimony of several soldiers reprinted in McPherson, *Negro's Civil War*, 221–25.

29. James H. Brewer, *The Confederate Negro* (Durham, N.C.: Duke University Press, 1969).

30. Benjamin Quarles, *The Negro in the Civil War* (New York: Russell & Russell, 1953), 38–40. For more on the Native Guards, see Lawrence Lee Hewitt, "An Ironic

Route to Glory: Louisiana's Native Guards at Port Hudson," in Smith, *Black Soldiers in Blue*, 76–106.

31. Reprinted in McPherson, *Negro's Civil War*, 248.

32. Special Field Order #15, issued on January 16, 1865.

33. See Herbert Aptheker, "Negro Casualties in the Civil War," *Journal of Negro History* 32 (January 1947): 12, 47–48; and McPherson, *Negro's Civil War*, 241.

~

CHAPTER FOUR

Spanish-American and Philippines-American Wars: Is This a White Man's War?

1 8 9 8 - 1 9 0 2

The passage of the Emancipation Proclamation, followed by the Union army's defeat of the Confederacy, created a sense of optimism among African Americans. Their yearning for full citizenship, equality and independence could finally be satisfied. But regrettably, less than a decade later, Northern-led Reconstruction efforts that had encouraged equal rights in voting, public accommodations and employment gradually ended when Rutherford Hayes and Samuel Tilden entered into a compromise on the presidential election of 1876. In return for the presidency, Hayes agreed to grant home rule to the oppressive South. Foremost in the minds of Southern lawmakers was to draft new state constitutions and pass laws that would disenfranchise Blacks and force them into unreasonable employment conditions, often akin to the servitude experienced during slavery. For instance, in 1883 the Supreme Court overturned the Pubic Accommodations Bill of 1875, which required equal access to public facilities. Then in a stunning decision, the Supreme Court gave legal sanction to Jim Crow segregation laws in its *Plessy v. Ferguson* (1896) decision. As a result of these acts, laws that mandated separate accommodations on buses and trains and in hotels, theaters and schools were deemed constitutional across the country.

African American attempts to vote and become elected officials were stifled. States instituted such measures as the poll tax, literacy tests and grandfather clauses to prohibit African Americans from voting. When those measures failed, the KKK resorted to outright violence to, in effect, terrorize Blacks into submission. The KKK was well known for their "nightrides" of violence and lynching Black people who were considered threats to white supremacy. Lynchings rose to unprecedented levels. From 1884 to 1900, there had been more than 2,500 lynchings in the South.[1] The loss of Black voting power led to a decrease of African American elected officials. During 1869 to 1901, two Blacks served in the Senate and twenty in the House of Representatives. By the end of Reconstruction, only a handful of Blacks held minor offices in communities with large Black populations, but none were elected to national or state offices until the 20th century.[2]

The response from African American leaders to these assaults was articulated by such noted figures as Frederick Douglass and founder of the Tuskegee Institute, Booker T. Washington. Upon Douglass's death in 1895, Washington became the preeminent African American leader. However, in contrast to Douglass's emphasis on political agitation to promote equality, Washington maintained that Blacks should acquiesce to white social rules on segregation and access to higher education, while emphasizing industrial training and economic development.[3] Washington thus encouraged Blacks to end the kind of political activism that might alienate whites and lead to more violence.

Monroe Trotter, editor of the newspaper the *Guardian*, and W. E. B. Du Bois cofounded the Black protest organization the Niagara Movement in 1905 to challenge Washington's views. Trotter caused a stir in 1903 when he interrupted Washington's speech at a Boston church with several tough questions. Accused of continued disorderly conduct, Trotter was also arrested. The event, widely reported in newspapers, became known as the "Boston Riot." W. E. B. Du Bois agreed with many of Trotter's criticisms of Washington, and argued that Washington was misguided in his assertion that Blacks should seek economic equality first. Du Bois instead insisted that economic security was not enough, and that Blacks must attend institutions of higher learning to attain intellectual, political and economic power.

Another challenger to Washington was Bishop Henry McNeil Turner of the First African Methodist Episcopal Church, who expressed some of the most nationalist ideas of that time. Based on pure pessimism about the commitment of the U.S. to end racial discrimination, Turner called on Black people to emigrate to Africa and stop worshipping a white image of God.[4]

Leaving the South to handle its own affairs, the national government focused on industrialization and expansion. Industrialization depended on power-driven machinery and factory production. Advances in iron- and steel-making, the expansion of the railroads, and innovations in electricity and the sciences improved the efficiency and productivity of industry. New communication tools like the telegraph and telephone allowed for further economic activity and expansion. U.S. capitalists became increasingly focused on finding new areas to build and invest to earn more profits. Consequently, a wave of expansionism was unleashed over North America. As the U.S. stretched out to the west, native populations were displaced often through violent clashes and negotiated treaties, rendering them homeless and hopeless.

The U.S. also sought to prohibit further European expansion in the western hemisphere. President James Monroe delivered the "Monroe Doctrine" in the State of the Union message to Congress on December 2, 1823. Essentially, his "doctrine" informed European powers that not only was America unavailable for European colonization, but that any effort to extend European political influence into the New World would be considered by the United States as a threat to its safety.[5] In effect, the United States would not interfere in European wars or internal affairs, and expected Europe to reciprocate the gesture. Also in the 19th century, the ideology of "Manifest Destiny" gained acceptance among the masses of citizens. Manifest Destiny has as its underpinning the idea that the United States had a divinely inspired mission to expand, particularly across the North American frontier toward the Pacific Ocean. Manifest Destiny justified expansion of U.S. power across North America and it promoted nationalism and racism as well.

The twin ideas embedded in the Monroe Doctrine and Manifest Destiny led to U.S. acquisition of land in the Pacific Island region, including Midway, Wake and Howland. However, European powers still claimed rights to some western lands. Spain's claim to island nations such as Cuba and Puerto Rico led to hostilities with the U.S. government.

The civil unrest in Cuba began in earnest during the Ten Years' War in 1868 when Cuban nationals began to challenge the brutal dictatorship of the Spanish government.[6] By 1878, Spanish troops had crushed the rebellion, but later signed the Treaty of Zanjon with the Cubans in 1878 that officially terminated the war. In 1895, five leaders from the Ten Years' War (Salvador Cisneros, Calixto Garcia, Maiximo Gomez, Antonio Maceo and Jose Marti) regrouped to continue the war against Spain. In 1898, violent rioting in Havana gained the attention of the American press, raising concern for U.S. citizens and U.S. investments of more than $50 million in plantations and sugar refineries there.

The U.S. became more alarmed when Spain sent General Valeriano Weyler to put down the insurrection. Having difficulty separating the insurgents from those loyal to Spain, Weyler placed a large number of the rural population in concentration camps. The Spanish crackdown on the insurgency resulted in the deaths of more than 50,000 people from poverty, starvation and disease.

The U.S., in an attempt to show Spain its willingness to support the Cubans militarily as well as to protect its property, dispatched the battleship U.S.S. *Maine* to Havana in January 1898. On February 15 of that same year, the battleship exploded, killing 268 Americans, 22 of whom were Black sailors. This heinous explosion sparked an American outcry against the assumed provocateur, Spain. The cry "Remember the *Maine!* To hell with Spain!" expressed the rage of Americans. Ironically, army engineering studies published in 1986 would conclude that the tragedy was actually the result of an accidental explosion on board the ship.[7]

Within three weeks of the explosion, Congress passed the "Fifty-Million-Dollar Bill" to prepare the U.S. military for war and declared that all the navy's ships were to remain fueled, staffed and ready for deployment. On April 19, President William McKinley requested a declaration of war from Congress. Three days later, he initiated a naval blockade of Cuba. Soon thereafter Congress officially recognized Cuba's independence and declared war on Spain, pursuant to the president's request.

African Americans expressed a myriad of emotions as they articulated their views on the war, including anger and empathy for the Cubans whose struggles against racism and injustice paralleled their own. Spain was characterized as exhibiting barbaric tendencies to the recognizably Black nation. Providence, Rhode Island, attorney Charles G. Baylor characterized the rebellion in Cuba "from the beginning, an Afro-Cuban Socialist uprising against Spanish tyranny, capitalistic greed and rapacity, the church being the mainstay and prop of the entire infernation."[8] Other African Americans questioned if they should enlist as soldiers in the U.S. war to defeat Spain. Certainly, an affirmative response meant that they would show the world their solidarity with the Cuban rebels. Furthermore, their participation might become an opportunity to improve their own conditions in the U.S. J. L. Thompson, editor of the *Iowa Bystander*, wrote in April 1898 that the present war "may serve as a lesson to their southern brothers as to what loyalty, true and equal manhood is, and we hope hereafter to be more willing to grant equal justice and freedom to their neighbors and citizens."[9] Thompson believed that African Americans would gain the respect of whites and lawmakers by demonstrating their patriotism and loyalty to the U.S. South Carolinian politician D. August Straker called on all Black Americans to display the same patriotism that had characterized their response to every national crisis of the past so as not to cast doubt on the "patriotism of the race." Moreover, said Straker, "the war with Spain over Cuba could end our race troubles."[10] Following that same line of thinking, in a letter to Secretary of the Navy John D. Long, Booker T. Washington maintained that Blacks should participate in the war "to render service to our country that no other race can," because unlike whites, they were accustomed to the dangerous climate of Cuba. He also offered to recruit 10,000 "loyal, brave, strong black men in the south who crave an opportunity to show their loyalty to our land . . . "[11]

On the other side, many African Americans opposed U.S. policy on Spain in Cuba, arguing that the U.S. had imperialist designs on the island-nation. During a meeting of the Afro-American Council in Washington, D.C., Ida B. Wells said that "Negros should oppose expansion until the government was able to protect the Negro at home."[12] John Mitchell Jr. of the *Richmond Planet* was concerned about the resources that would be used to support the war, resources that would not be used to promote the uplift of Blacks in the U.S. He stated, "The war-scare has cost this country fifty million of dollars. What will a war cost?"[13] Other opponents denounced the enlistment of Black soldiers in a war abroad, especially considering the government's failure to protect Blacks from white mob violence inside the U.S. Calvin Chase, noted Black Republican and editor of the *Washington Bee*, argued that African Americans had their own war to wage against injustice in the U.S. He quipped, "The Negro has no reason to fight for Cuba's independence. He is opposed at home. He is in as much need of independence as Cuba is."[14]

The proponents of African American enlistment prevailed in the debate. Thousands of Blacks responded to President McKinley's call for volunteers. The governors of most states from the North and the South, however, first ignored African American attempts to enlist. The failure to enlist African Americans was further compounded by "the fact that few belonged to the state militias, and the volunteer army was made up primarily of militiamen."[15] The governor of Georgia was well known for his refusal to mobilize any Black militiamen for the federal war.[16]

African American leaders protested and lobbied government officials to enlist their people as soldiers. As a consequence of that pressure or when whites failed to meet quotas needed by states, African Americans were able to enlist. In the end, it took an act of Congress to authorize ten all-Black volunteer regiments, of which four actually served. Thus in addition to the four regular Black army regiments, four volunteer regiments provided service in the war. The new regiments were recruited primarily from the South and were known as "immune" regiments—so named because of the belief that because of their African heritage and years of exposure to tropical diseases they would be immune to the diseases rampant in Cuba, such as malaria and yellow fever. This idea was most likely related to the myth spread during slavery that slaves could withstand certain diseases in various parts of the South. Eventually, after scores of African American soldiers fell sick, the old myth that Blacks were immune to yellow fever was disproved. At the end of the Cuban invasion, an epidemic of yellow fever broke out. White soldiers had outright refused to work as volunteer nurses in the hospitals, but members of the 24th eagerly stepped forth, perhaps believing the pseudo-scientific theory about African American resiliency in such conditions. Unfortunately, more than half of the 471 members of the 24th contracted yellow fever.[17]

The four regular African American regiments that served in the Spanish-American War were army veterans from previous wars. Often referred to as the Buffalo Soldiers, the 9th and 10th cavalry and the 24th and 25th infantry were summoned fresh from service in the western plains where they fought against several Native American nations. Having spent twenty to thirty years in this effort, they were now seasoned veterans, and by many accounts amongst the most qualified and courageous soldiers in the U.S. forces. They were named Buffalo Soldiers by the Cheyenne Indians, who respected them as warriors.[18]

Even though the Spanish-American War was widely considered a naval war, there were a number of notable ground battles that gained recognition for African American soldiers. Some of these significant campaigns were the battles of Las Guaiman, El Caney, San Juan Hill, Santiago and Kettle Hill. One of the most honorable mentions of African American soldiers came from Lieutenant Theodore Roosevelt, organizer of the First U.S. Volunteer Cavalry, also known as the Rough Riders and well known for their heroic deeds. Although Roosevelt's Rough Riders have become the premier battalion of the war, on one Cuban mission the Rough Riders were rescued by the all-Black 10th Cavalry. At one point when white soldiers were reluctant to move forward in the charge of two hills, African American soldiers pushed them aside and pressed on, sustaining heavy losses. Their sacrifices helped to ensure victory in the most decisive point of the war. Theodore Roosevelt acknowledged the bravery of the 10th Cavalry in several statements.[19] Unfortunately, Roosevelt later retreated from his initial public praise of the African American soldiers under his leadership when he sought to reach out to white voters during his presidential campaign of 1900.[20]

The four regiments set a high standard for African American soldiers. Black officers served as commanders for the first time, while more than seven African Americans were awarded the Medal of Honor.[21] On nearly every battlefield their spirit left observers amazed. First Sergeant M. W. Saddler of the 25th Infantry reported from Santiago that "The Spaniards fully appreciated the fighting qualities of those whom they called 'smoked Yankees' and 'negretter soladas.' In one skirmish, the Spaniards began to fire over their heads, for they knew that shooting at the Black soldiers was pointless, as 'powder and steel' would not stop them."[22]

But despite their spirited service, Black soldiers were subjected to racial discrimination and harassment. Forced to abide by the army's racist policies, African American soldiers faced constant insults from white soldiers and were often ordered out of restaurants and other public facilities. African American soldiers expressed their frustration in letters. In the book *Smoked Yankees*, a soldier who referred to himself as "Ham" discussed the ordeal of Black soldiers stationed in Camp Haskell near Macon, Georgia, who clashed with locals intent on maintaining their Jim Crow customs. An outbreak of violence and lynching resulted from the mixture of Black soldiers and the local whites. Ham commented on the unfairness of the justice system that prosecuted many of those cases. He stated, "Haven't a week passed since we have been in this pest hole of the South that some of Uncle Sam's black boys in blue, haven't been 'justifiably homicided,' at least this is the only word that seems to strike the minds of all juries who try cases for 'killing nigger soldiers . . . '" Another writer, referred to as "Black Man," discussed the racism of white officers. He asserted that "white officers found it too distasteful to use the sinks used by colored officers, so another sink for white officers was dug and housed in, that meant the needless waste of more than five hundred feet of dressed lumber."[23]

The Spanish-American War lasted 113 days. At its closing, the U.S. and Spanish Peace Commissions signed a treaty on December 10, in which the U.S. acquired Puerto Rico, Guam and the Philippines. In March, Congress passed the Army Act, which authorized the president to enlist U.S. volunteers for service in the Philippines.

The Philippines

McKinley's colonial policy in the Philippines was predicated on the idea of "benevolent assimilation," which meant that the U.S. would treat the native inhabitants "in a firm but kind manner, demonstrating respect for both human and property rights."[24] But the virulent racism practiced by many U.S. soldiers made an already difficult situation untenable for the Filipinos, who were not interested in trading in their Spanish masters for American masters. Hence, led by Emilio Aqunaldo, the Filipinos rebelled against U.S. colonization.

Although skirmishes had already occurred, the official Philippines-American War began in February 1899. The U.S. established a "pacification policy," designed to provide soldiers with a standard for moral behavior and to dispense justice fairly. But those natives who resisted were to be treated as criminals and punished harshly.[25]

The imperialist rationale was perhaps best exemplified by British novelist Rudyard Kipling in his poem "The White Man's Burden," published in 1899.[26] In the poem, Kipling described the white man's burden to save the unfortunate, darker peoples of the world by introducing them to Western civilization and controlling them and their territory. Kipling began his poem by stating:

> Take up the White Man's burden—
> Send forth the best ye breed—
> Go bind your sons to exile
> To serve your captives' need;
> To wait in heavy harness,
> On fluttered folk and wild—
> Your new-caught, sullen peoples,
> Half devil and half child. . . .[27]

Believing that U.S. policy was rooted in racism, it was common for African Americans to denounce the war. And they responded to Kipling's poem with anger and mockery. H. T. Johnson, a well-known Black clergyman and editor of the influential *Christian Recorder*, wrote a poem mocking Kipling's:

> Pile on the Black Man's Burden.
> 'Tis nearest at your door;
> Why heed long bleeding Cuba,
> or dark Hawaii's shore?
> Hail ye your fearless armies,
> Which menace feeble folks
> Who fight with clubs and arrows
> and brook your rifle's smoke.
>
> Pile on the Black Man's Burden
> His wail with laughter drown
> You've sealed the Red Man's problem,
> And will take up the Brown,
> In vain ye seek to end it,
> With bullets, blood or death
> Better by far defend it
> With honor's holy breath.[28]

Even still, Kipling's view was shared by U.S. officials. Governor Theodore Roosevelt said of Kipling's work that it was "poor poetry but a good sense of the expansionist standpoint."[29] In reference to the Filipinos, Virginia Senator John Daniel declared that Filipinos were people "not only of all hues and colors, but there are spotted people there, and what I have never heard of in any country, there are striped people there with zebra signs upon them."[30] It was this sort of characterization that buttressed support for imperialism and justified the view that it was the duty of the U.S. to save nations of color from their barbaric inferiority and lack of self-governance.

Although some conservative African Americans remained loyal to U.S. policy in the Philippines, anti-imperialist voices in the Black community received enormous attention. Bishop Henry McNeal Turner attacked African American soldiers for helping to suppress the rebellion against U.S. colonization. He stated, "I boil over with disgust when I remember that colored men from this country that I am personally acquainted with are there fighting to subjugate a people of their own color and bring them to such a degraded state."[31]

Notwithstanding the criticism, in mid-1899, Black soldiers who had returned to their stations following the Cuban campaign embarked for the Philippines and participated in virtually every part of the war. Later, in 1900, the regular Black troops were joined by two regiments of Black volunteers, the 48th and 49th Infantries. They were recruited by the War Department at the request of the commander in the islands.

The African American soldier was caught in a serious quandary. Unlike in Cuba, African American soldiers could not lean on the assertion that their actions were to liberate the nation from the brutish Spaniards. It was clear in this instance that the war in the Philippines was waged to defeat the independence movement of people of color. While in the Philippines, Black soldiers watched American soldiers treat the Filipinos with the same disdain they had for the Black American soldiers who were their allies. It is not a stretch to say that Black soldiers identified with the Filipinos. Nor was the racism of whites lost on the Filipino insurgents, who regularly distributed posters addressed to The Colored American Soldier, "to remind him of the American practice of lynching and encourage him not to be the instrument of his white master's ambition to oppress another 'people of color.'"[32] In the *Cleveland Gazette*, H. C. Smith commented on a report by the *Dallas Texas Express* on Aguinaldo's feelings about submission to America. "The more Aguinaldo reads the reports of how the colored people are being cut up for souvenirs in Georgia and hanged and shot to death in the other states, the more determined he is not to put himself under the protection of such a country, and who in the h—l can blame him?"[33] W. E. B. Du Bois expressed his disgust with white soldiers who impregnated Filipino women but then left them to fend for themselves. The U.S. government and philanthropists were called on to support the children.

In order to diminish their complicity with U.S. aspirations in the Philippines, some African American soldiers deserted the military. The case of David Fagan is perhaps the most popular account of Black soldier desertion. At the age of 24, Corporal Fagan defected to the rebels, while other members of the 24th Cavalry were attempting to conquer the mountains of central Luzon. He later led insurgent troops against the U.S. troops. It is widely believed that his decision to defect was related to the racist quarrels he had continually with white superiors. Overall, twenty American soldiers defected to the Insurrectos, but only two Black privates, Edmond Dubose and Louis Russell, were executed as a result.[34]

The affinity that some African American soldiers felt for the Filipinos was also demonstrated by those who married and started families with Filipino women. T. Thomas Fortune reported on his trip through the Island of Luzon, "We stopped with an old black trooper at Carranglan. He had a native wife, kept a small store, called a canteen (in which there was no liquor) and cultivated a large rice plantation. Like all the Negroes we had so far met in our journey, he was coal black and seemed to be perfectly at home. He was happy and making money, and never expected to return to the United States—and what black man out of it and doing well, should?"[35] Era Bell Thompson's research showed that more than 1,000 Blacks remained in the Philippines after the surrender of the Filipino nationalists to the U.S. in 1902.[36] Some African Americans even argued that mass migration to the Philippines could be the solution to the oppression they faced in the U.S. Carter G. Woodson emigrated to the Philippines and taught school there for four years. T. Thomas Fortune further surmised that "under the proper arrangement, 5,000,000 Negroes could be located in the Island, taken out of the Southern states, where they are wronged and robbed and where the white man claims that they are in the way . . . "[37]

On September 6, 1901, in the midst of the Philippines war, President McKinley was shot during his second term and died eight days later. His vice president, Teddy Roosevelt, became president on September 14. By the end of that year, almost all of the Filipino nationalists on the island of Luzon had surrendered and taken the oath of allegiance to the United States. The American-Philippines War officially ended July 4, 1902.

The Brownsville Raid

After Theodore Roosevelt became president in 1901, he invited Booker T. Washington to the White House. African Americans were proud of that gesture and thought that their patriotism and loyalty to the U.S. would finally receive long overdue recognition. The leader of the Rough Riders would surely remember the devotion of Black soldiers in San Juan, as well as long after the official end of the war. But in 1906 such hopes were dashed, when President Roosevelt dismissed an entire 25th Infantry regiment, in what became known as the Brownsville Incident.

In August of that year, 170 men from the 25th Infantry who had recently returned from the Philippines were ordered for training in Fort Brown in Brownsville, Texas. But local people there greeted the soldiers with Jim Crow signs and random violence. One night, after an incident of racial harassment, random shots were fired from a band of "unidentified" men. A white man was killed and two others were wounded. Military cartridges were found at the scene, leading federal investigators to blame Black soldiers, whose presence had been a point of discontent for the local whites. Nonetheless, no soldiers confessed and no evidence was found linking Black soldiers to the crime. President Roosevelt, however, labeled the Black soldiers killers and accepted the recommendation by the War Department for their dismissal. With no trial and no chance of appeal, except for the three who were on leave, all of the 167 soldiers of the 1st Battalion were dishonorably dismissed and forever barred from serving the government as soldiers or civilians. It would be sixty-six years before a Black congressman could petition the White House for a pardon and reversal of the dishonorable discharges. Consequently, the sole surviving soldier, Dorsie Willis, age 86, was granted $25,000 in damages and medical care, though he had never been able to receive gainful employment because of the dishonorable discharge.[38]

Although there was a slight variance of perspectives by African Americans on the Spanish-American and Philippines-American wars, the commentary in this section reflects the fact that many African Americans refused to support U.S. goals. Bishop Henry McNeal Turner argued against the enlistment of Black soldiers in the war against Spain, asserting that the "Negro will be exterminated soon enough at best, without being over-anxious to die in the defense of a country that is decimating his numbers daily."[39] On the other side, Booker T. Washington pledged Black loyalty in his speech at the National Peace Jubilee of 1898. In this section we also hear from M. W. Saddler, a soldier reporting from the 25th Infantry from Santiago. Saddler comments on the bravery and patriotism of Black troops while he hoped that they would be remembered by Blacks, even though they died fighting in a foreign land. T. Thomas Fortune traveled to the Philippines to report on the conditions for potential Black immigration to the island, while W. E. B. Du

Bois castigated white soldiers who had children with Filipino women and then left them behind to return to the States. All of these occurrences at the end of the century prompted W. E. B. Du Bois's statement at the first Pan African Conference, held in London in 1900, that the problem of the 20th century would be "the problem of the color line."

BOOKER T. WASHINGTON
(1856–1915)

Booker Taliaferro Washington was a leading Black educator and the founder of the famous Tuskegee Normal and Industrial Institute. As a legendary author, Washington was noted for his autobiography Up from Slavery, *published in 1901. Washington influenced Southern race relations and was the dominant figure in Black public affairs from 1895 until his death in 1915. He was criticized by many scholars, including W. E. B. Du Bois, for taking the posture that African Americans should disregard the fight for civil and political rights in order to first acquire social and economic equality. However, Washington used his intelligence and influence to give voice to prejudice and discrimination, while he implemented some very substantial programs and policies. "An Address in the National Peace Jubilee" is an illustration of Washington's position on African Americans' patriotism, which he asserts has been demonstrated by their willingness to fight in America's wars.*

An Address in the National Peace Jubilee
October 16, 1898

Mr. Chairman, Ladies and Gentleman: On an important occasion in the life of the Master, when it fell to Him to pronounce judgment on the two courses of action, these memorable words fell from His lips; "And Mary hath chosen the better part." This was the supreme test in the case of an individual. It is the highest test in the case of a race or nation. Let us apply this test to the American Negro.

In the life of our Republic, when he has had the opportunity to choose, has it been the better or worse part? When in the childhood of this nation the Negro was asked to submit to slavery or choose death and extinction, as did aborigines, he chose the better part, that which perpetuated the race.

When in 1776 the Negro was asked to decide between British oppression and American independence, we find him choosing the better part, and Crispus Attucks, a Negro, was the first to shed his blood on State Street, Boston, that the white American might enjoy liberty forever, though his race remained in slavery.

When in 1814 at New Orleans, the test of patriotism came again, we find the Negro choosing the better part; Gen. Andrew Jackson himself testifying that no heart was more loyal and no arm more strong and useful in defense of righteousness.

When the long and memorable struggle came between union and separation, when he knew that victory on the one hand meant freedom, and defeat on the other his continued enslavement, with a full knowledge of the portentous meaning of it all, when the suggestion and the temptation came to burn the home and massacre wife and children during the absence of the master in battle, and thus insure his liberty, we find him choosing the better part, and for four long years protecting and supporting the helpless, defenseless ones entrusted to his care.

When in 1863 the cause of the Union seemed to quiver in the balance, and there was doubt and distrust, the Negro was asked to come to the rescue in arms, and the valor displayed at Fort Wagner and Port Hudson and Fort Pillow, testify most eloquently again that the Negro chose the better part.

When a few months ago, the safety and honor of the Republic were threatened by a foreign foe, when the wail and anguish of the oppressed from a distant isle reached his ears, we find the Negro forgetting his own wrongs, forgetting the laws and customs that discriminate against him in his own country, and again we find our black citizen choosing the better part. And if you would know how he deported himself in the field at Santiago, apply for answer to Shafter and Roosevelt and Wheeler. Let them tell how the Negro faced death and laid down his life in defense of honor and humanity, and when you have gotten the full story of the heroic conduct of the Negro in the Spanish-American war—heard it from the lips of Northern soldiers and Southern soldiers, from ex-abolitionist and ex-master, then decide within yourselves whether a race that is thus willing to die for its country, should not be given the highest opportunity to live for its country.

In the midst of all the complaints of suffering in the camp and field, suffering from fever and hunger, where is the official or citizen that has heard a word of complaint from the lips of a black soldier? The only request that has come from the Negro soldier has been that he might be permitted to replace the white soldier when heat and malaria began to decimate the ranks of the white regiment, and to occupy at the same time the post of greatest danger.

This country has been most fortunate in her victories. She has twice measured arms with England and has won. She has met the spirit of a rebellion within her borders and was victorious. She has met the proud Spaniard and he lays prostrate at her feet. All this is well, it is magnificent. But there remains one other victory for Americans to win—a victory as far-reaching and important as any that has occupied our army and navy. We have succeeded in every conflict, except the effort to conquer ourselves in the blotting out of racial prejudices. We can celebrate the era of peace in no more effectual way than by a firm resolve on the part of the Northern men and Southern men, black men and white men, that the trench which we together dug around Santiago, shall be the eternal burial place of all that which separates us in our business and civil relations. Let us be as generous in peace as we have been brave in battle. Until we thus conquer ourselves, I make no empty statement when I say that we shall have, especially in the Southern part of our country, a cancer gnawing at the heart of the Republic, that shall one day prove as dangerous as an attack from an army without or within.

In this presence and on this auspicious occasion, I want to present the deep gratitude of nearly ten millions of my people to our wise, patient and brave Chief Executive for the generous manner in which my race has been recognized during the conflict. A recognition that has done more to blot out sectional and racial lines that any event since the dawn of freedom.

I know how vain and impotent is all abstract on this subject. In your efforts to "rise on stepping stones of your dead selves," we of the black race shall not leave you unaided. We shall make the task easier for you by acquiring property, habits of thrift, economy, intelligence and character, by each making himself of individual worth in his own community. We shall aid you in this as we did a few days ago at El Caney and Santiago, when we helped you to hasten the peace we here celebrate. You know us; you are not afraid of us. When the crucial test comes, you are not ashamed of us. We have never betrayed or deceived you. You know that as it has been, so it will be. Whether in war or in peace, whether in slavery or in freedom, we have always been loyal to the Stars and Stripes.

HENRY MCNEAL TURNER
(1834–1915)

In 1834, Henry McNeal Turner was born free in South Carolina. He was taught to read and write, while working in a lawyer's office. He received his license to preach in 1853 and was recruited as a traveling minister for the Methodist Episcopal Church. While at Trinity College in Baltimore, Turner studied Latin, Greek, Hebrew and theology. Alongside his spiritual growth was the development of his radical political views. As the founder of the African Methodist Episcopal Church in Georgia, Bishop Turner was famous for projecting Black pride in his sermons; he was often quoted as stating, "God is a Negro." President Abraham Lincoln appointed Turner army chaplain—the first Black man to be assigned the position. After the Civil War, Turner worked with the Freedmen's Bureau in Georgia. In the 1868 elections, Turner was one of the several Black men elected to the state legislature who served briefly before being expelled as a result of white protest. In the following editorials, Turner, who eventually supported emigrationism, argues against African American participation in the war against Spain and the fight in the Philippines.

The Quarrel with Spain
July 1898

Being out of the country when the present war with Spain broke out, we could not define our position relative to the part the colored man should play upon the bloody programme.

Since our arrival home we have been asked a thousand times for our opinion, and we have simply replied that the war is now in progress and the black man is in it and it would be useless to say anything; but just as we expected, we see that he is made the butt of ridicule, his faults are magnified and he is still the bone of contention. He is being snubbed while even defending the stars and stripes. This is no news to us, however, for we knew it would be the case before we returned to [the] country, or before we had even heard a word uttered. We do not see what the Negro is so anxious to fight for anyway; he has no country here and *never will* have.

Much is being said about fighting poor little Spain, the eighth power of the world, for the purpose of humanity, that the Spanish are cruel and brutal in their treatment towards the Cubans. "Physician, heal thyself," very appropriately comes in here. Enough men have been lynched to death to reach a mile high if laid one upon the other, and enough women and children to form the head and foot slab if they should be arranged to stand upon the head of each other. The United States puts more people to death without law than all the other nations of the earth combined. So our humanitarianism is too ridiculous to be made a count in the argument of justification.

The Negro will be exterminated soon enough at best, without being over-anxious to die in the defense of a country that is decimating his numbers daily.

The colored man would far better be employed in remaining at home, marrying wives and giving the race sons and daughters, and perpetuating our existence, than rushing into a death struggle for a country that cares nothing for their rights or manhood, and wait till they are wanted, and then the nation will feel and know his worth and concede to him the respect due the defenders of a nation.

It is very likely that the Negro will be wanted before this little fuss is over, anyway, for we have but little doubt that the greater part of Europe will have a hand in this affair before it is ended, and should it so turn out the black man will be wanted, and inducements will be offered for his blood and bravery in common with other men. One thing can be said to the everlasting credit of Spain— a man is a man in her domain. We have been from one end of Spain to the other, and we have seen black men and black women enjoying every privilege that was being enjoyed by people of any other color. We have stopped at some of her finest hotels and have enjoyed such respect and honors that some Americans who were there exhibited their disapproval because we were seated at the table in the midst of them. We pretended not to notice it, however, although we *did* notice it.

Governor Atkinson of Georgia, who said that he would not enlist Negroes in this war, according to what we saw in the English paper before our arrival home, shows himself a greater friend of the Negro than those governors who are enlisting his aid and service. Governor Atkinson knows that the Negro has nothing for which he should fight, and he has too much respect for the Negro to encourage him to die for nothing.

The Negro and the Army
May 1899

The difficulties faced by Black soldiers during and after the Spanish-American War increased Turner's bitterness toward the United States. In this statement on the subject, he returns to the theme of the flag and makes assertions which, when repeated in 1906, attracted national attention and brought accusations of treason.

If this is a white man's government, and we grant that it is, let him take care of it. The Negro has no flag to defend. There is not a star in the flag of this nation, out of the forty-odd, that the colored race can claim, nor is there any symbol signalized in the colors of the flag that he can presume to call his, unless it would be the stripes, and the stripes are now too good for him. He is only regarded as entitled to powder and lead and the burning fagots. He has no civil social, political, judicial . . . right . . .

Those who did enlist some months ago were abused, misrepresented, and vilified when they even passed through the country, worse than brutes would have been. If they came out of the cars and walked about the depot, they were charged with trying to kill men, women, and children, and fire cities and villages. If they sat in the cars and failed to get out, the newspaper branded them with cowardice, and said they were afraid, they knew what would follow, while one town would telegraph the next that Negro soldiers would pass through, "Have your armed police at the railroad station, armed to [the] teeth and ready to shoot them down upon the slightest provocation." Yet the same towns were ready to supply them with all the rot-gut whisky they were able to purchase, to transform them into maniacs and human devils . . .

We now ask, in the face of these facts, and they are not half told, what does the Negro want to enlist, lay his life on the [altar] of the nation and die for? . . . While we are the first Africanite Chaplain in the history of the nation, and have once been proud of the flag of this nation as it waved and flaunted in the air, as a Negro we regard it a worthless rag. It is symbol of liberty, of manhood, sovereignty and of national independence to the white man, we grant, and he should be justly proud of it, but to the colored man that has any sense, any honor, and is not a scullionized fool, it is a miserable dirty rag. . . . Take no oath to protect any flag that offers no protection to its sable defenders. If we had the voice of seven thunders, we would sound a protest against Negro enlistment till the very ground shook beneath our feet.

M. W. SADDLER

Sergeant Saddler of the 25th Infantry extols the patriotism of the "Sons of Ham" in the following letter, which describes the contributions of his Black infantry regiment "in compelling the surrender of Santiago." Saddler admits that he was troubled by the prospect of fighting men of his "own hue and color." Ultimately Saddler justifies the service of African American troops in the Philippines by insisting that his goal was to demonstrate the fitness, handiness and courage of the Black soldier.

The Patriotism of the Sons of Ham
July 30, 1898

Dear Sir:

I wish to call attention to the heroic part the Twenty-fifth United States Infantry played in compelling the surrender of Santiago. We have no reporter in the division and it appears that we are coming up unrepresented.

On the morning of July 1, our regiment, having slept part of the night with stones for pillows and heads resting on hands, arose at the dawn of day, without a morsel to eat, formed line, and after a half day of hard marching, succeeded in reaching the bloody battleground at El Caney. We were in the last brigade of our division. As we were marching up we met regiments of our comrades in white retreating from the Spanish stronghold. As we pressed forward all the reply that came from the retiring soldiers was: "There is no use to advance further. The Spaniards are intrenched and in block houses. You are running to sudden death." But without a falter did our brave men continue to press to the front.

In a few minutes the desired position was reached. The first battalion of the Twenty-fifth Infantry, composed of companies C, D, G and H were ordered to form the firing line, in preference to other regiments, though the commanders were seniors to ours. But no sooner was the command given than the execution began. A thousand yards distance to the north lay the enemy, 2000 strong in intrenchments hewn out of solid stone. On each end of the breastwork were stone block houses. Our regiment numbered 507 men all told. We advanced about 200 yards undercover of jungles and ravines. Then came the trying moments. The clear battlefield was reached. The enemy began showering down on us volleys from their strong fortifications and numberless sharpshooters hid away in palm trees and other places . . .

Our men began to fall, many of them never to rise again, but so steady was the advance and so effective was our fire that the Spaniards became unnerved and began over-shooting us. When they saw we were "colored soldiers" they knew their doom was sealed. They were afraid to put their heads above the brink of their intrenchments for every time a head was raised there was one Spaniard less.

The advance was continued until we were within about 150 yards of the intrenchments; then came the solemn command, "Charge." Every man was up and rushing forward at headlong speed over the barbed wire and into the intrenchments, and the Twenty-fifth carried the much coveted position. So great was the loss of officers that Company C had to be commanded by its First Sergeant S. W. Taliaferro, the gallant aspirant for the commission from the ranks . . . The Company's commander was wounded early in the action by the explosion of a bombshell.

Thus our people can now see that the coolness and bravery that characterized our fathers in the 60's have been handed down to their sons of the 90's. If any one doubts the fitness of a colored soldier for active field service, when the cry of musketry, the booming of cannon and bursting of shells, seem to make the earth tremble, ask the regimental Commanders of the Twenty-fourth and Twenty-fifth infantries and Ninth and Tenth Cavalry. Ask Generals [Henry W.] Lawton, [Jacob F.] Kent and [Joseph] Wheeler, of whose divisions these regiments formed a part.

The Spaniards call us "Negretter Solados" and say there is no use shooting at us, for steel and powder will not stop us. We only hope our brethren will come over and help us to show to the world that true patriotism is in the minds of the sons of Ham. All we need is leaders of our own race to make war records, so that their names may go down in history as a reward for the price of our precious blood.

M.W. Saddler
First Sergeant, Co. D.
25th Inf.

T. THOMAS FORTUNE
(1858–1928)

Timothy Thomas Fortune was born to a skilled shoemaker and educated slave. While in his hometown of Marianna, Florida, Fortune attended Freedmen's Bureau schools. He later became a journalist and prospered as a spokesperson, advocate and leader. In his publications Fortune expressed displeasure with the distorted images of Blacks, Indians and women. He also frequently denounced the Republican Party. His close affiliation with public figures of the time such as Ida B. Wells, Bishop Henry M. Turner, Alexander Crummell, Marcus Garvey, and Booker T. Washington placed him in a league with the greatest Black leaders of the era. Through his personal relationship with Booker T. Washington, Fortune was appointed Special Immigrant Agent of the Treasury Department during the Theodore Roosevelt administration to study race and trade conditions in the Philippines. While there, against the advice of Booker T. Washington, Fortune spoke out against the racism shown toward the Filipinos by whites. He also surveyed the island to gain information about possibly emigrating African Americans there.

The Filipino:
Some Incidents of a Trip through the Island of Luzon
1904

After studying the people and the social and industrial conditions in Manilla as closely as my limited time and tireless industry would allow, I prepared to take a trip across the Island of Luzon. I knew nothing of the requirements or the hardships of such a trip, as I could find no one among the Americans who had taken it . . .

Conditions in the Cagayan valley are much the same as in the Pangasinan country. The land is rich, producing the finest tobacco in the world, and other valuable crops can be produced; but the natives have no knowledge of farming, and do not seem to care to work, so that there is industrial prostration everywhere. That part of Luzon could easily support 3,000,000 more people. Thus it appears, Luzon could support 7,000,000 more people than it now does. The Negro and the Filipino get along splendidly together, and I am convinced that if, under proper arrangement, 5,000,000 Negroes could be located in the Island, taken out of the Southern States, where they are wronged and robbed, and where the white man claims that they are in the way, it would be good for them, good for the Filipinos, who badly need rejuvenation of blood, and good for the United States, and we should take a long step forward in solving the Filipino problem and the Negro problem, both of which promise to cost the Nation more in blood and money in the future than in the past. The Philippines have got to have a competent labor population, and naturally the Negro should be placed in position to supply it, as the Republic owes him a proper chance to enjoy life, liberty and the pursuit of happiness, which it has not given him in this country, but seems now to be on a policy of crushing out entirely his manhood and citizen rights. The Chinese cannot be drawn upon, because American sentiment is against it and the Filipino people will have none of it. Give the American Negro a chance in the Philippine Islands, if he wants to go there.

W. E. B. DU BOIS
(1868–1963)

W. E. B. Du Bois was born in Great Barrington, Massachusetts, graduated cum laude from Harvard University in 1890 and attended the University of Berlin in 1892. In 1896 Du Bois became the first African American to receive a Ph.D. from Harvard University. W. E. B. Du Bois was one of the most prominent activists and political leaders of the 19th and 20th centuries. A supporter of political, civil and economic equality, Du Bois was well known for his public debates with Booker T. Washington and Marcus Garvey. In 1905 Du Bois challenged Washington's accomodationism by establishing the Niagara Movement. Du Bois was also a key founder of the National Association for the Advancement of Colored People in 1909. As a prominent Pan Africanist, Du Bois has been credited with assisting in the expansion and sustenance of the Pan-African Movement. In this commentary, Du Bois comments on the unscrupulous behavior of white American soldiers in the Philippines who fathered children but refused to support them. Du Bois's commentary references an appeal for funds to help take care of the children.

Philippine Mulattoes
1925

You will have noticed in the press a delicately worded appeal for funds. It would seem that there are some little children in need in the Philippines. Major General Wood, Governor of the Islands, is speaking in their behalf:

> Chief Justice William Howard Taft of the Supreme Court of the United States, former Governor General of the Philippines, W. Cameron Forbes, Major Gen. James G. Harbord, Major Gen. Hugh L. Scott, Martin Egan, Vice-President Charles G. Dawes and dignitaries of the Catholic and Protestant churches are typical of the men who have pledged their support to this drive for funds. General Wood has cabled:
> *The American people have been so generous in their responses to the cries of children all over the world that I have no hesitation in appealing to them for children of their own blood who are in need of help. Especially do I have profound confidence, as the problem involves the honor of the American nation.*

What is all this about? In plain, cold English, the American people in bringing Peace and Civilization to the Philippines have left 18,000 bastards in the islands! Isn't this fine work? Can you not see the Godly White Race struggling under the Black Man's Burden! Can you not see how Americans hate social Equality with brown women?

Why is America asked to support these illegitimate victims of white men's lust? Because the United States government, the War Department and Govenores

Wood, Taft and Forbes have somehow let American skunks scuttle from the island and leave their helpless and innocent bastards to beg and perish, and their deserted mothers to starve or serve as prostitutes to white newcomers.

Send, in God's name, America, two million dollars to Mary Frances Kern at 8 West Fortieth Street, New York, now; and send simultaneously two million protests to Washington to lambaste the heads of Congressmen who permit the holding of the Philippines as a house of prostitution for American white men under the glorious stars and stripes.

Notes

1. Ida B. Wells, "Our Country's Lynching Record," *Survey* 24 (January 1913); John Hope Franklin and Alfred A. Moss Jr., *From Slavery to Freedom: A History of African Americans*, 7th ed. (New York: McGraw-Hill, 1994), 282.

2. See William L. Clay, *Just Permanent Interests: Black Americans in Congress 1870–1991* (New York: Amistad, 1992), 12–43, for a detailed discussion on Blacks in Congress during Reconstruction.

3. The comments were delivered in Washington's "Atlanta Exposition Address" on September 18, 1865, at the opening of the Cotton State and International Exposition in Atlanta, Georgia. For a copy of the address, see Howard Brotz, ed., *African American Social and Political Thought 1850–1920* (New Brunswick, N.J.: Transactions Publishers, 1993), 356–59.

4. For critiques of Booker T. Washington's ideas by Fox, Trotter, Du Bois and Turner, see Stephen R. Fox, *The Guardian of Boston: William Monroe Trotter* (New York: Atheneum, 1970), 51–58; W. E. B. Du Bois, *The Souls of Black Folk* (New York: Penguin, 1996); and "Critique of the Atlanta Compromise," in *Respect Black: The Writings and Speeches of Henry McNeal Turner*, ed. Edwin Redkey (New York: Arno Press and the *New York Times*, 1971), 165–66.

5. Foster Rhea Dulles, *America's Rise to World Power: 1898–1954* (New York: Harper & Row, 1954), 9; "President's Annual Message," *Annals of Congress of the United States*, 18th Cong., 1st sess., 12–24, esp. p. 14.

6. For resources on the Spanish-American War and Cuba's fight for freedom, see Thomas Huge, *Cuba: The Pursuit of Freedom* (New York: Harper & Row, 1971); G. J. A. O'Toole, *The Spanish-American War: An American Epic* (New York: Norton, 1986); and Ivan Musicant, *Empire by Default: The Spanish-American War and the Dawn of the American Century* (New York: Henry Holt, 1998).

7. Jerry Keenan maintains there is still speculation on the causes of the explosion, but the prevailing wisdom doubts the Spaniards intentionally destroyed the ship. See Jerry Keenan, *Encyclopedia of the Spanish-American and Philippine-American Wars* (Santa Barbara, Calif.: ABC-CLIO, 2001), 217–23.

8. *Richmond Planet*, July 30, 1889. Reprinted in Herbert Aptheker, *A Documentary History of the Negro People in the United States*, vol. 2, *From the Reconstruction to the Founding of the N.A.A.C.P. in 1910* (Secaucus, N.J.: Citadel Press, 1990), 824.

9. Reprinted in George P. Marks III, *The Black Press Views American Imperialism (1898–1900)* (New York: Arno and the *New York Times*, 1971), 30.

10. D. Augustus Straker, *A Trip to the Windward Isle, or Then and Now* (Detroit: Press of James A. Stone and Co., n.d.), 7–9, 107–9. Also see Willard B. Gatewood Jr., *Black Americans and the White Man's Burden (1898–1903)* (Urbana: University of Illinois Press, 1974), 26, for more discussion of Straker's views.

11. Louis R. Harlan, ed., *Booker T. Washington Papers,* vol. 4, *Booker T. Washington to John D. Long,* March 15, 1898, 389.

12. Ida B. Wells, "Ida Wells Barnett against Expansion," *Cleveland Gazette,* January 7, 1899. Reprinted in Marks, *Black Press,* 109.

13. *Richmond Planet,* March 25–26, 1898. Reprinted in Marks, *Black Press,* 18.

14. Calvin B. Chase, *Washington Bee,* March 5, 1898. Reprinted in Marks, *Black Press,* 13.

15. Willard B. Gatewood Jr., *Smoked Yankees and the Struggle for Empire: Letters from Negro Soldiers* (Urbana: University of Illinois Press, 1971), 8–10.

16. Edwin S. Redkey, ed., *Respect Black: The Writings and Speeches of Henry McNeal Turner* (New York: Arno Press, 1971), 173–74.

17. Roger D. Cunningham, "Virginia's Black Immunes," *Historic Alexander Quarterly,* Summer 2000; William G. Muller, *The Twenty-Fourth Infantry: Past and Present* (Fort Collins, Colo.: Old Army Press, 1972). Gail Buckley also presents an interesting brief analysis of the "immunes" in *American Patriots: The Story of Blacks in the Military from the Revolution to Desert Storm* (New York: Random House, 2001), 148–49.

18. Evan S. Conner, *Son of the Morning Star: Custer and the Little Big Horn* (New York: North Point Press, 1997), 13–14. Also see Buckley, *American Patriots,* 113, for further discussion on the origins of the term "Buffalo Soldiers."

19. See Hershel V. Cashin et al., *Under Fire with the Tenth U.S. Cavalry* (New York: Arno Press and the *New York Times*), 80, 122 and 160.

20. Roosevelt's statements on Rough Riders can be found in George Kennan, *Campaigning in Cuba* (New York: Century Company, 1899), 144; in *Scribner's Magazine,* April 1899; and in Theodore Roosevelt, *The Rough Riders* (New York: Scribner, 1902), 94–96.

21. Jesse Johnson, *Black Armed Forces Officers 1736–1971: A Documented Pictorial History* (Hampton, Va.: Hampton Institute, 1971), 51–54.

22. Gatewood, *Smoked Yankees,* 57.

23. Letter from Blackman, Sixth Virginia Infantry, U.S. V., Camp Haskell, Georgia, December 13, 1898. Reprinted in Gatewood, *Smoked Yankees,* 146–49.

24. Keenan, *Encyclopedia,* 295.

25. For discussion on U.S. policies in the Philippines, see Keenan, *Encyclopedia,* esp. 295–96.

26. The poem coincided with U.S. ratification of the Senate treaty that gave the U.S. control of the island and the origins of the war.

27. Rudyard Kipling, "The White Man's Burden: The United States and the Philippine Islands," 1899, in *Rudyard Kipling's Verse: Definitive Edition* (Garden City,

N.Y.: Doubleday, 1929). Also see Gatewood, *Black Americans*, 183, for further discussion of President Roosevelt's and other responses to Kipling's poem.

28. *Voice of Missions* 7 (April 1899), 1. H. T. Johnson's poem is also reprinted in Gatewood, *Black Americans*, 184.

29. See Dulles, *America's Rise*, 48, and Garel A. Grunder and William E. Livezey, *The Philippines and the United States* (Norman: University of Oklahoma Press, 1951), 49.

30. 55th Cong., 3rd sess., *Congressional Record* 32, pt. 1, 1430.

31. Bishop Henry McNeal Turner, "The Philippine Insurrection" (1900), reprinted in *Respect Black: The Writings and Speeches of Henry McNeal Turner*, ed. Edwin S. Redkey (New York: Arno and the *New York Times*, 1971), 186–87. George P. Marks, "Opposition of Negro Newspapers to American Philippines Policy, 1899–1900," *Midwest Journal* 4 (Winter 1951–52): 1–25.

32. For an overview of the Black soldiers' experiences in the Philippines and for Black statements on white racism, see Scot Ngozi-Brown, "African American Soldiers and Filipinos: Racial Imperialism, Jim Crow and Social Relations," *The Journal of Negro History* 82:1 (Winter 1997), esp. 45–46. For a poster addressed to colored American soldiers, see Marks, *Black Press*, 155.

33. H. C. Smith, "Aqunaldo [sic] Knows What American 'Protection' Is," *Cleveland Gazette*, September 30, 1899. Reprinted in Marks, *Black Press*, 148. An example of Black support for U.S. policy, "Black Troops Should Go to the Philippines," is also found in Marks, *Black Press*, 131.

34. Discussion of Fagan's desertion is chronicled in Buckley, *American Patriots*, 158.

35. Thomas T. Fortune, "The Filipino: Some Incidents of a Trip through the Island of Luzon," *Voice of the Negro* 1 (June 1904): 243.

36. Era Bell Thompson, "Veterans Who Never Came Home," *Ebony*, October 1972, 105.

37. Carter G. Woodson's experience in the Philippines is described in Jacqueline Goggin, *Carter G. Woodson: A Life in Black History* (Baton Rouge: Louisiana State University Press, 1993), 16–18. Fortune, "The Filipino," 245–46.

38. John D. Weever, *The Brownsville Raid* (New York: Norton, 1970).

39. Henry McNeal Turner, "The Quarrel with Spain," *The Voice of Missions*, April 1896.

CHAPTER FIVE

⁓

World War I:
The Strange Fruit of War

1 9 1 4 - 1 9 1 8

The cause of the "Great War" is widely debated by historians, but the event commonly credited as the catalyst is the assassination of the heir to the Austro-Hungarian throne, Archduke Franz Ferdinand, in Sarajevo on June 28, 1914. He was assassinated by Gavrilo Princip, a member of a Serbian nationalist organization called the Black Hand, believed to be supported by the Serbian government. Ferdinand's death was quickly followed by an ultimatum from the Austro-Hungarians with a lengthy list of demands upon the Serbian government, including swift and just punishment against the participants in the assassination plot. Although Serbia conceded to most of the demands, the Austro-Hungarian government remained unsatisfied. On July 28, 1914, within three days of ending negotiations, Austria-Hungary declared war on Serbia.[1]

Within six weeks, the declaration of war on Serbia began a chain of events that had the entire European continent at war. Almost immediately, Russia, who was bound by a treaty to Serbia, announced that it would mobilize its army for war. Germany, who was allied to Austria-Hungary, viewed the actions of Russia as an act of war. By August 3, France, bound by treaty to Russia, declared war on Germany, who swiftly responded by invading Belgium because it provided the shortest route between Germany and Paris. Britain, who was allied to France and Belgium, was obligated to defend both countries. On August 4, after declaring war on Germany, Britain's colonies and dominions such as Australia, Canada, India, New Zealand and the Union of South Africa began to contribute financial and military assistance.

103

Nationalism, economic and military alliances, and imperialism were the reasons for the eventual partnerships formed during World War I. On one side of the conflict were the Central Powers, which included Austria-Hungary, Germany and the Ottoman Empire (now Turkey). On the opposing side were the Allies, which consisted of Belgium, France, Great Britian, Russia, Serbia and eventually the United States.

Under the leadership of President Woodrow Wilson, in 1914, the United States had first declared a policy of absolute neutrality. Europe had been at war for nearly three years before the United States actually became militarily involved in 1917. But the formidability of Germany as a sea power whose presence directly threatened America's commercial shipping in the Pacific and Atlantic oceans, the sinking of the *Lusitania* by the Germans—killing 195 Americans—and the United States' economic relationship with France eventually pushed America directly into the war. Addressing a special session of Congress on April 2, 1917, President Woodrow Wilson said:

> It is war against all nations. American ships have been sunk, American lives taken, in ways which it has stirred us very deeply to learn of, but the ships and people of other neutral and friendly nations have been sunk and overwhelmed in the waters in the same way. There has been no discrimination.
>
> . . . With a profound sense of the solemn and even tragical character of the step I am taking and of the grave responsibilities which it involves, but in the unhesitating obedience to that I deem my constitutional duty, I advise that the Congress declare the recent course of the Imperial German Government to be in fact nothing less than war against the government and people of the United States; that it formally accept the status of belligerent which has thus been thrust upon it; and that it take immediate steps not only to put the country in a more thorough state of defense but also to exert all its power and employ all its resources to bring the Government of the German Empire to terms and end the war.[2]

On April 6, 1917, by the time Congress had approved U.S. entry into the war, the Allies were in terrible need of assistance on the battlefields. They were outmanned by the German military and their united front was beginning to fall apart, as Italy was in talks to surrender as a separate entity from the Allies to Austria.

The first American soldiers arrived in St. Nazaire, France, in June 1917. At least half of them were immigrants and also illiterate. Americans were also seen as ill-mannered, sloppily dressed and under-trained. Nonetheless, the American soldiers held the respect of the French because they were considered great fighters.[3] The Germans, however, were ruthless. In November

1917, three young American soldiers had their throats slit and were nearly decapitated by knives of a German raiding party.[4] By this time, more than a million radios were in American homes across the nation, but these deaths, which were the first American casualties of the war, were not reported to the public because of the sheer brutality.

The need for supplies and equipment to support the Great War created a record demand for products, which prompted the U.S. to expand its war-related industries. A significant problem for industry leaders, however, was the slowing of European immigration to the U.S., on which companies relied for cheap labor. Because of the dearth of European laborers, white American employers were forced to hire African American workers. Lured by the prospect of employment opportunities in Northern cities, African Americans began to migrate in great numbers for work. They were drawn to the North for other reasons as well. Conditions in the South were worsening as the boll weevil damaged cotton crops, leaving crop owners unable to pay their workers. Mississippi and Alabama were also ravaged by floods that devastated their agriculture and therefore led to a decline in the need for workers.[5] Consequently, between the years of 1910 and 1930, the North saw its African American population increase by over 20 percent, as nearly a million participated in the Great Migration from the rural South into the Northern cities.

Quite obvious, even at a cursory glance, was the fact that while Europe was engaged in this unprecedented brutal war between nations, the U.S. was mired in its own bitter race war. Northbound African Americans who had left the Deep South were confronted with extreme racial violence. In 1917, there were 38 documented lynching parties and more than 58 the next year.[6] On July 2, 1917, an East St. Louis mob, angry because African Americans were being employed in a factory servicing government contracts, rioted and killed between 40 and 100 African Americans. Racist views were also expressed in American cultural productions, such as D. W. Griffith's *Birth of a Nation*. Heralded by mainstream movie critics, the film portrayed African Americans as lazy coon types and implied the rise of the Ku Klux Klan in the South was necessary to protect white women from perverted Black men.

Organizations established to help ease racial tensions stepped up their work during this era. The National Urban League, a social service organization, supported African American migrants by helping them find shelter, employment and other necessities. The National Association for the Advancement of Colored People (NAACP) agitated for Black political rights and fought against the appalling atrocities committed against African American people. Journalist Ida B. Wells led an international crusade against lynching. Wells, one of the two Black women who signed a petition which formed the

NAACP, was renowned for her writings and fiery speeches against racist violence. The Universal Negro Improvement Association (UNIA), founded by Marcus Garvey in 1914, excited the masses of poor and frustrated African Americans with the promise of a back-to-Africa movement. Garvey's insistence on racial dignity and self-determination attracted more than 6 million African people in the U.S. and in the Diaspora.[7]

African Americans were also battling President Woodrow Wilson's conservative administration. The Democratic president, elected in 1912, issued an executive order that segregated federal employees and phased most African Americans out of civil service jobs. One of the most famous protests against Wilson's policies was led in 1914 by Monroe Trotter, a Phi Beta Kappa graduate of Harvard and Boston newspaper editor. Wilson had Trotter and his delegation removed from the White House during a meeting because he regarded Trotter's comments as insulting. Printed in the *Crisis Magazine* was the encounter between Trotter and Wilson:

> *Mr. Monroe Trotter.* Mr. President, we are here to renew our protest against the segregation of colored employees in the departments of our National Government. We [had] appealed to you to undo this race segregation in accord with your duty as President and with your pre-election pledges to colored American voters. We stated that such segregation was a public humiliation and degradation, and entirely unmerited and far-reaching in its injurious effects. . . .

> *President Woodrow Wilson.* The white people of the country, as well as I, wish to see the colored people progress, and admire the progress they have already made, and want to see them continue along independent lines. There is, however, a great prejudice against colored people. . . . It will take one hundred years to eradicate this prejudice, and we must deal with it as practical men. Segregation is not humiliating, but a benefit, and ought to be so regarded by you gentlemen. If your organization goes out and tells the colored people of the country that it is a humiliation, they will so regard it, but if you do not tell them so, and regard it rather as a benefit, they will regard it the same. The only harm that will come will be if you cause them to think it is a humiliation.

> *Mr. Monroe Trotter.* It is not in accord with the known facts to claim that the segregation was started because of race friction of white and colored [federal] clerks. The indisputable facts of the situation will not permit of the claim that the segregation is due to the friction. It is untenable, in view of the established facts, to maintain that the segregation is simply to avoid race friction, for the simple reason that for fifty years white and colored clerks have been working together in peace and harmony and friendliness, doing so even through two [President Grover Cleveland] Democratic administrations. Soon after your in-

auguration began, segregation was drastically introduced in the Treasury and Postal departments by your appointees.

President Woodrow Wilson. If this organization is ever to have another hearing before me it must have another spokesman. Your manner offends me. . . . Your tone, with its background of passion.

Mr. Monroe Trotter. But I have no passion in me, Mr. President, you are entirely mistaken; you misinterpret my earnestness for passion.[8]

Even though the encounter made front-page news and subsequent rallies protested Wilson's poor treatment of Trotter, segregation of the federal service continued. African Americans also protested other policies of President Wilson, including his order to occupy Haiti and the killing of several hundred Haitians in the process. African Americans argued that Wilson's order was in violation of the country's sovereignty.[9]

On the issue of the armed forces, initially African Americans were not included in the draft by the marine or army forces. However, the army rescinded that policy in its new Selective Service Act two months later. The Act mandated the enlistment of all able-bodied men age 21 to 31. Many white Southerners resisted the draft and found ways to obtain release from duty with the help of the local draft boards, who practiced racial discrimination when handing out exemptions. As a result, African Americans were over-drafted. Approximately 400,000 African American soldiers represented 13 percent of the total draftees, although the racial group represented less than 10 percent of the population during that time.[10]

Many African Americans, however, were not averse to signing up for the war. More than 700,000 signed up for the Armed Services on the first registration day.[11] Suffering from poverty, unemployment and lack of educational opportunities, many viewed the military as an opportunity to move out of abject poverty. Robert Edgerton illustrates the conditions of African American volunteers in his book, stating that "Many men, particularly poor black farmers from the rural South, arrived in tattered overalls with bare feet."[12]

Despite the view that the military could possibly save them from a life of sharecropping and impoverishment, there were still major hurdles to cross for African Americans—namely receiving proper training, fair treatment and promotion opportunities. African Americans were eager to participate not only as enlistees but also as officers. Colonel Charles Young, a West Point graduate and the highest ranking African American, took his examination for promotion to full colonel, so that he might lead African American Buffalo Soldiers as their commander in the Great War. "But the military establishment and Wilson administration joined forces to deny Young the rank."[13] They feared that if Young went into war as a full colonel, he could possibly later become a brigadier general, which they could not permit. So Young was officially retired from the military when he tested for high blood pressure. Young was so offended by the forced retirement that he rode horseback from Ohio to New York to prove his physical fitness. Still, the retirement board would not overturn its decision.[14]

Indeed, it had been long argued that African Americans lacked the intellect and educational background required for the status of officer. To refute this reasoning, the NAACP organized 1,500 students from Howard University into the Central Committee of Negro College Men and launched a massive campaign lobbying Congress for a junior officers' training program. The strategy proved fruitful, when in June 1917 the War Department established a Black officers' training school in Des Moines, Iowa, for some 1,250 men. On October 14, 1917, 639 graduates were commissioned. Before that time the army had commissioned a mere six African Americans.[15]

Emmett Scott, longtime secretary to Booker T. Washington, was appointed as a special assistant to Secretary of War Newton Baker during World War I in order to oversee the recruitment, training and morale of African American soldiers. The appointment, which became the highest government appointment ever achieved by an African American, was clearly a political response to shield the Wilson administration from those individuals, who were angry about the government's refusal to end racial discrimination in the U.S. Hence, Scott was viewed by many as a "presidential appeasement."

Scott's first major assignment was Camp Lee in Virginia, where he found that African American soldiers were subjected to inferior conditions based entirely on race. Scott found white soldiers living in barracks, while African American soldiers lived in tents, many without even floors and bedding. The African American soldiers were also subjected to inferior medical treatment, unsanitary conditions and given inadequate clothing. And while whites received rigorous training, African Americans were assigned to labor units and were not even allowed to fire guns. Scott worked diligently to change the conditions at Camp Lee. He investigated numerous complaints and made recommendations for change. Another one of his functions was to make sure the soldiers and their families received adequate compensation and risk insurance. He also helped to "induce the War Department to make adequate and equal provision for the training of Negro officers in connection with the various camps and cantonments where the National Army was being developed."[16]

The irony of the African American predicament was easy to distinguish. As with every preceding war, African Americans debated the question of what should be their unified position on this new international conflict, considering their unique circumstances in their own country. W. E. B. Du Bois, cofounder of the NAACP and the editor of its *Crisis Magazine*, was initially a proponent of war. He relied, as had others, on the logic that through military bravery, racial prejudice could be dealt a fatal blow. Writing in the *Crisis* in July of 1918, Du Bois rallied his kindred men with the following exhortation:

> We of the colored race have no ordinary interest in the outcome. That which the German power represents today spells death to the aspirations of Negroes and all darker races for equality, freedom and democracy. Let us not hesitate. Let us, while this war lasts, forget our special grievances and close ranks shoulder to shoulder with our own white fellow citizens and the allied nations that are fighting for democracy.[17]

The special assistant to the secretary of war, Emmett Scott, agreed with Du Bois and stated in his official account of the war that "It was a marvelous thing to have occurred, that a race itself so long oppressed should have had the opportunity to help save others from oppression! It is something for every man and woman of the Negro race to be proud of, that our people did eagerly welcome this opportunity and play so glorious a part."[18]

Fervently opposed to Du Bois's call to arms on behalf of America were Asa Philip Randolph and Chandler Owens, both editors of the Black socialist newspaper the *Messenger*. In a critique of America's racial politics during wartime, in July 1918 they wrote, " . . . we are conscripting the Negro into the military and industrial establishments to achieve this end for white democracy four thousand miles away, while the Negro at home, though bearing the burden in every way, is denied economic, political, educational and civil democracy. And this, despite his loyalty and patriotism in the land of the free and the home of the brave!"[19] Attorney General A. Mitchell Palmer found no patience for such candor and labeled the pair "the most dangerous Negroes in America." Randolph and Owens were imprisoned in July 1918 under the Espionage Act, for interfering with troop recruitment.[20] They were sentenced to two and a half years' time, while the second-class mailing privileges for the *Messenger* were revoked.[21]

Notwithstanding their racial problems at home, African American soldiers landed on the battlefields of Europe with an insatiable drive to prove their loyalty to the principles of democracy, and to affirm their good character to those in the U.S. who questioned their value. They fought as if they were unaware of the experiences of their ancestors who had fought in previous U.S. wars.

At the onset of World War I, there were approximately 10,000 African Americans in the regular army, all members of the Buffalo Soldier 9th and 10th Cavalries and 24th and 25th Infantries. There were also 10,000 peacetime African American National Guardsmen and some 10,000 African Americans in the non-combat mess and stewards' branches of the navy. There were no African Americans in the marines, the Air Corps, the Army Field Artillery, or the Army Corps of Engineers. In total, four African American regiments were organized to participate in World War I. Two new Black army combat units were created—the 92nd and the 93rd divisions. Ultimately, the Black division consisted of the four infantry regiments plus artillery, engineer and other support units.[22]

As in previous wars, African American soldiers were assigned to segregated units; many were kept out of combat and assigned only to labor battalions. However, with the escalation of the war, the 93rd Division was sent to fight alongside the French troops. They were later joined by the all-Black 369th Infantry Regiment. Consistent with previous performances, African American soldiers fought courageously. "All four of the regiments 'lent' to the French distinguished themselves in battle, suffering 35 percent casualties. In April 1918, the 369th represented only 1 percent of American troops in France, but they held 20 percent of the front lines occupied by U.S. soldiers. Known to Germans as 'hell-fighters,' and to the French as 'men of bronze,' . . . they occupied front-line trenches for 191 days without yielding a foot of ground or having a single soldier taken prisoner."[23] The 369th Regiment became the most decorated American unit of the war by the French Army.[24] The first American soldier of any color to receive the Croix de Guerre was Sergeant Henry Johnson of the same regiment. The Croix de Guerre is a medal awarded by the French government to recognize acts of bravery in the face of the enemy. Overall, the medal was awarded to 171 Black troops.[25]

Regardless of their epic performance in battle, not a single African American soldier was awarded the Medal of Honor, the U.S.'s highest military honor in World War I.[26] Not until 1991, when President George H. W. Bush posthumously granted the Medal of Honor to Corporal Freddie Stowers of the 371st Regiment, would an African American hold such an honor. Stowers's bravery defies belief. Caught in a shrewd "faux surrender" by the Germans, Stowers lost half of his men in a matter of seconds. Though riddled with fatal machine-gun fire himself, he actually managed to rally his surviving men and motivated them to move forward.[27]

World War I saw an extremely high percentage of illiterate enlistees, both African American and white; and so the YMCA took up the charge of providing them with basic educational classes. As with every facet of the war, attention and resources were not distributed evenly. One Y secretary was assigned for every 279 white soldiers, but only one for every 1,267 Black soldiers.[28]

Nineteen African American women answered the call to serve, mostly as "secretaries" within the ranks of the YMCA. Addie D. Hunton and Kathryn M. Johnson spent almost fifteen months in France, working to address the needs of the American Expeditionary Forces. The two reported African American soldiers shedding tears upon seeing them in France.[29]

Throughout the war, U.S. newspapers expressed the fear that many whites held regarding African American alliances with foreign nations. The French became well known for their admiration of African American culture, which they were exposed to as a result of the African American bands that accompanied their regiments. The most famous was the band of the 369th Infantry, led by James Reese Europe, a prominent musician. Members of the Europe band included such notables as Bill Bojangles Robinson and Noble Sissle, a vocalist and partner of Eubie Blake. These bands introduced many Europeans to jazz, ragtime and African American music and dance styles. The popularity of African American music spread so much that African Americans were welcomed by French troops and embraced in French society. White troops often envied the relationship between French women and African American male soldiers, which frequently led to accusations of African American crimes against French women by white troops. Efforts to further thwart interaction between African American men and French women ultimately culminated in Order No. 40. This proclamation, issued by General Ervin, a commander of the 92nd Division, mandated that "Negros were forbidden to speak with or to French Women."[30] Despite the acceptance of James Europe's band in France, when they returned home after the war they were refused the opportunity to march in the New York National Guard's "Farewell to Little Old New York" parade.[31]

White fear of African American international alliances also led to a widespread rumor that there was a German plot to foment a Black revolution in the Southern states. Indeed, the Germans worked to demoralize African American troops. On September 12, 1918, the Germans scattered circulars targeting the 92nd Division, which refuted the idea that African American troops were fighting for democracy. One circular, which invited African Americans to come over to the German lines, said:

> What is Democracy? Personal freedom, all citizens enjoying the same rights socially and before the law. Do you enjoy the same rights as the white people do in America, the land of Freedom and Democracy, or are you rather not treated

over there as second-class citizens? Can you go into a restaurant where white people dine? Can you get a seat in the theater where white people sit? . . . Is lynching and the most horrible crimes connected therewith a lawful proceeding in a democratic country? Why, then, fight the Germans only for the benefit of the Wall Street robbers and to protect the millions that they have loaned to the British, French, and Italians.[32]

Whether fueled by Germans, the French or just the media, there was extraordinary concern about any degree of African American defiance in the South. Such fears were brought to life, when on August 22, 1917, soldiers from the 24th Regiment at Camp Logan stationed outside of Houston, Texas, reached their breaking point with the constant flow of racial injustices. The final straw occurred on the morning of August 23, when Private Alonzo Edwards discovered a white policeman, Lee Sparks, beating an African American woman. Edwards interfered, and in turn Sparks and other officers beat and arrested him. Corporal Charles Baltimore, an African American military policeman, went to the police to inquire about Edwards. He was also beaten and arrested. After learning of the controversy, white officers locked away the African American battalion's guns and ammunition. Nonetheless, some African American soldiers retrieved their weapons and marched to the police station in protest. Over the next two hours violence ensued. When the air cleared 15 whites, including 5 Houston policemen, were dead, while 12 others were injured. Four African Americans died as well.

The U.S. government's reaction to the crisis was swift. The entire 24th Infantry was shipped to Fort Huachuca, Arizona, under armed guard. Thirteen of the African American soldiers, including Baltimore, were condemned to die, as a result of their summary court-martial. Forty-one others were sentenced to life in prison and forty were held pending further investigation. After the NAACP's campaign for clemency, President Wilson commuted ten of the death sentences to life in prison. Efforts to clear the names and release the members of the 24th Infantry continued for decades. Finally, in 1938, President Franklin Roosevelt released the last prisoners.

In the midst of the Great War, the October Revolution, led by such noted figures as Vladimir Lenin and based on the ideas of Karl Marx, brought socialism to Russia. The effort to spread communism throughout the world led to even further suspicion of African Americans, many of whom were eager to communicate with those who advocated the overthrow of capitalism in the U.S. White American fears of any perceived Black power became even more entrenched.

World War I ended on November 11, 1918, with Germany signing an armistice with the Allies in a railroad car at Compiègne, France. On June 28, 1919, the Treaty of Versailles signaled the official end to World War I between the Allies and the Central Powers. At the end of the four years more than 10 million people had died.[33] The four African American regiments suffered 35 percent casualties. After the war ended, African American labor battalions were kept in France to search for and bury the dead. The white troops sailed home ahead of them.

Their treatment during the war made the return home bittersweet for many African American soldiers. William Hewitt, an African American private, wrote W. E. B. Du Bois on August 26, 1919, explaining his feelings about the war. "We regret that on October 1919 we will sail for our home in Petersburg, Virginia, United States of America where true democracy is enjoyed only by white people. Why did African American men die here in France 3,330 miles from their home? Was it to make democracy safe for the white people in America, with the black people left out?"[34] Hewitt's questions were answered by the sheer violence that continued throughout the country that year. Seventy-eight African Americans were lynched; fourteen were burned at the stake, eleven of which were African American soldiers. Race riots erupted in 28 cities across the nation—proof positive that race relations in America had indeed not improved sufficiently as a result of the war.

Yet the war and the Great Migration led to a flurry of African American activism that eventually gave birth to one of the greatest cultural periods in African American history—the Harlem Renaissance. Also during this period, W. E. B. Du Bois organized the Pan-African Congress (PAC) in Paris in 1919, which ran parallel to the Versailles Peace Conference and the emergent plans for the League of Nations. Fifty-seven delegates attended the PAC from 15 countries. Sixteen of the attendees were African Americans. The conference proposed an international committee to assume control of Germany's African colonies and an international code of laws to protect all peoples from imperialism. The second Pan-African Congress stimulated further interest in Pan Africanism throughout the world.

The remarks by African Americans on World War I provide vivid expressions of the African American experience during the beginning of the 20th century. The desire to work within the American political system to promote equality is illustrated in Emmett Scott's discussion of his appointment as a special assistant to the secretary of war. Scott readily accepts the charge of working to reduce frictions between the races, especially in the American military. W. E. B. Du Bois presents two racially charged perspectives on the war, first in his article "Close Ranks," which he wrote in July 1918 to compel African Americans to "forget our special grievances and close our ranks shoulder to shoulder with our white fellow citizens . . . ," then in his turnabout "Returning Soldiers," written in May 1919, in which he criticizes the U.S. government for racial bigotry. Jack Johnson, the former heavyweight boxing champion, details his service to the U.S. despite his exile from the country that sought to arrest him for violating the Mann Act. The Act prohibited the transport of women across state lines for immoral purposes. Johnson's arrest was a response to his payment for a railroad ticket for his white girlfriend, Belle Schreiber, to travel from Pittsburgh, Pennsylvania, to Chicago, Illinois. Upon his return from exile, Johnson was sent to Leavenworth Penitentiary in Kansas, to serve his sentence of one year. Despite his trials, Johnson remained loyal to the U.S. until his death in 1946.

Critiques of African American participation in the war came from a myriad of leaders and personalities. Such assessments had roots in general ideological disagreements with U.S. policy as well as in actual events that highlighted the precarious predicament of African Americans. A. Philip Randolph and Chandler Owen raised the question of who will profit from the war, and asked the common man, how can he benefit from his engagement? Later, they delineated the terms for peace that African Americans, African people and other nations of color should advocate. Ida B. Wells comments on the execution of 13 African American soldiers in Houston who fought back against the violence perpetrated upon them by white racists. She provides insight into her own experiences with the Secret Service as she sought to honor the 13 soldiers.

Of the three final documents in this section, two reflect the diverse standpoints of two highly respected African American organizations on World War I. In a leaflet, the NAACP recounts the efforts to support African American troops during the war. Countering that action are the words and deeds of Marcus Garvey. In 1922, Garvey criticized the integrationist perspective on war by demanding that Blacks stop fighting for other nations and fight for themselves. The last commentary in this section is a poem by Claude McKay written in 1919, entitled, "If We Must Die." The poem is a response to the racial violence committed against African Americans at the end of the war. African American communities were attacked and destroyed by white mobs, hundreds were lynched and millions of whites joined the Ku Klux Klan. McKay's outrage at these atrocities is expressed in his assertion that Blacks must fight back.

W. E. B. DU BOIS
(1868–1963)

William Edward Burghardt Du Bois was one of the most prolific African American intellectuals in history. He authored scores of significant books, including Souls of Black Folk *in 1903. In addition to his literary activities and profound scholarship, he was a noted political activist and Pan Africanist. In 1945, Du Bois presided over the historic Fifth Pan-African Congress held in Manchester, England. Eventually, Dr. Du Bois relinquished his American citizenship and became a citizen of Ghana. In this article, published in the* Crisis *Magazine, Du Bois asserts that African people have a special interest in the outcome of World War I, and therefore they should unify with whites to fight against German militarism.*

Close Ranks
July 1918

This is the crisis of the world. For all the long years to come men will point to the year 1918 as the great Day of Decision, the day when the world decided whether it would submit to military despotism and an endless armed peace—if peace it could be called—or whether they would put down the menace of German militarism and inaugurate the United States of the World.

We of the colored race have no ordinary interest in the outcome. That which the German power represents today spells death to the aspirations of Negroes and all darker races for equality, freedom and democracy. Let us not hesitate. Let us, while this war lasts, forget our special grievances and close our ranks shoulder to shoulder with our own white fellow citizens and the allied nations that are fighting for democracy. We have no ordinary sacrifice, but we make it gladly and willingly with our eyes lifted to the hills.

EMMETT JAY SCOTT
(1873–1957)

Emmett J. Scott, an activist and journalist, established the oldest weekly newspaper initiated by a person of African descent, the Houston Freeman. *While working with Booker T. Washington, he was appointed the secretary of Tuskegee Institute in 1912. President Wilson appointed Emmett J. Scott as special assistant to the secretary of war during World War I. In that capacity, Scott served as the liaison between the African American soldiers and the War Department. For a time he also worked at Howard University as secretary, treasurer and business manager. Scott wrote several books including* Booker T. Washington: Builder of a Civilization *(1916) and* Scott's Official History of the American Negro in the World War *(1919). The purpose of Scott's appointment is discussed in his following essay.*

The Negro and the War Department
1917

The Secretary of War recognizes that in the unqualified support of this group of Americans, whom I have the honor to represent, he, in Our Country's Defense, has behind him an asset of appreciable value in the prosecution of the present war. On the other hand, he is equally desirous that we, as American citizens, shall have full and free opportunity to participate, as officers, as soldiers, and as loyal, self-sacrificing citizens, in this, the greatest conflict of all the ages, and that now and hereafter we shall receive the rewards which justly follow upon services well rendered.

The reason which actuated the Secretary of War in this matter is, perhaps, most clearly stated by the Mobile News-Item, a southern white newspaper, in an editorial which appeared in its issue of October 5, 1917, under the caption: THE NEGRO RECOGNIZED. With due apology for citing this article, because of the personal reference therein made, I venture to quote the following extract:

> The appointment is a wise move and a wise selection. While the Government is coordinating all the interests of the country in the movement to win the war with Germany, it should not overlook the colored people. Thousands of them have been drafted and are being trained for duty in the trenches.
>
> They are to wear their country's uniform and represent their country in the greatest conflict of all times. Millions will stay at home tilling the fields and working in the country's industries. They have their problems no less than others, and it is well that one who knows them so intimately is to advise the Government how to meet those problems.

All who are conversant with the history of our race in this country know that there are and likely will be problems arising out of the presence of white and colored soldiers in National Army cantonments and in National Guard camps, aside from many other delicate matters which have, and will, come up during the progress of the war, involving relationships between the races. It is highly desirable that all these matters shall be equitably adjusted with the minimum of friction in order to produce the maximum of efficiency, to the end that all groups of Americans may work together in harmony and present a solid front to a dangerous and united foreign foe.

I am not unmindful of the fact that the Secretary of War has not sought to honor an individual but to recognize the just claims of a race. Therefore, acting in this representative capacity, it is highly essential and earnestly desired that I have behind me the loyal support of the thoughtful men and women of our race, and I shall value and appreciate at all times their counsel and suggestions.

A. PHILIP RANDOLPH
(1889–1979)
AND
CHANDLER OWEN
(1889–1967)

Asa Philip Randolph is celebrated as a trade unionist and founder of the Brotherhood of Sleeping Car Pullman Porters. He was also a civil rights leader and socialist. Randolph was born in Crescent City, Florida, but grew up Jacksonville, Florida. In 1911 he moved to Harlem, New York, and attended the City College of New York. While at City College, Randolph met Chandler Owen, a sociology and political science student at Columbia University. The two young men joined the Socialist Party in 1916 and founded the Messenger, a radical journal in 1917. Chandler Owen was born in Warrenton, North Carolina, graduated from Virginia Union University in 1913 and subsequently entered Columbia University. After becoming disenchanted with the Socialist movement, Owen attempted a political career by running for the New York assembly in 1920, and also ran unsuccessfully for a seat in the House. Owen moved to Chicago, where he became managing editor of the Chicago Bee and later started a public relations firm. Below are three editorials printed in the Messenger, which set forth Black radical views on World War I.

Who Shall Pay for the War?
November 1917

Who shall pay for the war? This is the question every man and woman called upon to fight; to sacrifice in any way for the prosecution of the war, should ask. But the question should not stay there. The next question should be: who profits from the war? For obviously, those who profit from the war ought to pay for it. But these questions must be followed with a third question, viz.: How can profits be made out of the war? The answer to this question is: by selling to the government those things which are needed to keep the war going; for instance, food and clothing for soldiers, steel for battleships, submarines, aeroplanes, coal for transports, etc., money to lend to the government.

Now, Mr. Common-man, do you own any of these things? If you don't then you cannot profit from the war.

Then you ought to see to it that the government confiscates all profits made out of this war to carry on this war. Let the government take 100 percent. and peace will come.

Negroes to Be at Peace Conference in Europe
January 1918

Upon examination of the causes of the war, political scientists discover that the rivalry for the rich lands and the abundant labor supply of the darker nations constitute the real bone of contention. It is the coal fields and oil wells of China, the rich agricultural products of India, the diamonds, rubber, copper, cocoa oil and dates of Africa, or the control of trade routes by way of Constantinople to these fields of wealth. In a word, it is the object and means of reaching the object which continually have engulfed the world in war—the present world war being no exception.

This economic greed and national imperialism has been masquerading behind the philanthropic veil of carrying civilization to the benighted lands of the darker races, as well as of releasing the wealth of these lands to satisfy the wants of European civilization. Sooner or later delegates gathered together in official or unofficial capacities will be around the green tables discussing terms of peace. Their avowed object is to organize the world for peace. We submit, however, that no permanent, durable and democratic peace can be organized which leaves the richest lands and the greatest supply of labor in the world a perpetual, unsettled bone of contention. We further submit that the psychology and intellectual equipment of the delegates must enable them to deal sympathetically and scientifically with the various questions of race and geographical adjustments which will arise.

Irishmen ought to be there to keep vigil on the Emerald Isles. Hindus ought to be there to make Britain make good her claim of fighting for the rights of smaller and weaker nations. Chinese ought to be there to save from the future ravage the Chinese Empire. Poles ought to be there with suggestions and methods for securing Polish autonomy. Turks ought to be there to prevent an international conspiracy to steal Constantinople. The Negro ought to be there to insist upon international equity as regards the treasures of Africa and its inexhaustible labor supply. He needs further to call upon America to make good her claims of fighting "to make the world safe for democracy."

Herein lies the reason for THE MESSENGER'S suggestion to initiate a campaign to send Negro delegates to the peace conference, and to send men who are acquainted with the problems which the peace delegates will be called upon to settle. THE MESSENGER would recommend only those men whose vision and grasp of world politics enable them to comprehend the importance of insisting upon the freedom and independence of Ireland no less vigorously than upon the freedom and development of the darker race.

Within the next thirty days some concrete, organized and constructive propaganda to this end will be launched by THE MESSENGER.

Peace Terms

We do not expect that out of the Peace Conference will come any justice to Africa or to subject peoples in general. The old school diplomats of the Metternich and Bismarck ilk are at the helm and they will pilot the international ship of peace upon the shoals of imperialism. The peace terms will be equitably revised, however, by the growing international class consciousness of the proletariat with a few years.

We, therefore, urge the following general principles as guides to the conference, conscious of the fact that they will be given a distorted application as conscienceless, undemocratic and unjust as the treaty of Brest-Litovsk:

1. A league of free nations (white and colored).
2. Self-determination for all peoples.
3. No punitive indemnities.
4. No annexations.
5. Freedom of the seas.
6. Internationalization of labor standards.
7. Unconditional withdrawal of Allied troops from Russia.
8. No intervention in Germany, Austria or the democratic countries of Europe.
9. Disarmament.
10. International abolition of conscription.
11. Abolition of secret diplomacy.
12. Universal suffrage without regard to race, color, sex, creed or nationality.

We realize that so long as the profit system continues there will be commercial conflicts which will result in war, and that there can be no honest application of the aforenamed principles.

Pro-Germanism among Negroes
July 1918

At the recent convention of the National Association for the Advancement of Colored People, a member of the Administration's Department of Intelligence was present. When Mr. Justin Carter of Harrisburg, Pa., was complaining of the race prejudice which American white troops had carried into France, this administration representative rose and warned the audience that the Negroes were under suspicion of having been affected by German propaganda.

In keeping with the ultra-patriotism of the oldline type of Negro leaders (?) the N.A.A.C.P. failed to grasp its opportunity. It might have calmly and frankly informed the Administration representative that the discontent among Negroes was not produced by propaganda, nor can it be removed by propaganda. The causes are deep and dark—though obvious to all who care to use their mental eyes. Peonage, disfranchisement, Jim-Crowism, segregation, rank civil discrimination, injustice of legislatures, courts and administrators—these are the propaganda of discontent among Negroes. The only way to remove this general unrest and widespread discontent among Negroes is to remove these cankerous causes.

The only legitimate connection between this unrest and Germanism is the extensive government advertisement that we are fighting "*to make the world safe for democracy.*" . . . while the Negro at home, though bearing the burden in every way, is denied economic, political, educational and civil democracy. And this, despite his loyalty and patriotism in the land of the free and the home of the brave!

Col. Robert G. Ingersoll once said: "Between inevitable evils we have the right of choice." The Negro may be choosing between being burnt by Tennessee, Georgia or Texas mobs or being shot by Germans in Belgium. We don't know about this pro-Germanism among Negroes. It may be only their anti-Americanism—meaning anti-lynching, which historians and scholars like Prof. Cutler of Yale concede to be strictly "American." We should like to assist the government to investigate this pro-Germanism among Negroes. It might bring to light the fact that they are still so absorbed in suppressing American injustices that their minds have not yet been focused upon Germany. Meanwhile we shall be on the watch for the real basis of this alleged pro-Germanism among Negroes should any new facts arise.

JOHN "JACK" ARTHUR JOHNSON
(1878–1946)

John Arthur Johnson, better known as Jack Johnson, was born to two former slave parents in Galveston, Texas. At the age of 15, Johnson won his first fight, a sixteen-round victory. Johnson became a boxing professional around 1897 and won victories in numerous fights against both Black and white opponents. Johnson eventually won the World Heavyweight Title on December 26, 1908. His triumph over white fighters caused high-raging emotions, and at one point sparked a race riot. Johnson's boxing ventures allotted him the pleasure to travel all around the world. While in Spain as a fugitive from the U.S., Johnson competed in several boxing matches. While there, he also worked secretly with the U.S. government as an agent during World War I.

Exile: 1913–1920

When the United States entered the war, I found an opportunity to serve the country from which I was a fugitive by conducting investigations of German submarine operations off the coast of Spain, and I also engaged in wrestling matches, in one of which I defeated the Castilian champion.

In my work as an American agent, I was employed by the American military attaché in Spain, Major Lang, and pursued my assignments under the direction of the intelligence department. At that time, German submarines were causing havoc with English and American shipping. The destructive boats were appearing as if by magic in numerous places on the sea. They were baffling allied naval experts by the suddenness with which they did their damage and the mysterious manner in which they disappeared. It was evident that they had bases somewhere on the west coast of Europe, or had devised hiding places so near the scene of their depredations that they constituted the greatest menace to the successful prosecution of the war by the allies. Feeling sure that the sub bases, or at least some of them, were on the Spanish coast, I was sent out to discover what I could.

I made no pretensions to military training nor had I any experience as a sailor, but the accumulated experience of my life-time served me well in these ventures, to traversing of rough water into dangerous and out-of-the-way places along the coast, infested not only by possible war enemies but by smugglers and others engaged in outlaw practices. Then, too, there was the danger of capture by the enemy and the possibility of death by promiscuous shooting which frequently took place between the furtive craft in those waters. I was in and out of various sea ports and spent considerable time at San Sebastian and San Tandier and visited several islands off the coast. I obtained much information which was of sufficient value to be communicated to the United Sates officials who in turn submitted it to the allies for use in resisting submarine warfare and safeguarding shipping. For my work and the information which I obtained I received due recognition from the officials under whose instructions I operated, and I had the great satisfaction of being of service to my native country, even though I was an exile . . .

The press was eagerly bent upon reciting anything savoring of the sensational where I was concerned. But when I performed some worthy service there usually was complete silence. Thus, when I was in Spain during the World War, and gave my service to American and allied officials in obtaining information about the activities of German submarines along the coast of Spain, there was only slight mention of my efforts. During the war, there were a number of stranded Americans in Spanish cities, many of whom I aided financially and otherwise, and who, but for me, would have been subjected to much suffering and discomfort. But my part in these little tragedies so far as I know, has never been recorded . . .

At Bridgeport, Connecticut, I put on a boxing exhibition not long ago for the benefit of a sanitarium where wounded and tubercular World-War veterans are being treated. Many entertainments and other methods of raising money for the benefit of these sufferers had been tried. My boxing program made more money for the sanitarium than all the previous entertainments combined. The trustees of the sanitarium will vouch for the truth of this statement . . .

Various organizations and war relief committees in England will give favorable reports of my activities during the World-War period when I was in England. I appeared in numerous boxing exhibitions, the proceeds of which were used to procure comforts for crippled, blind and tubercular soldiers. In these events I not only tendered my services without cost, but I defrayed my own expenses.

IDA B. WELLS
(1862–1931)

Ida Wells was born in Holly Springs, Mississippi. When Wells was 16, both her parents and a younger brother died of yellow fever. In order to keep the remaining children in her family together, Wells dropped out of high school and found employment as a teacher. In 1880, Wells moved to Memphis, where she continued teaching and also attended Fisk University in Nashville. Wells began her crusade for justice when she was asked to give up her seat on a train to a white man. She sued the railroad company and became a local hero in her hometown when the verdict came in her favor. Wells became famous for her campaign against lynching, which evolved into a worldwide movement. In this excerpt from her autobiography, Wells discusses her attempts to honor the African American soldiers of the 24th Infantry who had been unjustly discharged and later hanged as a result of the Brownsville Raid.

World War I and the Negro Soldiers
1917–1918

Nineteen seventeen, the Year our country went to war, found Chicago and Camp Grant alive with soldiers and with those who had been drafted. Some had already gone overseas and the boys of the regular army were in Texas awaiting transportation. Word was flashed through the country that they had run amuck and shot up the town of Houston, just as a few years before the Negro soldiers were accused of shooting up Brownsville and had been discharged by President Roosevelt for doing so.

The result of the court-martial of those who had fired on the police and the citizens of Houston was that twelve of them were condemned to be hanged and the remaining members of that immediate regiment were sentenced to Leavenworth for different terms of imprisonment. The twelve were afterward hanged by the neck until they were dead and, according to the newspapers, their bodies were thrown into nameless graves. This was done to placate southern hatred.

It seemed to me a terrible thing that our government would take the lives of men who had bared their breasts fighting for the defense of our country. I felt that a protest ought to be made about it, and I feared that unless the Negro Fellowship League did it it would not be done.

Accordingly, we decided to hold a memorial service for the men whose lives had been taken and in that way utter a solemn protest. We felt that the government itself could not help but heed if we had a crowded outpouring of our people, at a meeting which would reflect dignity and credit upon us as a race. My first act was to put in an order with a button manufacturer downtown in order to have the buttons ready for distribution at our coming memorial service.

I then called the pastors of several of our large churches and asked which one of them would donate us the use of a church for the Sunday afternoon. I had imagined that they all felt as I did about the matter but was again given one of the many surprises of my life when every single pastor refused to let us have the use of the church. I felt it all the more keenly because almost every church in town had military services urging the boys to go to war and every congregation had done its bit by organizing nurse training classes, by meeting trains with cigarettes and sweets to give our boys who were passing through, by patriotic demonstrations, by Liberty Loan drives, by every sort of means if need be in defense of this government. The churches all did their bit along that line; yet they couldn't see that it was a duty which they owed to the youth of our race to protest to the government when they had been badly treated.

Of course when I could not get a church in which to have the kind of meeting we wanted to stage, there was nothing for me to do but distribute the buttons to those who wanted to buy them and thus reimburse us the money we had spent in having them made.

One morning very soon after we began distributing those buttons, a reporter for the *Herald Examiner* came into the office and asked to see one. I gave it to him and told him that the purpose was to give every member of our race who wanted to wear one in protest an opportunity to do so. I did not tell him that I was distributing them in this way because I was unable to get a church in which to hold a meeting. I didn't want the white people to know that we were so spineless as to not realize our duty to make a protest in the name of the black boys who had been sacrificed to race hatred. And I am telling it here for the first time.

The reporter went away with a button, and in less than two hours two men from the secret service bureau came into the office with a picture of the button which I had given to the reporter. They inquired for me, showed me the button, and told me that they had been sent out to warn me that if I distributed those buttons I was liable to be arrested. "On what charge?" I asked. One of the men, the smaller of the two, said, "Why, for treason." "Treason!" said I. "I understand treason to mean giving aid and comfort to the enemy in time of war. How can the distribution of this little button do that?" "Why," he said, "if you were in Germany you would be shot; and we have to have your assurance that you are not going to distribute any more of them." I said, "I can't give you any such promise because I am not guilty of treason; but if you think I am, you know your duty—only you must be very sure of your facts."

The other fellow said, "Well, we can't arrest you, Mrs. Barnett, but we can confiscate your buttons. Where are they? Weren't you showing one to a man as we came in?" "Yes," I said, "but he has gone and he must have taken the button with him." He said, "I told my partner on the way out here that I thought I knew you people and that we would have no trouble with you. Will you give us the buttons?" I said no. "Why," he said, "you have criticized the government." "Yes," I said, "and the government deserves to be criticized. I think it was a dastardly thing to hang those men as if they were criminals and put them in holes in the ground just as if they had been dead dogs. If it is treason for me to think and say so, then you will have to make the most of it."

"Well," said the shorter of the two men, "the rest of your people do not agree with you." I said, "Maybe not. They don't know any better or they are afraid of losing their whole skins. As for myself I don't care. I'd rather go down in history as one lone Negro who dared to tell the government that it had done a dastardly thing than to save my skin by taking back what I have said. I would consider it an honor to spend whatever years are necessary in prison as the one member of the race who protested, rather than to be with all the 11,999,999 Negroes who didn't have to go to prison because they kept their mouths shut. Lay on, Macduff, and damn'd be him that first cries 'Hold, enough!'"

The men looked at me as if they didn't know what to do about it, but finally asked me to consult my lawyer, for he would probably advise me differently. They went away, but they didn't take the buttons with them.

Both of the daily papers came out next day with a most respectful notice toughing this incident. The *Herald Examiner* had reproduced the picture of the button, and both of them said that Mrs. Barnett said anybody who felt as she did about it and wanted to wear a button in protest of the treatment the government had meted out to those soldiers could get one from her. The men did not come back, and I continued disposing of the buttons to anybody who wanted them; and strange to say, I was never molested and no further reference was made to the incident.

W. E. B. DU BOIS
(1868–1963)

"Returning Soldiers" was published in Crisis Magazine, *of which Du Bois was founder and editor. In this editorial, Du Bois criticizes the poor treatment of African American soldiers after they returned from fighting in World War I.*

Returning Soldiers
May 1919

We are returning from war! Tens of thousands of black men were drafted into a great struggle. For bleeding France and what she means and has meant and will mean to us and humanity and against the threat of German race arrogance, we fought gladly and to the last drop of blood; for America and her highest ideals, we fought in far-off hope; for the dominant southern oligarchy entrenched in Washington, we fought in bitter resignation. For the America that represents and gloats in lynching, disfranchisement, caste, brutality and devilish insult—for this, in the hateful upturning and mixing of things, we were forced by vindictive fate to fight also.

But today we return! We return from the slavery of uniform which the world's madness demanded us to don to the freedom of civil garb. We stand again to look America squarely in the face and call a spade a spade. We sing: This country of ours, despite all its better souls have done and dreamed, is yet a shameful land.

It *lynches.*

And lynching is barbarism of a degree of contemptible nastiness unparalleled in human history. Yet for fifty years we have lynched two Negroes a week, and we have kept this up right through the war.

It *disfranchises* its own citizens.

Disfranchisement is the deliberate theft and robbery of the only protection of poor against rich and black against white. The land that disfranchises its citizens and calls itself a democracy lies and knows it lies.

It encourages *ignorance.*

It has never really tried to educate the Negro. A dominant minority does not want Negroes educated. It wants servants, dogs, whores and monkeys. And when this land allows a reactionary group by its stolen political power to force as many black folk into these categories as it possibly can, it cries in contemptible hypocrisy: "They threaten us with degeneracy; they cannot be educated."

It *steals* from us.

It organizes industry to cheat us. It cheats us out of our land; it cheats us out of our labor. It confiscates our savings. It reduces our wages. It raises our rent.

It steals our profit. It taxes us without representation. It keeps us consistently and universally poor, and then feeds us on charity and derides our poverty.

It *insults* us.

It has organized a nation-wide and latterly a world-wide propaganda of deliberate and continuous insult and defamation of black blood wherever found. It decrees that it shall not be possible in travel nor residence, work nor play, education nor instruction for a black man to exist without tacit or open acknowledgement of his inferiority to the dirtiest white dog. And it looks upon any attempt to question or even discuss this dogma as arrogance, unwarranted assumption and treason.

This is the country to which we Soldiers of Democracy return. This is the fatherland for which we fought! But it is *our* fatherland. It was right for us to fight. The faults of our country are our faults. Under similar circumstances, we would fight again. But by the God of Heaven, we are cowards and jackasses if now that that war is over, we do not marshal every ounce of our brain and brawn to fight a sterner, longer, more unbending battle against the forces of hell in our own land. We *return*.

We *return from fighting*.

We *return fighting*.

Make way for Democracy! We saved it in France, and by the Great Jehovah, we will save it in the United States of America, or know the reason why.

MARCUS GARVEY
(1887–1940)

Marcus Mosiah Garvey Jr. was born in St. Ann's Bay, Jamaica. Garvey moved to Kingston at age 14 and became a print shop apprentice. Influenced by Booker T. Washington and his own experiences with racism, in 1914 Garvey founded the Universal Negro Improvement Association (UNIA) to unify Africa for all of its descendants. He also began the Negro World, *a newspaper in which Pan Africanism was preached. Under the auspices of the UNIA, Garvey launched many businesses, including the Black Star Shipping Line in 1917. Garvey's efforts eventually gained the attention of the U.S. government. Under J. Edgar Hoover, the FBI was determined to hinder Garvey's success at any cost. In 1927, after serving half of his five-year prison term on trumped-up mail fraud charges, Garvey was deported to Jamaica by the executive order of President Calvin Coolidge and to the merriment of Hoover. He died in West Kensington, England. On November 25, 1922, Garvey spoke to a gathering in New York City about the principles of the UNIA. He also discussed his concern about Blacks fighting in wars which would not benefit their own nation or people. An excerpt from his remarks is reprinted here.*

The Principles of the
Universal Negro Improvement Association
1922

Over five years ago the Universal Negro Improvement Association placed itself before the world as the movement through which the new and rising Negro would give expression of his feelings. This Association adopts an attitude not of hostility to other races and peoples of the world, but an attitude of self-respect, of manhood rights on behalf of 400,000,000 Negroes of the world.

We represent peace, harmony, love, human sympathy, human rights and human justice, and that is why we fight so much. Wheresoever human rights are denied to any group, wheresoever justice is denied to any group, there the U.N.I.A. finds a cause. And at this time among all the peoples of the world, the group that suffers most from injustice, the group that is denied most of those rights that belong to all humanity, is the black group of 400,000,000. Because of that injustice, because of that denial of our rights, we go forth under the leadership of the One who is always on the side of right to fight the common cause of humanity; to fight as we fought in the Revolutionary War, as we fought in the Civil War, as we fought in the Spanish-American War, and as we fought in the war between 1914–18 [World War I] on the battle plains of France and Flanders. As we fought up the heights of Mesopotamia; even so under the leadership of the U.N.I.A., we are marshaling the 400,000,000 Negroes of the world to fight for the emancipation of the race and of the redemption of the country of our fathers . . .

That does not suggest anything that is unreasonable. It was not unreasonable for George Washington, the great hero and father of the country, to have fought for the freedom of America giving to us this great republic and this great democracy; it was not unreasonable for the Liberals of France to have fought against the Monarchy to give to the world French Democracy and French Republicanism; it was no unrighteous cause that led Tolstoi to sound the call of liberty in Russia which has ended in giving to the world the social democracy of Russia . . . It is therefore not an unrighteous cause for the U.N.I.A. to lead 400,000,000 Negroes all over the world to fight for the liberation of our country . . .

The Universal Negro Improvement Association is not seeking to disrupt any organized system of government, but the Association is determined to bring Negroes together for the building up of a nation of their own. And why? Because we have been forced to it. We have been forced to it throughout the world; not only in America, not only in Europe, not only in the British Empire, but wheresoever the black man happens to find himself, he has been forced to do for himself.

To talk about government is a little more than some of our people can appreciate just at this time. The average man does not think that way, just because he finds himself a citizen or a subject of some country . . . But we of the U.N.I.A. have studied seriously this question of nationality among Negroes—this American nationality, this British nationality, this French, Italian or Spanish nationality, and have discovered that it counts for nought when that nationality comes in conflict with the racial idealism of the group that rules. When our interests clash with those of the ruling faction, then we find that we have absolutely no rights. In times of peace, when everything is all right, Negroes have a hard time, wherever we go, wheresoever we find ourselves, getting those rights that belong to us, in common with others whom we claim as fellow citizens; getting that consideration that should be ours by right of the constitution, by right of the law; but in the time of trouble they make us all partners in the cause, as happened in the last war [World War I], when we were partners, whether British, French or American Negroes. And we were told that we must forget everything in an effort to save the nation.

We have saved many nations in this manner, and we have lost our lives doing that before. Hundred of thousands—nay, millions of black men, lie buried under the ground due to that old-time camouflage of saving the nation . . . All that we have received for what we have done, even in giving up our lives, is just what you are receiving now, just what I am receiving now.

You and I fare no better in America, in the British empire, or in any other part of the white world; we fare no better than any black man wheresoever he shows his head. And why? Because we have been satisfied to allow ourselves to be led, educated, to be directed by the other fellow, who has always sought to lead in the world in that direction that would satisfy him and strengthen his position. We have allowed ourselves for the last 500 years to be a race of followers, following every race that has led, in the direction that would make them more secure.

If we have been liberal minded enough to give our life's blood in France, in Mesopotamia and elsewhere, fighting for the white man, whom we have always assisted, surely we have not forgotten to fight for ourselves, and when the time comes that the world will again give Africa an opportunity for freedom, surely 400,000,000 black men will march out on the battle plains of Africa, under the colors of the red, the black and the green.

We shall march out, yes, as black American citizens, as black British subjects, as black French citizens, as black Italians or as black Spaniards, but we shall march out with a greater loyalty, the loyalty of race. We shall march out in answer to the cry of our fathers, who cry out to us for the redemption of our own country, our motherland, Africa.

NATIONAL ASSOCIATION FOR
THE ADVANCEMENT OF COLORED PEOPLE

On February 12, 1909, a call was issued to create an organization that would promote liberty, civil rights and suffrage for African Americans. As a result of that
call, the National Association for the Advancement of Colored People (NAACP)
was formed in 1909 in New York City by a group of Black and white citizens who
believed in fighting for social justice. Some of the organization's founders included
Ida Wells-Barnett, W. E. B. Du Bois and Mary White Ovington. Throughout its
existence, the NAACP has worked primarily through the American legal system to
end segregation. In mid-1918 the NAACP and its District of Columbia Branch—
chaired by Archibald H. Grimke—issued a four-page leaflet to set forth the work
that the NAACP had done for the 100,000 African American soldiers serving in
the "U.S. National and Regular Armies" during World War I.

What the N.A.A.C.P. Has Done for the Colored Soldier
1918

What Association did:

March, 1916: Appeal to the Chairman of the House Committee on Military
Affairs urging the creation of more colored regiments and the establishment of
two artillery regiments.

April, 1917: The same appeal to the Executive chiefs in Washington by the
National Secretary in person.

May, 1917: After repeated unsuccessful efforts to get colored men into the
regular training camps for officers, the association works for a separate training
camp and secures one at Des Moines, Ia.

September, 1917: Commissions help up at Des Moines Camp. Telegram sent
to the men at Des Moines urging them to stay until commissions are granted.
Personal work at Washington to press the matter of commissions.

September, 1917: Efforts through personal interviews with Secretary Baker to
secure reversal of the decision regarding Colonel [Charles] Young's retirement.
Unsuccessful.

October, 1917: 678 colored men secure commissions at Des Moines. Des
Moines Camp sends contribution of $272 to N.A.A.C.P.

November, 1917: Action against forcing colored men at Camp Meade to act
as stevedores and common laborers. Successful. Men transferred to heavy artillery.

February, 1918: Association takes steps to find out status of the five colored
soldiers sentenced to death by Houston court martial. Deputation goes to Washington, headed by James W. Johnson, Field Secretary, asking for clemency for

these men and for forty-one soldiers of the same regiment sentenced to life imprisonment. Secures a stay of sentence in the case of the five men.

February, 1918: Representative of Association again confers with War Department on Colonel Young case, and on status of colored soldier. Injustice of "Jim-Crow" railroad discrimination against colored soldiers urged. Assurances received that due proportion of colored men would be mobilized for fighting (combatant) service and no undue proportion organized into "service" battalions.

March, 1918: Takes up with Secretary of War case of Lieutenant Tribbett who was taken from a Pullman coach in Oklahoma.

April, 1918: Open letter of protest to the War Department against General [Adin] Ballou's order, Bulletin 35. Publicity secured throughout the country.

CLAUDE MCKAY
(1890–1948)

Claude McKay—poet, novelist and journalist—was born September 15, 1890, in Sunny Ville, Clarendon Parish, Jamaica, as Fester Claudius McKay. The youngest of eleven children, McKay began writing poetry at age 10. In 1912 McKay moved to the U.S. He was already an established poet with two volumes published, including Songs of Jamaica *and* Constab Ballads. *Later McKay became the editor of the left-leaning journal the* Liberator. *Unrest during the summer of 1919, or Red Summer, motivated McKay to write some of his most profound sonnets, including "If We Must Die." The poem was a response to attacks on Black communities by white mobs who destroyed their homes, schools and churches. Scores of African Americans were lynched, some of them while still wearing their U.S. army uniforms.*

If We Must Die
1919

If we must die—let it not be like hogs
Hunted and penned in an inglorious spot,
While round us bark the mad and hungry dogs,
Making their mock at our accursed lot.
If we must die—oh, let us nobly die,
So that our precious blood may not be shed
In vain; then even the monsters we defy
Shall be constrained to honor us though dead!
Oh, Kinsmen! We must meet the common foe;
Though far outnumbered, let us show us brave,
And for their thousand blows deal one deathblow!
What though before us lies the open grave?
Like men we'll face the murderous, cowardly pack,
Pressed to the wall, dying, but fighting back!

Notes

1. For a general discussion of World War I, see John Keegan, *The First World War* (New York: Knopf, 1999).

2. Charles F. Horne, ed., *Records of the Great War*, vol. 5 (National Alumni, 1923).

3. Gail Buckley, *American Patriots: The Story of Blacks in the Military from the Revolution to Desert Storm* (New York: Random House, 2001), 168.

4. Buckley, *American Patriots*, 168.

5. John Hope Franklin and Alfred A. Moss Jr., *From Slavery to Freedom: A History of African Americans*, 7th ed. (New York: McGraw-Hill, 1994), 305–6.

6. Franklin and Moss, *From Slavery to Freedom*, 307.

7. Jeannette Smith-Irvin, *Marcus Garvey's Foot Soldiers* (Lawrenceville, N.J.: Africa World Press, 1989), 9.

8. *The Crisis*, January 1915, 119–20. Reprinted in William Loren Katz, *Eyewitness: The Negro in American History* (New York: Pitman, 1967), 389–90.

9. Franklin and Moss, *From Slavery to Freedom*, 292–93.

10. Franklin and Moss, *From Slavery to Freedom*, 126.

11. Franklin and Moss, *From Slavery to Freedom*, 274.

12. Robert B. Edgerton, *Hidden Heroism: Black Soldiers in America's Wars* (Boulder, Colo.: Westview Press, 2002), 73.

13. Buckley, *American Patriots*, 175.

14. See Buckley, *American Patriots*, 175–76, for a more detailed discussion on Colonel Young's forced retirement. Also see Nancy G. Heinl, "Col. Charles Young: Pointman," *Army* 27 (March 1977): 30–33.

15. Franklin and Moss, *From Slavery to Freedom*, 29, and Kai Wright, *Soldiers of Freedom: An Illustrated History of African Americans in the Armed Forces* (New York: Black Dog & Leventhal, 2002), 130.

16. Emmett J. Scott, *Scott's Official History of the American Negro in the World War* (1919; New York: Arno Press, 1969), 64.

17. W. E. B. Du Bois, "Close Ranks," *Crisis Magazine*, June–July 1918.

18. Scott, *Official History*, 24.

19. A. Philip Randolph and Chandler Owen, "Pro-Germanism among Negroes," *The Messenger* 2:7 (July 1918): 13.

20. Wright, *Soldiers of Freedom*, 125.

21. Franklin and Moss, *From Slavery to Freedom*, 308.

22. Information on the organization of the Black troops for World War I can be found in Buckley, *American Patriots*, 165–66.

23. Edgerton, *Hidden Heroism*, 85.

24. Buckley, *American Patriots*, 164–65.

25. Robert Ewell Greene, *Black Defenders of America: 1775–1973* (Chicago: Johnson Publishing, 1974), 171.

26. Greene, *Black Defenders*, 171.

27. Buckley, *American Patriots*, 214–15.

28. Addie D. Hunton and Kathryn H. Johnson, *Two Colored Women with the American Expeditionary Forces* (Brooklyn, N.Y.: Brooklyn Eagle Press, 1918), 17–18.

29. Hunton and Johnson, *Two Colored Women*, 17–18.

30. Scott, *Official History*, 442.

31. Buckley, *American Patriots*, 94.

32. Franklin and Moss, *From Slavery to Freedom*, 300.

33. Keegan, *First World War*, 3.

34. William Hewlett, in Michel Fabre, *From Harlem to Paris: Black American Writers on France* (Urbana: University of Illinois Press, 1991), 53.

~

CHAPTER SIX

World War II:
Fighting for "Our America"
1941-1945

The decade following the Great War engendered peace and prosperity for millions of U.S. citizens. However, for the majority of African Americans it was a period of turmoil and instability. The great migration of African Americans that had begun after the turn of the century continued, shifting waves of them from the agricultural South to the industrial North. Ostracized by bias and racial hatred in the South, but seeing immense employment opportunities in the North, African Americans fled to the nation's big cities in droves, engorging the urban slums. It was not an easy transition, however. They were challenged—often with violence—by whites who felt their social status and livelihood were being threatened. Uncomfortable with the idea of granting equal rights to their new African American neighbors, white urbanites responded with racially discriminatory policies and violence.

African Americans fought back against threats to their survival in various ways. An important voice for African Americans—which had been in existence since the 1840s—was the Black press. Small and relatively uninfluential before 1910 because it lacked a large urban audience, the Black press grew between the World Wars.[1] Strongly advocating an end to discrimination, the publications were increasingly investigated by the likes of J. Edgar Hoover, who suffered from paranoia about radical content and the bourgeoning support by some African Americans for Bolshevism in Russia.

In addition to the groundswell of political activism during the earlier part of the 20th century, a Renaissance occurring in Harlem led to international recognition of the talents of Black artists—including jazz musicians, writers, painters and other cultural advocates. African American artists creatively articulated the Black experience through poetry, song, literature and theatre. Langston Hughes, Lorraine Hansberry and Zora Neale Hurston emerged as cultural icons and spokespersons. The indignation of the African American community was expressed in songs by such legendary artists as Billie Holiday, whose song "Strange Fruit" illustrated the horrors of lynching.

The Nation of Islam was founded by Wallace Fard Muhammad in 1930 as a religious, sociopolitical organization with the aim of elevating the spiritual, social and economic condition of Black people throughout the world. The organization had only received limited attention until Wallace Fard Muhammad mysteriously disappeared in 1934 and Elijah Muhammad, his messenger, became its leader. Under the "Messenger's" leadership, the Nation of Islam's membership ranks grew to more than 100,000 people and produced such charismatic leaders as Malcolm X and Minister Louis Farrakhan. Elijah Muhammad led the organization until his death in 1975.[2]

Irrespective of the "Red Scare," the U.S. was forced to concentrate on its domestic affairs as a result of the Stock Market Crash of 1929 and the Great Depression of the 1930s. The Depression devastated the country, rendering a large number of Americans almost penniless practically overnight. During the period of 1929–1933, unemployment in the U.S. soared from 3 percent of the workforce to 25 percent, while manufacturing output collapsed by one-third. Prices declined, especially for farm products. Heavy industry, mining, lumbering and agriculture were badly hit. The impact was much less severe in white-collar and service sectors, but every city and state suffered. By 1933 millions of Americans were out of work. Thousands of citizens roamed the country in search of food, work and shelter. Bread and soup lines became ordinary. "Brother, can you spare a dime?" went the refrain of the popular song by Yip Harburg. African Americans were especially hard hit. "In October 1933, between 25 and 40 percent of the African Americans in several large urban centers were on relief, a figure three or four times the number of whites on relief at that time."[3] In some Northern cities, whites called for African Americans to be fired from any job as long as there were whites out of work.

Still reeling from the blow inflicted by the losses of World War I, the U.S. was also hit hard by the economic fallout from the Depression, which further exposed its vulnerability. In response to this crisis, Presidents Warren G. Harding and Herbert Hoover established an isolationist international posture. To be sure, many Americans believed that their nation had been manipulated into going to war by domestic arms makers and foreign interests. Isolationism spread throughout the nation and was marked by the refusal of the U.S. to join the League of Nations—the first world organization designed to provide order to the global arena.

President Hoover worked to end the economic crisis by creating programs to aid businesses and farmers. He also instituted banking reform and provided loans to states for feeding the unemployed. However, at the same time, Hoover reiterated his view that caring for impoverished Americans was primarily a local and voluntary responsibility. Hoover's failure to adequately resolve the economic chaos ultimately led to his defeat in 1932. Franklin D. Roosevelt replaced Hoover in a crushing blow, winning 472 electoral votes to his 59.

Roosevelt responded to the country's economic crisis immediately. He implemented a remarkable series of new programs in the "first hundred days" of his administration. Coined the "New Deal" and based on Roosevelt's earlier affinity to Progressivism, the policies provided relief for destitute Americans, created jobs and stimulated economic recovery. The New Deal established governmental agencies that brought generous credit facilities to industry and agriculture. One such agency was the Federal Deposit Insurance Corporation (FDIC), which insured savings-bank deposits up to $5,000 and imposed severe regulations upon the sale of securities on the stock exchange. The Civilian Conservation Corps (CCC) was established to bring relief to young men by enrolling them in work camps across the country. They participated in a variety of conservation projects, including planting trees; maintaining national forests; eliminating stream pollution; creating fish, game and bird sanctuaries; and conserving coal, petroleum, gas, sodium and helium deposits. Work relief also came in the form of the Civil Works Administration. This organizational apparatus created more jobs, ranging from teaching to hiring contractors for highway repairs. The Agricultural Adjustment Act (AAA) provided economic relief to farmers, while the National Recovery Administration (NRA) was designed to end cutthroat competition by setting codes for fair competitive practices to generate more jobs and thus more buying.[4]

A crisis was also burgeoning in the international sphere. A fragile peace had been secured after World War I with the Treaty of Versailles in 1919, but little attempt was made to really reconcile the differences between the winners and the losers. The Treaty, which was ratified by the newly created League of Nations on January 10, 1920, required Germany to accept full responsibility for causing the war. Other terms imposed included disarmament, reduction of Germany's territory and elimination of its colonial rights. The Germans were humiliated and suffered economically as they attempted to settle its war debts and reparations. The melancholic state of the German people eventually contributed to the collapse of the new government in 1933 and Adolf Hitler's subsequent rise to power.

The Germans were attracted to Adolf Hitler's charismatic personality and nationalistic perspective. Hitler, who was the head of the National Socialist German Workers Party (Nazi Party) and was known as the Führer ("leader"), was appalled by Germany's capitulation after World War I and acceptance of the conditions imposed under the Treaty of Versailles. He convinced the German people that he was their savior from depression, the Communists, the Jews and other minorities. Hitler also adopted a policy of fascism and imposed state control over all aspects of life: political, social, cultural and economic. He received even more support from the German people as a result of his successful expansion of industrial production and civil improvement.

Under fascism, the nation, state or race is considered superior to its individual citizens, institutions or other groups. Hitler stressed German nationalism and promoted the notion that the Aryan (European master race) was superior over all other races. As leader of Nazi Germany, Hitler harassed and persecuted Jewish people and other minorities. The country also enacted legislation to restrict their civil, economic and citizenship rights. Jews feared Hitler and as a result thousands fled Germany.

In 1935, Germany violated the Treaty of Versailles by reintroducing conscription in the army. Hitler also set about rebuilding the navy and air force. Further treaty violations included reoccupying the demilitarized zone in the Rhineland—generally considered the land on both sides of the river Rhine in West Germany. In July 1936, when the Spanish Civil War began, led by General Francisco Franco, who orchestrated a rebellion against the leftist-leaning Popular Front government of Spain, Hitler sent in troops to support Franco. During that period, Italy under the leadership of Benito Mussolini had also become an expansionist fascist state. In 1935, Italy invaded the independent African nation of Ethiopia, which it had unsuccessfully tried to conquer in the 1890s. After Italy took the capital, Addis Ababa, on May 5, 1936, the Ethiopian leader, Emperor Haile Selassie, went into exile. Germany, Italy and Japan, who later made up the Axis powers of World War II, entered into the Tripartite Pact in 1940, which meant that each country was obligated to assist the other in case of outside aggression.

In addition to their loathing for Jews and Blacks, Adolf Hitler and the Nazis had a deep-seated hatred for Russian Communists. War between Germany and the Union of Soviet Socialist Republics (USSR) was inevitable. The USSR tested its strength by making its own territorial gains, including conquering Finland and the Baltic states. Then, in hopes of establishing a nonviolent relationship, on August 23, 1939, Germany and the USSR signed a secret nonaggression pact dividing up Poland. On April 13, 1941, the USSR and Japan signed a neutrality pact.

But Soviet leader Joseph Stalin could not avoid war with Germany. On June 22, 1941, Germany invaded Russia. Nazi Germany's invasion of the Soviet Union created an instant alliance between the Soviets and two other great powers, Britain and France, who had also declared war on Germany in 1939, two days after the German invasion of Poland. The United States responded by sending billions in aid to the Soviet Union.[5]

On the other side of the world, the military leaders of Japan embarked on their own series of conquests. In search of badly needed oil and other raw materials, Japan had invaded China as early as 1937, leading to the second Sino-Japanese war. The League of Nations was ineffective at stopping these aggressive actions. Even as Hitler built up Germany's military in 1935 and when the Axis powers united in 1936, the League of Nations lay relatively docile.

When Hitler initially began his aggression, the U.S. elected to stay out of war. President Roosevelt condemned Japanese actions in China and accepted apologies when Japanese airplanes sank an American gunboat on the Yangtze River—but he didn't impose any sanctions. However, as the aggression escalated in Europe and Asia, the U.S. began to make countermoves which gradually shifted away from neutrality.

What eventually triggered U.S. active participation in the international aggression was a dispute with Japan. Up until this point, U.S. policy toward the Asian front was ambiguous and guarded. Concerned more about Hitler, the U.S. did not want a two-sided dilemma—and countered Japan at this time with more cautious measures of economic and trade sanctions. Japan tried to negotiate with the U.S. to keep it out of war but the U.S. would only agree if further Japanese aggression stopped. That proved futile when Japan invaded southern Indochina—and the U.S. retaliated by freezing all U.S.-based Japanese funds. Approximately 18 months earlier, the U.S. had transferred a navy fleet to Pearl Harbor as a presumed deterrent to Japanese aggression. The Japanese, in turn, attacked U.S. military bases at Pearl Harbor on December 7, 1941. Within three days after this blow to the U.S. fleet, the country was at war with Japan as well as Germany and Italy.

Despite their domestic troubles, African Americans were growing increasingly aware of these alarming events. They were particularly concerned about how these changes would affect African people globally. Indeed, they were annoyed by the Treaty of Versailles's failure to provide any provision affirming world racial equality. In addition, when the charter for the League of

Nations was debated in 1919, the delegates rejected Japan's proposal to in-clude a clause in the document that would provide for "the equality of all na-tions and fair treatment of all peoples." This proposed clause received 11 fa-vorable votes out of the 17 member votes of the League of Nations Committee. However, the proposition met fierce opposition from the U.S. and Britain. Woodrow Wilson, who was chairman of the committee, refused the proposition on the grounds that such an important decision should have unanimous support. Other clauses in the charter were adopted on the prin-ciple of majority vote.[6] Even still, despite the failure of the world organiza-tion to act on behalf of racial equality, African Americans could not ignore Hitler's hatred of Jews and bias against African people.

The African American conflict against Hitler and fascism intensified soon after it was rumored that Hitler snubbed Jesse Owens, the African American gold medal winner at the 1936 Berlin Olympics.[7] After the Hitler snub, an editorial entitled, "Fascism Now Means Something," appeared in the *Crisis Magazine*.[8] Certainly, many African Americans were already aware of Hitler's notions of Aryan superiority and his call for racial purity. He had intention-ally and openly insulted African Americans when he criticized the German petty-bourgeoisie for their praise of Black achievement. Hitler quipped, "It doesn't dawn on this depraved bourgeois world that this is positively a sin against all reason; that it is criminal lunacy to keep on drilling a born half-ape until people have made a lawyer of him, while millions of members of the highest culture-race must remain in entirely unworthy positions . . . "[9] Ac-knowledging Hitler's racism, Kelly Miller, dean of Howard University's Col-lege of Arts and Sciences, wrote that "The racial policy of the Hitler move-ment is strikingly similar to that of the neo–Ku Klux Klanism of America."[10]

African Americans were equally concerned about Italy's invasion of Ethiopia in 1935 and therefore rallied to support Ethiopia by raising money and sending aid.[11] Although Italy defeated the African nation, the awareness stimulated Black international activism against fascism and racism.

In addition to the ongoing international concerns, the Spanish Civil War prompted African American involvement. Approximately 100 African Americans joined the 3,000 American volunteers organized under the Abra-ham Lincoln Brigade to defend the Popular Front Spanish government against General Franco's coup. Those African Americans who volunteered for the brigade were part of a small but significant Black Communist Left that came of age between World War I and the Depression. Several African American newspapers, most notably Pittsburgh's *Courier*, Baltimore's *Afro-American*, Atlanta's *Daily World* and Chicago's *Defender*, sided with the Span-ish Republic and occasionally carried feature articles about African American participation in the Lincoln Brigade.[12] Some African Americans sent medical supplies, money and other needed equipment. Paul Robeson and Langston Hughes visited Spain during the civil war and reported the details of the conflict to their community.[13] Although the U.S. did not enthusiastically support the Popular Front government of Spain, fearing a Communist takeover of that country, African Americans did not object to the U.S. official merger with the Allied nations—which included the United Kingdom, France, Poland, the Soviet Union, China and other smaller nations.

There was concern, however, about U.S. ability to readily help defeat the Axis powers, considering the country had entered the war rather late and was not organized for such large-scale military ventures. But after the attack on Pearl Harbor, winning the war became a priority. Industrial production increased in the U.S. to meet the need for weapons. Industry, labor, government agencies and think tanks joined together to gear up the military-industrial complex to unprecedented, innovative scales. In 1944, war production in the U.S. was twice that of Germany and the other Axis members. This mega-production had the ultimate effect of transforming both the prosperity and social make-up of America.

The oncoming war required personnel reinforcement. In 1940, President Roosevelt signed the Selective Training and Service Act, which required men between the ages 21 and 30 to register with local draft boards. Not surprisingly, the Selective Service Act represented the continued segregation of U.S. society and revealed the early attitude toward African American participation in the war. Previously, during the interwar period, the army not only remained segregated, but it had also adopted a policy of having a quota on African American enlistment in order to keep its numbers proportionate to their percentage in the country. Nevertheless, in the pre–World War II period the number of African Americans in military service never approached the quota.

Many of the racist policies of the U.S. military were based on a 1925 Army War College study that concluded African Americans were genetically inferior to whites, unfit to fight, unintelligent, submissive, suffered from low self-esteem, were easily manipulated and were likely to crumble in war situations. Those conclusions were justified with misleading information. For instance, low test scores were used to argue that African Americans were of low intelligence, while the report ignored the limited educational options for African Americans.

On the eve of Pearl Harbor, there were fewer than 5,000 African Americans in the army, constituting less than 6 percent. Only two were combat officers.[14] African American activists pushed Roosevelt for reforms. In response, Roosevelt used his executive powers to give African Americans positions in government.. Encouraged by his wife Eleanor, the president organized a "Black Cabinet," which included William H. Hastie, dean of the Howard University Law School, who was appointed assistant solicitor in the Department of the Interior and later became aide to the secretary of war. Ralph Bunche worked in the State Department, and Bethune was director of the Division of Negro Affairs of the National Youth Administration. By the mid-1930s, Roosevelt had appointed 45 African Americans to serve in his New Deal agencies. Not only did the number of African American appointments increase, but so did the quality of the jobs. Most important, Roosevelt bypassed Congress and, by executive order, established the Civil Rights Section of the Justice Department. The Civil Rights Section eventually began building a skilled bureaucracy of lawyers and other trained professionals to further advance civil rights in the U.S.

Certainly, urban African Americans were becoming politically important, so Roosevelt attempted to address their issues. Moreover, Mrs. Roosevelt publicly addressed the anxiety of African Americans. During a speech to a church in Washington shortly after the bombing of Pearl Harbor, Eleanor Roosevelt stated, "The nation cannot expect the colored people to feel the U.S. is worth defending if they continue to be treated as they are now . . . I am not agitating the race question . . . The race question is agitated because people will not act justly and fairly towards each other as human beings."[15]

Reluctantly, the War Department conceded that African Americans would be accepted into the army in the same proportion as their percentage in the general population.[16] But even this concession was deceptive, because African Americans were still segregated, restricted to serving in noncombat functions, could not become commissioned officers and were initially denied entrance into the more prestigious branches. Most African Americans served in auxiliary units such as transportation and the engineering corps, doing grunt work. They were given the least attractive facilities and resources in camps. Because they were primarily trained in the South, African American soldiers were subject to constant racist harassment. Amazingly enough, the Red Cross refused—under military advice—to accept African American blood until January 1942. And even after the Red Cross agreed to accept blood from African Americans, it was segregated from whites'. Their military capability and loyalty notwithstanding, African Americans were acutely aware of the irony: the U.S. would be fighting racist Hitler with a racially divided army.

African American activists protested the discriminatory rules of the Selective Service in a seven-point program submitted to President Roosevelt.

The document urged that "all available reserve officers be used to train recruits; that Black recruits be given the same training as whites; that the army accept officers and men on the basis of ability and not race; that specialized personnel, such as physicians, dentists and nurses, be integrated; that responsible Negroes be appointed to draft boards; that discrimination be abolished in the navy and air force; and that competent Negroes be appointed as civilian assistants to the secretaries of war and navy."[17]

Not all African Americans believed that the fight to desegregate the army was important. Some, such as Elijah Muhammad, argued that African Americans should not involve themselves in the war at all. Muhammad stated that it was wrong to fight a war abroad when it was so much more important to fight the war against discrimination at home. A conscientious objector, Muhammad spent more than four years in various jails and prisons for eight counts of sedition and draft violations.[18] Bayard Rustin, a founder of the Congress of Racial Equality, was also sentenced to three years in Lewisburg Prison for his objection to the war. Rustin registered as a conscientious objector in October 1940, stating in a letter to the Draft Board that the conscription "separates black from white—those supposedly struggling for common freedom. Such a separation also is based on the moral error that racism can overcome racism, that evil can produce good, that men virtually in slavery can struggle for a freedom they are denied."[19] Whether they believed in their anti-war ideas out of ideology or pacifism, many participants in the resistance movement were accused of sedition and investigated by the FBI. By the end of 1943, approximately 167 African American men had been convicted for various draft violations.[20]

The racism practiced during wartime became even more transparent when determining who received jobs and contracts in the defense industries. The country was pumping money into industry on a gigantic scale—and as employment blossomed, more labor was needed to fill jobs. The war machines not only pulled the African American population off the farms into Northern cities, but also to the West because many defense industry companies were based in Southern California. For African American women, as it would for their white counterparts, the war would be an opportunity for new modes of employment. They could now leave behind those domestic service jobs for better-paying, albeit more hazardous industrial jobs. However, one must note that the "jobs that became available to Blacks were those that whites had abandoned in favor of the higher paying defense plant jobs."[21]

A. Philip Randolph, the president of the Brotherhood of Sleeping Car Pullman Porters, proposed a mass "March on Washington" to fight against the discriminatory policies in the defense industries. Speaking in January 1941, he said:

> The Negro stake in national defense is big. It consists of jobs, thousands of jobs. It consists of new industrial opportunities and hope. This is worth fighting for . . . To this end we propose that 10,000 Negroes march on Washington.[22]

Scheduled for July 1941, the proposed march on Washington was the largest mobilization of African Americans since the activities of Marcus Garvey's UNIA of the 1920s. Leaders of the march mobilized college students, interracial groups and African American women and men to support the activities. The effort quickly gained support, with more than 100,000 African Americans committed.[23] The demands included a ban on racial discrimination in defense training courses and in companies with government contracts; an end to segregation in the armed forces; and withdrawal of the National Labor Relations Act's protection for labor unions that excluded African Americans.

If the march had taken place, it would have been embarrassing for President Roosevelt, who feared it could become a wartime public relations disaster. Accordingly, the president proposed minor changes in policy in an effort to get Randolph and other leaders to call off the march. Reaching no agreement, however, Roosevelt then issued Executive Order 8802, which granted all of the movement's demands—with the exception of union and military desegregation. The president even established the Fair Employment Practices Commission, with the mission to investigate discrimination. While the Executive Order was considered the first major presidential order to counter discrimination since Reconstruction, it did not result in radical change. The order was opposed by leaders of important military and government agencies. Moreover, Southern congressmen and general white Americans, many of whom believed that winning the war took precedence over racial issues, found ways to obstruct implementation of the order. White soldiers protested Black advancement throughout the military, and racial violence occurred at practically every post.

African Americans had no delusions about turning around racism overnight—but they believed that their activism would result in progress. What became known as the "Double V" campaign functioned as an expression of African American sentiments. They would fight for two victories—one over international fascism and the other over domestic racism.[24] A *Negro Digest Poll* showed that 59 percent of African Americans believed that the war for democracy overseas would aid in the fight for democracy at home.[25] As part of the Double V campaign, African Americans tackled the issue of desegregating the military. They wrote letters to federal government officials complaining about discrimination, and African American soldiers protested against the threats and violence to which they were often subjected.

During World War II, racial violence exploded in several major cities. One of the deadliest riots occurred in Detroit, Michigan, where thousands of African Americans had migrated to work in the booming industrial plants. The competition for jobs between Black and white workers resulted in the killing of thirty-four people in 1943. Racism also reared its ugly head after the Pearl Harbor attack. Questioning the loyalty of Japanese Americans, the U.S. government ordered that all Japanese Americans be placed in domestic internment camps through Executive Order 9066. More than 100,000 citizens and "aliens" of Japanese descent were removed from their residences and placed in the camps.[26]

The overwhelming manpower needs of the war, however, forced each branch of the armed services to make concessions, either accepting African Americans for the first time into the service, allowing them into officer training schools, and/or—equally important—validating them as ready for combat. "Between 1941 and 1945, the number of black enlisted personnel grew from 5,000 to over 900,000, and the number of black officers grew from 5 to over 7,000. Some 500,000 black men and women served overseas in North Africa, Europe and the Pacific."[27] African American women also found opportunities—and quotas were eventually lifted in the Nursing Corps.

African American soldiers served heroically and admirably during World War II—even though, as in the case of World War I, no African Americans were awarded the Medal of Honor.[28] One of the earliest war heroes was African American mess attendant Dorie Miller, who shot down enemy aircraft and saved the life of his captain during the attack on Pearl Harbor (but although given the Navy Cross, went unpromoted).[29]

One of the most notable groups of African American soldiers was the Tuskegee Airmen, who served in the Army Air Force. Formed in July 1941, the Tuskegee Airmen were proposed by the War Department as a combined all–African American pilot pursuit squadron (with Black officers) and training program at Tuskegee Army Air Field in Alabama. The era of the all-white air force had finally ended with the advent of the Tuskegee Airmen. For the first time, African Americans were accepted in the armed forces as military aviation pilots. By the end of the war, the Tuskegee program had graduated almost 1,000 African Americans. The highly praised program produced respected pilots who flew over 15,000 sorties, destroyed over 1,000 German aircraft, participated in some of the most important missions of the war and were officially recognized, receiving hundreds of air medals, including 150 Distinguished Flying Crosses.

The changes made to accommodate African American interests, however, did not rid the military of racism. In 1944, when two military cargo ships at Port Chicago, California, exploded, it was the worst domestic loss of life in the war—a total of three hundred and twenty sailors were killed, including 202 Blacks. Charging that only Blacks had been given ammunition loading assignments and little training, many of the surviving African American seamen mutinied. However, instead of addressing the charges of racism, military officials arrested and convicted the protesters. Expressing the sentiment of the African American community, in response to the legal action against the seaman, NAACP lawyer Thurgood Marshall said:

> This is not fifty men on trial for mutiny. This is the Navy on trial for its whole vicious policy towards Negroes . . . Negroes are not afraid of anything any more than anyone else. Negroes in the Navy don't mind loading ammunition. They just want to know why they are the only ones doing the loading! They wanted to know why they are segregated; why they don't get promoted.[30]

For a year after the U.S. became involved in the world conflict, it struggled with the Allies to oppose Axis military moves. In fact, it wasn't until the last half of 1942 that the Allies initiated a recognizable counteroffensive. Hitler's defeat at Stalingrad in early 1943 was considered a turning point. By the following year, the Allies took the lead—defeating the Germans in Africa, overtaking Italy and seeing hope in the Pacific Islands. Unlike World War I, the United States was an active and full-fledged ally—and setting a precedent for becoming the premier superpower. Germany fell by May of 1944, and the United States forced Japan's surrender when its air force dropped two atomic bombs on Hiroshima and Nagasaki on the mornings of August 6 and August 9. Japanese official figures show that the number of civilians killed in Japan proper were: Tokyo—97,031; Hiroshima—140,000; Nagasaki—70,000; and 86,336 in 63 other cities.[31] Japan sent notice of its unconditional surrender to the Allies on August 15, a week after the bombings.

The war in Europe ended in May 1945 and in the Pacific in August of that same year. The most influential conflict since the Civil War had affected the lives of practically every American. "Lasting twice as long as World War I, it cost 350 billion dollars, involved 14 million men and women in the armed forces, and added another 10 million people in the work force."[32] However, World War II was the most destructive in history. Estimates put the "number of deaths at an unimaginable 50 million people. The Soviet Union lost 13 million combatants and 7 million civilians. The Germans calculated losses of 3.6 million civilians and 3.2 million soldiers. The Japanese estimated 2 million civilian and 1 million military deaths. Six million Jews had been killed. The number of British and commonwealth deaths is calculated at 484,482. With 291,557 battle deaths and 113,842 non-hostile deaths from accident and disease, the United States suffered the fewest casualties among the major nations."[33] Major losses suffered by other nations including China, several countries in Eastern Europe, India, Australia and more made up the rest of the casualties.

As World War II came to an end, African Americans were not particulary hopeful about the possibility of racial peace. A *Negro Digest* poll taken in August 1944 found that the majority did not believe that racial peace would come to the U.S., even after conquering the Axis powers.[34] After defeating racism and fascism abroad, African Americans returned home to face more of the same racist practices as before the war began. Many "were denied equal opportunity for employment. They were less able to take advantage of G.I. mortgages due to housing segregation and they were less able to take advantage of the G.I. bill, which provided for college or vocational education, unemployment compensation and loans because they were less likely to have finished high school before the war."[35]

The United Nations was established in August 1945 at the end of World War II, to replace the largely ineffective League of Nations. The name United Nations was coined by President Franklin Delano Roosevelt in 1941 to describe the countries fighting against the Axis. It was first used officially on January 1, 1942, when 26 states joined in the Declaration by the United Nations, pledging themselves to the Atlanta Charter and vowing not to make peace separately with the Axis Powers. The founding conference was held in San Francisco (April 25–June 26, 1945). The UN charter was signed on June 26 and ratified by the required number of states in October of that same year. The purpose of the new organization was to prevent future aggression and promote humanitarianism. African American leaders hoped that the new organization would provide them with an international forum to express their concerns about racism in the U.S. and abroad. In addition to Ralph Bunche, who attended the conference in his official capacity as the acting chief of the Division of Dependent Territories of the Department of State, other noted African Americans observed the organizational proceedings in San Francisco. Among them were Mary McLeod Bethune of the National Council of Negro Women, W. E. B. Du Bois and Walter White of the NAACP, and Mordecai W. Johnson from Howard University.[36]

After World War II, African Americans had vowed to continue their fight for racial equality. They sought to use their newfound strength to hasten racial progress and revolutionize the country as it moved into the Cold War.

The commentary by African Americans in this section reflects the complexity of their concerns and experiences during the World War II era. African Americans struggled to end legal lynchings and segregation. They also supported ideas, causes and movements that might lead to independence and self-determination through their mass support of the Garvey Movement. Others embraced economic equality in their support of Bolshevism. Still others fought for an integrated United States that would be true to its declared principles of liberty and democracy for all. In the end, African Americans proved their support for those principles by their willingness to engage in battle at home and abroad.

The various perspectives of African American political thought and activism during World War II are demonstrated by its leaders and organizations. The first document in this section is a letter to the draft board written by the African American pacifist Bayard Rustin. In his letter, Rustin outlines the reasons why he became a conscientious objector and why he was willing to spend years in prison in defense of those views. Also included is A. Philip Randolph's call to African Americans and his justification for a march on Washington to protest discrimination in the defense industries. In his article "My America," Langston Hughes details the contradictions of Jim Crowism with the American democratic creed.

Max Yergan, a founder and former executive director of the Council on African Affairs, reflects the developing international consciousness of many African Americans. He asserts that the loyalty Blacks have shown to America's ideas are reflected in their sincere opposition to fascism, and therefore "the attitude of Negroes toward the war takes rank with the highest and best attitude in America." In agreement with Yergan is the statement of Congressman Adam Clayton Powell, who argues for the freedom of colonial peoples throughout the war. He declares that the U.S. and British governments, while fighting for democracy in principle, had never really promoted a "real democracy," especially when considering the treatment of people of color.

The final two entries are written by Walter White, executive director of the NAACP, and William Hastie, civilian aide to Secretary of War Henry L. Stimson. White reports on the status of African American servicemen on the battlefields in Europe during the war, while Hastie explains the reasons why he resigned his position.

A. PHILIP RANDOLPH
(1889–1979)

In 1941, A. Philip Randolph advocated for a massive march on Washington to protest the exclusion of African American workers from jobs in the defense industries. He agreed to call off the march only after President Franklin Roosevelt issued Executive Order 8802, which banned discrimination in defense plants and established the nation's first Fair Employment Practice Committee. In 1948, Randolph warned President Harry Truman that if segregation in the armed forces were not abolished, masses of African Americans would refuse induction. Soon Executive Order 9981 was issued to comply with his demands. In protest of the mistreatment of African Americans in the armed forces and labor discrimination during World War II, Randolph published the following statement in the Black Worker.

A Call to the Negro American to March on Washington
July 1, 1941

We call upon you to fight for the jobs in National Defense.

We call upon you to struggle for integration of Negroes in the armed forces, such as the Air Corps, Navy, Army, and Marine Corps of the Nation.

We call upon you to demonstrate for the abolition of Jim-Crowism in all Government departments and defense employment.

This is an hour of crisis. It is a crisis of democracy. It is a crisis of minority groups. It is a crisis of Negro Americans.

What is this crisis?

To American Negroes, it is the denial of jobs in Government defense projects. It is racial discrimination in Government departments. It is widespread Jim-Crowism in the armed forces of the Nation.

While billions of the taxpayers' money are being spent for war weapons, Negro workers are being turned away from the gates of factories, mines and mills—being flatly told, "nothing doing." Some employers refuse to give Negroes jobs when they are without "union cards," and some unions refuse Negro workers union cards when they are "without jobs."

What shall we do?

What a dilemma!

What a runaround!

What a disgrace!

What a blow below the belt!

Though dark, doubtful and discouraging, all is not lost, all is not hopeless. Though battered and bruised, we are not beaten, broken or bewildered.

Verily, the Negroes' deepest disappointments and direst defeats, their tragic trials and outrageous oppressions in these dreadful days of destruction and disaster to democracy and freedom, and the rights of minority peoples, and the dignity and independence of the human spirit, is the Negroes' greatest opportunity to rise to the highest heights of struggle for freedom and justice in Government, in industry, in labor unions, education, social service, religion and culture.

With faith and confidence of the Negro people in their own power for self-liberation, Negroes can break down the barriers of discrimination against employment in National Defense. Negroes can kill the deadly serpent of race hatred in the Army, Navy, Air and Marine Corps, and smash through and blast the Government, business and labor-union red tape to win the right to equal opportunity in vocational training and re-training in defense employment.

Most important and vital of all, Negroes, by the mobilization and coordination of their mass power, can cause President Roosevelt to issue an executive order abolishing discriminations in all government departments, Army, Navy, Air Corps and National Defense jobs.

Of course, the task is not easy. In very truth, it is big, tremendous and difficult.

It will cost money.

It will require sacrifice.

It will tax the Negroes' courage, determination and will to struggle. But we can, must and will triumph.

The Negroes' stake in national defense is big. It consists of jobs, thousands of jobs. It may represent millions, yes, hundreds of millions of dollars in wages. It consists of new industrial opportunities and hope.

This is worth fighting for.

But to win our stakes, it will require an "all-out," bold and total effort and demonstration of colossal proportions.

Negroes can build a mammoth machine of mass action with a terrific and tremendous driving and striking power that can shatter and crush the evil fortress of race prejudice and hate, if they will only resolve to do so and never stop, until victory comes.

Dear fellow Negro Americans, be not dismayed by these terrible times. You possess power, great power. Our problem is to harness and hitch it up for action on the broadest, most daring and most gigantic scale.

In this period of power politics, nothing counts but pressure, more pressure, and still more pressure, through the tactic and strategy of broad, organized, aggressive mass action behind the vital and important issues of the Negro. To this end, we propose that ten thousand Negroes march on Washington for jobs in National Defense and equal integration in the fighting forces of the United States.

An "all-out" thundering march on Washington, ending in a monster and huge demonstration at Lincoln's Monument will shake up white America.

It will shake up official Washington.

It will give encouragement to our white friends to fight all the harder by our side, with us, for our righteous cause.

It will gain respect for the Negro people.

It will create a new sense of self-respect among Negroes.

But what of national unity?

We believe in national unity which recognizes equal opportunity of black and white citizens to jobs in national defense and the armed forces, and in all other institutions and endeavors in America. We condemn all dictatorships, Fascist, Nazi and Communist. We are loyal, patriotic Americans all.

But if American democracy will not defend its defenders; if American democracy will not protect its protectors; if American democracy will not give jobs to its toilers because of race or color; if American democracy will not insure equality of opportunity, freedom and justice to its citizens, black and white, it is hollow mockery and belies the principles for which it is supposed to stand.

To the hard, difficult and trying problem of securing equal participation in national defense, we summon all Negro Americans to march on Washington. We summon Negro Americans to form committees in various cities to recruit and register marchers and raise funds through the sale of buttons and other legitimate means for the expenses of marchers to Washington by buses, train, private automobiles, trucks, and on foot.

We summon Negro Americans to stage marches on their City Halls and Councils in their respective cities and urge them to memorialize the President to issue an executive order to abolish discrimination in the Government and national defense.

However, we sternly counsel against violence and ill-considered and intemperate action and the abuse of power. Mass power, like physical power, when misdirected is more harmful then helpful.

We summon you to mass action that is orderly and lawful, but aggressive and militant, for justice, equality and freedom.

Crispus Attucks marched and died as a martyr for American independence. Nat Turner, Denmark Vesey, Gabriel Prosser, Harriet Tubman and Frederick Douglass fought, bled and died for the emancipation of Negro slaves and the preservation of American democracy.

Abraham Lincoln, in times of the grave emergency of the Civil War, issued the Proclamation of Emancipation for the freedom of Negro slaves and the preservation of American democracy.

Today, we call upon President Roosevelt, a great humanitarian and idealist, to follow in the footsteps of his noble and illustrious predecessor and take the second decisive step in this world and national emergency and free American

Negro citizens of the stigma, humiliation and insult of discrimination and Jim-Crowism in Government departments and national defense.

The Federal Government cannot with clear conscience call upon private industry and labor unions to abolish discrimination based upon race and color as long as it practices discrimination itself against Negro Americans.

MAX YERGAN
(1896–1975)

Max Yergan, while generally unknown to the public, was a target of government surveillance from 1937 through the 1960s. Yergan, an educator and civil rights leader, was associated with the YMCA for over 20 years. He served in India and East Africa before being stationed in South Africa from 1920 to 1936, where he campaigned for civil rights for Black South Africans. Yergan was also a leading figure in the Council of African Affairs, an organization set up to support African liberation. In this commentary, Yergan explains why he and many other African Americans supported the U.S. effort against fascism during World War II, even though they continued to suffer from discrimination at home.

Relation of Negroes to the War
(n.d.)

There is, without doubt, among American Negroes a deep and sincere loyalty to our country's cause. There is likewise a genuine opposition to Hitlerism and all fascism. That means that the attitude of Negroes toward the war takes rank with the highest and best attitude in America. Why is this true?

Because America is the home of the Negro people. With the oldest American Negroes can say, "This is *my* own, my native land". Any attack on America's defenses, whether at Pearl Harbor, the Philippines or elsewhere, is therefore the concern of Negro Americans.

Negroes also know how to hate the poisonous racial theories of Hitler and the brutal assault of fascism in Ethiopia, in China, in Spain. They know how to detest the murderous Hitler in Europe and in the Soviet Union. Therefore, because of their loyalty of their hatred of fascism, Negro people today can say without qualification, "Our country is at war. We stand by our country."

The loyal and enthusiastic attitude of Negroes toward the war is not to be confused with their struggle for full democratic rights. Negroes have always struggled end will always struggle for the highest democratic, the highest American status.

Nor is the loyalty of Negroes conditioned by the degree to which they have or have not attained democratic rights. Those who would enter upon this sort of bargain for Negroes do a serious injustice to the Negro people and play into the hands of the enemies of Negroes as well as of national victory and fuller democracy for our country.

This does not mean that, even now, the struggle for the highest American status for Negroes has to be decreased. Our government and our country must well understand that discriminations stand in the way of the fullest expressions of loyalty and enthusiasm for our county's cause. Negroes, like the Chinese and

Russians, can have that spirit to fight unto death when that spirit is born of their freedom, of their full untrammeled American status.

This is what we Negroes say to our President and to our fellow-Americans: Remove all discriminations in order that we may all the more effectively fight for our country and fight against fascism.

BAYARD RUSTIN
(1912–1987)

Bayard Rustin was raised primarily by his grandparents, who were activists with close ties to prominent figures such as W. E. B. Du Bois and James Weldon Johnson. As a young man, Rustin fought Jim Crow in his hometown of West Chester, Pennsylvania. He also fought to free the Scottsboro boys of Alabama, who were charged with raping two white women. Rustin eventually became an official member of the American Communist Party. As a strong believer in the power of nonviolent resistance to achieve social change, Rustin helped to found the Congress of Racial Equality (CORE). Rustin also worked alongside A. Philip Randolph and Martin Luther King Jr. during the civil rights movement. Because he adhered to the guidelines of pacifism, Rustin refused to join the armed forces, and was therefore sentenced to three years in Lewisburg Prison. Here is Rustin's letter to the Draft Board, explaining his reasons for becoming a conscientious objector.

Letter to the Draft Board
1943

Local Board No. 63
2050 Amsterdam Avenue
New York, N.Y.

Gentlemen:

For eight years I have believed war to be impractical and a denial of our Hebrew-Christian tradition. The social teachings of Jesus are: (1) Respect for personality; (2) Service the "summum bonum"; (3) Overcoming evil with good; and (4) The brotherhood of man. These principles as I see it are violated by participation in war.

Believing this, and having before me Jesus' continued resistance to that which he considered evil, I was compelled to resist war by registering as a Conscientious Objector in October 1940.

However, a year later, September 1941, I became convinced that conscription as well as war equally is inconsistent with the teachings of Jesus. I must resist conscription also.

On Saturday, November 13, 1943, I received from you an order to report for a physical examination to be taken Tuesday, November 16, at eight o'clock in the evening. I wish to inform you that I cannot voluntarily submit to an order springing from the Selective Service and Training Act for War.

There are several reasons for this decision, all stemming from the basic spiritual truth that men are brothers in the sight of God:

1. War is wrong. Conscription is a concomitant of modern war. Thus conscription for so vast an evil as war is wrong.
2. Conscription for war is inconsistent with freedom of conscience, which is not merely the right to believe, but to act on the degree of truth that one receives, to follow a vocation which is God-inspired and God-directed.

Today I feel that God motivates me to use my whole being to combat by non-violent means the ever-growing racial tension in the United States; at the same time the State directs that I shall do its will; which of these dictates can I follow—that of God or that of the State? Surely, I must at all times attempt to obey the law of the State. But when the will of God and the will of the State conflict, I am compelled to follow the will of God. If I cannot continue in my present vocation, I must resist.

3. The Conscription Act denies brotherhood—the most basic New Testament teaching. Its design and purpose is to set men apart—German against American, American against Japanese. Its aim springs from a moral impossibility—that ends justify means, that from unfriendly acts a new and friendly world can emerge.

In practice further, it separates black from white—those supposedly struggling for a common freedom. Such a separation also is based on the moral error that racism can overcome racism, that evil can produce good, that men virtually in slavery can struggle for a freedom they are denied. This means that I must protest racial discrimination in the armed forces, which is not only morally indefensible but also in clear violation of the Act. This does not, however, imply that I could have a part in conforming to the Act if discrimination were eliminated.

Segregation, separation, according to Jesus, is the basis of continuous violence. It was such an observation which encouraged him to teach, "It has been said to you in olden times that thou shalt not kill, but I say unto you, do not call a man a fool"—and he might have added: "for if you call him such, you automatically separate yourself from him and violence begins." That which separates man from his brother is evil and must be resisted.

I admit my share of guilt for having participated in the institutions and ways of life which helped bring fascism and war. Nonetheless, guilty as I am, I now see as did the Prodigal Son that it is never too late to refuse longer to remain in a non-creative situation. It is always timely and virtuous to change—to take in all humility a new path.

Though joyfully following the will of God, I regret that I must break the law of the State. I am prepared for whatever may follow.

I herewith return the material you have sent me, for conscientiously I cannot hold a card in connection with an Act I no longer feel able to accept and abide by.

Today I am notifying the Federal District Attorney of my decision and am forwarding him a copy of this letter.

I appreciate now as in the past your advice and consideration, and trust that I shall cause you no anxiety in the future. I want you to know I deeply respect you for executing your duty to God and country in these difficult times in the way you feel you must. I remain

Sincerely yours,
Bayard Rustin

P.S. I am enclosing samples of the material which from time to time I sent out to hundreds of persons, Negro and white, throughout our nation. This indicates one type of the creative work to which God has called me.

ADAM CLAYTON POWELL JR.
1908–1972

Adam Clayton Powell Jr. was born November 29, 1908, in New Haven, Connecticut, to Adam Clayton Powell Sr. and Mattie Fletcher Schaefer. In 1941, Powell became the first African American member of the New York City Council, and then in 1945 became the first African American elected to the House of Representatives from New York. As the chairman of the Education and Labor Committee, Powell fought for minimum wage increases, education and training for the deaf, vocational training, and standards for wages and work hours. In this commentary, Powell argues that the best way for the U.S. to defeat the Axis powers and Nazism is to fairly enlist the support of Black, brown and yellow people. Powell supports the notion that winning the peace abroad is just as important as pursuing real democracy at home. Therefore, African Americans must commit to winning the war.

Is This a "White Man's War"?
April 1942

Until December 7, 1941, the American Negro was not even interested in the present war "to make the world safe for Democracy." This was due, first, to the British Empire's centuries-old record of exploitation and broken promises; and secondly, to the fact that America itself had not yet been made safe for democracy.

It is pretty hard for a Negro, or for any other thinking individual, to believe the British Empire's claims to democracy. The centuries of oppression of brown people in Asia and Asia Minor and black people in Africa give the lie to this claim. During the last World War Great Britain promised India dominion status, Arabia sovereignty, and the Jew a national home. Although these promises were made by the Crown's direct representatives, they were never kept. Colonel Lawrence of Arabia retired as a disillusioned idealist, disillusioned by his own empire's duplicity. More recently, when the farm workers of the British West Indies revolted and demanded the staggering salary of $1.00 a day, His Majesty's battlewagon *The Hood* steamed into the harbor of Barbados and trained its sixteen inch guns on the Negro section while British troops spilled the blood of hundreds who had the impudence to resist.

The Hogarth Press of London has just published a book entitled, *The Colour Bar in East Africa* by Norman Lays. In this book we learn that in East Africa there are less than 100,000 whites ruling over close to 17,000,000 blacks. These blacks cannot vote or organize into labor unions, even though this is their native land. We are reminded that "colour bars are found only in British Africa;

they do not exist in French Portuguese and Belgian Africa." Around the time that Great Britain decided to fight Germany "His Majesty signed two orders in Council that dealt with land in Kenya. One proclaimed the exclusive ownership by Europeans forever of so-called settled areas." Today, any native of East Africa who wants to live on the land that can be cultivated must "work for the owner at least 180 days in the year entirely free, as the owner chooses." So much for "democracy" in action in Africa.

But what of ourselves? The American way of life has always been a dual one. In many sections of the United States democracy has never been given a chance to work. It has been supplanted by Crackerocracy. Historically, through the 77 years of the Negro's freedom, he has been politically disfranchised, socially ostracized, educationally mis-educated, economically exploited and in the field of religion, has been met with hypocrisy.

The plight of the Jew in Germany compared to that of the Negro in America is ominously close. Ten million Negroes in the South, thanks to exclusion from Democratic primaries, cannot vote; five millions in the North are so gerrymandered that they can elect only one Negro Congressman. One of the great artists of our time was refused permission to sing in the Capital of the United States by the Daughters of the American Revolution in an auditorium ironically called Constitution Hall. There are scores of counties in the South that do not provide any education for Negroes over the sixth grade. The state of Mississippi, for instance, spends six times as much for the education of a white child as it does for a Negro. In fact no later than 1934 the total expenditure per Negro child for school buildings, maintenance, school books, teachers' salaries, school buses etc., was $7.00 per year. Economically, we have been exploited: "the last to be hired and the first to be fired." In the Army we are shunted into Jim Crow regiments; in the Navy—despite the radio's hourly blast of "Volunteers Needed"— we stand in long lines before the information desks only to be told that no Negroes are wanted in the Navy. The Air Corps has one squadron for Negroes in Montgomery, Alabama, which might be called "The Lonely Eagles." There are few, if any, jobs in defense industries. Four hundred industries in New York State working on defense contracts, in answer to a state questionnaire, replied that 97% of them would not employ Negroes.

The Negro vs. Nazism

Yet despite the apathy toward the war and its professed aims, which this kind of treatment naturally induces, it must be said that the American Negro recognized Hitler long ago; we recognized him immediately because he was a cheap imitation of the Hitlers that we have had here in America for years. Hitler was, and is, just another name for Cole Blease, Gene Talmadge and the The Man Bilbo. Nazism is just another word for crackerocracy. The Gestapo is the German name for Ku Klux Klan. Concentration camps must have found their pattern from our Georgia prison camps, and pogroms are very familiar to us, though we call them lynching or mob violence. Hitlerism is merely an old story with new labels.

Yet despite our lack of enthusiasm for the British Empire's brand of democracy, and despite the fact that America has kicked us around more than any other group of people, the Negroes have been and are today the most loyal element in this democracy. We have refused through the years and through recent months to allow ourselves to be used by anti-democratic forces. There are no Fifth Columnists in our ranks. The thinking Negro knows that if America loses the war, his plight as a Negro will be much worse than it is now. Under democracy, however poorly realized, the Negro does have a fighting chance. Politically, socially, educationally, culturally and spiritually, what we believe in and follow is the direct opposite of what the Nazis, the Fascists and the Japanese militarists believe in. If Hitler did win—and he won't—the Japanese themselves would be the first to suffer under him, for there can be no room in a "Nordic" philosophy of life for the little brown or yellow men.

Democracy must wage a two-fold battle—a battle on far flung foreign fields against Hitler, and a battle on the home front against Hitler, and a battle on the home front against Hitlerism. We must begin by stamping out Hitlerism in our own ranks. Negroes must be constantly on guard against crackpots and self-styled "nationalistic" leaders who may attempt to seize this opportunity to whip our emotions into a frenzy against democracy. Secondly, Hitlerism must be stamped out in the armed forces. How can white Americans expect to have a tolerant world after this war when there is racial prejudice within the ranks of those who are fighting? Third, Hitlerism must be stamped out in the Defense Industries. The Metal Trades Union of the A.F. of L., for instance, that does not allow Negroes to join, should have its charter revoked. Leaders of C.I.O and A.F. of L. unions, especially those who have just been appointed by the President to his Victory Labor Committee, should demand that Negroes be given an opportunity to work in all defense industries.

But the problems of winning the peace and strengthening democracy at home cannot be separated from the immediate task of winning the war. In so far as the war is being lost today by the democracies, it is because of our failure to counter the aggression of the Axis by enlisting the positive support of the yellow, brown and black races that make up the vast majority of people on this earth. Hong Kong, Singapore and Java have been lost; India, China, Arabia and Egypt are in peril, because of this failure. Englishmen who still think of colonial people in terms of "White Man's Burden," Americans who persist in discriminating against Negroes in the very defense industries and armed forces that are conducting the war, are in a poor position to enlist such support. And as Mrs. Pearl Buck recently pointed out in her famous attack on racial discrimination, the very worst way to meet the problem is to offer no broader post-war promise to these peoples than a "Union Now" of exclusively Anglo-Saxon hegemony. Before it is too late—and that means *now*—the democracies must guarantee that a free Palestine, a free India, a free China, a free Arabia, a free East Indies, a free Africa, a free West Indies shall be represented with commensurate powers at the peace table.

Two Battles as One

To execute any of that which I have recommended will pose problems and cause difficulties. But even supposing that the war can be won by less fundamental means, of what value is victory abroad if we lost democracy at home? Wipe out American Hitlerism now and there will never be a nation nor a combination of nations able to stand up against the united morale and solidarity of the people of this democracy. People of this country, let us make democracy total, not totalitarian. When Abraham Lincoln brooded over the crisis of our land, he said there was only one government that would never perish from the earth. That would be the government "of the people, by the people and for the people."

LANGSTON HUGHES
1902–1967

Langston Hughes was born as James Mercer Langston Hughes in Joplin, Missouri. He was raised primarily by his nationalistic maternal grandmother, Mary Langston. Langston Hughes is best known for his political and social commentary interwoven in vivid poems and narratives and his insightful and descriptive story-telling of the oppressed conditions of the "American Negro." The renowned poet first emerged on the literary scene in 1921 in the Crisis. His first book of poetry, The Weary Blues, was released in 1926. His disdain for the horrendous treatment of his people led to his intrigue with the Communist party and other organizations aimed at social justice. Hughes wrote well over thirty works of art in the genres of poetry, novels, nonfiction and plays. In this commentary, Hughes describes the dreadfulness of the Jim Crow system, including its application in the military. Hughes also compares the experiences of recent immigrants to those of African Americans to show how immigrants frequently receive greater rights and treatment from fascist-minded white Americans.

My America
1944

This is my land, America. Naturally, I love it—it is home— and I am vitally concerned about its mores, its democracy, and its well-being. I try now to look at it with clear, unprejudiced eyes. My ancestry goes back at least four generations on American soil and, through Indian blood, many centuries more. My background and training is purely American—the schools of Kansas, Ohio, and the East. I am old stock as opposed to recent immigrant blood.

Yet many Americans who cannot speak English—so recent is their arrival on our shores—may travel about our country at will securing food, hotel, and rail accommodations wherever they wish to purchase them. *I may not.* These Americans, once naturalized, may vote in Mississippi or Texas, if they live there. *I may not.* They may work at whatever job their skills command. *But I may not.* They may purchase tickets for concerts, theatres, lectures wherever they are sold throughout the United States. *Often I may not.* They may repeat the Oath of Allegiance with its ringing phrase of "Liberty and justice for all," with a deep faith in its truth—as compared with the limitations and oppressions they have experienced in the Old World. I repeat the oath, too, but I know that the phrase about "liberty and justice" does not fully apply to me. I am an American—*but I am a colored American.*

I know that all these things I mention are not *all* true for *all* localities *all* over America. Jim Crowism varies in degree from North to South, from the mixed schools and free franchise of Michigan to the tumbledown colored schools and open terror at the polls of Georgia and Mississippi. All over America, however, against the Negro there has been an economic color line of such severity that since the Civil War we have been kept most effectively, as a racial group, in the lowest economic brackets. Statistics are not needed to prove this. Simply look around you on the Main Street of any American town or city. There are no colored clerks in any of the stores—although colored people spend their money there. There are practically never any colored street-car conductors or bus drivers—although these public carriers run over streets for which we pay taxes. There are no colored girls at the switchboards of the telephone company—but millions of Negroes have phones and pay their bills. Even in Harlem, nine times out of ten, the man who comes to collect your rent is white. Not even that job is given to a colored man by the great corporations owning New York real estate. From Boston to San Diego, the Negro suffers from job discrimination.

Yet America is a land where, in spite of its defects, I can write this article. Here the voice of democracy is still heard—Wallace, Willkie, Agar, Pearl Buck, Paul Robeson, Lillian Smith. America is a land where the poll tax still holds in the South—but opposition to the poll tax grows daily. America is a land where lynchers are not yet caught—Bundists are put in jail, and majority opinion condemns the Klan. America is a land where the best of all democracies has been achieved for some people—but in Georgia, Roland Hayes, world-famous singer, is beaten for being colored and nobody is jailed—nor can Mr. Hayes vote in the State where he was born. Yet America is a country where Roland Hayes *can* come from a log cabin to wealth and fame—in spite of the segment that still wishes to maltreat him physically and spiritually, famous though he is.

This segment, the South, is not all of America. Unfortunately, however, the war with its increased flow of white Southern workers to Northern cities, has caused the Jim Crow patterns of the South to spread *all* over America, aided and abetted by the United States Army. The Army, with its policy of segregated troops, has brought Jim Crow into communities where it was but little, if at all, in existence before Pearl Harbor. From Camp Custer in Michigan to Guadalcanal in the South Seas, the Army has put its stamp upon official Jim Crow, in imitation of the Southern states where laws separating Negroes and whites are as much a part of government as are Hitler's laws segregating Jews in Germany. Therefore, any consideration of the current problems of the Negro people in America must concern itself seriously with the question of what to do about the South.

The South opposes the Negro's right to vote, and this right is denied us in most Southern states. Without the vote a citizen has no means of protecting his constitutional rights. For Democracy to approach its full meaning, the Negro *all over* America must have the vote. The South opposes the Negro's right to work in industry. Witness the Mobile shipyard riots, the Detroit strikes fomented by

Southern whites against the employment of colored people, the Baltimore strikes of white workers who objected to skill to rate upgrading. For Democracy to achieve its meaning, the Negro like other citizens must have the right to work, to learn skilled trades, and to be upgraded.

The South opposes the civil rights of Negroes and their protection by law. Witness lynchings where no one is punished, witness the Jim Crow laws that deny the letter and spirit of the Constitution. For Democracy to have real meaning, the Negro must have the same civil rights as any other American citizen. The three simple principles of Democracy—the vote, the right to work, and the right to protection by law—the South opposes when it comes to me. Such procedure is dangerous for *all* America. That is why, in order to strengthen Democracy, further the war effort, and achieve the confidence of our colored allies, we must institute a greater measure of Democracy for the eight million colored people of the South. And we must educate the white Southerners to an understanding of such democracy, so they may comprehend that decency toward colored peoples will lose them nothing, but rather will increase their own respect and safety in the modern world.

I live on Manhattan Island. For a New Yorker of color, truthfully speaking, the South begins at Newark. A half hour by tube from the Hudson Terminal, one comes across street-corner hamburger stands that will not serve a hamburger to a Negro customer wishing to sit on a stool. For the same dime a white pays, a Negro must take his hamburger elsewhere in a paper bag and eat it, minus a plate, a napkin, and a glass of water. Sponsors of the theory of segregation claim that it can be made to mean equality. Practically, it never works out that way. Jim Crow always means less for the one Jim Crowed and an unequal value for his money—no stool, no shelter, merely the hamburger, in Newark.

As the colored traveler goes further South by train, Jim Crow increases. Philadelphia is ninety minutes from Manhattan. There the all-colored grammar school begins its separate education of the races that Talmadge of Georgia so highly approves. An hour or so further down the line is Baltimore where segregation laws are written in the state and city codes. Another hour by train, Washington. There the conductor tells the Negro traveler, be he soldier or civilian, to go into the Jim Crow coach behind the engine, usually half a baggage car, next to trunks and dogs.

That this change to complete Jim Crow happens at Washington is highly significant of the state of American democracy in relation to colored peoples today. Washington is the capital of our nation and one of the great centers of the Allied war effort toward the achievement of the Four Freedoms. To a southbound Negro citizen told at Washington to change into a segregated coach the Four Freedoms have a hollow sound, like distant lies not meant to be the truth.

The train crosses the Potomac into Virginia, and from there on throughout the South life for the Negro, by state law and custom, is a hamburger in a sack without a plate, water, napkin, or stool—but at the same price as the whites pay—

to be eaten apart from the others without shelter. The Negro can do little about this because the law is against him, he has no vote, the police are brutal, and the citizens think such caste-democracy is as it should be.

For his seat in the half-coach of the crowded Jim Crow car, a colored man must pay the same fare as those who ride in the nice air-cooled coaches further back in the train, privileged to use the diner when they wish. For his hamburger in a sack served without courtesy the Southern Negro must pay taxes but refrain from going to the polls, and must patriotically accept conscription to work, fight, and perhaps die to regain or maintain freedom for people in Europe or Australia when he himself hasn't got it at home. Therefore, to his ears most of the war speeches about freedom on the radio sound perfectly foolish, unreal, high-flown, and false. To many Southern whites, too, this grand talk so nobly delivered, so poorly executed, must seem like play-acting.

Liberals and persons of good will, North and South, including, no doubt, our President himself, are puzzled as to what on earth to do about the South—the poll-tax South, the Jim Crow South—that so shamelessly gives the lie to Democracy. With the brazen frankness of Hitler's Mein Kampf, Dixie speaks through Talmadge, Rankin, Dixon, Arnall, and Mark Ethridge.

In a public speech in Birmingham, Mr. Ethridge says: "All the armies of the world, both of the United States and the Axis, could not force upon the South an abandonment of racial segregation." Governor Dixon of Alabama refused a government war contract offered Alabama State Prison because it contained an anti-discrimination clause which in his eyes was an "attempt to abolish segregation of races in the South." He said: "We will not place ourselves in a position to be attacked by those who seek to foster their own pet social reforms." In other words, Alabama will not reform. It is as bull-headed as England in India, and its governor is not ashamed to say so.

As proof of Southern intolerance, almost daily the press reports some new occurrence of physical brutality against Negroes. Former Governor Talmadge was "too busy" to investigate when Roland Hayes and his wife were thrown in jail, and the great tenor beaten, on complaint of a shoe salesman over a dispute as to what seat in his shop a Negro should occupy when buying shoes. Nor did the governor of Mississippi bother when Hugh Gloster, professor of English at Morehouse College, riding as an inter-state passenger, was illegally ejected from a train in his state, beaten, arrested, and fined because, being in an over crowded Jim Crow coach, he asked for a seat in an adjacent car which contained only two white passengers.

Legally, the Jim Crow laws do not apply to inter-state travelers, but the FBI has not yet gotten around to enforcing that Supreme Court ruling. En route from San Francisco to Oklahoma City, Fred Wright, a county probation officer of color, was beaten and forced into the Texas Jim Crow coach on a transcontinental train by order of the conductor in defiance of federal law. A seventy-six-year-old clergyman, Dr. Jackson of Hartford, Connecticut, going South to attend the National Baptist Convention, was set upon by white passengers for merely passing through a white coach on the way to his own seat. There have been many similar attacks upon colored soldiers in uniform on public carriers. One such attack resulted in death for the soldier, dragged from a bus and killed by civilian police. Every day now, Negro soldiers from the North, returning home on furlough from Southern camps, report incident after incident of humiliating travel treatment below the Mason-Dixon line.

It seems obvious that the South does not yet know what this war is all about. As answer Number One to the question, "what shall we do about the South?" I would suggest an immediate and intensive government-directed program of pro-democratic grades of the grammar schools to the universities. As part of the war effort, this is urgently needed. The Spanish Loyalist Government had trench schools for its soldiers and night schools for civilians even in Madrid under siege. America is not under siege yet. We still have time (but not too much) to teach our people what we are fighting for, and to begin to apply those teachings to race relations at home. You see, it would be too bad for an emissary of color from one of the Latin American countries, say Cuba or Brazil, to arrive at Miami Airport and board a train for Washington, only to get beaten up and thrown off by white Southerners who do not realize how many colored allies we have—nor how badly we need them—and that it is inconsiderate and rude to beat colored people, anyway.

Because transportation in the South is so symbolic of America's whole racial problem, the Number Two thing for us to do is study a way out of the Jim Crow car dilemma at once. Would a system of first, second, and third class coaches help? In Europe, formerly, if one did not wish to ride with peasants and tradespeople, one could always pay a little more and solve that problem by having a first class compartment almost entirely to oneself. Most Negroes can hardly afford parlor car seats. Why not abolish Jim Crow entirely and let the whites who wish to do so, ride in coaches where few Negroes have the funds to be? In any case, our Chinese, Latin American, and Russian allies are not going to think much of our democratic pronunciamentos as long as we keep compulsory Jim Crow cars on Southern rails.

Since most people learn a little through education, albeit slowly, as Number Three, I would suggest that the government draft all the lending Negro intellectuals, sociologists, writers, and concert singers from Alain Locke of Oxford and W. E. B. Du Bois of Harvard to Dorothy Maynor and Paul Robeson of Carnegie Hall and send them into the South to appear before white audiences, carrying messages of culture and democracy, thus off-setting the old stereotypes of the Southern mind and the Hollywood movie, and explaining to the people without dialect what the war aims are about. With each, send on tour a liberal white Southerner like Paul Green, Erskine Caldwell, Pearl Buck, Lillian Smith, or William Seabrook. And, of course, include soldiers to protect them from the fascist-minded among us.

WALTER WHITE
1893–1951

Walter Francis White was born in Atlanta, Georgia. White graduated from Atlanta University and worked for an insurance company. The first protest organized by White was against the Atlanta Board of Education because of its plans to close down a Black middle school to fund the construction of a new white high school. In 1918, White became the assistant secretary for the NAACP's national staff after starting a chapter of the organization in Atlanta. White rose through the ranks of the NAACP and became its executive secretary in 1931. As leader of this great organization, White spearheaded many civil rights campaigns, from anti-lynching legislation to fair housing and fair employment. White also wrote several books: The Fire in the Flint *(1924);* Flight *(1926);* Rope and Faggot: A Biography of Judge Lynch *(1929); and* A Rising Wind *(1945). In this address, delivered on July 16, 1944, before the Emergency War Conference—a special NAACP meeting—Executive Secretary White reports on his travels to the battlefields in Europe during the war. The purpose of his mission was to investigate the status and experiences of African American servicemen.*

White Supremacy and World War II
1944

On this 952nd day of America's participation in a war to save the world from the military aggression and racial bigotry of Germany and Japan, the United Nations with a comparable master race theory of its own moves on to victory. The growing certainty of that victory intensifies determination to permit no fundamental change in the attitude of "white" nations toward the "colored" peoples of the earth.

This is the harsh reality of the report I must unhappily bring you from visits to battlefronts stretching from England to the Middle East. In that reality lies not only continued misery and exploitation for black and brown and yellow peoples who constitute two-thirds of the population of the world. In it exists as well the virtual certainty of another and bloodier and costlier world war in the not too distant future.

Permit me now to report tersely to you on my trip overseas since last we met in annual conference and to tell you how your sons and fathers and husbands and friends are faring. I covered as a war correspondent more than twenty thousand miles in the European, North African, Italian and Middle East Theatres of Operations. I talked with many thousands of officers and soldiers, white and Negro, ranging in rank from G.I.'s of engineering units who had just stepped off the boat from America to the Supreme Allied Commander, General Eisenhower.

I shared with them the unique fraternity of enemy bombs dropping nearby and the ultimate democracy where race or color do not count—when men huddle together in a slit trench as enemy planes strafe at the rate of 3200 fifty-calibre bullets per minute per plane.

I wish it were possible for me to tell you truthfully that the alchemy of war and fighting to destroy Nazism had transformed the racial behavior of Americans in the armed services overseas. I cannot do so. We have merely transplanted to other lands the American pattern, both good and bad. As is true at home, there are some officers and enlisted men, from North and South, who are decent human beings who believe in and practice democracy. A decidedly encouraging note is the number of G.I.'s who, brought face to face with death, are re-examining their racial and other opinions. Some of them are beginning to realize that race is a global question which must be faced and solved. Unfortunately, our War and Navy departments, threatened by Congressional reactionaries and bigots, have manifested but slight and grudging recognition of the existence of this enlightened minority in the armed services. Basically, the root of all our difficulties overseas is in insistence on racial segregation.

As long as our government insists on segregation in an army and navy allegedly fighting for democracy, the chasm between the races will be perpetuated and broadened with resultant bitterness on both sides. When ten or eleven million men return after the war is over, our government cannot escape responsibility for whatever happens since it is in large measure responsible for immature racial, political, economic and social thinking among these men whose every act they have directed for the period of their army and navy service.

What some of us like to believe is that a minority of American soldiers overseas have deliberately fomented brawls with colored soldiers, and spread malicious falsehoods about Negroes among the citizens of countries where these men have been stationed. Among them are that all Negroes have tails, that they are illiterate and diseased and inferior, and even that Negroes are so sub-human that they cannot speak English but communicate their thoughts, if any, by grunting and barking. It is fortunate for America that colored soldiers had self-control and sense enough to treat this campaign as a joke. In some areas Negro soldiers, learning on arrival of the fanciful tales about themselves which had been spread in advance of their coming, barked at the English people of the neighborhood. Belying their reputation of being slow to catch on to a joke, the English soon began to bark back in a kind of warm, friendly language of friendship.

In Italy I ran across a deliberate printed campaign of vilification of Negro American soldiers. Large green placards appeared mysteriously one day on billboards in Naples, allegedly put out by the "Comitate Italiano-Americano," whose full name, translated, is the Italian-American Committee for the Preservation of the Italian race. The Placard vilified Negroes, declaring them to be inferior because their skins were black and warned Italians that they would not receive much consideration or help if they treated American Negro soldiers as equals.

When I was in England, virtually all of the Negro soldiers there were so-called service troops—members of quartermaster, engineer, port battalion and trucking units. It was strongly urged that Negro combat troops as well be brought to the European theatre and given opportunity to participate in the invasion of the Continent. You have recently seen Army photographs of Negro combat troops on the Normandy beachheads, and you heard at the opening session of this conference General Eisenhower's tribute to the part Negroes are playing with other Americans in beating Hitler.

One of the most galling practices to Negro soldiers overseas is the designation of certain towns and other places as "off limits." This practice sorely limited already greatly limited areas in which soldiers could find diversions while on leave. An order has been issued by General Eisenhower forbidding such practices.

Some prejudiced officers have utilized court martial to intimidate Negro soldiers. This has been true both here and overseas. It has been strongly urged upon the War Department that special boards of review of such cases be established and that on them shall serve able Negro lawyers, appropriately commissioned, to insure justice. It is our intention to follow up this recommendation to the end that no officer of the United States Army will dare utilize the machinery of the court martial to implement his prejudices.

Another source of dissatisfaction I found was the tendency to transform Negro combat units into service units. We have reason to believe that facts presented on this issue will check this process.

These are but some of the specific problems and the specific actions which your Association attempted to take on them. There are others which are in process of correction. But all of these and other problems are but the surface manifestations of the basic evil—segregation. If I were asked to state my most fundamental criticism not only of our Army and Navy, but of our whole governmental attitude, it would be this—that white America has so little faith in the inherent decency of white Americans. Wherever I went overseas, I found many young, intelligent, decent Americans, both northern and southern, who are disturbed by the race problem. They would like to bring their practice of democracy into line with their profession of it. But they fear that to do so would get them into difficulties with their superior officers. I believe the time has come for our government and all its agencies to stop basing their racial patterns on the lowest common denominator of American thought and action on this question. Unless it does so, I predict broadening of the chasm between the races which can only result in greater hatred, more friction and a weakening of the whole democratic structure.

One final word regarding the framing of the peace and the post-war years. I am happy to announce that the distinguished American scholar, Dr. W. E. B. Du Bois, will return to your N.A.A.C.P. on September 1 as Director of Special Research. His first and chief responsibility will be the preparation of material, in cooperation with a distinguished committee of Negro and white Americans, for presentation of the Negro's cause to the peace conference or peace conferences. If the peace treaty is based on the perpetuation of white overlordship over the peoples of the earth, another war is inevitable. On behalf of the Negroes not only of American, but of Africa, the West Indies and other parts of the world, we shall make our voice heard in an effort to save the framers from the folly of another Versailles Treaty.

WILLIAM H. HASTIE
(1904–1976)

William H. Hastie received his law degree from Harvard Law School and taught students such as Thurgood Marshall at Howard University. In private practice, Hastie argued a number of civil rights cases. In 1937, President Franklin Roosevelt appointed him as a judge of the Federal District Court in the Virgin Islands, making him the country's first African American federal magistrate. In 1941, Hastie became an aide to Henry L. Stimson, secretary of war, and worked to reform discriminatory military policies and practices. In 1943, Hastie resigned from this position to protest discrimination and inequality in the military. Below Hastie sets forth the reasons for his resignation.

Why I Resigned
1943

Reactionary policies and discriminatory practices of the Army Air Forces in matters affecting Negroes were the immediate cause of my resignation as Civilian Aide to the Secretary of War.

The Army Air Forces are growing in importance and independence. In the post war period they may become the greatest single component of the armed services. Biased policies and harmful practices established in this branch of the army can all too easily infect other branches as well. The situation had become critical. Yet, the whole course of my dealings with the Army Air Forces convinced me the further expression of my views in the form of recommendations within the department would be futile. I, therefore, took the only course which can, I believe, bring results. Public opinion is still the strongest force in American life.

To the Negro soldier and those who influence his thinking, I say with all the force and sincerity at my command that the man in uniform must grit his teeth, square his shoulders and do his best as a soldier, confident that there are millions of Americans outside of the armed services, and more persons than he knows in high places within the military establishment, who will never cease fighting to remove every racial barrier and every humiliating practice which now confront him. But only by being at all times a first class soldier can the man in uniform help in this battle which shall be fought and won.

When I took office, the Secretary of War directed that all questions of policy and important proposals relating to Negroes should be referred to my office for comment or approval before final action. In December, 1940, the Air Forces referred to me a plan for a segregated training center for Negro pursuit pilots at Tuskegee. I expressed my entire disagreement with the plan, giving my reasons in detail. My views were disregarded. Since then, the Air Command has never on its own initiative submitted any plan or project to me for comment or recommendation. What information I obtained, I had to seek out. Where I made proposals or recommendations, I volunteered them.

This situation reached its climax in late December, 1942, when I learned through army press releases sent out from St. Louis and from the War Department in Washington that the Air Command was about to establish a segregated officer candidate school at Jefferson Barracks, Mo., to train Negro officers for ground duty with the Army Air Forces. Here was a proposal for a radical departure from present army practice, since the officer candidate training program is the one large field where the army is eliminating racial segregation.

Moreover, I had actually written to the Air Command several weeks earlier in an attempt to find out what was brewing at Jefferson Barracks. The Air Command replied as late as December 17, 1942, giving not even the slightest hint of any plan for a segregated officer candidate school. It is inconceivable to me that consideration of such a project had not then advanced far enough for my office to have been consulted, even if I had not made specific inquiry. The conclusion is inescapable that the Air Command does not propose inform, much less counsel with, this office about its plans for Negroes . . .

To date, all Negro applicants, a number of them well and fully qualified, for appointment as army service pilots have been rejected. Two applicants were actually instructed to report for training. They did so but were sent home as soon as it was discovered that they were Negroes. I am advised that this matter is receiving further study. The simple fact is that the Air Command does not want Negro pilots flying in and out of various fields, eating, sleeping and mingling with other personnel, as a service pilot must do in carrying out his various missions.

Negro medical officers in the Air Forces are getting only part of the special training in aviation medicine which is available. They are not admitted to the principal school of aviation medicine at Randolph Field.

Even the branch school program in which it is represented that Negro officers share without discrimination is in fact discriminatory. Many white officers enrolled at branch schools of aviation medicine have the opportunity of full time resident study. The Negro officer is permitted to commute periodically from his home station at Tuskegee for work at the Maxwell Field branch school. Such grudging partial tender of makeshift schemes may be expected to continue unless a genuine change of racial attitude and policy occurs in the Air Command.

While Negro trainees and cadets at the Tuskegee Air Base have done well from a strictly technical point of view, they have suffered such demoralizing discrimination and segregation that, in my judgment, the entire future of the Negro in combat aviation is in danger. Men cannot be humiliated over a long period of time without a loss of combat efficiency.

Specifically, Negro and white officers serving at Tuskegee in the common enterprise of training Negroes for the combat have separate messes. They are not permitted to have quarters in the same building. Separate toilet facilities have been provided. If the group of white officers at Tuskegee insist upon this and I have no evidence that they do—they are psychologically unsuited to train Negroes for combat. If they do not insist, the racial attitude of the local commands, or of higher authority is all the more apparent.

Despite original design to advance Negro officers and to place them in posts of administrative responsibility at Tuskegee as rapidly as they should qualify, that design is not being carried out in the post administration, except in the station hospital.

Early in the history of the Tuskegee project, a Negro soldier guarding a warehouse was disarmed and arrested by civilian authorities. A new commander was appointed. He disarmed Negro military policemen assigned to patrol duty in the town of Tuskegee. A recent member of the Alabama state police force was assigned to Tuskegee as an army officer with duties related to his civilian experience. The Negro solder was embittered, but the prejudiced community was somewhat mollified.

Fundamentally, it seems to me the Air Command has either failed to comprehend or failed to care that its policies and prejudices are tending to tear down rather than build up the pride, dignity and self respect which Negro soldiers like all other soldiers must possess if they are to achieve maximum combat efficiency.

Military men agree that a soldier should be made to feel that he is the best man, in the best unit in the best army in the world. When the Air Command shall direct its policies and practices so as to help rather than hinder the development of such spirit among its Negro soldiers, it will be on the right road.

Notes

1. Patrick S. Washburn. *A Question of Sedition: The Federal Government's Investigation of the Black Press during World War II* (New York: Oxford University Press, 1986), 14, 29.

2. Claude Andrew Clegg II, *An Original Man: The Life and Times of Elijah Muhammad* (New York: St. Martin's, 1997), 114.

3. John Hope Franklin and Alfred A. Moss Jr., *From Slavery to Freedom: A History of African Americans*, 7th ed. (New York: McGraw-Hill, 1994), 384.

4. M. J. Heale, *Franklin D. Roosevelt: The New Deal and War* (New York: Routledge, 1999).

5. Doris Kearns Goodwin, *No Ordinary Time* (New York: Simon & Schuster, 1995), 262, 404, 477.

6. Harold Nicolson, *Peacemaking 1919* (New York: The Universal Library, 1965) and Azza Salama Layton, *International Politics and Civil Rights Policies in the United States: 1941–1960* (New York: Cambridge University Press, 2000).

7. Clarence Lusane, *Hitler's Black Victims* (New York: Routledge, 2003), 228. Note that Lusane raises questions about the truth of the "snub," in his discussion of Blacks

and Hitler. Brenda Gayle Plummer, *Window on Freedom* (Chapel Hill: University of North Carolina Press, 2003), 67, states that Jesse Owens later publicly praised Hitler. Kelly Miller, "Hitler—The German Ku Klux," *Norfolk Journal and Guide* 7 (April 1933): 3.

8. "Fascism Now Means Something," *Crisis*, September 1936, 273.

9. Adolf Hitler, *Mein Kampf* (New York: Houghton Mifflin, 1943), 430.

10. Miller, "Hitler," 3.

11. Joseph Harris, *African American Reactions to the War in Ethiopia: 1936–1941* (Baton Rouge: Louisiana State University Press, 1994).

12. Robin Kelly, "This Ain't Ethiopia, but It'll Do," in *African Americans in the Spanish Civil War*, ed. Danny Duncan Collum (New York: Macmillan, 1992), 18.

13. Collum, *African Americans*, 19.

14. Robert Mullen, *Blacks in America's Wars* (New York: Monad, 1973), 51, and Franklin and Moss, *From Slavery to Freedom*, 386.

15. *Washington Star*, January 9, 1942; quoted in Goodwin, *No Ordinary Time*, 328.

16. Memorandum, Assistant Secretary of War Robert P. Patterson to the President, October 8, 1940, Modern Military Records Branch, National Archives, Washington, D.C. Reprinted in Bernard C. Nalty and Morris McGregor, *Blacks in the Military: Essential Documents* (Wilmington, Del.: Scholarly Resources, 1981), 107–8.

17. Franklin and Moss, *From Slavery to Freedom*, 387.

18. Clegg, *Original Man*, 93, 97.

19. Bayard Rustin, "Letter to the Draft Board," in *Time on the Cross: The Collected Writings of Bayard Rustin*, ed. Devon W. Carbado and Donald Weise (San Francisco: Cleis, 2003), 11–13.

20. *Selective Service Conscientious Objector*, vol. 1 (Washington, D.C.: Government Printing Office, 1950), 261, 264–65.

21. Mullen, *Blacks in America's Wars*, 53.

22. Account of the speech is in Goodwin, *No Ordinary Time*, 248, located in Franklin D. Roosevelt Library, Office File 93, "Call to Negro Americans," July 1, 1941.

23. Jervis Anderson, *A. Philip Randolph: A Biographical Portrait* (New York: Harcourt Brace Jovanovich, 1972), 249–61.

24. The *Pittsburgh Courier* and other Black newspapers were vital to the Double V campaign, by headlining military racism. The Black Press was criticized for spotlighting acts of discrimination and equating them with Nazi practices. See "Double 'V' for a Double Victory Campaign Gets Country-Wide Support," *Pittsburgh Courier*, February 14, 1942. For more detailed discussion of the Double V campaign, see Gail Buckley, *American Patriots: The Story of Blacks in the Military from the Revolution to Desert Storm* (New York: Random House, 2001), 272–73, and Neil A. Wynn, *The Afro-American and the Second World War* (New York: Holmes and Meier, 1993), 101.

25. *Negro Digest* 1 (December 1942): 68–69.

26. Francis Biddle, *In Brief Authority* (Garden City, N.Y.: Doubleday, 1948), 219.

27. Buckley, *American Patriots*, 280, and Franklin and Moss, *From Slavery to Freedom*, 390.

28. Robert Ewell Greene, *Black Defenders of America: 1775–1973* (Chicago: Johnson, 1974), 185.

29. Kai Wright, *Soldiers of Freedom: An Illustrated History of African Americans in the Armed Forces* (New York: Black Dog & Leventhal, 2002), 154.

30. Robert Allen, *The Port Chicago Mutiny* (New York: Warner, 1989), 119.

31. John W. Dower, *War without Mercy: Race and Power in the Pacific* (New York: Pantheon Books, 1986).

32. Wynn, *Afro-American*, 12. Also see Heale, *Franklin D. Roosevelt*, 66–68, for the impact of World War II on the American economy.

33. Goodwin, *No Ordinary Time*, 62. Also see Martin Gilbert, *The Second World War* (New York: Holt, 1989), 746.

34. *Negro Digest* 2 (August 1944): 48.

35. Mullen, *Blacks in America's Wars*, 59–60.

36. Franklin and Moss, *From Slavery to Freedom*, 407.

CHAPTER SEVEN

~

Korean War:
Coming In from the Cold

1 9 5 0 - 1 9 5 3

The end of World War II led to significant changes in the geopolitical face of the world. Powerful nations began to align themselves into two philosophically different camps: communism, represented by the Soviet Union and China, and capitalism, dominated by nations in the West, ostensibly directed by the United States. Expressing his concern about the rise of communism in Eastern Europe, during a 1946 speech at Westminster College in Fulton, Missouri, former prime minister of Great Britain Winston Churchill warned that an "iron curtain is drawn down upon their front . . . We do not know what is going on behind."[1] Americans too were alarmed and feared that communism would gain further control of Asia. The fears of the Western nations were justified. On October 11, 1949, the Red Army led by Communist leader Mao Tse-tung defeated Chiang Kai-shek, the nationalist and pro-Western leader of China. Chairman Mao established the People's Republic of China as a Communist nation and instituted a "cultural revolution" to make Marxist ideology compatible with an agrarian economy.

The battle for ideological and economic supremacy in the world culminated in a "Cold War" that was led and sponsored by the United States, China and the Soviet Union. These crusading nation-states used economic assistance, intimidation, propaganda, assassination, low-intensity military operations and proxy wars as tactics. The Cold War, as opposed to direct armed encounters, was seen as the alternative to World War III, or a major nuclear conflict. Throughout the Cold War, both sides engaged in an arms race that resulted in the proliferation of nuclear and conventional weapons.

The Korean War took place from June 25, 1950, to July 27, 1953.[2] It was a proxy war between the U.S. and its allies on one side, and the Communist powers of the People's Republic of China and the Soviet Union on the other. The principal combatants were North Korea, supported by China and the Soviet Union, and South Korea, supported by the United States, the United Kingdom and the Philippines. Other nations sent troops to the war zone under the auspices of the United Nations.

Prior to the proxy war, Korea had been ruled by Japan from 1910 until the end of World War II in 1945. The United States and the Soviet Union, on the same side in World War II, had both declared war on Japan. As the war came to a close, the U.S. and the Soviet Union agreed to divide Korea along the 38th parallel. The peninsula was divided into zones of control in the north and south under the administration of the two major powers. Japanese forces north of that line would surrender to the Soviet Union and those south of that line would surrender to the United States.

Although the partition was not considered permanent, the Western nations engineered UN-supervised elections which replaced the indigenous, left-wing government that had formed, with one led by anti-Communist Syngman Rhee. The Soviet Union, in turn, supported the rise of a Communist government led by Kim Il-sung in the northern part. Kim Il-sung built the North Korean army into a formidable offensive organization. On June 25, 1950, with the support of Soviet leader Joseph Stalin, North Korea invaded South Korea to force unification of the split countries.

The invasion surprised the United States and the other Western powers. During the preceding week Secretary of State Dean Acheson had given a speech before the National Press Club, in which he outlined the defense needs of the U.S. Neither Korea nor Taiwan was mentioned by Acheson as part of his government's "defense perimeter."[3]

Upon learning of the surprise invasion, U.S. President Harry S. Truman reacted quickly. Anti-communism was already becoming a part of American domestic politics, with real or imagined Communists thought to be infiltrating the country. Truman, a Democrat, was under severe domestic pressure for being too soft on communism. According to Republican leaders, the Democrats had already "lost China," and conservative senator Joseph McCarthy of Wisconsin declared that the U.S. State Department was "infested" with Communists.[4] The president's quick response reflected his desire to gain support for the "Truman Doctrine," which advocated the idea that the U.S. should oppose communism everywhere it sought to expand.

President Truman committed U.S. forces to Korea and sent General Douglas MacArthur to command them. American civilians were immediately evacuated to Japan. Instead of pressing for a congressional declaration of war, which Truman considered too alarmist and time-consuming, the U.S. president went to the United Nations for approval to respond to the attack. Because the Soviets were boycotting the United Nations at the time in protest of the exclusion of the People's Republic of China (PRC) from the international body, the U.S. persuaded the United Nations Security Council to demand a North Korean withdrawal. Without the Soviet and Chinese veto, on June 27, the United Nations voted to provide military assistance to South Korea in order to repel the attack and restore their peace and security.[5]

Although the official response to the North Korean attack was a United Nations multinational action, 90 percent of the troops were either from the U.S. or South Korea. General Douglas MacArthur arrogantly boasted that he could win the war single-handedly. MacArthur drove the North Koreans back to the dividing line and eventually captured the North Korean capital in November of that year. Truman then ordered American troops to cross the 38th parallel and press on to the Chinese border. China responded in November 1950 with a huge counterattack that decimated U.S. troops. MacArthur then requested permission to invade mainland China, but Truman rejected the idea. MacArthur was subsequently accused of a flawed war strategy and holding an unauthorized meeting with ROC President Chiang Kai-shek. By December, MacArthur's overly optimistic plans had been deflated. In 1951 Truman fired him for insubordination.[6] Matthew Ridgeway, who succeeded MacArthur, managed to regroup United Nations forces for an effective counter-offensive. A series of attacks inflicted heavy casualties on Chinese and North Korean units, as United Nations forces advanced some miles north of the 38th parallel. What started as a limited action under a mandate from the U.N. General Assembly for a "unified and democratic Korea" had escalated into a campaign to rid South Korea of the Communist menace.

Not only did the Cold War result in extreme international turmoil, but it created tumult in U.S. domestic affairs. Suspicion about Communist penetration of federal agencies triggered the creation of the Federal Employee Loyalty Program in 1947, established by Truman to root out subversive workers in government service. The program instituted a loyalty review board to investigate government workers and fire those found to be disloyal. As a result, hundreds of employees were dismissed and thousands more felt compelled to resign. By 1953, 80 percent of states had imposed loyalty tests of some kind on their residents.[7] In 1949, the Justice Department prosecuted 11 leaders of the Communist Party, who were convicted and jailed under the Smith Act of 1940, which prohibited groups from conspiring to advocate the violent overthrow of the government. Claudia Jones, an African American communist, was also deported under the Smith Act. Jones, a Trinidadian by birth, immigrated to the U.S. with her parents when she was eight years old. After spending four years in jail for violating the Smith Act, Jones was expelled from the U.S. She then relocated to England, where she became a leading political activist.[8]

Meanwhile, Congress also began to investigate claims of disloyalty. Led by Joseph McCarthy, the House Un-American Activities Committee (HUAC) investigated communist infiltration in U.S. society, with special emphasis on the entertainment industry.[9] Prominent film directors, actors and screenwriters were called as witnesses. Those who refused to cooperate were imprisoned on contempt charges. The HUAC investigation resulted in an entertainment industry blacklist, in which those suspected of having Communist sentiments or affiliations began to experience difficulty gaining and maintaining employment in the industry. HUAC admitted in 1948 that it had compiled dossiers on 300,000 individuals; a year later the figure was a million.[10] Then in 1950, the Internal Security Act, also known as the McCarran Act, was passed. The act, named after Nevada's Senator Pat McCarran, called for severe restrictions against Communists and the registration of all Communist organizations with the office of the attorney general. The suspect organizations had to provide specified information to government agents, such as lists of their members and fingerprints. The McCarran Act also established the Subversive Activities Control Board to determine which individuals and organizations should comply with the law. Those individuals and organizations who failed to satisfy the requirement of the act could be subjected to criminal prosecution and fines.[11] In 1968, Congress repealed the registration requirements of the law as a result of several U.S. Supreme Court decisions that declared certain aspects of the law unconstitutional.

Moreover, the United States received worldwide attention as a result of two troublesome trials. In August 1948 *Time* magazine editor Whittaker Chambers, a former Communist, accused ex-State Department official Alger Hiss of being a spy and a member of the Communist Party. Hiss sued Chambers for slander, but after two trials he was convicted of perjury in 1950 and jailed for 44 months. In 1951, U.S. citizens and Communist party members Julius and Ethel Rosenberg were convicted of espionage for stealing atomic secrets for the Soviet Union. They were executed two years later. The Hiss and Rosenberg trials and convictions provoked decades of debate.

U.S. government officials also had to contend with the attempts by African Americans to provoke international inquiry into its domestic affairs. African American activists submitted several petitions to the UN during the first few years of its existence. Although the UN had no power over domestic issues, the petitions embarrassed the U.S. The National Negro Congress (NNC) presented the first petition in June 1946 "seeking relief from racial oppression."[12] President Truman reacted to the first petition by holding meetings with civil rights leaders about their concerns. He then formed a Committee on Civil Rights, which issued a report on October 29, 1947, entitled "To Secure These Rights." The report focused on the denial of four essential rights, including security and safety rights, the right to full citizenship, the freedom of expression and the right to equality of opportunity.[13]

The second petition was written by W. E. B. Du Bois and submitted under the aegis of the NAACP in October 1947. The petition, entitled "An Appeal to the World: A Statement on the Denial of Human Rights to Minorities in the Case of Citizens of Negro Descent in the Unites States of America and an Appeal to the United Nations for Redress," linked racial injustice in the U.S. to colonialism in Africa and asked the world to support the cause of justice. Du Bois wrote:

> Discrimination practiced in the United States against her own citizens and to a large extent a contravention of her own laws, cannot be persisted in, without infringing upon the rights of the peoples of the world and especially upon the ideals and the work of the United Nations.[14]

Although the U.S. blocked the second petition from submission to the General Assembly, it still received widespread publicity. "Requests for a copy of and permission to publish the petition came from everywhere—from national organizations and the news media to international organizations and the foreign press. Countries interested included Belgium, Czechoslovakia, Denmark, Egypt, Ethiopia, Haiti, India, Liberia, Mexico, Norway, Pakistan, Poland, Russia, South Africa, Greece, Italy, France, and China."[15]

A third petition to the UN also engendered the wrath of the State Department. The Civil Rights Congress under the leadership of William Patterson delivered a petition to the United Nations Committee on Human Rights in Geneva, Switzerland, in 1951. The petition charged the U.S. with genocide against African Americans and provided documentation of 153 killings, 344 violent crimes and other human rights abuses against Black people from 1845 to 1951. In addition to listing the genocidal acts of the American government against African Americans, the document stated:

> This genocide of which your petitioners complain serves now, as it has in previous forms in the past, specific political and economic aims. Once its goal was the subjugation of American Negroes for the profits of chattel slavery. Now its

aim is the slitting and emasculation of mass movements for peace and democracy, so that a reaction may perpetuate its control and continue receiving the highest profits in the entire history of man. That purpose menaces the peace of the world as well as the life and welfare of the Negro people whose condition violates every aspect of the United Nations' stated goal—the preservation "of peaceful and friendly relations among nations" by the promotion of "respect for human rights and fundamental freedoms for all without distinction as to race . . . "[16]

The petition called upon the UN to force the U.S. to account for its crimes. It was signed by 94 individuals, among whom were George Crockett Jr., later a distinguished judge in Detroit who went on to serve many terms in the U.S. Congress; New York City Communist councilman Benjamin J. Davis Jr.; Ferdinand Smith, Black leader of the National Maritime Union; Dr. Oakley C. Johnson of Louisiana; Aubrey Grossman, the labor and civil rights lawyer; Claudia Jones, a Communist leader in Harlem later deported under the McCarran Act; W. E. B. Du Bois; and Paul Robeson. Family members of individuals who had been lynched were also signatories to the document. After the petition was submitted by William Patterson, an avowed Communist, his passport was seized by the U.S. government.

African Americans who spoke out against racism were viewed as subversives and as a consequence, they became targets of the U.S. campaign to oust communism from the U.S. Paul Robeson and W. E. B. Du Bois found "their ability to travel overseas was curtailed in the early 1950s. The State Department confiscated their passports, effectively denying them access to an international audience."[17] Paul Robeson's passport was revoked after he criticized President Truman's decision to send troops to Korea, arguing that "if we don't stop our armed adventure into Korea today—tomorrow it will be Africa. For the maw of the war makers is insatiable. They aim to rule the world or ruin it. Their slogan is all or none."[18] The State Department also barred him from entering Canada, where he was scheduled to perform.

Du Bois's troubles with the State Department began after the Second World War. His work on the petition to the UN was well known, but after he became chairman of the New York City–based Peace Information Center in 1950, he received even more attention from the U.S. government. In July of that year, after collecting one million signatures for a global petition to ban the use of nuclear weapons, the Peace Center was labeled a Communist-front organization by the Justice Department. Du Bois was charged as an agent of a foreign principal within the United States and his passport to travel outside of the country was revoked.[19] Eventually, in 1958, the Supreme

Court of the U.S. ruled that the State Department could not demand the signing of loyalty oaths as a basis for issuing passports and Du Bois's was reissued.

The dancer Josephine Baker also used her international fame to call attention to America's racial problems. Baker lectured on U.S. racial discrimination throughout the world. In Uruguay, "she told an audience that most Negroes in the United States were unhappy." In Argentina, she "announced that she would campaign against racial discrimination . . . "[20] The U.S. State Department became increasingly concerned about Baker's impact on international audiences, but could not officially withhold her passport because she had given up her U.S. citizenship and become a citizen of France in 1937. Therefore, U.S. government officials developed other strategies to thwart her international effectiveness. Scheduled appearances in countries such as Peru and Colombia were called off at the last minute. Embassy personnel in Havana, Cuba, worked to cancel her contract and reported that Baker had made statements to the Argentine press that were unfavorable to the U.S. They also expressed concern that Baker might use the Cuban press to make additional accusations against the U.S. Despite U.S. attempts to bar her from Cuba, Baker showed up in Havana anyway and "blamed the cancellation of her contracts on the United States government."[21] While in Cuba, Baker met with President Batista, who did not support her critiques of America. The day after the meeting, Baker was arrested. "Military intelligence officers seized books and pamphlets from her room, took her to headquarters, and interrogated her about her Communist leanings."[22] Irrespective of her troubles with the U.S. government, France demonstrated its support for Baker. She was awarded the Medal of the Resistance with the Rosette and named a Chevalier of the Legion of Honor by the French government for her hard work and dedication.

Other African American celebrities who aroused the suspicion of the U.S. government included other greats like the jazz musician Louis Armstrong. Incensed over Arkansas Governor Orval Faubus's call to the National Guard in order to stop African American children from integrating classes in Little Rock at Central High School on September 4, 1957, Armstrong said, "The way they are treating my people in the South, the government can go to hell."[23] Armstrong was eventually placed under FBI surveillance and the State Department cancelled his U.S.-sponsored visit to the Soviet Union.[24]

Cold War politics also affected relationships within the African American community. Discord over U.S. foreign policy and the Cold War led to W. E.

B. Du Bois's dismissal from the NAACP in 1948. Du Bois advocated the position that the NAACP should focus more attention on the liberation struggles in Africa, and pay special attention to how the Cold Warriors might use the continent in the Cold War. In disagreement with Du Bois, NAACP Executive Secretary Walter White aligned the NAACP with the Truman Doctrine of anti-Soviet expansionism.[25] Du Bois, in turn, accused White of refusing to take a clear stance on imperialism and colonialism. Subsequently, Du Bois was dismissed from the NAACP.

The Council on African Affairs (CAA) also split as a result of disagreements on issues related to the Cold War. Established to keep the issue of colonial liberation on the U.S. agenda and to provide links to anti-colonial and African liberation networks, the CAA attracted the support of noted individuals such as Mary McLeod Bethune, E. Franklin Frasier and Alphaeus Hunton. Paul Robeson and Max Yergan, both founders of the organization, eventually split over the Truman Doctrine, the CAA's increasingly close relationships with African liberation movements and the issue of Communist affiliation. The tear in their relationship ruptured after the attorney general added the CAA to its list of subversive organizations to be monitored in 1947. Yergan responded to the pressure by working to disassociate the organization from Communist and other left-wing organizations. Paul Robeson refused to allow the U.S. government threats to affect the organization's mission and affiliations. As the rancor between the leaders continued, Yergan was eventually suspended by the board and expelled from the organization in September 1948.[26]

African American leaders, above all, considered U.S. racial policies and the discriminatory activities of the U.S. military as a prime example of the hypocrisy between the American ideals of democracy and its practices. Although the army received a policy report in 1946 that recommended integration, little change actually happened. The leadership of the armed services remained divided on the issue—with the more progressive recognizing that racial segregation did not produce the best fighting men. On the contrary, racial discrimination led to an acceptance of inadequate performance from white servicemen. In fact, Black soldiers, who made up just 10 percent of the army by 1950, were the army's scapegoat. They were poorly trained, given only service and supply jobs, and frequently punished at a rate disproportionate to their numbers.

African Americans accelerated their battle against segregation after the Universal Military Training Bill of 1947 was proposed, requiring registration for the draft. African American activists were afraid that the proposal might lead to military slavery. A. Philip Randolph of the League for Non-Violent

Civil Disobedience against Military Segregation argued that it was immoral for African Americans to serve in a segregated military and that they would respond with mass civil disobedience if those conditions were not addressed. Testifying before the Armed Services Committee of the U.S. Senate in March 1948, Randolph stated:

> Well, now, I consider that if this country does not develop the democratic process at home and make the democratic process work by giving the very people whom they propose to draft in the Army to fight for their democracy, then that democracy is not the type of democracy that ought to be fought for, and, as a matter of fact, the policy of segregation in the armed forces and in other avenues of our life is the greatest single propaganda and political weapon in the minds of Russian and international communism today."[27]

An NAACP poll conducted among African American male college students found that 71 percent were sympathetic to civil disobedience against the draft. *Newsweek Magazine*'s survey also indicated strong support for Randolph's proposal.[28]

The potential for mass activism, which might lead to violence; the succession of African American petitions for redress from the United Nations; and the fear that African American international activism might permanently damage U.S. foreign relations—especially with Third World nations—rendered a response from the Truman administration. President Truman formed the first presidential Committee on Civil Rights and recommended to Congress that it establish a permanent civil rights commission, outlaw lynching and protect the right to vote.[29] The Committee further recommended that the armed forces immediately stop discrimination and segregation. In July 1948, Truman nixed the negative reaction to the report by issuing Executive Order 9981, which mandated equal rights for all personnel in the U.S. armed forces.

Truman's actions on civil rights gained him the support of African American voters and was important for his win in the 1948 presidential race. The president ran against Republican Thomas Dewey, who was slated to win, and the progressive candidate Henry Wallace. African American leftists like Paul Robeson and W. E. B. Du Bois supported Wallace because they were displeased with Truman's refusal to take action against the brutal lynchings that had occurred after World War II. Even so, Truman won the support of Black mainstream leaders, including Walter White of the NAACP and Channing Tobias, a director of the Phelps-Stokes fund. Overall, African American support for Truman "had been overwhelming. He polled more than two-thirds of the Black vote, a percentage higher than ever attained by

Franklin Roosevelt. In such crucial states as Ohio and Illinois it could be said that the Black voter had been quite as decisive as anyone in bringing about a Truman victory."[30]

Segregation in the military was being phased out by the time the Korean War erupted. Each of the armed services shifted to the new policy—but at a slow pace. Even still, military integration did not eliminate discrimination. African Americans continued to face segregationist attitudes and were still treated poorly.

As the fighting escalated on the Korean peninsula and white regiments suffered casualties on the front, African American soldiers were called in to fill in the ranks, a move that was welcomed by white commanders because they needed bodies. However, the white divisions blamed the Black troops when they performed poorly. And African Americans were easy scapegoats for failure, which played out in unequal rendering of court martial convictions. At one point, African Americans were receiving twice as many court martial convictions as whites. A group of 24th Infantrymen petitioned the NAACP to review the convictions. NAACP legal counsel Thurgood Marshall, the future first African American Supreme Court justice, traveled to Korea to investigate and then published his findings in the May 1951 issue of the Crisis Magazine. Marshall found "the military's justice system to be rife with prejudice."[31] He found that one soldier had been given a life sentence after only forty-two minutes of a trial. Even Eisenhower said before a Senate Armed Services Committee: "When you pass a law to get someone to like someone, you have trouble."[32]

Despite the criticisms of African American troops, the all-Black 24th Infantry, which was the last of the Buffalo Soldiers and the only African American infantry regiment to fight in the Korean War, distinguished itself with the first American war victory, capturing Yech'on, a town on the Naktong River in South Korea. The sixteen-hour battle was the first combat assignment for most of the regiment. The 24th kept the troops of the opposing army at bay until the South Koreans could take over.[33] One of its members, Private William Thompson, won a Congressional Medal of Honor, with a total of five Black soldiers and one sailor eventually being awarded the same medal. Daniel Chappie James Jr., a former protestor of segregation in the air force, flew 101 missions during the Korean conflict before being shot down during an unarmed reconnaissance mission. In October 1950 Lieutenant James earned a Distinguished Flying Cross for his efforts. Eventually James climbed to the rank of major. After flying 78 combat missions in Vietnam, he became the nation's first Black four-star general and was placed in charge of the North American Air Defense Command.[34] In 1953, while the Korean

War was still raging, the air force assigned Benjamin O. Davis Jr. to take command of the 51st Fighter-Interceptor Wing in Suwon AB, South Korea. Davis was promoted to brigadier general and became the first Black to earn a star in the U.S. Air Force.

On October 1, 1951, the 24th Infantry Regiment was officially deactivated. By the end of the war, the army had over 13 percent African American representation with 95 percent of the troops in integrated units.[35]

After a bitter election campaign, Dwight D. Eisenhower was elected president on November 29, 1952. Once in office, Eisenhower quickly began work to fulfill his campaign promise to end the war. The president traveled to North Korea to negotiate. Joseph Stalin died on March 5 of that same year and the Soviet Council of Ministers and the Presidium of the Supreme Soviet declared a new form of collective leadership. Using the threat of nuclear weapons to stop the war, and pressure from the Soviets, an armistice was declared in July 1953, effectively ending the armed conflict in Korea. The terms for the truce essentially re-divided the Korean peninsula roughly along the same lines that it was before the conflict.

Korea became known as the "forgotten war," as a result of the widespread attention given to the ensuing war in Vietnam. However, millions of people died in the three years of the Korean conflict. There were 520,000 North Korean casualties while more than 900,000 Chinese troops died. "The worst of the casualties occurred among the civilians in North Korea and South Korea. Although the figures are not precise, there were probably significantly more than four million civilians killed during the Korean War."[36] Approximately 33,914 American troops died and 103,284 were wounded by the time the armistice was signed.

As the Korean War was drawing to an end, segregation was being challenged on all fronts inside the U.S. Significant legal challenges led the Supreme Court to end segregation in its decision of *Brown v. Board of Education of Topeka, Kansas* (1954), thereby overturning legalized segregation ensconced by its decision in *Plessy v. Ferguson* in 1896. The next year, the civil rights movement exploded throughout the South.

Although early in his administration Dwight Eisenhower had refused to endorse civil rights publicly, he found himself embroiled in controversies surrounding race. African ambassadors were consistently insulted by America's segregation laws as they sought to travel, reside and eat at America's restaurants and hotels along the interstate highways. The storm surrounding the Little Rock Nine's efforts to integrate Central High School was broadcast around the world. Articles appeared in newspapers and magazines from India to London. As a consequence of the racial tumult inside the U.S., international opinion polls demonstrated the low opinions other nations shared about U.S. racial polices. A November 1957 report found that in Norway, "82 percent of respondents had a very bad opinion of the way the United States treated African Americans."[37] Similar results were found in Great Britain, France and West Germany.

African Americans expressed a myriad of concerns regarding the Korean War. Paul Robeson openly denounced U.S. involvement in Korea during a speech sponsored by the CAA. Robeson warned that unless U.S. intervention in Korea was stalled, the superpower would have free reign in Asia, and the next would be Africa. Robeson's activism helped to bring international attention to racism in the United States. Mary McLeod Bethune expressed her concern about the potential for nuclear war as a consequence of the Korean conflict. In her commentary, Bethune also explains the reason why she accepted membership on the President's Defense Advisory Council. Thurgood Marshall provides an account of his conversation with General MacArthur after he investigated the court martial of 32 African American soldiers. The conversation confirmed the racist sentiments held by MacArthur and therefore bolstered the complaints of African American soldiers. Finally, Lieutenant Beverly Scott describes his experiences during the Korean War and the bloody battle at Heartbreak Ridge. In his narrative, Scott reflects on his experiences as an African American soldier during the Korean War.

PAUL ROBESON
(1898–1976)

Paul Robeson was an African American athlete, singer, actor and advocate for human rights. In college at Rutgers University, Robeson was named to the All-American football team and graduated valedictorian of his class. Robeson went on to play professional football and earn a degree at Columbia Law School. He decided to use his artistic talents to support oppressed peoples after he experienced racism at the law firm where he worked. Robeson supported the anti-fascist forces in the Spanish Civil War and protested the Cold War between the U.S. and the USSR. In the late 1940s, when dissent was scarcely tolerated in the U.S., Robeson openly questioned why African Americans should fight in the army of a government that tolerated racism. Because of his outspokenness, he was accused by the House Un-American Activities Committee (HUAC) of being a Communist. In 1950, the U.S. revoked Robeson's passport, leading to an eight-year battle to re-secure it and to travel again. The following speech was given at a rally sponsored by the Civil Rights Congress at Madison Square Garden, New York City. It was published as a press release by the Council of African Affairs on June 29, 1950.

Denounce the Korean Intervention
June 28, 1950

A new wind of freedom blows in the East. The people rise to put off centuries of domination by outside powers, by the robber barons and white-supremacists of Europe and America who have held them in contempt and, too long, have crushed their simplest aspirations with the mailed fist. We may as well tell oceans' waves to stand still as to try to stop the tide of freedom flowing in the East. The peoples' will for freedom is stronger than atom bombs and we may be sure the people of Korea, Indo-China, the Philippines and Formosa will not treat their invaders lightly any more.

We have supported, not only the bankrupt Chiang in China, but all the little Chiangs—equally corrupt and lacking in favor among their peoples—all over the Far East. And the American people must resent this forced alliance of our proud nation with the dishonorable quislings who stand, momentarily, in the way of their peoples' strivings for freedom and independence.

Our place has always been on the side of the Lafayette, the heroes of the French Revolution, Toussaints, the Kosciuskos, the Bolivars—not Quislings of Europe and the Chiangs, the Bao Dai's and the Syngman Rhee's of Asia. The meaning of the President's order that the lives of our airmen and sailors must be sacrificed for the government's despicable puppet in Korea, shall not be lost to the millions in the East whose day of freedom is not far off. And it will not be lost to the millions of Americans who must insist louder than ever for peace in the world, for real freedom everywhere, for security and brotherhood.

Least of all will the meaning of the President's order be lost to the Negro people. They will know that if we don't stop our armed adventure in Korea today— tomorrow it will be Africa. For the maw of the warmakers is insatiable. They aim to rule the world or ruin it. Their slogan is all or none.

It has already meant our intervention not only in Korea, but in Formosa, the Philippines and Indo-China with arms, ships, aircraft, and men.

I have said before, and say it again, that the place for the Negro people to fight for their freedom is here at home—in Georgia, Mississippi, and Alabama, and Texas—in Chicago ghetto, and right here in New York's Stuyvesant Town!

Only this past Monday a united coalition of all the progressive forces in South Africa conducted a one-day demonstration against the government's policy of racial zoning. The people were called upon to quit their work and to devote the day to prayers, meetings and other activities against the reincarnation of Hitlerism which plagues their land.

How terrible a travesty on our democratic traditions for Negro youth to be called on one day to put down these brave African peoples! What mockery that black Americans should one day be drafted to protect the British interest in Nigeria whose proud people cannot be held in bondage for another ten years!

Fail to stop the intervention in Korea, and that day may come!

Fail to win our government to a policy of withdrawal from Indo-China, Formosa and the Philippines—a policy of recognition of the People's Republic of China—and that day may not be far off!

It is for us to take our place in history at the side of the popular masses who fight for freedom and independence. How long before we Americans shall emulate the brave freedom fighters of South Africa? How long before we shall have our Freedom Day, where the people in every church and synagogue shall pray for freedom; when no one will work but all will speak and sing and talk and meet and petition for the freedom of the Trenton 6, the Martinsville 7, Willie McGee, the Groveland 3, Mrs. Ingram, George Marshall, Carl Marzani, Eugene Dennis and his colleagues, the Hollywood Ten and the leaders of the Joint Anti-Fascist Refugee Committee—for amnesty and peace?

The working masses of America stand for life, not death. We stand for the right of peoples to determine their own destinies.

The people of the world are soberly determined that they shall have peace, and the people shall prevail. It falls upon our shoulders here in the United States to halt our government's intervention on behalf of the corrupt Rhee regime, no less than it was the responsibility of the British workers to prevent their government's joining the Civil War on the side of Jeff Davis' Confederates. The British workers fulfilled their jobs. We will not fail in ours now.

The fight goes on all around the world—for peace, for increased activity in gathering signatures to the Stockholm petition, for letters and telegrams to the President demanding amnesty for the victims of the cold war—for a decent world and a good life for all the world's peoples!

THURGOOD MARSHALL
(1908–1993)

On July 2, 1908, in Baltimore, Maryland, Thurgood Marshall was born as the grandson of a slave. In 1925, Marshall enrolled in Lincoln University, a historically Black college. He later applied to the University of Maryland Law School, but was denied because of the color of his skin. Fortunately that same year he was accepted to Howard University's Law School. Marshall became the Chief Counsel for the NAACP and in 1954, won his best-known case, Brown v. Board of Education. After this great victory, which annihilated the separate but equal doctrine, President Kennedy nominated Marshall to the U.S. Court of Appeals for the Second Circuit. After serving in the U.S. Solicitor General's office, Judge Marshall became a member of the U.S. Supreme Court in 1967. When the U.S. military deployed troops to Korea in 1950, the all-Black 24th Infantry Regiment was among them. A newspaper reporter from Baltimore's Afro-American first informed Thurgood Marshall that more than 50 Black soldiers had been arrested in Korea, a number out of proportion to the average arrests of white soldiers. In 1951, the NAACP sent Marshall into the war zone to investigate and he eventually helped to clear most of the soldiers' charges. Here is an excerpt of Justice Marshall's comments and observations spoken during an oral history interview.

Reminiscences of Thurgood Marshall:
The Korean War Court Martial
1951

Q: Justice Marshall, you were mentioning your travels, to Korea, Kenya, and there have been others, I believe. Do you want to talk about Korea first?

Marshall: Well, in the Korea situation—as I remember—it was the latter part of 1950. A newspaper reporter, a Negro from the *Afro-American* in Baltimore called me, on his return from Tokyo, and reported that there was something going on which brought about the arrest of fifty or more Negro soldiers in Korea. The NAACP decided that I should look into it. I found enough substance to warrant going over, but in applying for a passport, a Mrs. [Ruth B.] Shipley of the state department—who had a built-in dislike for Negroes and the NAACP—would not give me a passport. She even had the FBI to check me out, and they gave me a clean bill of health, but she still wouldn't grant it. And then she got General [Douglas] MacArthur to refuse me an entry permit, and that blocked it, and I decided the best thing to do would be to go to President Truman, and I did. He ordered that the passport be issued.

But it was delivered to me as I getting on the plane, and when I got on the plane, I opened up the passport and looked at it, and it said, "Not good for travel to Korea."

I figured I might have some trouble, and I did. But when I got to Tokyo, after trouble of getting located, I began meeting with Inspector General Zondell, the inspector general of the Far East Command, and the Assistant Inspector D. D. Marin. They were extremely cooperative, decent, well-trained investigators, and of course lawyers. They arranged for me to interview all of the Negroes who were then in Tokyo stockade, and the procedure was that I would go by the Dai-Ichi building, which [was] the headquarters for the Army, each morning, discuss the day's work with General Zondell and [Colonel] Martin. From there, I would go to the stockade and interview the prisoners, one at a time. Come back in the afternoon, work up my work sheets, and then be ready to report back to the solicitor general in the morning.

The reason for this was that many leads that were gotten from the prisoners had to be run down by the inspector general's office. This went on for several weeks, I've forgotten now how many, until I talked to some sixty or eighty people involved.

I found enough to warrant a trip to Korea, and then I had to go to MacArthur's chief of staff, the name slips me for the moment, who was also very cooperative; and he arranged for me to go to Korea, and Colonel Martin went along with me.

Just prior to that, I was given an audience with General MacArthur, and I found it very interesting. I questioned him about the continuation of segregation in the Army, and he said he was working on it. And I asked him how many years he'd been working on it, and he didn't really remember how many.

I reminded him that at the very time we were talking, the Air Force was completely integrated, and the Navy was quite integrated, and the only group not integrated was the Army. He said that he didn't find the Negroes qualified, and when he found them qualified, they would be integrated.

Well, we didn't part very friendly. I guess I told him what I thought, and he told me what he thought. And he being the boss, he cancelled, and I left.

Well, getting back to the trip—when I got to Korea, we went all the way up from Tejon to just below Seoul, where the enemy was. We were in the area where there was great movement, and at times you'd go into one place, and the next time you'd get there, they'd tell you, you can't go in because the enemy was there.

This was for the purpose of interviewing people, Negroes, in these service units. The stories were almost unbelievable. On the big hill, I believe it was Pork Chop Hill, the casualties were between eighty-five and ninety-five percent, which is high for anybody, and they were constantly being pushed around. The Negroes were just getting it in the neck.

Then I was investigating these court-martials, and eventually I got on the track, and I found where they were stored, down near Tejon. Colonel Martin, the deputy inspector general who I said was willing to cooperate, arranged for me to get to the warehouse where these records were kept. I got there just as they were about to be shipped away, I don't know where.

But once the inspector general clamped down on them, we got them, and I spent days going through them, and they were unbelievable. There were records of trials, so-called trials, in the middle of the night where the men were sentenced to life imprisonment in hearings that lasted less than ten minutes. They were the old well-known drumhead court-martials, done in the heat of passion and in the heat of war. There were fifty or sixty involved. One death penalty case. I remember in particular: the record showed that this man was charged with being absent in the presence of the enemy. Instead of being charged with AWOL, he was charged with cowardice in the presence of the enemy. And fortunately for him, he produced two witnesses: a major in the Medical Corps and a lieutenant in the Nurse Corps, both of whom testified that he was in a base hospital the very day that he was supposed to be AWOL.

And despite their testimony, he was convicted and given life imprisonment.

You could go through them like that. I took my notes. I worked on these records. And I came back to Tokyo, and back to the Untied States, and fortunately in the judge advocate general's office of the Army, we were able to bust every one of the convictions. Although we didn't get them all out scot-free, we got most of them out scot-free, and the others [with] a very short term.

To me, that was very important. It was good experience, to be with the military and to be up in actual warfare. It wasn't what I relished, but I learned a whole lot.

Now, the next experience with the military—no, this was before. This was in World War II. Outside of San Francisco, at the naval establishment of Yerba Buena Island, fifty Negro seamen were charged with mutiny because they refused to load ammunition during the time of war.

MARY MCLEOD BETHUNE
(1875–1955)

Mary McLeod Bethune was born July 10, 1875, as the fifteenth of seventeen children in Maysville, South Carolina. During Bethune's childhood she worked in the cotton fields with her family. She was educated at Maysville Presbyterian Mission School, Scotia Seminary and the Moody Bible Institute (Dwight Moody's Institute for Home and Foreign Missions). Later she married Albertus Bethune and their union produced a son. Bethune opened the Daytona Normal and Industrial Institute in 1904, with only a few students. She raised funds, ran the school, taught the students, and the school grew. In 1923, Bethune merged her all-girl academy with the Cookman Institute for men in Jacksonville to become Bethune-Cookman College. Bethune was active in a myriad of organizations. She served as the president of the National Association of Colored Women, leader of the Black Women's Club Movement, director of the Negro Affairs in the National Youth Administration from 1936 to 1944, consultant to the U.S. Secretary of War and Interracial Affairs for the charter conference of the U.N., vice president of the NAACP and founder of the National Council of Negro Women. Bethune was also a part of the "Black Cabinet" during Franklin D. Roosevelt's presidency and worked very closely with Eleanor Roosevelt. In the two editorials below, Bethune articulates a concern for the nation's soldiers and stresses that the American people must show them respect. She also declares her support for the president's goal of preparing an adequate defense by joining his Civil Defense Advisory Commission.

Warns Those on Home Front of Their Debt to Boys in Korea
September 16, 1950

Every American who is loyal to his flag and believes in the Declaration of Independence must be gravely concerned with the mounting threat to our democratic way of life and with the immediate need for defending it.

As the call goes out from the Armed Forces of the nation to men and women in towns and cities and country villages, the responsibility for the defense of a free world rests not only upon those of us who are called to active service, but upon those of us who are left behind to keep the strength of democracy unbroken at home.

It is our responsibility to see that those who are called from our hearthstones are fully sustained with all the resources that we are capable of giving, in the anxious days between the call to the colors of our country and the United Nations, and the foxholes and trenches and mortar-filled roads—the highways of the sea and the danger-filled skies of the battle front.

We have a duty to see that these youths are not forsaken nor neglected—in time of peace or in time of war. Our "peace strength" is your boy and your neighbor's boy, ready to meet an emergency. Our "war strength" is more of these same boys, yours and mine, alerted for action. We have a duty to them at all times. The uniform of his country should make no young man unacceptable to his neighbors.

It is ours to watch out for the boys out of reach of home—giving them a friendly word, a welcome to a decent home, to wholesome recreation and entertainment, for those days on leave that mean to so many of them only aimless, lonely drifting. Many of those same boys will be back home, one day, better or worse for their experience with their fellows while in the service of their country. What will they have to look back upon as our measure of their worth? All of the encouragement and comfort and opportunity that can be given to our boys, to keep their morale high, we are called upon, every one of us, to give.

I pray God that the day has passed when a soldier of any rank—a sailor or marine of any rank, a flier of any rank, will be snarled at and shunned and tossed about. Our organizations have a great humane task to do to meet this need.

This need, for cherishing and stimulating the men and women of our Armed Forces, applies to all Americans, of every race and creed and national origin. But there is another unfortunate situation in which the Negro in the service is singled out for rejection. Victorious in arms, he has been crushed in spirit—refused a place on the publicly-displayed rolls of the defenders of his nation, in the democracy he has bled to protect. It happened in my town. It has happened in hundreds of other towns across the nation. And as the sounds of battle roll in from the East there is evidence that this spirit of separation is developing again.

Our concern over the call to arms needs to be two-fold. For that call is much more than a test of whether our boys can fight hard and shoot straight. It is an even greater test of whether we can work together—and think straight.

The Huge Job of Civil Defense
Is Protection of All the People
May 15, 1951

On Tuesday and Wednesday of last week I attended the Civil Defense conference in Washington, at the Statler hotel, where I later met many friends. There were 1,200 delegates at the Conference, representing 250 national organizations totaling 50 million members.

Addressing the conference, the President of the United States warned that extended hostilities might very well mean a first atomic war, because, as he said, if there is another war, that is the kind of war it will be.

Both the President and Vice President Barkley reminded the delegates that while this country might survive and even win such a war, it would be at a terrible cost in civilian casualties, because not even the best possible air defense could completely or even largely block an enemy attack by air. In the event of war, we must be prepared, whenever the test may come, to reduce casualties and prevent panic by training now.

Losses from atomic attack, said the President, would constitute disaster in spite of all we could do. He pointed out that in addition to the capital at Washington—an almost certain target—many of our great industrial centers such as New York, Chicago, Cleveland or Seattle might actually be destroyed, although victory might eventually be ours.

The prevention of all-out war and the achievement of peace are our only real protection against atom bombing or any of the other frightful manifestations of war, said the President. The Vice-President, Congressman McCormack, Speaker Rayburn and Secretary of Labor Tobin all urged the delegates to help prepare the country against the eventuality of a war in which "every man, woman and child" would be involved. Civil Defense Administrator Caldwell said that a strong civil defense would help to convince an aggressor that his bombs would not destroy our morale.

As I pointed out in this column much earlier, this year, organizations—church, fraternal, women's or civil—can help greatly by getting proper information from the Civil Defense administration at Washington, if local offices have not been established, and moving it speedily through their memberships and contacts, until, directly or indirectly, it reaches every family in the group, and spreads out in a widening circle throughout our American communities.

As the President spoke, I seemed to recall that he was from Missouri. If so, he gave no evidence of the fact that he needed to "be shown." On the contrary, he seemed urgently anxious that other Americans should take heed and realize that their country and their homes were vulnerable to attack, and learn to protect them without having to be shown by the horrors of experience.

I am sure that the leaders of the nation did not take their time to meet with the delegates in order to try to "scare" a group of highly intelligent people. The reason is very sobering. A little thought and we all must realize that there would be no warning of attack. We must do our utmost, through our representatives in the Congress, and by discouraging irresponsible statements from platforms, in the press and on the air, to prevent war. Part of prevention is preparation for the defense of all the people.

As my part, I have accepted membership on the President's Civil Defense Advisory Commission, together with five other members at large, six governors of States, and six mayors and shall do all I can to push our vitally needed program of defense.

BEVERLY SCOTT

Beverly Scott was born in Statesville, North Carolina, and attended Bluefield State College in West Virginia before entering the U.S. Army. He received his commission as a lieutenant in 1946. After his tour in Korea he served at duty stations around the world. He was a senior advisor to the Thai army in Thailand and South Vietnam from 1963 to 1965, and served on the staff of the Army Inspector General in Vietnam in 1968. Scott recalls his experience on Heartbreak Ridge in Korea as one of the most miserable of his entire life. This judgment reflected not just the particular ferocity of the enemy in those areas, the consistently bad weather and the dreary living conditions, but also the fact the Beverly Scott was an African American soldier.

Black Officer in a White Man's Army
1951

I want to make something clear from the beginning. From the first day I went in the army I had no thought of getting out. I saw the army as something I could do extremely well. I fitted in. The army offered everything I like in life. I like order, I like structure, I like organization, I like discipline, I like judgment on the basis of performance.

And it was honorable. There was no better institution in American life, no better one anywhere, than the army for the Black man in the forties and fifties. Things weren't perfect, but they were better than any civilian institution. You had more leverage in the army. You always had somebody you could go to and complain about bad treatment. A Black man couldn't do that in civilian life. Especially in the South.

From almost my first day in the army I planned to go to officer candidate school. I got my orders for OCS around Christmas of 1945. Graduated in July 1946. A nineteen-year-old second lieutenant.

OCS was my first experience with living in an integrated society. There were no all-Black officer candidate schools. Most of my bunk-mates were white, and that was my first experience with meeting white people on a person-to-person basis. Previous to that all my experience with whites had been adversarial. Growing up in rural North Carolina, I'd done all kinds of menial jobs as a boy, and I was always subjected to insults and names. We had white neighbors living across the creek from our house, and all us kids did was fight.

OCS was the first time I'd ever competed with guys who had gone to Yale and Harvard and the various prep schools. It was a very enlightening experience. Frankly, it set the tone for the rest of my life, because OCS taught me that I could successfully compete with these people.

When the war in Korea broke out I was at Fort Knox, Kentucky, helping train Black troops. I was an infantry officer, always had been. But in Korea they immediately began experiencing severe communications problems, because the men over there didn't know how to handle their radios or lay wire properly. They told us they needed school-trained communications officers. That became one of the army's highest priorities. So I was sent to Fort Benning, Georgia, to learn communications.

I graduated from Benning in December 1950, and a month later I was in Korea as a common officer with the 25th Infantry Division.

Basically what I did was try and teach the infantry officers in my battalion the basics of radio communications. Few of them accepted what I told them. It might have been partly because I was Black and they were White, but mostly it was them not wanting to admit they were doing things wrong. But they were. They always tried to talk with the radio out of range. And they didn't understand the business of laying wire.

The radio operations seldom had any training. A company commander would grab hold of a rifleman and say, "Here, you carry this radio." That was all the training they got, and consequently most radio operators didn't know good procedure, didn't know how to keep the transmissions short, or how to tune the radio so it was zeroed in on the proper frequency. I tried to bring some professionalism to the battalion's communications, and eventually it got that way.

The 24th Regiment was the only all-Black regiment in the division, and as a Black officer in an all-Black regiment commanded by whites I was always super sensitive about standing my ground. Being a man. Being honest with my soldiers. I felt that the Black soldiers were depending on me to look out for them, that if I didn't look out for them nobody would.

Most of the white officers were good. Taken in the context of the times, they were probably better than the average white guy in civilian life. But there was still that patronizing expectation of failure. White officers came to the 24th Regiment knowing or suspecting or having been told that this was an inferior regiment.

And there were always the really outright racist sons of bitches. But you didn't deal with those people. You maintained a strictly professional relationship and had no interpersonal dealings at all with that kind of officer.

I served as the 1st Battalion communications officer all through the spring and summer of 1951, when the 24th was on the line constantly. The 24th fought well. As a common officer I was not in a foxhole on the front line, but I was damn close to it, and I saw no instances of the mass cowardice that some people claimed the regiment displayed earlier in the war. Those men did their jobs as well as any white unit fighting at that time.

In September we got word that the 24th was going to be deactivated. Nobody told us why, the order just came down. It was probably inevitable, though, that the regiment would be broken up, because by now General Ridgway was pushing hard for real integration in the army. And there were other generals

202 ~ Chapter Seven

around who may not have cared much for integration, but who refused to believe that all-Black units could fight, and who wanted them disbanded for that reason.

Anyway, they pulled us off the line about the middle of September and moved us back in reserve. While we were back there we started turning in our equipment. Everyone in the 24th was transferred to the remaining regiments in the division, with the 24th being replaced in the division by the 14th Regiment from Japan.

I was transferred to the 14th, and right away I experienced some problems. People in the 14th didn't want anybody from the 24th. I was a technically qualified communications officer, which the 14th said they needed very badly, but when I go there, suddenly they didn't need any commo officers.

Then their executive officer said, "We got a rifle platoon for you. Think you can handle a rifle platoon?"

What the hell do you mean, can I handle a rifle platoon? I was also trained as an infantry officer. He knew that. I was a first lieutenant, been in the army six years, almost all that time in the infantry. If I had been coming in as a white first lieutenant the question never would have been asked.

In any case, I became the first Black platoon leader in the 14th Regiment. I was the only Black officer in the battalion. I never had any problems with my men; they were mostly Hispanics, and when they saw that I knew what I was doing, and wasn't going to get them killed or shot unnecessarily, they relaxed and accepted me.

My relationship with the other officers was cool. Especially with the company commander. For a while I wasn't talked to. I was watched very closely. I should have been made the executive officer of the company, since I outranked all the other lieutenants, and it was customary to have the second-highest in rank as the company exec. But I wasn't given the job.

I saw right away it was going to be pretty tough for me.

It was now the fall of 1951. We'd just moved to the Iron Triangle area. Three towns arranged in a triangle around a long valley, the valley surrounded by steep hills.

That valley had been one of the main invasion corridors to the south, but the truce talks had started, and now they were digging in. Every morning we'd see fresh piles of dirt on the ridges. You never saw the Chinese, but you saw the dirt. They were always digging, and they churned out that dirt like worms.

We were digging in too, until what you had were two armies facing each other from opposing trenchlines. Between the two trenchlines there was maybe five hundred or six hundred yards of no man's land. And what the war came down to for us was patrolling that no man's land.

It was a miserable time. Just a miserable, miserable time. We lost men almost every day, killed or wounded, and it was hard to see the point. The lines stayed exactly where they were.

After we'd been in our positions for about a month, word came down that we were going to make this big attack. We were going to attack all the way up the Iron Triangle to Pyongyang, to straighten out the line, and I'll tell you, we truly believed that was going to be our last action of war. We were absolutely convinced we would never survive an attack like that. The Chinese were not going to be dislodged on those hill masses. It would have been impossible to get them out of there. We'd been patrolling those hills for a month, and we'd never gotten more than halfway up any one of them before taking heavy fire and a lot of casualties.

But the order came down that we were going to attack. We were pulled back off the line, re-outfitted, issued fresh ammunition, we recalibrated our weapons, we spent about two days—cold, wet, miserable days—rehearsing the attack. And you never saw so many long faces, including my own. We felt certain we were being ordered to our deaths.

At the last minute, for reasons unknown to us, the attack was called off, and I don't think I could begin to describe the relief we felt. I read later that there had been a breakdown in the truce talks, and that this attack was to be part of a major offensive all along the front. But new overtures were made in the talks, and the attack was called off.

Shortly after this we moved to Heartbreak Ridge. We had to cross a valley to get there, and the entire road through that valley, over two miles of it, was covered with camouflage netting. It was like a long dim tunnel, and it was very depressing to see, because it meant that we were going into positions where the enemy would be looking down our throats.

It turned out to be even worse than that. Our trenches in that sector were only about twenty meters in front of theirs. We were eyeball to eyeball. Just twenty meters of no man's land between us. We couldn't move at all in the daytime without getting shot at. Machine-gun fire would come in, grenades, small-arms fire, all from within spitting distance.

It was like World War 1. We lived in a maze of bunkers and deep trenches. Some had been dug by previous occupants of the ridge. Some we dug ourselves. There were bodies strewn all over the place. Hundreds of bodies frozen in the snow. We could see the arms and legs sticking up. Nobody could get their dead out of there.

On Heartbreak it was just a matter of holding our positions. We'd send out a patrol once in a while, but only at night. It was suicide to move around in the daytime. Many times they'd attack us at night, so nobody slept after dark. You stayed wide awake. During the day we'd get shelled by artillery or mortars, or get sniped at, so you never got any real sleep.

Added to that, we were fighting North Koreans. There was a distinct difference between fighting them and fighting the Chinese. The Chinese were normal soldiers, in the sense that when they saw they couldn't do something they'd pull back. The North Koreans would come at you even when they couldn't do anything. Even when they knew it was hopeless and that they were going to be killed. They'd come right into your hole, try and shoot you or stab you or bite you if they didn't have a weapon. Just fanatical as hell. Maybe thirty or forty of them would come straight at us in a kind of banzai attack, where they'd all get killed, but it was just to distract us while more of them were trying to sneak around us somewhere else. And they were vicious people. They mutilated bodies. They shot prisoners. Just nasty, nasty people.

Heartbreak Ridge was bad news any way you looked at it.

But I finally made exec while I was up there. We had a new CO by that time, a big Polish guy from Pennsylvania who was making a real effort to be fair. A replacement came in, a lieutenant named Stevens who had been wounded in World War II on Okinawa and who'd been called up from the reserves. He was a nice guy, a real handsome guy. We all called him Steve. When he came to the company our exec was moved up to battalion, and I was made the executive officer while Steve took over my old platoon.

At this time the army required that we have one hot meal a day. I suppose it was for morale purposes. Conditions on Heartbreak were so miserable otherwise. You could choose either breakfast or supper—that is, you could eat your hot meal before the sun came up or after it went down. But to get to the mess tent you had to walk down the reverse slope of the hill, and the North Koreans were always lobbing mortar rounds over there. It was just random fire, but it was something you had to be careful about.

Steve and I got to be pretty close friends, and since we both preferred to eat our hot meal in the morning, each morning we'd walk down the hill together. And as we walked down we'd talk about various issues, or about the platoon, things that needed to be done, or the personalities of the men, who you could rely on and so forth.

On this one particular morning, I guess it was a week or two after Steve got there, I couldn't get my razor going. I used an electric razor plugged into an old radio battery, and the battery was acting up, so I sent Steve on ahead of me.

Finally I got myself shaved, and as I was walking down the hill a big blast blew apart the mess tent. A mortar round had landed right on it. The explosion killed a number of cooks, and it also blew Steve's legs off.

He'd been sitting at the mess table, where I'd have been sitting if that battery hadn't acted up, and the blast just kind of sheared him off below the hips.

I was one of the first to reach him. I helped get him out, and he was a mess. He survived the wound, but he didn't want to, because as were taking him out he saw his legs still lying there under the table. He'd been a newspaper reporter from Vallejo, California, and I think he eventually went back to his work in Vallejo, but after they took him away I never had any contact with him again.

By this time, March of 1952, I had been in Korea longer than anybody in the division. You needed thirty-six points to rotate. You got four points for every month of line duty, so after nine months on line you had thirty-six points. I think

I had something like fifty-two points by this time, but they kept telling me, "Well, we don't have a replacement for you."

That was nonsense, so one morning while I was back picking up the company payroll I stopped by the Inspector General's office and complained about being treated unfairly. I left a note asking that they look into my case and find out why I couldn't rotate home when I'd been there longer than anybody in the division.

The next time I went down there I got word from the IG to report to Yongdungpo to go home.

I didn't even go back to the company. I called my platoon sergeant and some of the other guys on the telephone, told them goodbye and left.

Notes

1. Telegram of May 12, 1945, Prime Minister Churchill to President Harry S. Truman, in *Cabinet Papers*, No. 44. See Martin Gilbert, *Churchill and America* (New York: Free Press, 2005), 354, for further discussion on Churchill's quote and perspective.

2. For a discussion of the Korean War, including source documents, see Sonia G. Benson, *Korean War Almanac and Primary Sources* (New York: Gale, 2002).

3. Major Robert Sawyer, *Military Advisors in Korea: KMAG in Peace and War, Office of the Chief of Military History* (Washington, D.C.: U.S. Government Printing Office, 1962), 100.

4. Benson, *Korean War Almanac*, 14.

5. Benson, *Korean War Almanac*, 199.

6. See excerpts from "President's Address: Korean War Dismissal of General Douglas MacArthur," in Benson, *Korean War Almanac*, 277–80. Also see pages 90–92 for additional discussion on the reasons for MacArthur's dismissal.

7. M. J. Heale, *McCarthy's America: Red Scare Politics in State and Nation, 1935–1965* (Athens: University of Georgia Press, 1998), 28. For additional data on loyalty oaths and programs, see Chapter 2.

8. For more information on the life of Claudia Jones, see Buzz Johnson, *I Think of My Mother: Notes on the Life and Times of Claudia Jones* (London: Karia Press, 1985).

9. For a detailed discussion of the Red Scare in America and the House Un-American Activities Committee, see David Caute, *The Great Fear: The Anti-Communist Purge under Truman and Eisenhower* (New York: Simon & Schuster, 1978).

10. Sidney Lens, *Permanent War: The Militarization of America* (New York: Shocken Books, 1987), 47.

11. Caute, *Great Fear*, 38–39.

12. W. E. B. Du Bois, National Negro Congress, "First Petition to the United Nations from the African American People" (1946). Reprinted in Herbert Aptheker, *A Documentary History of the Negro People of the United States*, vol. 5, *From the End of World War II to the Korean War* (New York: Citadel, 1993), 135–41.

13. Minnie Finch, *The NAACP: Its Fight for Justice* (Metuchen, N.J.: Scarecrow Press, 1981), 117.

14. W. E. B. Du Bois, NAACP, "An Appeal to the World." Reprinted in Aptheker, *Documentary History*.

15. Azza Salama Layton, *International Politics and Civil Rights Policies in the United States, 1941–1960*. (Cambridge, UK: Cambridge University Press, 2000), 57. See also Paul Gordon Lauren, "Seen from the Outside: The International Perspective on America's Dilemma," in *Window on Freedom: Race, Civil Rights, and Foreign Affairs, 1945–1988*, ed. Brenda Gayle Plummer (Chapel Hill: University of North Carolina Press, 2003), 29–30.

16. William L. Patterson, ed. *We Charge Genocide: The Crime of Government against the Negro People* (New York: Civil Rights Congress, 1951), 27.

17. Mary L. Dudziak, *Cold War Civil Rights: Race and the Image of American Democracy* (Princeton, N.J.: Princeton University Press, 2000), 61.

18. Council on African Affairs press release, "Robeson Denounces Korean Intervention," June 29, 1950, in *Paul Robeson Speaks*, ed. Philip S. Foner (New York: Brunner/Mazel, 1978), 252–53.

19. David Lettering Lewis, *W .E. B. Du Bois: The Fight for Equality and the American Century 1919–1963* (New York: Henry Holt, 2000), 547, 552.

20. Jean Claude Baker and Chris Chase, *Josephine* (New York: Random House, 1993), 319. Also see Dudziak, *Cold War Civil Rights*, 67–75, for more discussion on Baker's international activism.

21. Dudziak, *Cold War Civil Rights*, 73.

22. Baker and Chase, *Josephine*, 322.

23. Gary Giddins, *Satchmo* (New York: Doubleday, 1988), 160–65; Hughes Panassie, *Louis Armstrong* (New York: Scribner, 1971), 34–36.

24. Dudziak, *Cold War Civil Rights*, 66.

25. Penny M. Von Eschen, *Race against Empire: Black Americans and Anti-Colonialism 1937–1957* (Ithaca, N.Y.: Cornell University Press, 1997), 116–18.

26. Von Eschen, *Race against Empire*, 115–16. Also see "Council on African Affairs Faces Split on Policies," *Chicago Defender*, February 28, 1948, 13.

27. "A. Philip Randolph's Call for Draft Resistance," *Congressional Record*, Senate, April 12, 1948, 4312–13. Reprinted in Aptheker, *Documentary History*, 332–36.

28. *New York Times*, June 5, 1948; "Crisis in the Making," *Newsweek* 31 (June 7, 1948), 28–29. For further discussion on the polls see Richard M. Dalifume, *Desegregation of the U.S. Armed Forces: Fighting on Two Fronts 1939–1953* (Columbia: University of Missouri Press, 1969), 169.

29. Layton, *International Politics*, 76–80.

30. David McCollough, *Truman* (New York: Simon & Schuster, 1992). Also see Ronald W. Walters, *Black Presidential Politics in America: A Strategic Approach* (Albany: State University of New York Press, 1988), 24.

31. Kai Wright, *Soldiers of Freedom: An Illustrated History of African Americans in the Armed Forces* (New York: Black Dog & Leventhal, 2002), 223.

32. Clark Clifford and Richard Holbrook, *Counsel to the President* (New York: Random House, 1991), 167.

33. Gail Buckley, *American Patriots: The Story of Blacks in the Military from the Revolution to Desert Storm* (New York: Random House, 2001), 352.

34. Wright, *Soldiers of Freedom*, 221.

35. Buckley, *American Patriots*, 367.

36. Benson, *Korean War Almanac*, 199.

37. See Dudziak, *Cold War Civil Rights*, 141, for additional information on international opinion of the United States on the issue of race, especially note 66 on page 288. Information on world opinion of the U.S. was included in the report by the Office of Research and Intelligence, United States Information Agency, Post–Little Rock Opinion on the Treatment of Negroes in the U.S., January 1958.

CHAPTER EIGHT

∼

Vietnam War:
Red, White, Black and Blue
1 9 5 6 – 1 9 7 5

The Vietnam War was fought in the milieu of the greatest social unrest in recent U.S. history. The racial climate in the country was changing rapidly
during the early years of the Vietnam War. The Supreme Court's landmark
decision in *Brown v. Board of Education* (1954) which declared the United
States' "separate but equal" system unconstitutional, helped to propel the
modern civil rights movement into existence.[1] The senseless violence occurring in small towns all over the South also stimulated mass action by African
Americans. One tragedy that epitomized the viciousness of the South was
the lynching of fourteen-year-old Emmett Till, an African American male
visiting Mississippi from Chicago. On August 28, 1955, a few days after allegedly making an inappropriate comment to Carolyn Bryant, a white
woman in a grocery store, Till was kidnapped at gunpoint in the middle of
the night by Bryant's husband and his half-brother, J. W. Milam. The body of
the fourteen-year-old boy was found three days later in the Tallahatchie
River mangled and shot.[2] Till's mother, Mamie Bradley, overwhelmed with
grief and anger, held a public, open-casket funeral to display the cruelty of
racism. Thousands of people attended the memorial service in Chicago and
those who did not attend were able to witness the crimes of the South
through pictures of the disfigured corpse of Emmett Till, which had been
published in newspapers and magazines throughout the world.

Shortly after being acquitted by an-all white jury, Till's two murderers sold
their confessions to *Look Magazine*. In the article, the assassins took pride
in their ability to escape punishment for murder.[3] The African American

community, on the other hand, became even more determined to fight the racist violence and unfair laws that allowed crimes like the murder of Emmett Till to go without penalty. From 1955 to 1968, African Americans engaged in nonviolent direct action to defeat legal racism and discrimination in the U.S., using such tactics as mass protests, boycotts and demonstrations.

National organizations such as the Southern Christian Leadership Conference (SCLC), Congress of Racial Equality (CORE), the National Urban League (NUL), the National Association for the Advancement of Colored People (NAACP) and the Student Non-Violent Coordinating Committee (SNCC) led the fight for change. Local groups, such as the Women's Political Council in Montgomery, Alabama, brought cases of discrimination to national attention and also provided grassroots support to the nationwide movement for civil rights.

Dr. Martin Luther King Jr. emerged as the central and most celebrated leader of the civil rights movement. At the age of 26, while completing his doctoral studies at Boston University, King accepted the offer to become pastor of Dexter Avenue Baptist Church in Montgomery in 1954. Soon thereafter King was thrust into the national spotlight after Rosa Parks, a secretary of the NAACP, refused to give up her seat on a bus to a white man. In concert with local leadership, King organized a bus boycott under the auspices of the Montgomery Improvement Association (MIA), a newly formed group established to organize the boycott. Meanwhile, attorneys from the NAACP Legal Defense Fund worked diligently on defeating legalized segregation on the buses. As a result of the combined pressure, on June 4, 1956, the federal district court ruled that Alabama's racial segregation laws for buses were unconstitutional in *Browder v. Gayle*. However, an appeal kept segregation intact and so the boycott continued until November 13, 1956, when the Supreme Court upheld the lower court's ruling. This victory led to a city ordinance that allowed public transportation passengers to sit down on a first-come, first-served basis.

Rooted in the teachings of Mahatma Gandhi, Jesus Christ and the methods of CORE pacifists, Martin Luther King Jr. spread the gospel of the nonviolent direct action. King's oratorical and leadership skills, which mobilized millions of Americans, eventually earned him a Nobel Peace Prize in 1964.

As the decade of the 1950s came to an end, the work of civil rights activists had resulted in important changes in the country, including the passage of the 1957 Civil Rights Bill that established the Civil Rights Section of the Justice Department. The legislation also empowered federal prosecutors to obtain court injunctions against interference with the right to vote and established a federal Civil Rights Commission with authority to investigate discrimination and recommend curative action.

The decade of the 1960s proved to be one of the most tumultuous for civil rights activism, as Black and white people challenged segregation with freedom rides, sit-ins and voter education and registration drives. The nonviolent activists frequently encountered violence in their fight for civil rights. Although they won several victories, including the passage of the 1964 Civil Rights Act, which struck down discrimination in public accommodations, and the 1965 Voting Rights Act, which set forth special enforcement provisions to secure the right to vote for all citizens, the U.S., particularly the South, became a war zone. Violence and riots surrounded a Black student who sought to enroll at the University of Mississippi on October 1, 1961. President Kennedy sent 5,000 federal troops into Mississippi to quell the violence. On June 12, 1963, Mississippi's 37-year-old NAACP field secretary was murdered outside his home in Jackson. Then, on September 15, 1963, four little African American girls were killed in a senseless bombing at the 16th Street Baptist Church, a popular location for holding civil rights meetings in Birmingham, Alabama. Also in Neshoba County, Mississippi, the bodies of two whites and one African American were found in an earthen dam, six weeks into a federal investigation backed by President Johnson. James E. Chaney, 21; Andrew Goodman, 21; and Michael Schwerner, 24, had been working to register African American's to vote in Mississippi. After investigating the burning of a Black church, they were arrested by the police on speeding charges, incarcerated for several hours and then released. After their release the three activists were found murdered and the evidence pointed to members of the Ku Klux Klan. Malcolm X, the Black nationalist leader and founder of the Organization of Afro-American Unity, was shot to death at the Audubon in Harlem, New York, on February 21, 1965.

Incensed by the violent response to demands for basic civil rights, many prominent African American individuals and organizations began to eschew nonviolence as an appropriate tactic. Members of SNCC, led by Stokely Carmichael and H. Rap Brown, denounced nonviolence and the fight for civil rights with their battle cry "Black Power." The Black Panther Party for Self-Defense was founded in 1966 to defend Black people "by any means necessary." They drafted a 10-point platform which demanded radical ideas such as "freedom for all black men held in federal, state, county and city prisons and jails, and that black people be tried in court by a jury of their peer group or people from their Black communities."[4] Riots and rebellions erupted in several cities in the South and North. In Harlem, Watts, Detroit and Newark, the violence resulted in at least 99 deaths, 10,200 arrests and more than $35 million in property damage.[5] In his quest to repress further disturbances, President Lyndon B. Johnson announced the creation of the National Advisory

Commission on Civic Disorders, also known as the Kerner Commission, so named after its leader Governor Otto Kerner Jr. of Illinois. After studying the disturbances, the Kerner Commission issued a report that found the primary cause of the disturbances was white racism, which resulted in pervasive discrimination and segregation that excluded "Negros" from economic progress.[6]

While the battle over racism ensued inside the U.S., a conflict was brewing in Indochina that came to a boiling point during the early 1960s. The hostilities were rooted in French colonialism and the realities of the Cold War. Beginning in the 1840s and lasting until the 1880s, the French had gained control of Indochina in a series of colonial wars. During World War II the United States supported the Allied forces against the Japanese, who had been granted military access to the Tonkin in Indochina during September 1940, after the French surrender to Germany. The agreement gave the Japanese better access to China during the Sino-Japanese War and allowed them further opportunities to dominate the Pacific region and other portions of Southeast Asia.

From the perspective of the U.S., Japan's occupation of Indochina was a strategic problem. Certainly, Japan's control of Indochina threatened U.S. access to the vital resources of the country, but the essential reason for U.S. intervention was to support its relationship with France.[7] The U.S. supported the French government's attempt to regain its colonial holdings in Indochina, which consisted of Vietnam, Cambodia and Laos. Hence, the U.S. intervened in the conflict by freezing Japanese assets in America and providing intelligence on Japanese military movements and ship locations to the Allied forces fighting in Japan. The work of the U.S. was conducted by the Office of Strategic Services, which later became the Central Intelligence Agency.[8]

U.S. bombing of Hiroshima and Nagasaki led to the Japanese surrender in 1945. Soon thereafter, France attempted to reassert itself in the region, but was met with fierce opposition by the indigeonous population who aspired for independence from colonial rule. Vietnamese nationalists organized as the "Viet Minh" fought under the leadership of Ho Chi Minh, a Vietnamese revolutionary who later became prime minister and then president of North Vietnam. While living in France, Ho became active in the Vietnamese community and a member of the French Socialist Party. In 1919, he petitioned the leaders at the Versailles peace talks for equal rights in French Indochina, but was ignored. In his early years, Minh had also traveled to such places as England, the U.S. and Hong Kong. While touring the U.S., Ho Chi Minh was reported to have visited Harlem, where he attended meetings of Marcus Garvey's UNIA. While in the U.S., Ho also became familiar with the brutal racial violence of the Ku Klux Klan and wrote an article that described the lynching of African Americans. After visiting the U.S., Ho openly criticized U.S. and European racial practices.[9] Ho later returned to Vietnam in 1941 to lead the Viet Minh Independence Movement.

During World War II, the United States had supported Ho Chi Minh and the Viet Minh in resistance against the Japanese.[10] But after the war and the end of Japanese occupation in Vietnam, the U.S. chose to back France's effort to regain its colonial hold over Indochina. On September 2, 1945, using the Declaration of Independence as his foundation, Ho Chi Minh announced the independence of the Democratic Republic of Vietnam. He further declared that "All men are created equal. They are endowed by their Creator with certain inalienable rights, among these are Life, Liberty, and the pursuit of Happiness."[11] Vietnamese independence was recognized by the Communist governments of China and the Soviet Union. Ho Chi Minh later became president of North Vietnam with the capital located in Hanoi.

Not willing to acquiesce, the French battled the indigenous population for control of Indochina. But the French assault only increased the popularity of Ho Chi Minh, who was seen as a liberator. Covertly, U.S. President Harry Truman bolstered the French effort, and at one point U.S. taxpayers were underwriting 80 percent of the cost of the occupation.[12] The U.S. also supported Ho Chi Minh's challenger in the South, Bao Dai, the last emperor of the Nguyen Dynasty, by extending diplomatic recognition to his French-backed government on February 7, 1950. U.S. actions were rationalized by its stated objective to stop the spread of communism.

The French hold on the territory began to slip as the fighting spirit of the Viet Minh proved more than a match for French industrialized military might. Bitter fighting lasted until March 1954, when the Viet Minh won a decisive victory against French forces at the gruelling 56-day Battle of Dien Bien Phu, near the Laotion border. The Peace Agreement signed at the Geneva Conference of 1954 signaled an official end to the war. Representatives from the U.S., the Soviet Union, the United Kingdom, France, the People's Republic of China, the Democratic Republic of Vietnam (DRV), which later became the government of North Vietnam, and the State of Vietnam, which later became the government of South Vietnam, Laos and Cambodia all attended the conference to settle their differences. The "Agreement" partitioned the North and South Vietnam at the 17th parallel until internationally supervised elections could be held in July 1956 to elect a leader for a new, unified nation.[13] France relinquished any claim to territory in Indochina. Laos and Cambodia also became independent in 1954, as part of the Geneva Agreement.

The Democratic Republic of Vietnam in the North was controlled by the Viet Minh, while Bao Dai was granted leadership over the State of Vietnam in the South. The U.S., the United Kingdom and France supported the Southern leadership, while the Eastern bloc countries of the Soviet Union and China supported the North. The events of 1954 not only marked the end of French involvement in the region, but also the beginnings of a serious commitment on behalf of the U.S. government to South Vietnam.

In the South, Bao Dai installed Ngo Dinh Diem as his prime minister. Soon thereafter Dai was ousted from power in a referendum to determine who should lead Vietnam. In the referendum, which was sponsored by Prime Minister Diem and supported by the U.S., Diem won over 90 percent of the vote.

Meanwhile in the U.S., Harry Truman declined to run for the presidency in 1952. Adlai Stevenson from Illinois was the Democratic Party nominee, but was defeated by General Dwight Eisenhower—the former Supreme Commander of the Allied Forces in Europe. Eisenhower had also earned the position as the first Supreme Commander of the North Atlantic Treaty Organization (NATO). Running on a pledge to resolve the crisis in Korea, Eisenhower won 444 electoral votes to Stevenson's 89.

As president, Eisenhower did not depart from Truman's policy of containment, but actually supported the idea with his famous "domino theory." Using this approach, Eisenhower asserted that blocking DRV success in Vietnam would prevent the fall of neighboring states to Communist control. Accordingly, Eisenhower's administration expanded U.S. economic and military assistance to South Vietnam, despite Diem's authoritarian and autocratic style of government.[14] Eisenhower's Secretary of State John Foster Dulles then spearheaded the creation of the Southeast Asia Treaty Organization in September 1954, which pledged U.S. security protection to the region. On the other side, the Eastern bloc countries backed Ho Chi Minh.

As preparations for the coming elections began, Ngo Dinh Diem and Ho Chi Minh both worked to eliminate their rivals. In January 1956, Diem launched a brutal crackdown against Viet Minh suspects in the countryside and rounded up their supporters who were located in the South. Those arrested were hauled before "security committees" with many suspects, imprisoned, tortured and executed. Meanwhile in North Vietnam, Ho Chi Minh instituted reform policies that centered on redistributing land from the wealthy to the poor. Some landowners were hauled before "people's tribunals" and sent to labor camps and ideological cleansing programs.

Fearing that Ho Chi Minh might win the national elections, Diem denounced the Geneva agreement in 1955 and refused to cooperate with the upcoming elections.[15] The U.S. supported Diem's decision and his subsequent pronouncement that he was the new president of the Republic of Vietnam.

Although scholars debate the actual beginning of the Second Indochina War, also referred to as the Vietnam War, the disagreements between the U.S. and Ho Chi Minh escalated during the Kennedy administration. It was also during this period that Ho Chi Minh declared a People's War to unite all of Vietnam. The National Liberation Front (NLF), also known as the Viet Cong (Vietnamese Communist), was established as an insurgent organization fighting the Republic of Vietnam and its allies during the war. American forces typically referred to members of the NLF as "Charlie."

Over the next three years guerilla warfare ensued between the North and South in Vietnam. North Viet Minh guerillas procured weapons from the East, while the South received support from the West. On July 8, 1959, Viet Minh soldiers killed two American advisers, Major Dale Buis and Sergeant Chester Ovnand, at Bien Hoa in South Vietnam. They were the first American deaths by hostile action in the Second Indochina War. The U.S. press provided more coverage of the Vietnam War and U.S. citizens began to pay more attention to the conflict.[16]

On January 20, 1961, John Fitzgerald Kennedy was inaugurated as the 35th U.S. president, with Lyndon Johnson serving as his vice president. Kennedy defeated Richard Milhous Nixon narrowly, only winning by two-tenths of a percentage point (0.2%) of the popular vote and 303 electoral votes to Nixon's 219. Kennedy labeled his domestic program the "New Frontier." It ambitiously promised government intervention to improve the economy, federal funding for education, health care for the elderly and an end to racial discrimination.

On the war against communism, Kennedy favored a strong anti-Communist foreign policy. During a campaign address in Raleigh, North Carolina, on September 17, 1960, Kennedy stated that we must "act to spread freedom as well as to react against the spread of communism."[17] Kennedy also compared the Soviet Union's high economic growth to the U.S., criticized Republicans for the missile gap between the two countries and lamented Soviet superiority in the space program, which was evidenced by their successful Sputnik program.

Once in office, Kennedy followed Eisenhower's foreign policies on communism. Before he left office, Eisenhower had begun preparations to invade Cuba with the goal of unseating its Socialist leader, Fidel Castro. Kennedy attempted to carry out the operation just three months into his presidency by supporting, with military assistance, the bombing of Cuban airfields and the invasion of Cuban beaches by Cuban pilots in exile. The incident quickly became a foreign policy disaster for President Kennedy.

On Indochina, Kennedy increased weapons shipments and sent more military advisors and special forces to the region. By the end of 1962, approximately 11,300 U.S. military personnel were stationed in South Vietnam, up from 3,200 the previous year.[18] However, Kennedy began to question his stance on the Diem regime when a conflict arose between the Catholic president and the Buddhist leaders over the display of Buddhist flags during the birthday celebrations of Buddha. Catholic Archbishop Ngo Dinh Thue, the brother of President Diem, ordered the flags be taken down. The Buddhists demonstrated in protest, especially since a similar order had not been issued during Catholic celebrations. During the demonstrations, a confrontation between the government and Buddhist demonstrators resulted in the death of nine members of the crowd.[19] Kennedy, however, did not have the time to change the direction of U.S. policy in Vietnam. President Diem was killed in a coup in 1963 and Kennedy was assassinated that same year. Upon Kennedy's death, Vice President Lyndon Baines Johnson immediately assumed the presidency.

Johnson's primary concerns were domestic. He envisioned a "Great Society," which would work to eliminate poverty and racial injustice. To operationalize his goals, Johnson initiated a set of domestic programs that included Job Corps, Head Start, Upward Bound, Neighborhood Youth Corps, Medicare/Medicaid and a host of anti-poverty programs. Johnson had also resolved to deal with the racial crisis engulfing the country. In that regard, he urged Congress to pass the 1964 Civil Rights Act, the 1965 Voting Rights Act and fair housing legislation. However, Johnson's Great Society initiative was never fully funded because of the drain on government resources as a result of increased spending on the Vietnam War.

Johnson was the fourth president to encounter the war in Vietnam. Operating in the tradition of those who came before him, Johnson declared that he would not "lose Vietnam." In a speech in Baltimore on April 7, 1965, Johnson said, "we are there because we have a promise to keep. Since 1954 every American President has offered support to the people of South Viet-Nam. We have helped to build, and we have helped to defend. Thus, over many years, we have made a national pledge to help South Viet-Nam defend its independence. And I intend to keep that promise."[20] Accordingly, Johnson strengthened U.S. presence in the region by instituting an air campaign and sending more troops, and his administration worked covertly with Laos and Cambodia to undermine communism. By the end of 1964, there were 23,300 American military personnel in South Vietnam.[21]

A major turning point for U.S. involvement in Vietnam occurred as a result of the conflict in the Gulf of Tonkin in August 1964, when two naval ships, the *Maddox* and *Turner Joy*, stationed ten miles off the coast of North Vietnam, were attacked by the NLF. In response, the U.S. Congress, at the behest of President Johnson, overwhelmingly passed the Gulf of Tonkin Resolution, which allowed the president "to take all necessary measures to repel any armed attack against the forces of the United States and to prevent further aggression."[22] The resolution, which passed August 7, 1964, unanimously in the House and 98-2 in the Senate, granted President Johnson enormous power to wage an undeclared war in Vietnam. The Tonkin Resolution was the only congressional authorization for the war.

U.S. involvement in Vietnam escalated even further under the Johnson administration. The first U.S. combat troops arrived in Vietnam on March 8, 1965, when 3,500 marines landed at China Beach to defend the American air base at Da Nang. Then on March 9, 1965, President Johnson authorized the use of napalm, a petroleum-based anti-personnel bomb that showers hundreds of explosive pellets upon impact. On July 24, 1965, the first U.S. jet was shot down. President Johnson increased the number of U.S. military personnel in South Vietnam to 125,000.[23] Then on January 7, 1966, the State Department issued Fourteen Points setting forth the parameters for which the United States could begin negotiations for peace. In the Fourteen Points the Johnson administration requested a conference on Southeast Asia, during which negotiations could occur without preconditions. Because the U.S. did not disavow continued support for South Vietnam, in the interim, Ho Chi Minh denounced Washington's Fourteen Points in a letter to Communist leaders.[24]

Another essential turning point in the war occurred as a result of the Tet Offensive in 1968. The Tet Offensive took place during the Tet holiday, which celebrates the beginning of the Lunar New Year at the end of January or beginning of February. Because Tet is the most important Vietnamese holiday, a ceasefire usually occurs. However, in 1968, the NLF coordinated a series of offensive attacks in concert with its allies against the South Vietnam army and United States military. During the operation, the NLF captured and executed South Vietnamese government officials and sympathizers. South Vietnamese troops and three U.S. Marine battalions counter-attacked. After heavy fighting, the battle ended with a North Vietnamese defeat. The NLF suffered devastating losses, and never regained their former strength. Although the South Vietnamese and the West had won that military battle, President Johnson understood that the Tet Offensive was a political failure for his administration. The "general uprising" he had assumed would ignite among South Vietnamese peasants against the NLF did not materialize. Instead, the NLF pressed on despite their losses for four months.

During this period television coverage of the devastation led to further erosion of support among Americans for continuing the war. A haunting photograph of an NLF guerrilla being shot in the head by Brig. Gen. Nguyen Ngoc Loan, the Chief of South Vietnam's National Police, appeared on the front page of several American newspapers.[25] Then a massacre of over 300 civilians that had occurred in My Lai on March 16, 1968, by soldiers of the U.S. Army, which had been successfully concealed for a year, was uncovered in a series of letters from Vietnam veteran Ronald Ridenhour. The initial report by participants at My Lai stated that 69 NLF soldiers were killed and makes no mention of civilian causalities. However, after intense public outcry, the army investigated the charges and found that during an airborne assault against suspected Viet Cong encampments in the Quang Ngai Province, U.S. Army personnel killed hundreds of civilians. Although Captain Ernest L. Medina, First Platoon Leader; Lt. William Calley; and 14 others were brought to trial by the army, news photos of the carnage, showing a mass of dead children, women and old men led to more emotional and violent antiwar protests in the U.S.[26]

Critics of the war came from Republicans and Democrats alike. Robert F. Kennedy, the former attorney general and senator from New York who was also the younger brother of the slain President John F. Kennedy, began to question the morality of the war. A previous supporter of his brother's policies, Robert Kennedy later called for a halt of the bombings in order to create an environment conducive for negotiations.[27] Kennedy announced his candidacy for the presidency on March 16, 1968, after polls indicated that he was more popular than President Johnson. The Vietnam quagmire and loss of confidence in his presidency were cited as the reasons President Johnson declined to seek reelection.[28]

The antiwar movement was led by religious, pacifist, disarmament, human rights, antiwar, student and civil rights organizations. Groups such as the Clergy and Laity Concerned about Vietnam (CLCV), the American Friends Service Committee (AFSC), the Fellowship for Reconciliation (FOR), Students for a Democratic Society (SDS), the Committee for a Sane Nuclear Policy (SANE), CORE and the Black Panther Party (BPP) provided early leadership for the burgeoning movement. The anti–Vietnam War protestors held teach-ins, sit-ins and demonstrations throughout the U.S. One of the first early, large protest demonstrations was held by SDS—a white student organization—on April 17, 1965. More than 20,000 people participated. On October 21, 1967, a peaceful rally of 50,000 people held in Washington, D.C., ended in considerable violence with "protesters throwing eggs and bottles, and guards clubbing protestors."[29] Organizations affiliated with communism and more radical groups also engaged in antiwar activity. The Weath-ermen, a group of about 300 white activists, embarked on a wave of bomb-ings. Always providing warning of their potential targets, they "claimed to bomb only corporate, military, or government buildings (Socony Oil, the Bank of America, ROTC buildings) . . . "[30] The Weathermen were noted for their alliances with members of the Black Liberation Army (BLA) and the Republic of New Afrika (RNA).[31]

Prominent African American individuals and organizations were intri-cately involved in the antiwar protest during its formative stage. Actors and activists, such as Ruby Dee, Ossie Davis, Coretta Scott King and James Farmer, participated in a SANE-sponsored march in Washington, D.C., on Thanksgiving weekend in 1965.[32] During the spring of 1967, the atrocities occurring in Vietnam finally rended a public address from Dr. Martin L. King Jr. Although he had spoken against the Vietnam War previously, his address from the pulpit of the prestigious Riverside Church in New York City re-ceived the most attention. King's sermon "Time to Break Silence" on April 4, 1967, criticized U.S. policy in Vietnam and set forth his many reasons for disavowing the war. King stated:

> Somehow this madness must cease. We must stop now. I speak as a child of God and brother to the suffering poor of Vietnam. I speak for those whose land is being laid to waste, whose homes are being destroyed, whose culture is being subverted. I speak for the poor of America who are paying the double price of smashed hopes and death and corruption in Vietnam. I speak as a citizen of the world, for the world as it stands aghast at the path we have taken. I speak as an American to the leaders of my own nation. The great initiative in this war is ours. The initiative to stop it must be ours . . . [33]

King was applauded by critics of the war for taking what they considered a principled and moral stance. Undoubtedly he was one of the most respected leaders in the world and surely his public denouncement of U.S. policy in Vietnam would receive enormous attention and credibility. But, holding a different opinion of King's statements were many of his closest advisors and friends who expressed disappointment with his open criticism. Some even distanced themselves from King and the SCLC. The events of that period were recounted by Manning Marable in his book, *Race, Reform and Rebellion*. According to Marable:

> Ralph Bunche urged King either to cease his attacks on the Johnson adminis-tration, or to relinquish his role as a civil rights leader. Rustin, who was ap-pointed director of the A. Philip Randolph Institute, vilified King's stance on

the war. NAACP and Urban League officials privately and publicly attacked King and defended Johnson. Black Republican Edward Brooke, elected to the Senate from Massachusetts on an anti-war platform, swung behind the Vietnam War in 1967 and joined the anti-King chorus. Carl Rowan drafted a vicious, brutal essay against King which appeared in *Reader's Digest Magazine*.[34]

The famed baseball player Jackie Robinson criticized King as well. Concerned that the government and other benefactors of the movement would react negatively to King's statements, the NAACP board voted unanimously not to unite the civil rights and antiwar movements, and attorney and SCLC fundraiser Stanley Levinson advised King that his position on Vietnam could bankrupt the organization. King responded to Levinson, "I don't care if we don't get five cents in the mail."[35] Nonetheless, King's antiwar statement led to increased involvement of people in antiwar demonstrations held soon after and SCLC revenues increased slightly as well. Marches held in New York and San Francisco on April 15, 1967, by the Spring Mobilization to End the War in Vietnam, showed an increase in turnout, with estimates ranging from 100,000 to 400,000 participants.[36]

King's critique of the war was thorough and scathing, and many observers marked it as a critical turning point in his career. In fact, one year to the exact date, King was murdered in Memphis, Tennessee, on April 4, 1968. The assassination of King led to violence, riots and protests in over 100 American cities. Then on June 5, 1968, Robert F. Kennedy was shot and mortally wounded in Los Angeles by Palestinian Sirhan Sirhan, who opposed Kennedy's support for Israel. Robert Kennedy's assassination occurred just after he won the California Democratic presidential primary election.

Richard Milhous Nixon became the fifth president to supervise the conflict in Vietnam. During the presidential election of 1968, Nixon ran on a conservative law and order ticket, which appealed to many voters angry about the violent riots and demonstrations taking place across the country. Nixon also devised a "Southern strategy," which was designed to appeal to white, Southern, middle-class voters. His challengers were George Wallace, the nominee of the American Independent Party and former governor of Alabama, who ran on an anti-desegregationist and pro-Vietnam platform. The Democratic candidate was Johnson's vice president, Hubert H. Humphrey, who campaigned on continuing the Great Society programs. The Vietnam War became a central issue during the campaign and led to divisions within the Democratic Party. Hubert Humphrey tried to distance himself from Johnson's policies in Vietnam, by calling for an end to U.S. bombings. Nonetheless, war protestors hounded Humphrey during the 1968 Democratic Convention held in Chicago and clashed violently with the police. Wallace received 45 electoral votes and almost 10 million popular votes. Nixon won the 1968 election with 301 electoral votes.

Upon assuming the office of the presidency, Nixon planned to disengage the U.S. from the war by first drawing down American troops from Vietnam. His plan, labeled Vietnamization, pledged continued equipment and training to the South Vietnamese, while at the same time strengthening their army in order to turn the fighting over to them. Surprisingly, in March 1969, Nixon ordered bombings of Cambodia to destroy the headquarters and large numbers of soldiers of the NLF. The Cambodian invasion ignited protest among young Americans. On May 4, 1970, at Kent State University, a mass student protest against the Cambodian action escalated into violence resulting in the shooting and killing of four students by the Ohio National Guard. Nine other students were wounded as well. "Within the week of the Kent State killings thirty ROTC buildings were destroyed by fire or bombs. The National Guard, heavily armed, was called out at twenty-one campuses."[37] More than 500 college campuses canceled school in response to the violence and 51 did not reopen at all during that semester.[38] In August of that same year Nixon sent his national security adviser Henry Kissinger to Paris to begin secret discussions with the North Vietnamese. Ho Chi Minh died on September 2, 1969, six years before the country was unified.

For some African Americans, joining the war effort was viewed as a portal to opportunity, economically and socially. Enlistment in the armed forces could bring economic benefits, stature and respect. Certainly, if African Americans were again willing to stand at the threat of death to fight those targeted as the country's enemy, then white America would no longer deny them the full benefits of citizenship. Moreover, by joining the military during this period of lawful integration, it would be possible for African Americans to gain an education, move up in the ranks and acquire officer status, without the stigmas that had been previously attached to the race. John F. Kennedy encouraged that feeling among African Americans when he said, in a radio address to the nation in 1963: "Today we are committed to a worldwide struggle to promote and protect the rights of all who wish to be free. And when Americans are sent to Viet-Nam or West Berlin, we do not ask for whites only. It ought to be possible, therefore, for American students of any color to attend any public institution they select without having to be backed up by troops."[39]

Unlike previous wars, the Vietnam War marked the first major combat deployment of an integrated military. As a result of the battles won by civil rights activists to desegregate the military, by 1953 all new draftees of all races lived in similar conditions, ate together, showered together and trained together, even taking orders from the same African American and white officers. African Americans also served in a myriad of positions in all branches of the military. They were represented in the navy, army, air force and marine corps in all ranks up to colonel, admiral and general. Even still, there was a paucity of African American officers. In 1962, the largest number of African American officers was 3.2 percent in the army, while enlisted men made up 12.2 percent of its population. In the marines, African Americans made up 7.6 percent of enlisted personnel and only 0.2 percent of the officers.[40]

Even though the war was seen as a path toward integration by some African Americans, others publicly opposed the military quandary. Concerns were raised about the "true" motives of the U.S., especially since racism was still prevalent within the country. Activists like Eldridge Cleaver, the former minister of information for the Black Panther Party, asserted that the war's enthusiasts were men and organizations most noted for their racism, including Congressman Strom Thurmond, Arkansas Governor Orval Faubus and members of the John Birch Society. Cleaver wrote in his book *Soul on Ice*:

> Those who most bitterly oppose Negro progress are also the most ardent advocates of a belligerent foreign policy, the most violent castigators of critics of American escalation of war against the Vietnamese people, the hardest to die of the die-hard enthusiasts of armed intervention in the internal affairs of the Dominican Republic and Latin America generally.[41]

Others raised questions about the financial cost of the war and its relationship to African American poverty. A *Newsweek Magazine* poll reported in 1969 that African Americans believed by 7 to 1 that the cost of the Vietnam War directly affected the amount of money that could be spent on antipoverty programs at home.[42]

Anxiety was also articulated about the disparity in the number of African Americans drafted in proportion to their population. "In the 1960s proportionately more blacks (30 percent) than whites (18 percent) from the group qualified for military service were drafted."[43] It was clear that the Southern draft boards remained opposed to African Americans serving equally on the draft boards. An African American male would be drafted regardless of his place in society, whereas a white man could obtain draft deferments easier or avoid the draft by entering the National Guard.[44] Protest against the draft gained national attention when Muhammad Ali, an international people's champion and media darling, shocked the nation by declaring his refusal to serve in Vietnam. This was in stark contrast to the patriotism that had been shown by the preceding people's champion Joe "Brown Bomber" Louis, who had served in the army during World War II. Ali, a towering figure from the African American community, stood firm in his conviction, willing to relinquish his championship title, along with the revenue and privilege that came along with it, and to shoulder the consequent three and a half years of imprisonment.

Similar questions were raised about the high numbers of African Americans being disproportionately killed in the war. After training in military camps, African Americans were generally assigned to combat units. As the war continued into the late 1960s, they began to complain of being disproportionately assigned to combat more than their white counterparts.[45] At one point, African Americans made up 9.8 percent of the military, yet were 14.1 percent of total U.S. fatalities.[46] According to Staff Sergeant Don F. Browne, the uneven number of African Americans dying in combat was even noticed by the Viet Cong. He explained in the book *Bloods: An Oral History of the Vietnam War by Black Veterans*, "To play on the sympathy for the black soldier, the Viet Cong would shoot a white guy, then let the black guy behind him go through, then shoot the next white guy."[47]

Another concern was the deterioration of discipline and morale which resulted from the constant criticisms of the war and the doubt of soldiers about their role in process. Marijuana and heroin were used by soldiers who disregarded military rule. There were also instances of troops refusing to obey direct orders, and some engaged in brutal attacks against those in authority. A common form of attack by rebellious troops was "fragging," in which officers would be killed by fragmentation grenades. Colin Powell, who would later become a high-ranking officer in the military and the first African American secretary of state, even admitted to moving his cot every night to hinder attacks from both the Viet Cong and soldiers who increasingly resented the authority of their officers.[48]

Other concerns raised by African American human and civil rights activists were related to the issue of sovereignty and human rights for indigenous peoples. In his article the "War Crimes Tribunal," James Baldwin asks if "small nations, in this age of super-states and super-powers, will be allowed to work out their own destinies and live as they feel they should."[49] Finally, some African Americans considered the fight for domestic rights and against the Vietnam War as interconnected. Stokely Carmichael said, "The struggle is international. We well know what happens in Vietnam affects our struggle here and what we do affects the Vietnamese people . . . Our destiny cannot be separated."[50]

Ironically, the assassination of Martin Luther King on April 4, 1968, brought great racial turmoil to the armed forces. When the news of King's assassination spread, over 125 American cities immediately erupted into violence, requiring more than 68,000 troops to restore order.[51] But African American soldiers rioted as well. White service men were said to have donned Ku Klux Klan–like outfits, burned crosses, and raised the Confederate flag. Major Colin Powell wrote at the time that while it was understood why African American soldiers rioted, they still had a duty to the country.

The Vietnam War, although it had no official beginning, ended with the signing of the Paris Peace Accords on January 27, 1973, by the governments of North Vietnam, South Vietnam and the United States. As a result of international pressure, a reluctant South Vietnam was forced to sign the "Agreement on Ending the War and Restoring the Peace in Vietnam." The new president of South Vietnam, Nguyễn Văn Thiệu, elected in 1967, protested the agreement because it established a permanent North Vietnamese diplomatic presence in Saigon, while there was no such South Vietnamese counterpart in Hanoi. The Paris Peace agreement also restricted U.S. aid to South Vietnam to replacement quotas only, but there were no such restrictions made upon the Soviet Union and Communist China in their support of North Vietnam. These concessions led to the impression that the North Vietnamese had "won the war," and greatly contributed to rumors that the U.S. was deserting South Vietnam.

Thiệu's fears came true. U.S. withdrawal of their military forces left South Vietnam vulnerable. As a consequence, the military leaders of North Vietnam successfully launched a main-force offensive from its border base areas in Laos and Cambodia that quickly overwhelmed the government in Saigon. With no assistance coming from President Nixon, who was embroiled in the Watergate scandal, which eventually led to his resignation on August 7, 1974, South Vietnam capitulated to the North in April 1975. Vice President Gerald Ford became the new U.S. president. By the time the war ended, more than 1 million Vietnamese were dead and 300,000 missing. The U.S. lost 58,226 military personnel and more than 153,000 were wounded seriously enough to require hospitalization.[52] Although the figures are debated, African American casualties ranged from 12.5 percent to 14 percent.[53]

The documents in this section are a reflection of the commentary by African Americans on the Vietnam War. Ralph Bunche, a Nobel Peace Prize winner for his work in the United Nations Middle East Peace Process and an unparalleled champion of equality for peoples of color at home and abroad, asked, "Would the United States be engaged in that war, if the North Vietnamese and the National Liberation Front were white?" Similar to Bunche, noted Black power advocates, Black nationalists and Black Marxists provided a critique of the Vietnam War. Black Panther Party Minister of Defense Huey Newton considered the U.S. assault on Vietnam a criminal act. On behalf of the Black Panther Party, Newton sent a letter to the National Liberation Front of South Vietnam offering to send troops from his vanguard revolutionary internationalist party to Vietnam to fight against U.S. aggression. Nguyen Thi Dinh, deputy commander of the SVN People's Liberation Armed Forces, accepted Newton's offer for assistance.

Nation of Islam Leader Malcolm X expressed moral outrage at U.S. aggression. Malcolm X was killed in February 1965, before the large-scale multi-racial antiwar movement came to fruition. However, his analysis of the war can be found within his various public addresses. During one speech, "Two Minutes on Vietnam," Malcolm X laments the amount of time he was given to address such an important subject. In addition to Malcolm X, Muhammad Ali, the heavyweight boxing champ of the world, also a member of the Nation of Islam, criticized the Vietnam War. Ali became a conscientious objector to the war and served several years in prison.

Although African American leaders, outside of the military, en masse rejected the war, there were some civilians who spoke out publicly in support of U.S. actions. Alan Keyes, an African American conservative and former ambassador to the Economic and Social Council of the United Nations and then U.S. assistant secretary of state for International Organizations under President Ronald Reagan, revealed his overwhelming support for U.S. policy in his commentary "Blessings of Peace." The journalist Carl Rowan's scathing critique of Dr. King's attempt to link the Vietnam War to U.S. domestic policy is also included in this section.

The country that thousands of African American soldiers left behind to fight an unforgiving war was not the same nation they returned to. The nonviolent protests of Dr. Martin Luther King Jr. had long taken a back seat to groups who demanded self-defense and more radical change, such as the Black Panther Party, the Revolutionary Action Movement (RAM) and the Nation of Islam. "Black Power" and "By Any Means Necessary" became the battle cries for the warriors of the African American community. Specialist 4 Haywood T. Kirkland spoke about his feelings after Vietnam: "I was getting more of a revolutionary, militant attitude. It had begun when I started talking with friends before leaving 'Nam about being a part of the struggle of black people. About contributing in the world since Vietnam was doing nothing for black people. They killed Dr. King just before I came home. I felt used."[54] Like many African American Vietnam veterans, Kirkland eventually turned to crime, pulling one of the largest mail truck robberies in the history of the District of Columbia.

But the U.S. had undoubtedly changed. The majority of African Americans determined to work toward integrating into the country, found ways to align themselves with institutions that had the capacity to promote real change. By 1972 there were 2,264 African American elected officials on the municipal level and 14 African American members in Congress, representing an increase of 21.7 percent from the year previous.[55] Black studies departments emerged throughout the nation to challenge Eurocentric representations of history and enlighten African Americans of their past, present and future. The Black Arts Movement also flourished. Great poets such as Sonia Sanchez and Nikki Giovanni and award-winning authors such as Maya Angelou and Gwendolyn Brooks became household names. African Americans began to integrate into the corporate sector as high-level managers and entrepreneurs.

As in previous wars, African Americans linked U.S. domestic policies with U.S. activities abroad. Viewing the war as a struggle against racism, white supremacy and imperialism, African Americans joined the two movements. They saw no reason to fight or spend valuable resources fighting against those seeking self-determination. The Vietnam War ultimately changed the U.S. by creating an environment that required leaders to respond to its citizens. The war changed African Americans, who fought injustice at home and abroad without apology. The Vietnam War also laid the foundation for a new all-volunteer military, which would require the participation of its minority citizens to survive.

ALAN L. KEYES
(1950–)

Born in a naval hospital on Long Island in New York, Keyes was the fifth child of a U.S. Army sergeant and a teacher. Resulting from his father's military career, the Keyes family traveled frequently. Keyes later worked in the U.S. Foreign Service, was appointed ambassador to the Economic and Social Council of the United Nations and then became U.S. assistant secretary of state for International Organizations under President Ronald Reagan. Keyes is noted for his activism on behalf of the Republican Party and for his outspoken conservative politics. Keyes, a radio talk show host, also ran several unsuccessful campaigns for various political offices, including the U.S. presidency. Below are excerpts made by Keyes in the midst of the Vietnam War, in which he expresses support for the noble work of servicemen and the sacrifices they make on behalf of their country.

The Blessings of Liberty, the Blessings of Life
1967

The sky is hung with the gray clouds of death, so heavy that even the rays of the sun cannot penetrate their leaden veil. While on the earth there are the clouds of a thousand boisterous arms, each sending its messenger of death into the breasts of those within its reach. Perhaps it is Trenton; perhaps New Orleans, then again it might be Argonne or the Marne, Verdun or Iwo Jima. Here falls a soldier, there another, the light of life gone from their faces and their souls, the fluids of their existence moistening the earth to which they fall. All the battlefields of freedom are speckled with their inert forms, and bathed in their precious blood, each one a sacrifice in defense of that sacred and elusive trust men have termed liberty. These men were Americans who died defending the land that has become as one with that liberty, the land whose Constitution established the framework under whose auspices that liberty has flourished.

Thus have Americans chosen to die in defense of their Constitution, yet death is the termination of life and our Constitution today is a living, vital document. The Constitution survived because Americans were willing to die for it but it has increased its vigor and its worth because men have lived for it. They are willing not only to give their lives for their system but to it . . .

What are the blessings of liberty? They are those rights derived from the principle of democracy which insures to the people the right to declare their own destinies, the right to set their own hands to the shaping of their destinies.

. . . The desire within each of us to look upon our future and say, "I shall shape it." The Constitution gives voice to the muted and aid to the defenseless, it gives redress to the offended and protection to the accused, it insures the equity of all, and the rights of those under its protection, it gives . . . nothing. It is the people who must give all if that Constitution is to survive. The Constitution becomes little more than a scrap of quixotic parchment, unless we who are its life give it meaning. Its blood is our blood, its mind is our mind and if we do not live for it and by it, it shall perish . . .

The byword of democracy is action. No amount of past glory was ever substituted for this action. Many are tempted to use the glory of the past and the dead as an excuse for the sullied visage of the present. It is not for us to draw our pretexts from the past but our example. Look again upon those renowned fields of past conflict, look again upon those who gave their lives for this land, its government and its Constitution. Do not take heart from them, for that is within you, do not take courage from them, take action. Even today some may be asked to die, but there is more, much more that can be given to this land, to its Constitution and to ourselves. A man can die only once, but he can live a thousand times in the deeds that he performs. This then is our injunction from the past, our message from the glorious dead, it is to act, to speak, to live for that to which they gave their lives.

We must make this our goal, and in doing so we shall cement our destinies with a long and glorious future. Our cry shall be, "I lived as an American, to make those dreams expressed by past generations a reality." Thus shall the Constitution live on. It shall grow strong from our strength, and exalted from our dedication. Our actions shall reflect the high aspirations which we nurture for this system under which we live. Ours shall be the legacy of the past and the promise of the future, but only if we labor to make it so. Only by action was the legacy formed and preserved, and only by action will that legacy be perpetuated. Thus shall we promulgate the freedom that others worked to transmit to us. Thus shall we insure to ourselves, and through us to all the world, the blessings of liberty.

MALCOLM X
(1925–1965)

Malcolm Little was born in Omaha, Nebraska, but grew up in Lansing, Michigan. As a child he witnessed his home being burned down by the Ku Klux Klan. Two years later his father was murdered and his mother was subsequently placed in a mental institution. Many of his younger years were spent in Michigan detention homes, and his early teen years with a sister in Boston, Massachusetts. After an arrest for burglary, Malcolm Little was sent to prison. While in prison, he converted to the Nation of Islam. After his release Malcolm X became the Honorable Elijah Muhammad's foremost lieutenant. Because of remarks concerning the assassination of President John F. Kennedy, in November of 1963 he was suspended from the Nation of Islam. Malcolm X finally parted with the organization in the spring of 1964 and founded the Muslim Mosque, Inc., and later the Organization of Afro-American Unity (OAAU). He was assassinated on February 21, 1965. The following is Malcolm X's response to a question regarding his opinions on Vietnam. This statement was given in New York City at the Militant Labor Forum in 1965.

On Vietnam
January 7, 1965

Address to Vietnam for two minutes? It's a shame—that's one second. It is, it's a shame. You put the government on the spot when you even mention Vietnam. They feel embarrassed—you notice that? They wish they would not even have to read the newspapers about South Vietnam, and you can't blame them. It's just a trap that they let themselves get into. It's John Foster Dulles they're trying to blame it on, because he's dead.

But they're trapped; they can't get out. You notice I said "they." They are trapped, they can't get out. If they pour more men in, they'll get deeper. If they pull the men out, it's a defeat. And they should have known it in the first place.

France had about 200,000 Frenchmen over there, and the most highly mechanized modern army sitting on this earth. And those little rice farmers ate them up, and their tanks, and everything else. Yes, they did, and France was deeply entrenched, had been there a hundred or more years. Now, if she couldn't stay there and was entrenched, why, you are out of your mind if you think Sam can get in over there.

But we're not supposed to say that. If we say that, we're anti-American, or we're seditious, or we're subversive, or we're advocating something that's not intelligent. So that's two minutes, sir. Now they're turning around and getting in a worse situation in the Congo. They're getting into the Congo the same way they got into South Vietnam. They put Diem over there. Diem took all of their money, all their war equipment and everything else, and got them trapped. Then they killed him.

Yes, they killed him, murdered him in cold blood, him and his brother, Madame Nhu's husband, because they were embarrassed. They found out that they had made him strong and he was turning against them. So they killed him and put big Minh in his place, you know, the fat one. And he wouldn't act right, so they got rid of him and put Khanh in his place. And he's started telling Taylor to get out. You know, when the puppet starts talking back to the puppeteer, the puppeteer is in bad shape.

MUHAMMAD ALI
(1943–)

The world heavyweight boxing champion, Muhammad Ali, whose "slave name" was Cassius M. Clay Jr., registered for the draft in 1960. In 1966 he was classified 1-A (qualified for military service only in an emergency after a physical exam). Ali immediately filed Form 150, a claim for conscientious objector status. Nonetheless, he was convicted in June and sentenced to five years in prison and a $10,000 fine for refusing to be inducted into the armed forces. Below is a transcript of the administrative hearing on August 23, 1966, before Judge Lawrence Grauman, who was appointed by the Justice Department as the hearing officer for Ali's appeal.

Conscientious Objector
August 23, 1966

. . . I was raised as a Baptist and while being raised as a Baptist I never understood the teachings of the Christian preacher, and I never understood why Heaven was in the sky and I never understood why Hell was under the ground and I never understood why so-called Negroes had to turn their cheeks and have to take all the punishment while everyone else defends themselves and fought back . . .

I never understood why when I went to the Olympics in Rome, Italy, and won the Gold Medal for great America and came back to Kentucky, I couldn't go in a downtown restaurant, and I always wondered why everything in it was white.

I always wondered these things and I am saying this to tell you why I accepted the religion of Islam the minute I heard it when in 1961, while I was walking down the streets of Miami, Florida, a Muslim walked up to me and asked me would I like to come to Muhammad's Mosque and listen to the teachings of Islam and listen to why we are the lost people . . . and this sounded interesting and, by me being a person of common sense, I went to the Mosque to listen and immediately, on entering the Mosque—I would say the first half hour after being there—I immediately wanted to know what I could do to become a member . . .

The minister of the Mosque was preaching on the subject of why are we called Negroes . . . I asked questions on the subject and he gave me good answers and he also said that we do not have our own names . . . and all intelligent people on earth are named after their people of their land and their ancestors . . . We call ourselves Culpepper, Mr. Tree, Mr. Bird, Mr. Clay, Mr. Washington, and he said these were names of our slave masters, and by me being an intelligent man and the Lord blessing me with five senses, I have to accept it because there have been write-ups in the Louisville papers where my father and [I] were named after great white slave father named Cassius Marcellus Clay.

So, I had to accept this, and he also told us that the proper name of God is Allah and that Honorable Elijah Muhammad was taught by Allah for three and one half years to teach the so-called Negroes the true knowledge of his God, the true knowledge of his religion, true knowledge of his names and his future and not to force himself on whites and not to beg whites to come clean up rats, but to clean up our own neighborhoods, respect our women, do something for ourselves, quit smoking, quit drinking, and obey the laws of the land and respect those in authority.

Immediately, I had to check and see who is Elijah Muhammad. . . . So after finding out who he was, I had to convince myself that he was a divine man from God because I knew I would have to give up a lot . . .

At least six hours of the day I'm somewhere walking and talking, or going to schools or colleges all over the country, Muslim temples, and there are some fifty odd mosques all over and constantly—in Chicago, I have this thirty-passenger bus that, daily, we go out bringing in busloads of people to the Mosque. And now I'm talking to the Blackstone Rangers, which is the worst Negro group in the wilderness of North America who have killed at least one hundred boys since they've been in Chicago, and the police—nobody could handle them and I was blessed with, all praise due Allah, I was lucky enough to round up twenty-one of the ringleaders and . . . they say they are ashamed for the way they have been shooting and killing and . . . I have convinced them to come together. So this is what I do as far as ministering and talking is concerned. . . . But when I'm really in training and in camp for fights, a week or two before the fight I don't have time, not too much time, because I really burn a lot of energy debating and answering questions, so during training we don't do too much ministering . . . When they say that "You would not bring in five hundred people," inasmuch as I do sometimes, "You would not bring these five hundred people if you were not the champ," well if it is not for Allah and the teachings of Islam, I would not be champ and I could not hold my title so strongly after being champion. . . . On the average it's about thirty people a night.

. . . It's the teaching of Islam that has given me the proudness and boldness to say, "I'm the Greatest," and lift my chin and which has enabled me to be one of the most popular athletes on earth . . . and this is the only thing now keeping me out of night clubs and places that serve alcoholics like liquor and demonstrations where I could become popular in leading people.

. . . I have, I would say, and excuse the expression, caught more hell for being Muslim, even before the Army talk came up, with my wife and boxing, and the movie rights that I turned down, the advertisements, the TV commercials, the royalties and endorsements that I have had to turn down and I have all this before the Army came up and it's not just saying that I would not participate in war, but we actually believe it and feel it. . . . We are awfully serious in anything we say about fighting a war, adultery, or fornication, or drinking alcohol, cursing, using profanity, or anything that is against the teachings of the Holy Qur'an and the Honorable Elijah Muhammad, and Allah is who we really fear. . . . I was registered as a Muslim about three weeks prior to the first Sonny Liston fight and then if I had gone to any type of war or done anything morally or spiritually that wasn't in accord with the teachings of the Honorable Elijah Muhammad I would say I . . . was a conscientious objector the hour that I first heard the teachings of the Honorable Elijah Muhammad. . . . But I would be lying to you if I said to you that at the moment I was determined that I would be a conscientious objector because war was not pending at that time. I had nothing to worry about and I had nothing about war on my mind . . .

. . . The only time I really thought about it—the only time that I was conscious that I would have to make a decision was the first time they mentioned going to take a physical.

. . . The first time I failed I had no need to say anything. They said I wasn't fit. The second time . . . I took the test in Kentucky and they advised me and said I wasn't fit. Then they reclassified me [1-A]. I came out with that outburst and my lawyer went in with the conscientious objector bit and it was known then. . . . I have no need the first two times that I was called up, because they never accepted me, but I'm sure that if they had called me when I was in Miami and I had passed the test then I would have had to just say I'm a conscientious objector. But I didn't know nothing about the law and if I knew the right procedures at the time I would have moved accordingly. But I'm new—I'm learning each day about how this appeal and things go, but I didn't know at the time. I had no idea how they worked.

. . . When I go in a ring, my intention is not to be violent in the way of fighting to kill, or going to war, or hurting [anyone] physically; it's not of my faith. We have a referee in the ring, and I'm known as a scientific fighter and as a fast, classy boxer, and we have three judges and we have an ambulance and we have doctors and we are not one nation against another or one race against another or one religion against another. It's just the art of boxing, and more people get killed in at least ten other sports than they do boxing. But I don't consider myself a violent man because next month I will be in the ring with Carl Mildenberger of Germany, prancing and dancing and moving and jabbing and if he hit me low, points will be taken away. In war you shoot, you kill, you fight, and you kill babies and you kill old ladies and men and there's no such thing as laws and regulations.

Mentally, some fighters are violent; mentally, some fighters go in the ring angry and they have a grudge and they are violent in their approach towards a fellow and many of them lose their head and get beaten, but I never get violent. I never lose my head and I'm known for being a calm, cool boxer and I never feel as though I'm violent and I never fight and act like I'm violent. . . . I don't consider them blows of violence, not me. . . . Now football players, they elbow each other and they run over each other and they cheat each other and break each other's backs and they are paralyzed, and I don't think that's referred to as intentionally going out to do violence. As far as hitting a man is concerned, my intention is not to really hurt [anyone]. In war it's your intention to kill and to hurt and put another man out.

. . . It would be no trouble for me to accept conscientious objector [status] on the basis that I'll go into the armed services boxing exhibitions in Vietnam, or traveling the country at the expense of the government or living in the easy life and not having to get out in the mud and fight and shoot. . . . If it wasn't against my conscience to do it, I would easily do it. I wouldn't raise all this court stuff and I wouldn't go through all of this and lose and give up millions that I gave up and my image with the American public, that I would say is completely dead and ruined because of us in here now, and so I wouldn't turn down so many millions and jeopardize my life walking the streets of the South and all of the Americans with no bodyguard if I wasn't sincere in every bit of what the Holy Qur'an and the teachings of the Honorable Elijah Muhammad tell us and it is that we are not to participate in wars . . . on the side of nonbelievers, and this is a Christian country and this is not a Muslim country. . . . The Holy Qur'an teaches us that we do not take part . . . in any part of war unless declared by Al-lah himself, or unless it's an Islamic World War, or a Holy War, and it goes as far (the Holy Qur'an is talking still) as saying we are not even as much as aid the infidels or nonbelievers in Islam, even to as much as handing them a cup of water during battle.

. . . Many people confuse the teachings of the Honorable Elijah Muhammad with the teachings of hate, and the only hate I know, as far as the teachings of the Honorable Elijah Muhammad is concerned, is that we hate the way that we've been treated for four hundred years. We hate the way that our pregnant women are being kicked around the streets; we hate the way innocent Negroes have been shot and lynched and killed outright, but the killers are not—never been caught. We hate that we're the first fired and last hired and we hate the way we have served so faithfully for this country in all wars and have spent three hun-dred and ten long years [in] enabling America to have fifty of the richest states on the planet. . . . We do not hate white people. We hate the way certain peo-ple have treated and we also, now, have a better knowledge of ourselves. We have a better knowledge of nature. We have a better knowledge of where we should go, where we shouldn't go, what we should do, what we shouldn't do.

So, we are taught by the Honorable Elijah Muhammad that if a wild lion broke in, say this courtroom now, I would break out—not because I hate lions. I don't have a chance to hate the lion. I just know his nature is not like mine and we can't get along. . . .

So, we do not hate white people. We want to go for ourselves and do for our-selves and get some of this earth that we can call our own like other intelligent civilized humans do on the planet Earth. . . . We are not haters. [The Honorable

Elijah Muhammad] teaches us to love. We don't break laws. We are in no riots, no demonstrations. We pray five times a day. We fast three days a week and we constantly worship at the Mosque three nights a week. We are peaceful people and we are not haters, but we are victims of hate.

The Holy Bible . . . teaches that though I dwell in the valley of the shadow of death I fear no evil, and we are taught by the Honorable Elijah Muhammad that [no] one dwells in the shadow of death [than] the so-called Negro is here in the wilderness of North America. . . . So, by our teaching and by we believing in God, whose law is self-preservation, we are taught not to be the aggressor, but defend ourselves if attacked, and a man cannot defend himself if he knows not how, and we are taught that not only America, but all countries, all civilized governments have armies and have guns around their shores, not necessarily to attack or be the aggressor, but to defend America or our country or whatever it may be if we are attacked. So we, the Muslims, to keep in physical condition, we do learn how to defend ourselves if we are attacked since we are attacked daily through the streets of America and have been attacked without justification for the past four hundred years.

. . . We are only preparing for the war of Armageddon divinely. We are taught that the battle will be between good and right, truth and falsehood, and we are taught that the battle will be between God and the Devil. . . . If it will be a physical war we will look foolish with what we call military training, which is judo and learning how to wrestle and box and run. The war of Armageddon will be a real nuclear war, and nothing that judo can do and nothing that karate can do or take part in. So therefore, this is for our health and self-defense while we are here if we are attacked. But when Armageddon itself comes . . . we won't participate in putting out physical energy ourselves.

. . . It is impossible for us to prepare for Armageddon since we don't make bullets, we don't make guns, we don't control food. It's foolish for us, or for an intelligent government to think that we, the ten per cent of America, are hiding in some secret little meeting places in this country preparing to fight these atomic bombs, the jets, these helicopters all types of guns you have that haven't been revealed to the public yet. . . . But as far as putting it out in a war, it would be like a beanshooter running up against a big German tank, so we are only preparing for Allah in a spiritual way.

. . . We just hope that we are spiritually and physically and internally and mentally and morally able to get on the side of Allah and the Honorable Elijah Muhammad when Armageddon starts.

MARTIN LUTHER KING JR.
(1929–1968)

Born in Atlanta, Georgia, Martin Luther King Jr.'s father and grandfather had been ministers involved in fighting for civil rights. Graduating from Morehouse College in 1948, King Jr. considered careers in medicine and law, but chose the ministry. While a seminarian he became deeply interested in the nonviolent philosophies and strategies of Mahatma Gandhi. In 1955, King tested Gandhi's practices on U.S. soil, when the Montgomery bus boycott began after NAACP secretary Rosa Parks refused to relinquish her seat to a white passenger. In 1957, King cofounded the Southern Christian Leadership Conference (SCLC). In 1964, King received the Nobel Peace Prize. The following are excerpts from King's anti–Vietnam War speech made at the historic Riverside Church in New York.

A Time to Break the Silence
April 4, 1967

I come to this magnificent house tonight because my country leaves me no other choice . . . The recent statements of your executive committee [Clergy and Laity Concerned about Vietnam] are the sentiments of my own heart . . . "A time comes when silence is betrayal." That time has come for us in relation to Vietnam . . .

I have seven major reasons for bringing Vietnam into the field of my moral vision. There is at the outset a very obvious connection between the war in Vietnam and the struggle I, and others, have been waging in America. A few years ago there was a shining moment in the struggle . . .

Then came the build-up in Vietnam, and I watched the program [the War on Poverty] broken and eviscerated as if it were some idle political plaything of society gone mad on war, and I knew that America would never invest the necessary funds or energies in rehabilitation of its poor so long as adventures like Vietnam continued to draw men and skills and money like some demonic destructive suction tube. So I was increasingly compelled to see the war as an enemy of the poor and to attack it as such.

Perhaps the more tragic recognition of reality took place when it became clear to me that the war was doing far more than devastating brothers and their husbands to fight and to die in extraordinarily high proportions relative to the rest of the population. We were taking the Black young men who had been crippled by our society and sending them 8,000 miles away to guarantee liberties in Southeast Asia which they had been repeatedly faced with cruel irony of watching Negro and white boys on TV screens as they kill and die together for a nation that has been unable to seat them together in the same schools. So we watch the brutal solidarity burning the huts of the poor village, but we realize that they would never live on the same block in Detroit. I could not be silent in face of such cruel manipulation of the poor.

My third reason moves to an even deeper level of awareness, for it grows out of my experience in ghettos of the north over the last three years—especially the last three summers. As I have walked among the desperate, rejected and angry young men I have told them that Molotov cocktails and rifles would not solve their problems. I have tried to offer them my deepest compassion while maintaining my conviction that social change comes most meaningfully through non-violent action. But they asked—and rightly so—what about Vietnam? They asked if our own nation wasn't using massive doses of violence to solve its problems, to bring about the changes it wanted. Their questions hit home, and I knew that I could never again raise my voice against the violence of oppressed in the ghettos without having first spoken clearly to the greatest purveyor of violence in the world today—my own government. For the sake of the hundreds of thousands trembling under our violence, I cannot be silent . . .

And as I ponder the madness of Vietnam and search within myself for the ways to understand and respond with compassion, my mind goes constantly toward the people of that peninsula. I speak now not of the soldiers of each side, not of the junta in Saigon, but simply of the people who have been living under the curse of war for almost three continuous decades now. I think of them too because it is clear to me that there will be no meaningful solution there until some attempt is made to know them and hear their broken cries.

They must see Americans as strange liberators. The Vietnamese people proclaimed their own independence in 1945 after a combined French and Japanese occupation, and before the communist revolution in China. They were led by Ho Chi Minh. Even though they quoted the American Declaration of Independence in their own document of freedom, we refused to recognize them. Instead, we decided to support France in its re-conquest of her former colony.

Our government felt then that Vietnamese people were not "ready" for independence, and we again fell victim to the deadly western arrogance that has poisoned the international atmosphere for so long. With the tragic decision we rejected a revolutionary government seeking self-determination, and a government that had been established not by China (for whom the Vietnamese have no great love) but clearly indigenous forces that included some communists. For the peasants this new government meant real land reform, one of the most important needs in their lives.

For nine years following 1945 we denied the people of Vietnam the right of independence. For nine years we vigorously supported the French in their abortive effort to re-colonize Vietnam.

Before the ends of the war we were meeting 80 per cent of the French war costs. Even before the French were defeated at Dien Bien Phu, they began to despair of reckless action, but we did not. We encouraged them with our huge financial and military supplies to continue the war even after they had lost the will. Soon we would be paying almost the full costs of this tragic attempt at re-colonization.

After the French were defeated it looked as if independence and land reform would come again through the Geneva agreements. But instead there came the United States, determined that Ho should not unify the temporarily divided nation, and the peasants watched again as we supported one of the most vicious modern dictators—our chosen man, Premier Diem. The peasants watched and cringed as Diem ruthlessly routed out all opposition, supported their extortionist landlords and refused even to discuss re-unification with the North. The peasants watched as all this was presided over by U.S. influence and then by increasing numbers of U.S. troops who came to help quell the insurgency that Diem's methods had aroused. When Diem was overthrown they may have been happy, but the long line of military dictatorships seemed to offer no real change—especially in terms of their need for land and peace.

The only change came from America as we increased our troop commitments in support of governments which were singularly corrupt, inept and without popular support. All the while the people read our leaflets and received regular promises of peace and democracy—and land reform. Now they languish under our bombs and consider us—not their fellow Vietnamese—the real enemy. They move sadly and apathetically as we herd them off the land of their fathers into concentration camps where minimal social needs are rarely met. They know they must move or be destroyed by our bombs. So they go—primarily women and children and the aged.

They watch as we poison their water, as we kill a million of their crops. They must weep as the bulldozers roar through their areas preparing to destroy the precious trees. Wander into the hospitals, with at least 20 casualties from American firepower for one "Vietcong"-inflicted injury. So far we may have killed a million of them—mostly children. They wander into the towns and see thousands of children, homeless, without clothes, running in packs on the streets like animals. They see the children degraded by our soldiers as they beg for food. They see the children selling their sisters to our soldiers, soliciting for their mothers.

What do the peasants think as we ally ourselves with the landlords and as we refuse to put any action into our many words concerning land reform? What do they think as we test out our latest weapons on them, just as the Germans tested out new medicine and new tortures in the concentration camps of Europe? Where are the roots of the independent Vietnam we claim to be building? Is it among these voiceless ones?

We have destroyed their two most cherished institutions: the family and the village. We have destroyed their land and their crops. We have cooperated in the crushing of the nation's only non-communist revolutionary party political force—unified Buddhist Church. We have supported the enemies of the peasants of Saigon. We have corrupted their women and children and killed their men. What liberators!

Now there is little left to build on—save bitterness. Soon the only solid physical foundations remaining will be found at our military bases and in the concrete of the concentration camps we call fortified hamlets. The peasants may well wonder if we plan to build our new Vietnam on such grounds as these? Could we blame them for such thoughts? We must speak for them and raise the questions they cannot raise. These too are our brothers.

Perhaps, the more difficult but no less necessary task is to speak for those who have been designated as our enemies. What of the National Liberation Front—that strangely anonymous group we call VC (Viet Cong) or Communists? What must they think of us in America when they realize that we permitted the repression and cruelty of Diem which helped to bring them into being as a resistance group in the South? What do they think of our condoning the violence which led to their own taking up of arms? How can they believe in our integrity when now we speak of "aggression from the North" as if there were nothing more essential to the war? How can they trust us when now we charge them with violence while we pour every new weapon of death into their land? Surely we must understand their feelings even if we do not condone their actions. Surely we must see that the men we supported pressed them to their violence. Surely we must see that our own computerized plans of destruction simply dwarf their greatest acts.

How do they judge us when our officials know that their membership is less than 25 percent communist and yet insist on giving them the blanket name? What must they be thinking when they know that we are aware of their control of major sections of Vietnam and yet we appear ready to allow national elections in which this highly organized politicized parallel government will have no part? They ask how we can speak of free elections when the Saigon press is censored and controlled by the military junta. And they are surely right to wonder what kind of new government we plan to help form without them—the only party in real touch with the peasants. They question our political goals and they deny the reality of a peace settlement from which they will be excluded. Their questions are frighteningly relevant. Is our nation planning to build on political myth again and then shore it up with the power of new violence?

Here is the true meaning and value of compassion and non-violence when it helps us to see the enemy's point of view, to hear his questions, to know his assessment of ourselves. For from his view we may indeed see the basic weakness of our own condition, and if we are mature, we may learn and grow and profit from the wisdom of the brothers who are called the opposition.

So, too, with Hanoi. In the North, where our bombs now pummel the land, and our mines endanger the waterways, we are met by a deep understandable mistrust. To speak for them is to explain this lack of confidence in western words, and especially their distrust of American intentions now. In Hanoi are the men who led the nation to independence against the Japanese and the French, the men who sought membership in the French commonwealth and were betrayed by weakness of Paris and the willfulness of the colonial armies. It was they who led a second struggle against French domination at tremendous costs, and then were persuaded to give up the land they controlled between the 13th and 17th parallel as a temporary measure at Geneva. After 1954 they watched us conspire with Diem to prevent elections which would have surely brought Ho Chi Minh to power over a United Vietnam, and they realized they had been betrayed again.

When we ask why they do not leap to negotiate, these things must be remembered. Also it must be clear that the leaders of Hanoi considered the presence of American troops in support of the Diem regime to have been the initial military breach of the Geneva Agreement concerning foreign troops, and they remind us that they did not begin to send in any large number of supplies or men until American forces had moved into the tens of thousands.

Hanoi remembers how our leaders refused to tell us the truth about the earlier North Vietnamese overtures for peace, how the President claimed that none existed when they had clearly been made. Ho Chi Minh has watched as America has spoken of peace and built up its forces, and now he has surely heard of increasing international rumors of American plans for an invasion of the North. He knows the bombing and shelling and mining we are doing are part of traditional pre-invasion strategy. Perhaps only his sense of humor and irony can save him when he hears the most powerful nation of the world speaking of aggression as it drops thousands of bombs on a poor weak nation more than 8,000 miles away from its shores.

At this point I should make it clear that while I have tried these last few minutes to give a voice to the voiceless on Vietnam and to understand the arguments of those who are called enemy, I am as deeply concerned about our troops there as anything else. For it occurs to me that what we are submitting them to in Vietnam is not simply the brutalizing process that goes on in any war where armies face each other and seek to destroy. We are adding cynicism to the process of death, for they must know after a short period there that none of the things we claim to be fighting for really are involved. Before long they must know that their government has sent them into a struggle among Vietnamese, and the more sophisticated surely realize that we are on the side of the wealthy and the secure while we create a hell for the poor.

Somehow this madness must cease. We must stop now. I speak as a child of God and brother to the suffering poor of Vietnam. I speak for those whose land is being laid to waste, whose homes are being destroyed, whose culture is being subverted. I speak for the poor of America who are paying the double price of smashed hopes and death and corruption in Vietnam. I speak as a citizen of the world, for the world as it stands aghast at the path we have taken. I speak as an American to the leaders of my own nation. The great initiative in this war is ours. The initiative to stop it must be ours . . .

In 1957 a sensitive American official overseas said that it seemed to him that our nation was on the wrong side of a world revolution. During the past 10 years we have seen emerge a pattern of suppression which now has justified the presence of U.S. military "advisors" in Venezuela. This need to maintain social stability for our investments accounts for the counter-revolutionary action of American forces in Guatemala. It tells why American helicopters are being used against rebels in Peru. It is with such activity in mind that the words of the late John F. Kennedy come back to haunt us. Five years ago he said, "Those who make peaceful revolution impossible will make violent revolution inevitable."

Increasingly, by choice or by accident, this is the role our nation has taken— the role of those who make peaceful revolution impossible by refusing to give up the privileges and the pleasures that come from the immense profits of overseas investment.

I am convinced that if we are on the right side of the world revolution, we as a nation must undergo a radical revolution of values. We must rapidly begin the shift from a "thing-oriented" society to a "person-oriented" society. When machines and computers, profit motives and property rights are considered more important than people, the giant triplets of racism, materialism, and militarism are incapable of being conquered.

A true revolution of values will soon cause us to question the fairness and justice of many of our past and present policies. On the one hand we are called to play the Good Samaritan on life's roadside; but that will be only an initial act. One day we must come to see that the whole Jericho Road must be transformed so that men and women will not be constantly beaten and robbed as they make their journey on Life's highway. True compassion is more than flinging a coin to a beggar; it is not haphazard and superficial. It comes to see that an edifice which produces beggars needs re-structuring. A true revolution of values will soon look uneasily on the glaring contrast of poverty and wealth. With righteous indignation, it will look across the seas and see individual capitalists of the West investing huge sums of money in Asia, Africa and South America, only to take the profits out with no concern for the social betterment of the countries, and say: "This is not just." It will look at our alliance with the landed gentry of Latin America and say: "This is not just." The Western arrogance of feeling that it has everything to teach others and nothing to learn from them is not just. A true revolution of values will lay hands on the world order and say of war: "This way of settling differences is not just." This business of burning human beings with napalm, of filling our nation's homes with orphans and widows, of injecting poisonous drugs of hate into the veins of peoples normally humane, of sending men home from dark and bloody battlefields physically handicapped and psychologically deranged, cannot be reconciled with wisdom, justice, and love. A nation that continues year after year to spend more money on military defense than on programs of social uplift is approaching spiritual death . . .

These are revolutionary times. All over the globe men are revolting against old systems of exploitation and oppression and out of the wombs of a frail world new systems of justice and equality are being born. The shirtless and barefoot people of the land are rising up as never before. "The people who sat in darkness have seen a great light." We in the West must support these revolutions. It is a sad fact that, because of comfort, complacency, a morbid fear of Communism, and our proneness to adjust to injustice, the Western nations that initiated so much of the revolutionary spirit of the modern world have now become the arch anti-revolutionaries. This has driven many to feel that only Marxism has the revolutionary spirit. Therefore, Communism is a judgment against our failure to make democracy real and follow through on the revolutionaries that we initiated. Our only hope today lies in our ability to recapture the revolutionary spirit and go out into a sometimes hostile world declaring eternal hostility to poverty, racism, and militarism. With this powerful commitment we shall boldly challenge the status quo and unjust mores and thereby speed the day when "every valley shall be exalted, and every mountain and hill shall be made low, and the crooked shall be made straight and the rough places plain."

A genuine revolution of values means in the final analysis that our loyalties must become ecumenical rather then sectional. Every nation must now develop an overriding loyalty to mankind as a whole in order to preserve the best in their individual societies . . .

CARL THOMAS ROWAN
(1925–2000)

Carl T. Rowan was born in Ravenscroft, Tennessee. He was a well-known journalist, writer, and radio and television commentator who was one of the first African American officers in the U.S. Navy during World War II. Rowan graduated from Oberlin College and earned a master's degree in journalism from the University of Minnesota. Renowned for his extensive reporting on the civil rights movement, Rowan was considered an "insider" who was accepted into several presidential administrations. Rowan joined the Kennedy administration in 1961 as deputy assistant secretary of state for public affairs; served as U.S. ambassador to Finland and then director of the United States Information Agency. Rowan, a syndicated columnist for over 100 newspapers, was a frequent panelist on public affairs television shows. He was also the author of several books, including South of Freedom *(1953),* Wait Till Next Year: The Life Story of Jackie Robinson *(1960),* Breaking Barriers: A Memoir *(1991), and* Dream Makers, Dream Breakers: The World of Justice Thurgood Marshall *(1993). In this article, Rowan sets forth his criticism of Martin Luther King's activism against the Vietnam War.*

Martin Luther King's Tragic Decision
September 1967

What has caused him to jeopardize, by his ill-advised pronouncements on Vietnam, the movement he has so ably served? Another distinguished Negro looks at the man and his motives.

On a crisp, clear evening last April 4, the Rev. Martin Luther King stood in New York City's Riverside Church and delivered the most scathing denunciation of U.S. involvement in Vietnam ever made by so prominent an American. He labeled the United States "the greatest purveyor of violence in the world today" and accused it of "cruel manipulation of the poor." He said that the people of Vietnam "watch as we poison their water, as we kill a million acres of their crops."

He stated that U.S. troops "may have killed a million South Vietnamese civilians—mostly children." He said that American soldiers "test out our latest weapons" on the peasants of South Vietnam "just as the Germans tested out new medicine and new tortures in the concentration camps of Europe." He accused President Johnson of lying about peace overtures from Hanoi, and urged Americans to become "conscientious objectors."

Reaction across the nation and around the world was immediate and explosive. Radios Moscow and Peking picked up King's words and spread them to distant capitals. In the White House, a Presidential aide shouted, "My God, King has given a speech on Vietnam that goes right down the commie line!" President Johnson, reading the wire-service reports, flushed with anger.

Civil-rights leaders wrung their hands and began to plan steps to take the already splintered movement for Negro equality out from under the onus of King's broadside. Such prominent Negroes as Roy Wilkins, executive director of the National Association for the Advancement of Colored People, Ralph Bunche, Nobel Prize-winning United Nations under-secretary, and Sen. Edward Brooke disagreed publicly with King. The directors of Freedom House called the program that King advocated "demagogic and irresponsible in its attack on our government." The *Washington Post*, long supporter of King, said, "Dr. King has done a grave injury to the great struggle to remove ancient abuses from our public life. He has diminished his usefulness to his cause, to his country and to his people."

What sort of person is this man who has been awarded a Nobel Peace Prize and denounced as a knave, all within three years? What do Martin Luther King and his recent actions mean to the nation and to the searing disputes that now rend the civil-rights movement? . . .

"Breastplate of Righteousness." How did King rise to the pinnacle? He had charisma—a down-to-earth sincerity, an ability to wear the mantle of the church in such a way as to suggest a special closeness to God. He won the grudging admiration of white Americans and the support of millions of foreigners through his dignity, his willingness to take verbal abuse, to go to jail quietly—and to turn the other check in the process—in order to achieve his goals. He seemed impervious to provocation. He earned the reputation of a selfless leader whose devotion and wisdom were larger than life.

When a group of badgered, beaten Negroes in Gadsden, Ala., were on the verge of violence, King asked them to put down their arms. "Get the weapon of non-violence, the breastplate of righteousness, the armor of truth, and just keep marching," he pleaded. They did. And when the young minister said to whites, "We will match your capacity to inflict suffering with our capacity to endure suffering. We will not hate you, but we cannot in all good conscience obey your unjust laws," he disarmed many who held latent hostility toward the Negro.

"There is no arrogance in him, no intellectual posturing," reported the *New York Times* in 1961. "He voices no bitterness against the whites who have handled him roughly." If he became involved in crisis after crisis—the restaurant sit-in Atlanta in 1960; demonstrations in Albany, Ga., in 1961; the explosive Birmingham protests of 1963; the Selma, Ala., march of 1964—it was because, as one of his aides said, "You've got to have a crisis to bargain with. To take a moderate approach, hoping to get white help, doesn't work."

The Halo Slips. But, inexplicably, something began to happen after a while. King seemed to develop an exaggerated appraisal of how much he and his crisis techniques were responsible for the race-relations progress that had been made.

He could, indeed, make a pretty convincing argument that it was the crisis he and his followers precipitated in Birmingham in 1963 that capped the Negro's revolution and won the support necessary for the passage of the civil-rights laws of 1964 and 1965. But other Negro leaders, while not belittling demonstrations, argued that the Negro could never forgo a reliance on the law. They pointed out that Negroes might still be walking instead of riding buses in Montgomery had the lawyers not won their case in the Supreme Court. They said that the Negro had to continue to seek strong legislation and just court decisions. They argued that the cause required a shrewd, sometimes sophisticated wooing of public opinion.

Negroes had, in fact, begun to grow uneasy about King. He no longer seemed to be the selfless leader of the 1950's. There was grumbling that his trips to jail looked like publicity stunts. When arrested in Albany, Ga., in 1961, he had declared dramatically that he would stay behind bars until the city desegregated public facilities. Two days later, he was out on bail. In St. Augustine, Fla., after getting Negroes fired up for massive demonstrations, he went to jail amid great fanfare. But two days later he was bailed out again, so he could receive an honorary degree at Yale University.

Sinister Murmurings. King really gave both critics and admirers serious cause for concern in 1965, when he began to talk about foreign policy. In July of that year, he told a Los Angeles group that the issues of racial injustice, poverty and war are "inextricably bound together." When advisers expressed doubts about the wisdom of linking the three, he retorted: "One cannot be just concerned with civil rights. It is very nice to drink milk at an un-segregated lunch counter—but not when there is strontium 90 in it."

A month later, he announced that he intended to write President Ho Chi Minh of North Vietnam, and the leaders of South Vietnam, Russia and the United States in an effort to move the war to the conference table.

Then, in September 1965, he called on Arthur Goldberg, chief U.S. delegate to the United Nations, and urged the United States to press for a U.N. seat for Communist China. Also, he asked for a halt in American air strikes on North Vietnam, and he recommended negotiations with the Vietcong. At this point, even some of his strongest supports began to demur.

The New York *Herald Tribune* said: "Dr. King is already committed to a massive, unfinished task in an area in which he has great influence. He can only dissipate that influence by venturing into fields that are strange to him." In a harsher comment, liberal columnist Max Freedman asked, "Is he casting about for a role in Vietnam because the civil-rights struggle is no longer adequate to his own estimate of his talents?" NAACP leader Roy Wilkins, Whitney Young, executive director of the Urban League, Socialist leader Norman Thomas, and Bayard Rustin, a chief planner of the great civil-rights march on Washington in 1963 and himself a pacifist, all pleaded in vain with King not to wade into the Vietnam controversy.

Why did King reject the advice of his old civil-rights colleagues? Some say it was a matter of ego—that he was convinced that since he was the most influential Negro in the United States, President Johnson would *have* to listen to him and alter U.S. policy in Vietnam. Others revived a more sinister speculation that had been whispered around Capitol Hill and in the nation's newsrooms for more than two years—talk of communists influencing the actions and words of the young minister. This talk disturbed other civil-rights leaders more than anything else.

I report this not to endorse what King and many others will consider a "guilt by association" smear, but because of the threat that these allegations represent to the civil-rights movement. When King was simply challenging Jim Crow, murmurings that he was associating with, or influenced by, "enemies of the United States" had only limited impact. Most Congressmen and editors knew that American Negroes did not need a communist to tell them that they disliked being herded into the rear of buses, the balconies of theaters, the back doors of restaurants or a ramshackle school across the briar patch. But now that King has become deeply involved in a conflict where the United States is in direct combat with communists the murmurings are likely to produce powerfully hostile reactions. They cannot help but imperil chances of passage of the civil-rights bill that would protect civil-rights workers in the South and make housing discrimination illegal.

New Strain. King answered his critics. He had become convinced, he said in his April 4 speech at New York's Riverside Church, that America would never invest the necessary funds or energies in rehabilitation of its poor "so long as adventures like Vietnam continue to draw men and skills and money like some demonic destructive suction tube." He told the Riverside audience that "we are taking black young men who have been crippled by our society and sending them 8000 miles away to guarantee liberties in Southeast Asia which they have not found in southwest Georgia and East Harlem."

The latter is an old cry that some Negroes have uttered in every American war. But in no conflict has a Negro with King's prestige urged Negroes to shun battle because they have nothing to fight for. King must have assumed that the "new Negro," full of frustration as he is, would be sympathetic to this argument. But a recent Harris survey showed that almost one of every two Negroes believes that King is wrong—and another 27 percent reserved judgment.

I find this opposition to King remarkable considering the amount of emotion and anger involved in the Negro revolution. It suggests that most Negroes are proud of the integrated performance of colored GIs in Vietnam; that most Negroes still think of America as *their* country and do not want to seem unpatriotic.

Beyond doubt, King's speech at Riverside Church and his subsequent remarks have put a new strain and new burdens on the civil-rights movement. He has become *persona non grata* to Lyndon Johnson, a fact that he may consider of no consequence. It is also likely that his former friends in Congress will never again listen to or be moved by him the way they were in the past. This, too, may not bother King. But it can make the difference between poverty and well-being for millions of Negroes who cannot break the vicious circle of poverty and un-preparedness that imprisons them unless the President provides leadership and Congress provides the circle-breaking programs and laws.

Martin Luther King has alienated many of the Negro's friends and armed the Negro's foes, in both parties, by creating the impression that the Negro is disloyal. By urging Negroes not to respond to the draft or to fight in Vietnam, he has taken a tack that many Americans of all races consider utterly irresponsible.

It is a tragic irony that there should be any doubt about the Negro's loyalty to his country—especially doubt created by Martin Luther King, who has helped as much as any one man to make America truly the Negro's country, too.

RALPH BUNCHE
(1904–1971)

Born in Detroit, Michigan, just after the turn of the century, Bunche grew up confronting the realities of race and class in the U.S. His father, a barber, had an all-white clientele. His grandmother, who could pass for white, had been born into slavery. At ten the family moved to Albuquerque, New Mexico, and then eventually to Los Angeles. Bunche attended UCLA on a basketball scholarship and graduated summa cum laude. He earned master's degrees in government and international relations at Harvard University. Afterwards he joined the faculty at Howard University. During World War II, Bunche served in the Office of Strategic Service, and was very active in the planning of the United Nations in 1945. In 1947, Bunche joined the permanent secretariat at the United Nations. In 1950, he was awarded a Nobel Peace Prize for his negotiation of the Arab-Israeli truce. The following is an excerpt of Bunche's last speech, delivered in 1969 at the Fifth East-West Philosophers Conference in Honolulu, Hawaii. The focal point of the speech is on race and the Vietnam War. Bunche also expresses his concern for oppressed people of color throughout the world.

On Race and Vietnam
July 10, 1969

The Vietnam War has very deep racial implications. There, the United States is fighting "yellow" men who are also considered Communists. This makes it rather easy for Americans to rationalize their involvement and to broadcast daily the number of those despised little yellow men that the American and South Vietnamese forces have killed. The derogatory name Americans give their North Vietnamese opponents is "Viet Cong," which literally means, I understand, "yellow bandits." Would the United States be engaged in that war if the North Vietnamese and the National Liberation Front were white?

The black Americans who have fought, or are asked to fight in Vietnam, found themselves in a paradoxical position. They must employ every violent means at hand to maim and kill the enemy—North Vietnamese and the South Vietnamese enrolled in the National Liberation Front. This is to protect the rights and freedom of 17 million South Vietnamese, a considerable number of whom obviously resent and resist American presence in their country. On the other hand, there are 22 million black Americans whose Constitutional rights are being violated flagrantly and persistently. But the black veteran from Vietnam, like all other blacks, is not permitted to do very much about that. He cannot resort to force in his own country, certainly. He cannot "disturb the peace" and must respect "law and order," although white citizens are not compelled to respect the law of the Constitution where its application to black citizens is concerned. The black veteran, along with all others, may in some places even be denied permission to demonstrate or to march peacefully in protestation against racism and racial injustice. The government requires black citizens to fight for the South Vietnamese but will not even empower the issuance of a cease-and-desist order to white employers who flagrantly deny employment to black men and women solely on grounds of race. That, in the eyes of the senator from Abraham Lincoln's state, Everett Dirksen, would be intolerable "harassment" of business . . .

Now, after a long-enduring faith and patience without parallel, I think, in human history, the black citizen has lost his patience—and his fear—and is, I am afraid, also losing his faith in the American establishment and system insofar as their promises to him are concerned. He is demanding, not appealing, nowadays, and his demands begin to take unexpected courses—courses which could only be born out of profound frustration and complete disillusionment.

HUEY P. NEWTON
(1942–1989)

Born in Monroe, Louisiana, as an infant Newton and his family moved to Oakland, California. Illiterate when he left high school, Newton eventually learned to read and later studied at Oakland City College and San Francisco Law School. Along with Bobby Seale, in October of 1966 Newton cofounded the Black Panther Party for Self-Defense. In 1974, after he was charged with murder, Newton escaped to Cuba for three years. He was acquitted of the charges after his return to the U.S. In 1980, Newton earned a Ph.D. from the University of California, with a dissertation titled "War against the Panthers: Study of Repression in America." Below is a letter written to the National Liberation Front of South Vietnam by Huey Newton on behalf of the Black Panther Party. In the letter, Newton offers assistance to the North Vietnamese in their war against imperialism and U.S. aggression. The reply from Nguyen Thi Dinh, deputy commander of the SVN People's Liberation Armed Forces, which recognizes the work of the members of the Black Panther Party as comrades-in-arms, is included in this passage.

Letter to the National Liberation Front of South Vietnam
August 29, 1970

In the spirit of international revolutionary solidarity the Black Panther Party hereby offers to the National Liberation Front and Provisional Revolutionary Government of South Vietnam an undetermined number of troops to assist you in your fight against American imperialism. It is appropriate for the Black Panther Party to take this action at this time in recognition of the fact that your struggle is also our struggle, for we recognize that our common enemy is the American imperialist who is the leader of international bourgeois domination. There is not one fascist or reactionary government in the world today that could stand without the support of United States imperialism. Therefore our problem is international, and we offer these troops in recognition of the necessity for international alliances to deal with this problem.

Such alliances will advance the struggle toward the final act of dealing with American imperialism. The Black Panther Party views the United States as the "city" of the world, while we view the nations of Africa, Asia and Latin America as the "countryside" of the world. The developing countries are like the Sierra Maestra in Cuba and the United States is like Havana. We note that in Cuba the people's army set up bases in the Sierra Maestra and choked off Havana because it was dependent upon the raw materials of the countryside. After they won all the battles in this countryside the last and final act was for the people to march upon Havana.

The Black Panther Party believes that the revolutionary process will operate in a similar fashion on an international level. A small ruling circle of seventy-six major companies controls the American economy. This elite not only exploits and oppresses Black people within the United States; they are exploiting and oppressing everyone in the world because of the overdeveloped nature of capitalism. Having expanded industry within the United States until it can grow no more, and depleting the raw materials of this nation, they have run amuck abroad in their attempts to extend their economic domination. To end this oppression we must liberate the developing nation—the countryside of the world—and then our final act will be the strike against the "city." As one nation is liberated elsewhere it gives us a better chance to be free here.

The Black Panther Party recognizes that we have certain national problems confined to the continental United States, but we are also aware that while our oppressor has domestic problems these do not stop him from oppressing people all over the world. Therefore we will keep fighting and resisting within the "city" so as to cause as much turmoil as possible and aid our brothers by dividing the troops of the ruling circle.

The Black Panther Party offers these troops because we are the vanguard party of revolutionary internationalists who give up all claim to nationalism. We take this position because the United States has acted in a very chauvinistic manner and lost its claim to nationalism. The United States is an empire which has raped the world to build its wealth here. Therefore the United States is not a nation. It is a government of international capitalists and inasmuch as they have exploited the world to accumulate wealth this country belongs to the world. The Black Panther Party contends that the United States lost its right to claim nation-hood when it used its nationalism as a chauvinistic base to become an empire.

On the other hand, the developing countries have every right to claim nation-hood, because they have not exploited anyone. The nationalism of which they speak is simply their rightful claim to autonomy, self-determination and a liberated base from which to fight the international bourgeoisie.

The Black Panther Party supports the claim to nationhood of the developing countries and we embrace their struggle from our position as revolutionary internationalists. We cannot be nationalists when our country is not a nation but an empire. We contend that it is time to open the gates of this country and share the technological knowledge and wealth with the peoples of the world.

History has bestowed upon the Black Panther Party the obligation to take these steps and thereby advance Marxism-Leninism to an even higher level along the path to a socialist state, and then a non-state. This obligation springs both from the dialectical forces in operation at this time and our history as an oppressed Black colony. The fact that our ancestors were kidnapped and forced to come to the United States has destroyed our feeling of nationhood. Because our long cultural heritage was broken we have come to rely less on our history for guidance, and seek our guidance from the future. Everything we do is based upon functionalism and pragmatism, and because we look to the future for salvation we are in a position to become the most progressive and dynamic people on the earth, constantly in motion and progressing, rather than becoming stagnated by the bonds of the past.

Taking these things under consideration, it is no accident that the vanguard party—without chauvinism or a sense of nationhood—should be the Black Panther Party. Our struggle for liberation is based upon justice and equality for all men. Thus we are interested in the people of any territory where the crack of the oppressor's whip may be heard. We have the historical obligation to take the concept of internationalism to its final conclusion—the destruction of statehood itself. This will lead us into the era where the withering away of the state will occur and men will extend their hand in friendship throughout the world.

This is the world view of the Black Panther Party and in the spirit of revolutionary internationalism, solidarity and friendship we offer these troops to the National Liberation Front and Provisional Government of South Vietnam and to the people of the world.

A Reply:
Report
Letter from Nguyen Thi Dinh:
October 31, 1970
To: Mr. Huey P. Newton
Minister of Defense
Black Panther Party

Dear Comrade:

We are deeply moved by your letter informing us that the Black Panther Party is intending to send to the National Liberation Front and the Provisional Revolutionary Government of the Republic of South Vietnam an undetermined number of troops, assisting us in our struggle against the U.S. imperialist aggressors.

This news was communicated to all the cadres and fighters of the PLAF in South Vietnam; and all of us are delighted to get more comrades-in-arms, so brave as you, on the very soil of the United States.

On behalf of the cadres and fighters of the SVN PLAF I would welcome your noble deed and convey to you our sincere thanks for your warm support to our struggle against U.S. aggression for national salvation. We consider it as a great contribution from your side, an important event of the peace and democratic movement in the United States giving us active support, a friendly gesture voicing determination to fight side-by side with the South Vietnamese people for the victory of the common cause revolution.

In the spirit of international solidarity, you have put forward your responsibility towards history, towards the necessity of uniting actions, sharing joys and sorrows, participating in the struggle against U.S. imperialism.

You have highly appreciated the close relation between our both uncompromising struggles against U.S. imperialism, our common enemy. It is well known now that the U.S. government is the most warlike, not only oppresses and exploits the American people, especially the Black and the coloured ones, but also oppresses and exploits various peoples the world over by all means, irrespective of morality and justice. They have the hunger of dollars and profits which they deprived by the most barbarous ways, including genocide, as they have acted for years in South Vietnam.

In the past years, your just struggle in the U.S. has stimulated us to strengthen unity, and rush forward towards bigger success. . . . Dear Comrades, our struggle yet faces a lot of hardships, but we are determined to overcome all difficulties, unite with all progressive forces, to heighten our revolutionary vigilance, to persist in our struggle, resolutely to fight and win. We are sure to win complete victory.

So are our thinkings: At present, the struggles, right in the United States or on the SVN battle-fields, are both making positive contributions for national liberation and safeguarding the world peace. Therefore, your persistent and ever-developing struggle is the most active support to our resistance against U.S. aggression for national salvation.

With profound gratitude, we take notice of your enthusiastic proposal; when necessary, we shall call for your volunteers to assist us.

We are firmly confident that your just cause will enjoy sympathy, warm and strong support of the people at home and abroad, and will win complete victory; and our ever closer coordinated struggle surely stop the bloody hands of the U.S. imperialist and surely contribute winning independence, freedom, democracy, and genuine peace.

Best greetings for "unity, militancy, and victory" from the SVN people's liberation fighters.

Nguyen Thi Dinh,
Deputy Commander
Of the SVN People's
Liberation Armed Forces
Republic of South Vietnam

Notes

1. Sources on the civil rights movement: Harvard Sitkoff, *The Struggle for Black Equality* (New York: Hill & Wang, 1981); Taylor Branch, *Parting the Waters: America in the King Years 1954–63* (New York: Simon & Schuster, 1988); Taylor Branch, *Pillar of Fire: America in the King Years 1963–65* (New York: Simon & Schuster, 1998); Manning Marable, *Race, Reform and Rebellion: The Second Reconstruction in Black America, 1945–1990* (Jackson: University Press of Mississippi, 1991); and Clayborne

Carson, ed., *Civil Rights Chronicle: The African American Struggle for Freedom* (Lincolnwood, Ill.: Legacy, 2003).

2. Mamie Till Mobley and Christopher Benson, *Death of Innocence: The Story of the Hate Crime That Changed America* (New York: Random House, 2003); Stephen Whitfield, *A Death in the Delta: The Story of Emmett Till* (Baltimore, Md.: Johns Hopkins University Press, 1991).

3. William Bradford Huie, "The Shocking Story of Approved Killing in Mississippi," *Look Magazine*, January 24, 1956.

4. Black Panther Party 10-Point Platform in *Off the Pigs: The History and the Literature of the Black Panther Party* (Metuchen, N.J.: Scarecrow Press, 1976), 54–57.

5. James Ciment, *Atlas of African American History* (New York: Checkmark Books, 2001), 173.

6. U.S. Riot Commission, *Report of the National Advisory Commission on Civil Disorders, New York Times* ed. (New York: Dutton, 1968), 10.

7. "Statement of Policy by the National Security Council on United States Objectives and Courses of Action with Respect to Southeast Asia," document 13, in *The Pentagon Papers*, Gravel ed., vol. 1 (NSC 124/2, June 25, 1952), 384–90.

8. Stanley Karnow, *Vietnam: A History* (New York: Penguin, 1997).

9. For Ho Chi Minh's views on race relations in America and Europe, see William J. Duiker, *Ho Chi Minh* (New York: Hyperion, 2000), 50–51; Bernard B. Fall, *The Two Viet-Nams: A Political and Military Analysis* (New York: Praeger, 1963), 87–88; David Dellinger, "Conversations with Ho," *Liberation*, October 1969, 3–4.

10. George McTurnan Kahin and John W. Lewis, *The United States in Vietnam: An Analysis in Depth of the History of America's Involvement in Vietnam* (New York: Dial, 1969), 11–17; Gerald J. DeGroot, *A Noble Cause: America and the Vietnam War* (New York: Pearson Education, 2000).

11. Ho Chi Minh, *Selected Works*, vol. 3 (Hanoi, 1960–1962), 17–21.

12. Kahin and Lewis, *The United States in Vietnam*, 32.

13. "Agreement on the Cessation of Hostilities in Vietnam, July 20, 1954," in *Further Documents Relating to the Discussion of Indochina at the Geneva Conference, June 16–July 21, 1954*. Miscellaneous No. 20 (1954), Command Paper 9239 (London: Her Majesty's Stationery Office, 1954). Reprinted in Kahin and Lewis, *The United States in Vietnam*, 348–76.

14. William Duiker, *Historical Dictionary of Vietnam* (Metuchen, N.J.: Scarecrow Press, 1988), 201. Edwin E. Moise asserts that Diem received 98 percent of the vote; see *Historical Dictionary of the Vietnam War* (Lanham, Md.: Scarecrow Press, 2001), 275.

15. Moise, *Historical Dictionary of the Vietnam War*, 15.

16. Moise, *Historical Dictionary of the Vietnam War*, 52–53.

17. Maxwell Meyersohn, comp., *Memorable Quotations of John F. Kennedy* (New York: Crowell, 1965), 50–53.

18. Moise, *Historical Dictionary of the Vietnam War*.

19. Daniel C. Hallin, *The Uncensored War: The Media and Vietnam* (Berkeley: University of California Press, 1989), 43.

20. Department of State Bulletin, *President Johnson's Baltimore Speech, April 1965* (Washington, D.C.: U.S. Government Printing Office, April 26, 1965). Reprinted in Kahin and Lewis, *The United States in Vietnam*, 423.

21. Moise, *Historical Dictionary of the Vietnam War*.

22. Department of State Bulletin, *Joint Resolution, U.S. Congress, "Tonkin Gulf Resolution*, August 7, 1964 (Washington, D.C.: U.S. Government Printing Office)

23. Moise, *Historical Dictionary of the Vietnam War*.

24. "Ho Chi Minh's Letter to Communist Leaders, January 24, 1966." Hanoi Radio, January 28, 1966. Reprinted in Kahin and Lewis, *The United States in Vietnam*, 438.

25. "Grim and Ghastly Picture," *New York Daily News*, Feb. 3, 1968; George A. Baily and Lawrence W. Lichty, "Rough Justice on a Saigon Street: A Gatekeeper Study of the NBC's Tet Execution Film," *Journalism Quarterly* 49 (Summer 1972): 274.

26. For additional discussion of the media coverage of the Vietnam War and the My Lai massacre, see William M. Hammond, *Reporting Vietnam: Media and Military at War* (Lawrence: University Press of Kansas, 1998), 187–200.

27. Jack Newfield and Robert Kennedy: *A Memoir* (New York: Dutton, 1969), 70–71, 125–29, 134–41.

28. David L. Anderson, *The Columbia Guide to the Vietnam War* (New York: Columbia University Press, 2002), 131.

29. Moise, *Historical Dictionary of the Vietnam War*, 35.

30. Nancy Zaroulis and Gerald Sullivan, *Who Spoke Up? American Protest against the War in Vietnam 1963–1975* (Garden City, N.Y.: Doubleday, 1984), 314.

31. Zaroulis and Sullivan, *Who Spoke Up?* 314.

32. Zaroulis and Sullivan, *Who Spoke Up?* 63.

33. "Martin Luther King Jr.: A Time to Break Silence, Nov. 2, 1967," in *Freedomways Reader*, ed. Esther Cooper Jackson (Boulder, Colo.: Westview, 2000), 173.

34. Marable, *Race, Reform and Rebellion*, 104. For additional information on criticisms of King from his allies, see David L. Lewis, *King: A Biography* (Urbana: University of Illinois Press, 1978), 357–58.

35. Lewis, *King*, 357.

36. Zaroulis and Sullivan, *Who Spoke Up?* 110.

37. For additional information on the Kent State Protest, see Zaroulis and Sullivan, *Who Spoke Up?* 319–23.

38. Zaroulis and Sullivan, *Who Spoke Up?* 319–23.

39. President John F. Kennedy, "Radio and Television Report to the American People on Civil Rights," The White House, June 11, 1963, 468.

40. Peter Bergman, *The Chronological History of the Negro in America* (New York: Harper & Row, 1969), 576.

41. Eldridge Cleaver, *Soul on Ice* (New York: Dell, 1968), 166.

42. "Report from Black America—A *Newsweek* Poll," *Newsweek Magazine*, June 30, 1968.

43. John Hope Franklin and Alfred A. Moss Jr., *From Slavery to Freedom: A History of African Americans*, 7th ed. (New York: McGraw-Hill, 1994), 488.

44. Robert B. Edgerton, *Hidden Heroism: Black Soldiers in America's Wars* (Boulder, Colo.: Westview Press, 2002), 180.

45. Edgerton, *Hidden Heroism*, 182.

46. Bergman, *Chronological History*, 613.

47. For Staff Sergeant Don F. Browne's comments see Wallace Terry, *Bloods: An Oral History of the Vietnam War by Black Veterans* (New York: Ballantine, 1984), 167.

48. Colin Powell with Joseph E. Persico, *My American Journey: Colin Powell* (New York: Random House, 1995), 133.

49. James Baldwin, "The War Crimes Tribunal," in *Vietnam and Black America: An Anthology of Protest and Resistance*, ed. Claude Taylor (New York: Anchor, 1973), 101.

50. Stokely Carmichael, "Black Power and the Third World," printed in a pamphlet by the Southern Student Organizing Committee (Nashville, Tenn.: Southern Student Organizing Committee, 1967), 1.

51. Bergman, *Chronological History*, 609.

52. Moise, *Historical Dictionary of the Vietnam War*, 75–77.

53. Moise, *Historical Dictionary of the Vietnam War*, 75–77, and Stanley I. Kutler, ed., *Encyclopedia of the Vietnam War* (New York: Macmillan, 1997), 105.

54. Specialist 4 Haywood T. "The Kid" Kirkland, in Terry, *Bloods*, 101.

55. Joint Center for Political Studies, "Number of Blacks in Selected Categories of Elected Officials, 1970–1985" (Washington, D.C.).

~

CHAPTER NINE

Persian Gulf War:
Civil Rights, Human Wrongs

1991

The end of the Cold War and the demise of communism did not signal a resolution to the problems of racial injustice and inequality in the U.S. Segregation and disparate treatment had taken their toll on the African American community. When compared to white Americans, African Americans still experienced disproportionate unemployment, poverty, and inferior education and healthcare. By the late 1970s, the median wealth of Black households was $24,608, well below the median figure for whites at $68,891.[1] Millions of African Americans lived in overcrowded apartments, without adequate services such as heat and plumbing facilities. African Americans also suffered from higher death rates than whites from tuberculosis, hypertension, sexually transmitted diseases and infant mortality.[2] Despite these disparities, a subtle backlash against affirmative action programs occurred. Eventually, critics of the program gained legal backing from the Supreme Court in its landmark ruling in *Regents of the University of California v. Bakke* (1978). Allan Bakke, a white applicant to the University of California at Davis School of Medicine, was denied admission on the basis of the school's affirmative action policy. Bakke charged the university with "reverse discrimination," and claimed that the school did not consider his strong academic record, in comparison to several "disadvantaged" students who had scored lower on the entrance exam. The Supreme Court overturned the university's quota system, and after *Bakke*, similar quota and set-aside programs in employment and government contracts were declared illegal.

One way in which African Americans mobilized against the racial back-lash was to support political candidates who appeared sympathetic to their plight. Jimmy Carter, a Southerner, benefited from African American elec-toral mobilization when he ran for the Democratic nomination for president in 1976. Carter was endorsed by noted Black leaders such as Congressman Andrew Young and former SNCC activist John Lewis, and 78.8 percent of African American delegates had pledged to support Carter even before the 1978 Democratic Convention.[3] Even though Carter was a pro–civil rights candidate, he was still able to maintain the support of whites throughout the race. Another bonus for Carter was that his Republican opponent, President Gerald Ford, had been severely weakened by his pardon of former President Nixon for his role in the Watergate scandal.

As the 39th president of the U.S., Jimmy Carter appointed African Amer-icans to high-level positions at rates much higher than the Nixon and Ford administrations combined.[4] He was most highly praised for his appointments of Andrew Young as ambassador to the United Nations and Patricia Roberts Harris, former dean of Howard University's Law School, as the first Black woman to serve as a cabinet member in her appointment as the secretary of the Department of Housing. Carter also appointed attorney Clifford Alexan-der to serve as secretary of the army. Alexander, the first African American to lead a service branch, became well known for his refusal to sign a promo-tions list compiled by the Army Review Board after he discovered that there were no African American candidates on the list.[5]

Aside from the high-profile appointments, Carter's relationship with African Americans deteriorated during his presidency. Unemployment for non-whites edged upward to 13.6 percent and thousands more African American families fell below the federal poverty levels. Carter was also ac-cused of failing to work aggressively on behalf of the Balanced Growth Act of 1976, known as the Humphrey-Hawkins Bill, which would have mandated full employment for American citizens, and declared that the federal gov-ernment should "meet human and national needs" such as day care, public housing and public transportation. The act further called for the creation of a Job Guarantee Office, which would be "responsible for actually enforcing the right of all able and willing adults to a job."[6] Although a watered-down version of the measure was eventually passed, African American leaders had to pressure Carter to lobby on its behalf.

Disappointment with Carter's performance was evidenced by low African American voter turnout during the 1980 primaries. Political scientist Hanes Walton noted that "blacks turned out in the 1976 primaries from 30–40 per-cent of their voting strength. By the 1980 presidential primaries, this had declined to below 20–30 percent."[7] Walton attributes African American inactivity during the primaries to Carter's "perceived bad performance." Vernon Jordan, executive director of the National Urban League, stated during an address to the 1977 annual meeting that the Carter administration had "fallen short of blacks' expectations in terms of policies, program, and people."[8]

African Americans did not support Carter's opponent either. In 1980, Ronald Reagan, the former governor of California and movie actor, was "elected with the lowest percentage of Black votes of any previous Republican candidate. Fewer than one out of every ten Blacks had voted for him."[9] Reagan defeated Carter by what were considered landslide margins. About 51 percent of the popular vote went to Reagan and 41 percent for Carter. However, Reagan won 91 percent of the electoral vote, because Carter's support was not concentrated in any electoral regions. Carter only won six states and the District of Columbia.[10]

There were additional reasons for Carter's loss. Domestically, he was dogged by the high interest rates and double-digit inflation that the country experienced during his presidency. He also received constant criticism for the high levels of government spending and the rising price of imported oil. Carter created more disaffection from the business community when he signed legislation bolstering the Social Security system through a staggered increase in the payroll tax.

On international affairs, during the early years of the Carter presidency, he departed from his predecessor's emphasis on containing the Soviet Union and worked to promote human rights. During a speech in May 1977 at Notre Dame University in Indiana, Carter indicated that his foreign policy would be liberated from the inordinate fear of communism. According to Carter, "For too many years we have been willing to adopt the flawed and erroneous principles of our adversaries, sometime abandoning our values for theirs . . . This approach failed, with Vietnam the best example of its intellectual and moral poverty."[11] Led by U.S. Ambassador to the United Nations Andrew Young and Secretary of State Cyrus Vance, the Carter administration worked to actualize the concept of a "global community." Consequently, under Carter, the U.S. supported majority rule in Rhodesia, South Africa and Namibia, three countries dominated by a white minority. Because the threat of atomic annihilation had been subdued, Carter entered into negotiations with Leonid Brezhnev, the leader of the Soviet Union, to ratify the Strategic Arms Limitations Talks (SALT II) Treaty, which sought to curtail the manufacturing of nuclear weapons. Although both parties reached an agreement and held a signing ceremony, the treaty was never ratified after the Soviet Union invaded Afghanistan late in 1979. In response to the invasion, the U.S. boycotted the Moscow Olympics under Carter's orders. After that, Carter moved farther to the right and began to rebuild U.S. military power.[12]

On other global issues, President Carter continued Richard Nixon's policy of "normalizing" relations with the People's Republic of China, granting the country full diplomatic and trade relations, thereby ending official relations with the Republic of China. Carter also unofficially recognized Taiwan through the Taiwan Relations Act. Furthermore, the Carter administration succeeded in having the Senate approve the Panama Canal Treaty, which handed over the canal to the people of Panama. Perhaps his proudest accomplishment was the Camp David Accords, which signaled a peace agreement between Israel and Egypt.

One of the lowest points for the Carter administration was the Iranian hostage crisis. Beginning on November 1, 1979, thousands of protestors in Iran gathered around the U.S. embassy in Tehran to demonstrate against the U.S. and Israel. The protests were sparked by the U.S. agreement to allow the deposed Shah of Iran into the United States for cancer treatment. On November 4, approximately 500 Iranian students seized the main embassy building. U.S. Marines guarding the embassy were thoroughly outnumbered, and out of 90 occupants, 66 were taken captive, including three who were taken from the Iranian Foreign Ministry. Fourteen women, African Americans and non-U.S. captives were soon released, leaving 52 hostages remaining until their release in January 1981. The new fundamentalist Islamic leader of Iran, Ayatollah Ruhollah Khomeini justified the taking of the hostages as a reaction to American refusal to hand over the Shah for trial to answer for crimes committed against the "Iranian Nation." Carter struggled for 444 days to release the hostages and authorized a failed rescue attempt that eventually led to the resignation of Secretary of State Cyrus Vance.[13] Although Carter managed to negotiate release of the hostages on his last day in office, the Iran hostage crisis was seen as a sign of his weakness as president.

Another low point for President Carter, which especially hurt his relationship with African Americans, was the forced resignation of Andrew Young. On August 15, 1979, Young resigned from his post as U.S. ambassador to the UN amidst the uproar over his unauthorized conversation with the PLO observer at the UN, Zehdi Labib Terzi. According to those critical of Young, he had broken the U.S. pledge to have no dealings with the PLO until the organization accepted Israel's right to exist. In defending his actions, Young characterized his meeting with Terzi as inadvertent, and asserted that no substantive business was discussed. On the other side, Yehuda Blum, the Israeli delegate to the UN, believed that Young had violated U.S. policy, and on August 14, the Israeli government lodged a formal protest in Washington and Jerusalem.[14] The controversy had a negative impact on Black-Jewish relations. Israeli and Jewish American leaders supported the ouster of Young, while African Americans en masse began to question their relationship with the Jewish community.[15]

Ultimately, Carter lost his reelection campaign as a result of the economic slump experienced during his presidency, the disaffection of African Americans and the Iran hostage crisis. Ronald Reagan, on the other hand, won the election by appealing to corporate, pro-business and anti-communist sentiments. On the issue of his relationship with African Americans, Reagan was considered unfriendly and insensitive. During his campaign, Reagan appeared with former Dixiecrat leader Strom Thurmond. He also questioned the need for such policies as welfare, affirmative action and busing to promote integration.[16] Reagan's early appointees to the federal courts and Justice Department were critical of government efforts to implement civil rights legislation, and suggested that the racially exclusionary policies of white educational institutions such as Bob Jones University, located in South Carolina, might not violate the law.

As president, Reagan ignored liberal and progressive leaders who reflected the views of most African Americans and appointed African American conservatives to his administration. Clarence Thomas, a Black Republican, became the assistant secretary for civil rights in the Department of Education, while Colin Powell was appointed the national security advisor from 1987 to 1989. Clarence Thomas was later appointed as the head of the Equal Employment Opportunity Commission (EEOC), the organization charged with combating workplace discrimination. Thomas replaced Eleanor Holmes Norton, a pro–civil rights activist lawyer appointed under Carter. While head of the EEOC, Thomas literally worked to abolish the rules that would render the EEOC more effective. According to Anita Hill, the former employee of the EEOC who later charged Thomas with sexual harassment, Clarence Thomas "was part of the administration's transition team which had recommended the change in policy to reduce the burden an employer bore for supervisors who harassed their workers."[17] Thomas had also abandoned requirements that employers meet timetables and numerical goals in hiring minority workers. Moreover, during Thomas's tenure, the EEOC's budget and staff declined, which reduced its ability to investigate discrimination complaints.[18]

Civil rights leader Reverend Jesse Jackson challenged the conservative offensive by running for the Democratic presidential nomination in 1984 and 1988. Organized under the banner of the Rainbow Coalition, Jackson declared that his mission was to build a new functional Rainbow Coalition of the "rejected, spanning lines of color, sex, age, religion, race, region and national origin" to constitute the new majority in American politics.[19] The campaign challenged Reagan's budget cuts that reduced support for poor and minority Americans and Reagan's massive increase in military expenditures. On domestic issues, Jackson argued for voting rights enforcement, passage of the Equal Rights Amendment, corporate responsibility and a new emphasis on helping the poor.

On foreign affairs, Jackson declared that the basis of U.S. policy should rest on human rights and peace, which contrasted with his Democratic opponent Walter Mondale's emphasis on attaining a strong and secure United States. Jackson's foreign policy platform reflected the views of his center-left constituency. On the Middle East, Jackson called for mutual recognition of Israel and Palestine and advocated U.S. communication with the Palestine Liberation Organization (PLO). On Central America and the Caribbean, Jackson's supporters deplored U.S. aid and assistance to dictators and other destabilizing forces in the region, including the governments of El Salvador, Guatemala and radical rebel groups such as the Contras of Nicaragua. Jackson also denounced the U.S. invasion of Grenada in 1983, which the U.S. claimed was to rescue American medical students and to restore democracy in the island-nation that was led by the socialist-leaning New Jewel Movement. According to Jackson, the real goal of "Operation Fury" was to fight communism by replacing the new government with a pro-American regime.[20] In order to demonstrate his expertise in international affairs, Jackson flew to Syria and negotiated the rescue of U.S. Navy pilot Lt. Robert O. Goodman Jr., who was shot down and captured by the Syrians while engaged in air strikes.[21]

Although Jackson did not win the election, he received significant support in 1984 by winning 3.5 million votes, "almost four hundred delegates and a campaign schedule of events maintained in at least forty-four states and six foreign countries."[22] There is also evidence that Jackson's candidacy mobilized large numbers of new African American voters. According to election-day exit polls, about 12 percent of African Americans voted for the first time. In 1988, Jackson came in second place out of a field of eight candidates, losing only to Michael Dukakis, the governor of Massachusetts. Jackson, however, won seven million votes and registered two million more. The increased African American voter turnout led to the installation of Douglas Wilder as governor to Virginia. Wilder became the first African American governor elected to hold office in 1989.

During the height of the Jackson campaign, the African American community established its formidability in foreign affairs by its work to abolish apartheid in South Africa. In 1948, the South African government had formally instituted a policy of separating Blacks, whites, coloreds and Indians by law. Under the banner of "apartheid" the races were separated, each with their own homelands and institutions.[23] In practice, legislation and other rules developed under the apartheid system prevented non-white people from having a vote or influence in the country's policies. Whites reserved the most valuable and profitable land for themselves and divided the remaining 13 percent into "homelands" for Blacks and others. Hence, the majority population resided on less land, of poor quality, and suffered from inferior education, medical care and other public services.

Up until 1986, President Reagan pursued a policy of "constructive engagement" with the apartheid government, which essentially meant that through closer and improved relationships the U.S. could force the South African government to change. For this reason, Reagan vetoed congressional legislation that would have imposed economic sanctions on South Africa. The Jackson campaign responded to Reagan by advocating for sanctions, the release of political prisoners in South Africa and financial support for other African nations. With Randall Robinson at its helm, the newly formed African American foreign policy lobby Transafrica organized protests and advocated for divestiture of U.S. companies from South Africa. Other organizations such as Artists United against Apartheid in South Africa joined the effort by using their celebrity to bring more attention to the horrors of apartheid. The Congressional Black Caucus (CBC) repeatedly called for sanctions, but the Reagan administration refused to budge from its policy of constructive engagement. In 1986, Ronald Dellums, a member of the CBC from California, introduced the Comprehensive Anti-Apartheid Act, which called for sanctions against South Africa and set forth the preconditions for lifting them, including the release of all political prisoners. Reagan's veto of the bill was overridden.

After serving two terms, President Reagan's vice president and former CIA director George H. W. Bush defeated Democratic Governor Michael Dukakis of Massachusetts in the presidential election campaign of 1988. Bush's victory was predicated in part on his ability to label Dukakis a "tax and spend" liberal who was soft on crime. In order to further capitalize on white American fears of African Americans, the Bush campaign attacked Dukakis's opposition to capital punishment by highlighting the crimes of Willie Horton, a Black convicted murderer who raped and assaulted a white woman while on a weekend furlough. African Americans were insulted by the coded racial stereotypes and refused to support Bush's presidential bid, despite his pro–civil rights rhetoric. Eighty-six percent of African Americans voted for Dukakis, while Bush received 11 percent of their vote.[24]

Issues of race not only pervaded the Bush campaign, but were insidiously present throughout his tenure as president. Indeed, Bush sought to distinguish himself from Ronald Reagan's racial legacy at first. He met with African American leaders, including the CBC, on several occasions; increased the budget of the EEOC to $185 million—its largest fiscal allocation in history; and directed more federal funds to African American educational institutions. Bush also appointed African Americans to high-level positions, including Colin Powell as the first African American chairman of the Joint Chiefs of Staff and Arthur Fletcher, the former executive director of the United Negro College Fund, as chairman of the Civil Rights Commission. But ultimately Bush retreated to Reagan's racial policies by showing lukewarm support for civil rights. In 1990, the Bush administration proposed to prohibit colleges and universities from awarding scholarships based on race.[25] Bush also appointed African American conservatives to key positions, with what seemed to be the only prerequisite: that they show hostility to civil rights. A case in point was the nomination of Clarence Thomas, the former director of the EEOC as the second Supreme Court justice to replace Thurgood Marshall. Notwithstanding questions of Thomas's competence to hold the title of Supreme Court justice, given his lack of experience as a jurist, the NAACP, the Urban League and the National Organization for Women opposed the appointment based on Thomas's criticism of affirmative action and suspicions that Thomas might not be a supporter of *Roe v. Wade*. Thomas's appointment also set off a contentious national discussion on sexual harassment when his former employee, law professor Anita Hill, charged him with making sexually suggestive comments to her while she was employed as his assistant at the EEOC. During the Senate Judiciary Committee hearings on Thomas's confirmation, Hill testified against Thomas, setting off a national discussion on racism and sexism in America. Although Hill's testimony did not prevent Thomas's appointment, it stimulated more awareness of sexual harassment. Thomas was narrowly confirmed by the Senate.

Racial politics during the Bush administration reached a high point during the debates on the proposed Civil Rights Act of 1990, which was designed to counter a series of Supreme Court decisions that limited the rights of employees who sued their employers for discrimination. The act also modified some of the basic procedural and substantive rights of the 1964 Civil Rights Act by providing for the right to a jury trial on discrimination claims. It also introduced the possibility of emotional distress damages, while limiting the amount that a jury could award. On the grounds that the new legislation might lead to quotas, President Bush set off a storm of protest by civil rights leaders when he vetoed the act. However, one year later, Bush "signed a bill which most observers regarded as only modified version of that which he had vetoed the year earlier." Augustus J. Jones, author of "Kinder, Gentler? George Bush and Civil Rights," attributes Bush's change in position on the changed political and racial terrain, which forced him to demonstrate support for civil rights. Jones states:

> First Bush was under increasing pressure to demonstrate support for civil rights. In August, the Senate hearings on the nomination of Clarence Thomas to the Supreme Court featured a highly publicized fight over the issue of the nominee's alleged sexual harassment of his former subordinate, Anita Hill. Moreover, the November political season featured a gubernatorial election in Louisiana, with former Ku Klux Klan leader David Duke running under the Republican Party banner, despite disclaimers from Bush and the Republican Party organizations that Duke was no Republican. Second, the President faced the threat of Congress breaking his record of not having any vetoes overridden. In consequence, he acquiesced and signed the Civil Rights Bill of 1991.[26]

The Bush administration continued Ronald Reagan's policy of supporting destabilizing forces in the world in order to fight pro-Communist regimes. A case in point was U.S. policy toward Angola, in which the Bush administration continued U.S. support for the National Union for the Total Independence of Angola (UNITA), an anti-Communist rebel group headed by Jonas Savimbi, who was also backed by the South African government. Although several opportunities for a cease-fire existed, Savimbi refused to enter into a sincere agreement with the Angolan government as long as he was receiving funding from the U.S. African American spokespersons such as Randall Robinson repeatedly called on the U.S. government, and specifically its conservative congressmen, to end its support of Savimbi. According to Robinson, "They would never support such policies anywhere in Eastern Europe, or in any white country in the world . . . All the land mines these people have stepped on, all of the Stinger missiles that have killed all of these people, for which we are responsible because of the work of the DeConcinis and the Jesse Helmses and the Bob Doles."[27] However, instead of lessening its support for Savimbi in order to promote peace, U.S. aid actually increased from $30–45 million to between $50–60 million.[28] The war in Angola was so bloody that Angola led the world in the highest per capita amputee rates from land mines.[29]

Described as taking a very cautious and conservative approach on foreign policy, the Bush administration responded slowly to the tumult in the international arena. When Chinese troops fired on pro-democracy demonstrators in Tiananmen Square on the evenings of June 3–4, 1989, the Bush administration's "first concern was to avoid any damage to bilateral relations."[30] U.S.

policy response was to ban military exports and exchanges, while refusing to enact non-defense sanctions. The Bush administration also took a "wait and see" approach to the unraveling of the Soviet Union, under the new reform efforts of Mikhail Gorbachev who was the general secretary of the Communist Party of the Soviet Union. Under the banner of perestroika (economic restructuring) and glasnost (political openness) Gorbachev began to liberalize the Eastern Bloc in order to pursue economic reform after he assumed power in 1985. The public face of the Soviet Union's dissolution occurred in November 1989, with the fall of the Berlin Wall that separated East and West Germany. Elections and other reform measures were instituted in places like Poland, Hungary and Czechoslovakia. The Baltic states of Estonia, Latvia and Lithuania rebelled against Soviet domination as well. Instead of initiating military action against the Baltic states, Gorbachev renounced the "Brezhnev Doctrine"—the Soviet Union's policy of intervening with military force, if necessary, to preserve Communist rule in the region. Instead, he encouraged the local Communist leaders to seek new ways of gaining popular support for their leadership. President Bush, however, was criticized for not providing any direct input into the process, until his meeting with President Gorbachev in a Soviet ship off the coast of Malta, December 1989. Described as one of the most important international meetings since the founding of the UN in 1945, President George H. W. Bush and Soviet leader Mikhail Gorbachev decisively ended the Cold War.

According to President Bush, a "New World Order" had begun, in which international affairs could finally move away from nuclear rivalry and bipolarity, to one where international law and global consensus would be emphasized to accomplish objectives in the national interest.[31] Helping to define the "New World Order" was General Colin Powell. Born in the Bronx, New York, to Jamaican immigrants, Powell entered the U.S. Army in 1958 as a commissioned officer. After serving two tours of duty (1962–63, 1968–69) during the Vietnam War, Powell subsequently worked in several staff positions in the White House, including in the Office of Management and Budget. He also served as deputy secretary to Casper Weinberger, commander of the V Corps in Western Europe and assistant to the president for National Security Affairs. In 1989, Powell was promoted to four-star general, becoming the first African American to hold that rank.

Powell's Vietnam War experiences taught him several important lessons. After returning from the war and experiencing the rejection of the American public, which resulted from continued questions about the U.S. role in the conflict, and the seemingly unnecessary loss of lives, Colin Powell began to consider the requirements for efficient military combat. He determined that the bedrock of his military counsel would be to stress that certain pre-conditions must be met before U.S. forces are committed to battle: "(1) Commit only if our allies' vital interests are at stake. (2) If we commit, do so with all the resources necessary to win. (3) Go in only with clear political and military objectives. (4) Be ready to change the commitment if the objectives change, since wars rarely stand still. (5) Only take on commitments that can gain the support of the American people and the Congress. (6) Commit U.S. forces only as a last resort."[32] Subsequently referred to as the "Powell Doctrine," those points translated into the simple idea that before engaging in military action, the U.S. must: "Have a clear political objective and stick to it. Use all the force necessary, and do not apologize for going in big if that is what it takes. Decisive force ends wars quickly and in the long run saves lives."[33]

The Powell Doctrine was first implemented in 1989 against General Manuel Noriega of Panama. The U.S. relationship with Noriega went back to the 1960s, when he was a paid agent for the CIA, but the relationship soured when Noriega's role as a drug trafficker and as a conduit for the Contras of Nicaragua became public.[34] The U.S. was also concerned about Noriega's potential control over the Panama Canal. According to the Panama Canal Treaty, the U.S. would relinquish control of the Canal to the Panamanians in the year 2000, ending their operation of the ship canal since 1903. The Reagan administration encouraged a coup against Noriega and froze Panamanian assets, but to no avail. When President Bush took power, he was determined to remove Noriega from office. Bush ordered the capture and arrest of Noriega after a U.S. military officer was murdered by Noriega's defense forces and after several attempts to overthrow him failed, including an attempt to oust him electorally by financing elections, and a failed coup attempt by disaffected members of the armed forces was crushed. Under the banner of Operation Just Cause, on December 20, 1989, the U.S. invaded the country. Noriega was captured, taken to the United States, tried for drug trafficking, and imprisoned in 1992. He remains imprisoned in a federal prison in Miami, Florida. The Organization of American States voted 20–1, with five abstentions, in favor of a resolution condemning the intervention and calling for the immediate withdrawal of U.S. troops. "A similar resolution brought before the General Assembly of the United Nations passed 75–20, with 40 abstentions."[35] In line with these resolutions were the views of African American leaders on the invasion, which were decidedly in contrast to the Bush administration's view. Gus Savage, congressman of Illinois, called for a special congressional session to address possible misconduct by the U.S. in the Panama invasion. In addition to other critics, Savage claimed that "control of the Panama Canal, as well as control of Noriega's mouth, were the principal reasons behind the invasion."[36] Nonetheless, because the invasion did not result in a large number of casualties, the Powell Doctrine became viewed as the most efficient and effective way to wage war.[37]

The Gulf War (1990–1991) was a defining event for the Bush administration and perhaps set the foundation for African American expression on U.S. wars in this contemporary age. U.S. direct involvement in the crisis in the Gulf region began in 1990 after Iraq invaded its oil-rich neighbor to the south, Kuwait. Led by Saddam Hussein, "the Iraqi Army, which possessed the fourth largest ground force in the world at that time, had been assembling along the border with Kuwait for some time."[38] From the perspective of Saddam Hussein, his reasons for invading Kuwait were many, which included his charge that the Kuwaiti government was illegally "slant drilling" oil across the Iraqi border. In addition, Hussein's government was deeply in debt as a result of the costs of the eight-year war with Iran. Iraq had hoped to repay its debt by raising the price of oil through OPEC oil production costs, but Kuwait had increased production, knocking the price of oil further down. And finally under Hussein, Iraq reasserted its claim to Kuwaiti territory, which was left unresolved at the end of British colonialism in the region. The Iraqi perspective was that Kuwait had been arbitrarily severed from Iraq, and therefore Iraq had a right to the territory.

The irony of the Persian Gulf War was that Saddam Hussein's regime had been a foreign policy favorite of U.S. policy makers during the previous decade. When Islamic extremists overthrew the Shah of Iran in 1979 and created the possibility of political instability in the region, the U.S.—looking to build balance in what was perceived as unpredictable Middle East and Arab politics—backed Hussein almost to the time of the Kuwait invasion. The U.S. supplied Iraq with both military and non-military intelligence and technology during the war against Iran (1980–1988), and continued afterwards. For Iraq, the war against Iran was to combat Khomeini's desire to overthrow Iraq's Ba'ath Party. Iraq was also interested in ending the 1975 agreement that provided joint Iraq-Iran control over the Shatt al Arab Waterway that ran between the two countries.[39] However, the war left Iraq's economy in shambles and the issue of the waterway remained unresolved.

On the issue of the Iraq-Kuwait conflict, the two governments had attempted to negotiate a resolution to the issues dividing them, but in July 1990 when negotiations stalled, Iraq began to assemble troops on Kuwait's border. That same month, Hussein summoned U.S. Ambassador April Glaspie to a meeting where he discussed the escalating conflict with Kuwait.

According to Hussein, Glaspie expressed "no U.S. interest in the Iraq-Kuwaiti border dispute,"[40] leading him to believe that he would receive no retribution from the U.S. if he attacked Kuwait. On August 2, 1990, Iraqi troops invaded and occupied the country. Although the Kuwaiti army was quickly overwhelmed, enough time was bought for the Kuwaiti Air Force and the emir of Kuwait, Abdullah al-Sabbath, to escape to Saudi Arabia. Hussein then installed a new provincial government headed by Alaa Hussein Ali in the emir's place and annexed Kuwait. Thousands of Western visitors were detained as hostages to act as human shields to protect Iraq from a violent response to its actions.

Within hours of the invasion, the U.S. and Kuwaiti delegations requested a meeting of the UN Security Council, which passed Resolution 660 condemning the invasion and demanding a withdrawal of Iraqi troops. The U.S. was especially concerned about the security of Saudi Arabia, a vital interest because of its vast oil reserves and because it was an ally in the region. On August 5, President Bush told reporters that "This aggression will not stand," and "this is not a war for oil. This is war against aggression."[41]

The U.S. and Kuwaiti governments also assembled a broad coalition of other nations to support their fight against Iraq. This international-in-appearance opposition was then followed by trade sanctions and a UN resolution that required Hussein's army to leave Iraq by January 15, 1991, or face a military response. Knowing that Hussein might not back down, President Bush sought and won an authorization from Congress to deter Iraqi aggression. Iraq had already built the world's fourth-largest army, with as many as a million soldiers equipped with highly advanced weapons, much of it previously supplied—ironically—by Western nations and Russia. The Bush administration began to build a counter force of multinational allied troops.

Following the dictates of the Powell Doctrine meant that U.S. forces would be massive. Under the banner of Operation Desert Shield, the U.S. assembled the biggest wartime army since Vietnam, deploying approximately half a million troops to the desert. Complementing the U.S. military were contingents of Arab, Western and other nations.

Under the name of Operation Desert Storm, on January 17, 1991 (Baghdad time), the counterattack against Iraq began. Commanding first a high-tech allied air offensive whose pin-point accuracy and "smart bombs" almost made the war seem like a video game, Saddam's military was overpowered. Iraq's skies were decisively controlled quickly by allied jets and bombers; its command and military infrastructure were virtually destroyed; and its army—once such a strategic concern—generally gave up and surrendered, leaving the allies with more prisoners of war than they could handle. After just a month, Desert Storm was over. The occupiers of Kuwait fled while setting oil wells ablaze as they ran. Southern Iraq was temporarily occupied by coalition forces as Bush made the decision not to go after Saddam. President Bush declared that the intent of the coalition was not to overthrow him but instead force the Iraqi leader to sign a peace agreement.

For the first time in almost fifty years, the United States had won a war. The casualty figures reflected the superiority of the coalition forces over the Iraqi military. The U.S. Defense Intelligence Agency released preliminary figures that showed 100,000 Iraqi soldiers were killed and 300,000 wounded. Those numbers, however, have been disputed by other sources which suggest that the numbers were much lower. What is not in dispute is the casualties of the coalition forces. Less than 200 American lives were lost, while 467 were wounded in action. Forty-seven Saudis were killed with 220 wounded. Troops from the United Kingdom suffered 25 deaths and 45 were injured.[42]

African-Americans did not conceal their views on the crisis in the Persian Gulf. Certainly, the 24-hour-a-day coverage of the war by CNN gave all U.S. citizens a daily glimpse into every new development. In contrast to the majority of whites, it was common for African Americans to question U.S. policy in the Persian Gulf. A *Wall Street Journal*/NBC News poll in January 1991, the month of the actual invasion, showed that a "much higher percentage of black voters are skeptical of the war effort than white voters."[43]

African American voters first questioned the amount of time the Bush administration allotted for the sanctions to work, before actually waging war. Seventy-eight percent of white voters said the president had waited long enough before using military forces, while only 52 percent of Black voters agreed. Twice as many Blacks as whites—39 percent vs. 19 percent—thought the president should have given sanctions more time. Why risk shedding American blood when continued economic sanctions might work just as well? Congressman Ronald Dellums, a member of the CBC and the Armed Services Committee, said that "Economic sanctions against Iraq weren't given enough time, and U.S. diplomacy amounted to offering an ultimatum." Dellums felt so strongly that the U.S. was rushing to war, that he sought a federal court injunction under Article I, Section 8 of the Constitution to reaffirm sole congressional authority for any declaration of war against Iraq. In defending his lawsuit, Dellums stated, "From the outset, I have opposed a U.S. offensive war to undo the illegal and immoral Iraqi invasion of Kuwait. Because of my opposition, I am seeking a federal court injunction under Article I, Section 8 of the Constitution to reaffirm sole congressional authority for any declaration of war against Iraq."[44] Dellums was joined by 44 House Democrats in the lawsuit.[45]

Others challenged the Bush administration's justification for the intervention. Was Iraq being contained to defend democracy or to secure U.S. oil interests and Kuwait's huge investments in U.S. companies and banks? Two African American female army reservists believed so. Farcia DeToles and Azania Howse both filed for discharge on the grounds of conscientious objection with the Army Reserves on December 19, 1990. In her statement justifying her position, Howse said, "I understand now that wars waged by this country have nothing to do with freedom or democracy or human rights. What they have to do with is the domination of power to yield profits."[46]

Several African Americans pointed out what they perceived as the apparent contradictions between the government's support for Kuwaitis while ignoring the plight of African people who were suffering from war and oppression. During an interview for the article "Guns and Butter," written as part of a *Wall Street Journal* News Round-Up, entrepreneur Eugene Wiley of Atlanta stated:

> Most of the people who live in Kuwait are simply foreigners who work for the Kuwaitis. The Kuwaitis themselves are arrogant and wealthy and take advantage of others. The idea that we're "liberating" them is comical. The U.S. has been aware for 30 or 40 years of what's been going on in South Africa—scores of people being killed, denial of freedom of the press and other basic rights. But we haven't gone in to "liberate" the 25 million South Africans who are oppressed by six million whites. [47]

Damu Smith, a leader of the National African American Network against U.S. Aggression in the Gulf, also noted the contradiction in his assertion that unlike the U.S. response to the invasion of Kuwait, the U.S. "has been slow to respond to aggression against blacks in South Africa."[48] Expressing even more concern about the U.S. ignoring the plight of Africa during this period was Reverend Jesse Jackson, who proposed that UN peacekeeping troops be sent to Liberia, which was embroiled in a bloody civil war. While speaking at the United Methodist Church camp in Iowa, Jackson stated that "We cannot stand by and watch the slaughter of a people." President Bush's response to the crisis was to evacuate Americans from Liberia.[49]

One of the most common concerns of African Americans was the connection between the war cost and domestic social services cut-backs. Former mayor of Gary, Indiana, Richard Hatcher pointed out that "The irony is not lost upon blacks that just a few months ago the U.S. was saying it was broke and that it couldn't afford to do anything."[50]

Adding their voices to the antiwar chorus were more traditional civil rights leaders—including Coretta Scott King, widow of Martin Luther King. At Ebenezer Baptist Church in Atlanta, Georgia, where the Rev. Martin Luther King Jr. preached nonviolence, Mrs. King encouraged her listeners to oppose the war against Iraq. Mrs. King said, "This war is about oil and militarism: Don't let anyone tell you oil is not a consideration." She added, however, that the students should not abandon their support for American troops. "We do not seek to defeat people, but to defeat injustice. Oppose a policy, not a person. . . . The best way we can support the men and women who will be fighting is to continue to work for a peaceful solution."[51] Mrs. King also called on the government to put an end to the system that puts militarism ahead of education. In the annual "State of the Dream" speech at Ebenezer Baptist Church that year, Mrs. King expressed her concerns about government spending on the military rather than meeting the needs of common people. She said, "If self-funding programs such as Social Security are subtracted from the federal budget, the U.S. is spending 55 cents out of every taxpayer dollar on the military, compared to just 2 cents for education. The real hostages today are American schoolchildren, the nation's 3 million homeless people, the 20 million Americans who experience hunger every day and the 37 million Americans who have no health insurance."[52] On the anniversary of the King Holiday in 1991, Rev. Joseph Lowery, president of the SCLC, said, "Let us call upon the nations to spend our resources on medical supplies, not military supplies; to make tractors, not tanks; to beat missiles into morsels of bread to feed the hungry; to build housing, not foxholes."[53]

The legacy of Dr. Martin Luther King Jr. was connected to the war in many ways. Some considered the United Nations' deadline for Iraqi withdrawal from Kuwait on January 15, King's birthday, an affront to his legacy. In the meantime, there were still three states that had not instituted a paid King Holiday for state workers. To protest those state decisions, a march and rally was held in Phoenix, Arizona, which drew an estimated 20,000 people to push for passage of a state-sponsored holiday. The two other states without an official King Holiday at that time were Montana and New Hampshire.

Criticisms of the war also included resentment against President Bush personally for his failure to endorse legislation that would have further protected the rights of minorities and women within the U.S. Reverend Jesse Jackson charged President Bush with raising fears of a war in the Persian Gulf in order to divert the attention of Americans away from his anti–working class public policies. Bush vetoed the 1990 Civil Rights Bill, which not only would have restored fair treatment at the workplace for racial minorities, but also would have given working women new rights to sue for intentional sexual discrimination.[54] In addition, African Americans recalled how Bush had placed restrictions on minority college scholarships and ran an election campaign that promoted negative stereotypes about their community. Earlier, even General Colin Powell expressed his concern about the Willie Horton ads during Bush's presidential election campaign. When asked about the Willie Horton spot used against Dukakis, Powell considered it "a cheap shot" and said that it bothered him.[55]

At the heart of African American opposition to the war was the belief that many of its community members were forced to enlist in military service for economic reasons. Contrary to the previous wars, which relied on the draft for troops and other personnel, the fight in the Persian Gulf was the first wartime test of the all-volunteer, no-draft, no loopholes, "be all you can be" army. After Vietnam, President Nixon officially ended the military draft, and hence, the army of the Persian Gulf War exemplified the new military. The Pentagon hoped that the new recruits would be motivated by on-the-the job training, higher pay, college tuition offerings and other new benefits. Under the leadership of General Colin Powell, the effort to further down-size the military continued. Powell's downsizing strategy was premised on the idea that the country needed to establish a "base force," which would consist of only the minimum necessary to fight in an emergency situation and one or two other hot spots in the world.

Although the military had been downsized, "the percentage of black officers rose from 6.5 to 7.5, while white officers dropped from eight-nine percent to eighty-two percent of the total."[56] African Americans also held more prominent positions than at any other time in American military history. Even still, African Americans were still subjected to a "glass ceiling," with most of the soldiers receiving promotions in the lower and middle rungs. According to a study conducted by the Department of Defense, "Women and minority officers tend to be concentrated in administration and supply area, and underrepresented in tactical operations, the area that yields two-thirds of the general and flag officers of the Services."[57]

African Americans criticized the all-volunteer military primarily for the reason that it attracted recruits who had few other economic choices, making volunteerism an economic draft. The percentage of African Americans, for instance, fighting in the Persian Gulf, compared to the American population, was much higher than that for whites. In 1991, African Americans accounted "for 25% of the force, and all minorities for 32%. One of every 25 working eligible-age (18–44) white males is in the service, but one out of every 12 working black males of that age."[58] Echoing this concern was Congressman John Lewis of Georgia, who stated that "I think a great majority of black Americans are concerned with the Persian Gulf because so many young black men and women are there in many cases because of economic necessity."[59] Congresswoman Maxine Waters also emphasized the fact that voluntary military service is really for young people with few other job opportunities. Waters, who represents Watts and other areas of South Los Angeles, commented that many African Americans who join the military are "escaping the mean streets of the inner cities, gangs and drugs."[60]

And finally, members of the African American community openly voiced their concerns about "true equality" in the military. If the experiences of African Americans were really equal, then why were they more likely to be exposed to danger? Of the soldiers killed in the Persian Gulf War, 15 percent were Black, although they represent only 12 percent of the population.[61]

Certainly, as the polls suggest, not all African Americans were against the war. Celes King III, a World War II veteran and brigadier general in California's state military reserves, stated, "Hussein has to be stopped. I don't like war. I don't like to see young men killed. If, however, it does come to the reality of war, blacks should do our part."[62] Former UN Ambassador Donald F. McHenry, a professor at Georgetown University, agreed that Bush should have given sanctions more time to cripple Iraq, but believed "the president was going to have to use force anyway because I don't think Saddam Hussein had any interest in coming out [of Kuwait]."[63]

Juan Williams attributes the lack of African American support for the war to the public antiwar stance of the community's leaders, whom he accuses of attempting to divide the American public along racial lines. According to Williams, African Americans should be proud of their performance against Saddam Hussein.[64] Edwin Dorn of the Brookings Institution, who has studied the relationship between race and the military, concurred with Williams. Dorn believed that there was a lot more support for the war than was indicated. So many African Americans are more likely to know someone who is in the Gulf, and "there's a kind of individual or closer identification with fighting and dying."[65] Even John Lewis, a critic of what he perceived as "Bush's rush to war" stated that when he visited troops the week before the war began, he found Black soldiers to have "very high morale" and to be "upbeat." He also found "a great degree of interracial cooperation, a much greater sense of family, a greater sense of togetherness among the military people than I see in civilian life."[66]

Certainly, the military was the most integrated than at any other time in history and never before had African Americans held such prominent positions. Serving alongside General H. Norman Schwarzkopf Jr., who served as commander of the Coalition Forces, and Secretary of Defense Richard Cheney were General Colin Powell and the African American Lieutenant General Calvin Waller, who served as Desert Storm deputy commander. Prior to those appointments only a few African Americans had served at such high-ranking positions.

On the issue of race and African American soldiers during the war, some African Americans acknowledged their willingness to serve, but maintained that race still factored into their experiences. In the book *We Were There: Voices of African American Veterans, from World War II to the War in Iraq*, J. Alexander Martin, who served in the navy before becoming a cofounder of FUBU, an international sportswear company aimed at the hip-hop generation, was based on a ship that was 25 percent African American. He acknowledged that race was still a factor in his service, which was evidenced by the treatment he experienced from his African American superior, who was concerned that if he was not perfect, he would be treated unfairly. Martin stated that his superior was always on their backs, "trying to get us to work harder and be perfect. He treated us that way because some of the white officers looked down on us. He had to work hard to get where he was and he wanted us to work hard to be the best."[67]

First Lt. William J. Simmons Sr., a Gulf War veteran, wrote of his experiences during Operation Desert Storm as well. One of his early hints at racism occurred when his assistant commander told him that the South Carolina Army National Guard was "based on the 'good ol' boy system." Then he was assigned to duties to which "his white counterparts would not be subjected." Simmons held positions ranging from motor pool officer to safety committee participant and range control officer, even though he held a Bachelor's of Science degree in biology from the University of South Carolina.[68]

Lester Outterbridge served as a National Guard specialist during the Persian Gulf War as a dispatcher. Outterbridge suffers from Gulf War Syndrome, a mix of illnesses that troops who served in the Gulf have endured. It is generally believed that Gulf War Syndrome was caused by exposure to toxic debris from Iraqi chemical and biological weapons.[69] Now, Outterbridge runs a small support group for veterans who suffer from the same debilitating condition, and sees it as his duty to advocate for African American soldiers because so many lack support. According to Outterbridge, "You see a lot of black men out here who are in their late forties, fifties, even sixties living on the street. You know why? Because they gave up. They gave up on the American system because they think, I went over there, I came back messed up, and nobody wanted me."

African American commentary on the Persian Gulf War reflects the changes in the status of its community, and society. As African American elected officials rose in numbers, so did their influence in governmental policy. African American members of Congress began to hold key committee assignments on military and international affairs, including Donald Payne, who served on the International Relations Committee during the war, and Ronald Dellums, a member of the Armed Services Committee.

After his two presidential bids and his previous ventures in international politics, Reverend Jesse Jackson earned the position as one of the most prominent commentators and advisers on U.S. foreign policy. Two of Jackson's commentaries are included in this section. In the first, Jackson draws a connection between the domestic concerns of African Americans, women and the poor to President Bush's policies in the Persian Gulf. Jackson also challenges President Bush's racial policies, including the veto of the Civil Rights Bill of 1990, opposition to the Equal Rights Amendment and refusal to support other bills that would have sustained a woman's right to reproductive freedom. In a second commentary Jackson presents the reasons why he opposed Bush's January 15 deadline for Iraq to remove its troops from Kuwait. To be sure, Jackson accepted the proposal that the U.S. must be "willing to use our military if diplomacy fails," because "we can't watch Hussein waltz through our foreign policy and through our allies."[70] But, ultimately, Jackson surmised that our first response should be diplomatic, through the imposition of strong sanctions. Jackson became a key player in negotiations for the release of hostages in Iraq by appealing directly to President Saddam Hussein. As a result, President Hussein released 47 Americans and a large group of other foreigners as a result of Jackson's appeal.[71]

Conflict between traditional African American liberals and the new conservatives is illustrated in the responses of Andrea Young and A. Knighton Stanley to Juan Williams's commentary. In their article, Young and Stanley challenge Williams's castigation of Black leaders who spoke out against the Persian Gulf War. As antiwar proponents, the authors avowed that "We must speak out against the use of America's resources—material, human and financial—for violence and destruction. We have supported nonviolent strategies to rid the world of atrocities such as apartheid, and we support nonviolent strategies to reverse the occupation of Kuwait." They further challenged Williams's assertion that African American critics do not value integration. In their view, integration is necessary, but African Americans must not assimilate into a "dangerously flawed American mind-set which betrays rather than fulfills Dr. King's dream."

In Congressman Ronald Dellums's commentary, he sets forth several reasons for opposing the war and for filing a lawsuit against the president. Dellums reminds us that Dr. King urged us to abandon the mentality of war and to end our fascination with the technology of war. Also included in this segment is Azania Howse's statement justifying her application for discharge from the Army Reservists as a conscientious objector in 1990.

The final commentary in this section was written by Congressman Donald Payne from New Jersey, a member of the CBC, the International Relations Committee and its Subcommittee on the Western Hemisphere and Subcommittee on Africa. In his address to the American people, Payne outlined the contributions of African Americans to America's wars. According to Payne, that contribution in the past and in the present success of Desert Storm has earned them the right to benefit economically from the rebuilding of Kuwait. Specifically, Payne called on President Bush, Secretary of Defense Cheney, the secretary of the army and the heads of several U.S. government agencies involved in the reconstruction process to give favorable treatment to African American companies for the five-year rebuilding program.

JESSE JACKSON SR.
(1941–)

Reverend Jesse Jackson was born in Greenville, South Carolina. He attended the University of Illinois and then transferred to the Agricultural and Technical College of North Carolina (Greensboro), receiving a B.A. in sociology in 1964. In 1965, Jackson went to Selma, Alabama, to march with Martin Luther King Jr. and became a member of the SCLC. He moved to Chicago in 1966, did postgraduate work at the Chicago Theological Seminary and was ordained a Baptist minister in 1968. In 1966, Jackson helped to establish the Chicago branch of Operation Breadbasket, the economic arm of the SCLC, and served as the organization's national director from 1967 to 1971. In 1971, he founded Operation PUSH (People United to Serve Humanity). Reverend Jackson became the first African American to make an earnest bid to become the Democratic nominee for the U.S. presidency with his campaigns in 1983–84 and 1987–88. He was later appointed as the "special envoy of the president and secretary of state for the promotion of democracy in Africa" by President Bill Clinton. In an editorial written in 1990, Jackson charged President Bush with trying to "change the subject" on his unfair domestic policies by "raising fears of a war." In the second editorial Reverend Jackson comments on the deadline that the UN Security Council set for Iraqi withdrawal from Kuwait. According to Jackson, we must give peace a chance because "time is on our side."

Ignore Bush's Ploys: Vote for Change
1990

The 1990 election season has reached what ballplayers call "money time," the last moments when victory is on the line. In politics, the last days of a campaign are down and dirty, a time when anything goes. Too often, politicians, unable to offer hope and unwilling to offer direction, play on people's fears and peddle distraction.

In Washington, for example, President George Bush launched his electioneering by vetoing the 1990 civil rights bill, branding it a racial "quota" bill. The measure would have restored fair treatment at the workplace for racial minorities (while explicitly disavowing quotas). But it also would have given working women new rights to sue for intentional sexual discrimination. It was ardently opposed by the conservative Chamber of Commerce, which historically has fought against efforts to provide workers with rights in the workplace.

The posturing about racial quotas diverts attention from a veto that hurts working people. In the last 15 years, more and more wives and mothers have gone to work to help support their families. More than two-thirds of all married women now are employed.

Working women face persistent discrimination in hiring, firing, unequal pay and sexual harassment. Their families suffer accordingly. Bush's veto shuts the door on them, just as it shuts out religious and racial minorities.

If you get beyond the distraction, you begin to see the direction. To put it kindly, the president is removed from the realities facing everyday working families. Thus he vetoed the first minimum-wage increase, ignoring the working women often caught in low-paying jobs. He vetoed a bill that would have given working parents the chance to take unpaid leave to care for a newborn or sick child without losing their jobs. The president mused that maybe some businesses might offer such programs voluntarily.

Bush continues to oppose the Equal Rights Amendment and to veto any bill aiding women's right to choose an abortion.

The president offered another favorite distraction this week—tried and true rhetoric about "tax-and-spend liberals." Liberals, he said, "are still peddling that tired old saw about Republicans and the rich. Well, you and I know that is hogwash . . . I'm taking this message all across the country: We are for the working people in this country."

The president began his campaign tour at a San Francisco breakfast for "working people" able to ante up $25,000 per couple to hear his populist pitch. Not exactly your basic workers. The president knew his crowd: He pledged to stop any tax on millionaires and to fight once again for a capital gains tax cut for the wealthy. Workers who can afford to give away $25,000 will no doubt rally to that agenda.

Now the White House is trying to change the subject by raising fears of a war in the Persian Gulf. Bush has admitted that he finds foreign crises more interesting than domestic challenges. This poll-driven White House knows that the president gets higher approval ratings for his foreign policy than for the mess at home.

Politics is often tawdry, but seeking electoral advantage by playing on fears about the young men and women in the deserts of the Middle East carries matters to dangerous extremes.

Conservatives have found the politics of distraction effective. Working people can be divided by their fears. Cynicism and nastiness drives good people away from the voting booth, and the affluent vote in far greater numbers than those struggling to get by.

But one thing about democracy—it gives us the right to fight for the right. We can ignore the distraction and vote for a new direction.

An Ironic Deadline for the Gulf Crisis
1990

Jan. 15 is decision day in the Persian Gulf. Last week, the UN Security Council authorized the use of force if Iraq has not withdrawn from Kuwait by then.

President George Bush said President Saddam Hussein must "get the message" that the current standoff "is not going to go on forever" and that the UN resolutions will be enforced "with all means necessary." Jan. 15 also is the birth date of Dr. Martin Luther King Jr., the apostle of nonviolence, the winner of the 1964 Nobel Peace Prize. "Wars," King taught, "are poor chisels for carving out peaceful tomorrows . . . We must pursue peaceful ends through peaceful means."

An international embargo, respected by nations around the world, deprives Hussein of any fruits of his act. He has oil without customers, hotels without guests, industries without supplies. With each passing week, his military machine grows weaker from the absence of replacement parts and vital imports. Time is on our side.

Last week, Secretary of Defense Richard Cheney suggested that Hussein could "ride out" the sanctions, that there was "a price to be paid" for waiting for sanctions to work. But surely there is a higher price to be paid for not waiting.

If war starts, limbs will be lost, lives will be lost. Surely the reports that thousands of body bags have been shipped to the Saudi desert should give us pause.

Moreover, while the sanctions take effect, the time can be used not simply to wait, but to work. The embargo is necessary but not sufficient. We should seek negotiation instead of confrontation, take the initiative to resolve conflicts and stop the drift towards war.

The president sensibly has broken his "no talk" posture by offering to send Secretary of State Baker to Baghdad, but only, it is claimed, to ensure that Saddam Hussein "has gotten the message." The president demands unconditional enforcement of the UN resolutions condemning Iraqi aggression, with "no concessions." Yet UN Resolution 660 has three parts: It calls for unconditional withdrawal from Kuwait; it authorizes an international embargo of the aggressor; it calls for immediate negotiations to resolve outstanding differences between Iraq and Kuwait. We have embraced the first two but ignored the third.

Iraq must leave Kuwait without conditions. But all agree the Iraqis have legitimate grievances against Kuwait. If finding a way to resolve these differences helps end the crisis without war, the UN's mandate will be served and the world will have gained.

At the same time, we should continue to pursue a settlement of the Israeli-Palestinian conflict, following UN Resolution 242 that calls for trading land for peace, guaranteeing security for the Israelis and justice for the Palestinians. Resolution of this terrible conflict is vital to any future security and peace in the region. It is essential for the moral authority of the United Nations and the United States to be consistent on this question.

Hussein must not profit from his aggression. Yet we should not let his militarism disarm the peacemakers. The gulf crisis should not stop us from doing what is right, taking the peacemaking steps that we should have taken if the invasion had not occurred.

A war in the gulf would be a catastrophe of untold proportions. Even if the war is short, the hatreds engendered will be deep and destructive. War is not a chisel for building the future, but a bludgeon that destroys the present. As King taught with his life, the challenge of leadership is not to surrender to violence, but to act both to resist injustice and to build for peace.

We must seek a resolution that builds peace in this region—the birthplace of three of the world's great religions—which remains torn by violence and hatred. We must not let the arrogance of power and the impatience of political considerations to move us, in the name of life, to reduce our options to that of death.

ANDREA YOUNG
AND
A. KNIGHTON STANLEY

Andrea Young is a noted author, speaker and director of public policy for the National Black Child Development Institute in Washington, D.C. The daughter of Andrew Young and Jean Childs Young, Andrea Young is also an associate for foreign policy advocacy for the United Church of Christ. Dr. A. Knighton Stanley is the senior pastor of Peoples Congregational United Church of Christ in Washington, D.C. He is a graduate of Talladega College, with a master's from Yale University and a doctorate from Howard University. As a young activist he participated in the 1963 phase of the Greensboro, North Carolina, civil rights movement. He served as advisor to the local chapter of the Congress of Racial Equality (CORE). He is married to Andrea Young.

"Race and War in the Persian Gulf"
February 2, 1991

American Leadership has been deeply divided over the decision to go to war with Iraq. America's black leaders are no exception to that. This war is one on which reasonable persons disagree, and it is unreasonable for Juan Williams to castigate black leaders who have expressed their heartfelt opposition to the war [Juan Williams, "Race and War in the Persian Gulf," *Washington Post*, Outlook, Jan. 20, 1991].

As did we, Eleanor Holmes Norton, Jesse Jackson, Coretta Scott King and Joseph Lowery witnessed the destructiveness of the Vietnam War. We must speak out against the use of America's resources—material, human and financial—for violence and destruction. We have supported nonviolent strategies to rid the world of atrocities such as apartheid, and we support nonviolent strategies to reverse the occupation of Kuwait.

The leaders criticized by Williams are all fine examples of American leaders who are black and have taken up the cause of full equality for black Americans. We challenge the assumption that they are the leaders of black people only. The manager of Jesse Jackson's Minnesota campaign was recently elected to the U.S. Senate.

While Williams may disagree with Jesse Jackson, he must surely remember that Jackson's presidential campaign was based in large part on an internationalist foreign policy that would affirmatively engage the Third World in development. His opposition to this war is fully consistent with positions taken in the campaign and affirmed by millions of American voters.

For American leaders who have championed full equality for black Americans, it is impossible to ignore the contradictions of this war. The legacy of

American racism and cultural arrogance permeates the war. The disproportionate number of persons of color in the U.S. military must not be dissociated from the actions of the Bush administration in the arena of social justice. While African Americans go to war at the orders of the president, President Bush has shifted resources and protection away from our communities. He has abandoned the cities, vetoed the Civil Rights Bill and attacked minority scholarships. He has played on racial divisions for political gain.

This is a replay of a historical irony for African Americans. Valor in war, patriotic service and sacrifice for the freedom of others is a tradition dating back to Crispus Attucks. At the same time, blacks have had to struggle with the same segregation, racism and cultural arrogance in the military, that they face in the society. Black soldiers have returned from foreign wars to face discrimination, rather than adulation at home.

We also see the telltale signs of racism and cultural arrogance in the events leading up to this war. Iraq was a tool of U.S. policy so long as it was fighting Iran. Saddam Hussein's aggression was abetted by the administration's failure to elevate human rights in foreign policy considerations in the Third World and its focus on military security rather than economic development. While Iraq bears full responsibility for the invasion, the failure of American intelligence and diplomacy to comprehend Saddam's intention is not unrelated to the lack of racial and ethnic diversity in our foreign policy establishment. A U.S. foreign policy that valued human rights for all people of color could not have found an ally in Saddam Hussein.

Martin Luther King Jr. said that bombs that exploded in Vietnam would explode at home in inflation and unemployment. He called for a transformation of America away from materialism and militarism. He called for a beloved community based on justice and brotherhood. He did not call for black Americans to become part of some imagined mainstream.

Integration is necessary, but not sufficient. Assimilation, into a dangerously flawed American mind-set is a betrayal rather than a fulfillment of Dr. King's dream.

RONALD VERNIE DELLUMS
(1935–)

Oakland native Ronald Dellums was elected to the Berkeley City Council in 1967. Following his tenure on the city council Dellums was elected to Congress in 1971. Just weeks into his first term, Dellums set up a Vietnam War crime exhibit in his congressional office; shortly thereafter he called for a formal investigation into Vietnam war crime allegations. During his tenure in Congress he received immense criticism for his support of Fidel Castro, anti-apartheid legislation, Dellums and campaigns against defense projects. Despite the criticism, Dellums served as U.S. Representative from California without interruption for 27 years. The congressman was the lead plaintiff in the lawsuit, Dellums v. Bush (1990), which requested an injunction to prevent the president from initiating an offensive attack against Iraq without first securing congressional authorization. In this commentary, Dellums follows in the tradition of Benjamin Banneker, who argued that the U.S. should concentrate on finding alternatives to war.

Shedding the Mentality of War Brinkmanship Got Us into This, but We Could Still Step Back from the Edge of Ground Fighting
1991

I have opposed the application of offensive military force throughout the Persian Gulf crisis. I filed suit to protect against a unilateral decision by the President to use such force. I led the effort to continue economic sanctions in the place of a military offensive. I believe that negotiations and sanctions needed to be exhausted before we resorted to force.

When asked why I oppose the war now started, I invoke a speech that Dr. Martin Luther King Jr. delivered at the height of the Vietnam War. He warned that the bombs being dropped on the jungles of Vietnam were exploding in the ghettos and barrios of America. The significance of that statement lies in both its simplicity and its complexity. Its thrust is every bit as relevant today.

Simply put, King warned us that those bombs were killing the hopes and aspirations of many, particularly the poor, in this country. The pursuit of a military solution to the situation in Vietnam was at the direct expense of those Americans whose marginal existence depended to a great extent on federal programs.

Today, Dr. King would warn that the bombs falling in the Persian Gulf are exploding all across America. The middle and working classes now join the poor in feeling the effects of the nation's misplaced spending priorities. Our crisis in health care, housing, education, environment and the "safety net" programs all will be aggravated by Gulf War expenses now ranging from $500 million to $1 billion a day. As a result of the misplaced spending priorities driven by the mentality and the actuality of war, the people of our nation face the greatest threat to the quality of their lives in modern times.

Dr. King also urged us to abandon the mentality of war. We are at war because an enormous gamble failed. A gamble of brinkmanship, driven by the mentality of war. During this crisis we have been taken to this brink, the next brink, and so on, with assurances that we would not have to leap any farther. Now we stare into the abyss, brought to the brink of what would, by all accounts, be an incredible slaughter of human beings—Americans, allies and Iraqis—in a ground attack combined with an unrestrained air assault on entrenched Iraqi positions in Kuwait and Iraq.

The economic sanctions continue, even though the war is having a negative effect on the resolve of the coalition enforcing them. As no strategic goods are allowed in and no oil is allowed out of Iraq, the country's economy will continue to disintegrate under the weight of the sanctions, without an escalation of the war.

Dr. King also warned against our fascination with the technology of war. In the days since the beginning of this war, we have heard discussion of a kind of national "euphoria" as we collectively consumed the descriptions of the performance of our high-technology weaponry. We now face the more sober reality that even when the weaponry exceeds our expectations, the predictions of an early Iraqi capitulation have proved false.

I submit that an even more sober reflection is in order. We are actually experiencing a unique opportunity to look through a window at the future of war. Instead of becoming enamored of this technology, we should become profoundly frightened by it. As long as we remain fixated on perfecting the art and craft of war over the art and craft of diplomacy, we will remain caught in a spiral of violence that may escalate to the use of biological, chemical or even nuclear weapons.

The time to think beyond warfare is now. Otherwise, modern warfare may someday come to our own country, raining cruise missiles and high-technology death down on our own cities.

The harvest of a policy driven by the mentality of war finds fruit in increasingly anti-American Arab states. I agree with President Bush that America has a special role and a special responsibility in what he refers to as the "new world order." However, I believe that the United States should lead by example in searching for alternatives to war.

The decision to resort to brinkmanship is a failure of that responsibility. Respect for all of the lives that are being—and would be—extinguished should surely be great enough to drive nations to negotiate a solution to the current crisis. In the long run, peace is not just the withdrawal from hostilities, peace is the withdrawal from the mentality of war.

Dr. King's simple but profound statement lives with us today: eventually nations must peacefully coexist or violently annihilate each other. The search for peaceful coexistence is our moral obligation in the post–Cold War era.

AZANIA HOWSE

Azania Howse, a member of the U.S. Army Reserves, became a member of the peace movement in the Bay Area and a conscientious objector to the Persian Gulf War. In this article, she describes the reasons for her request to leave military service. She also chastises the U.S. for unnecessary violence against the Iraqi people, and argues that imperialism and a quest for domination are the reasons for Desert Storm. She considers the attack on Iraq an attack against people of color in the U.S., because of their high numbers in military service.

The War against Us All
1990

Farcia DeToles and I filed for discharge on the grounds of conscientious objection with the Army Reserves on December 19, 1990. As of today, our filings are still not completed. We are still in the Army Reserves.

As a matter of fact, we've just finished our two-week active duty training required by the Reserves. The officer who investigated our claims reported that we should be released from the military. Now we have to wait for our application to go to a higher headquarters to be reviewed and decided on. And while we wait, we are still required to attend monthly drills.

Attending these drills is one of the hardest things I've ever had to do. It's become so hard for me now because I'm not the same person I was before the tragic massacre this government committed against the Iraqi people.

I understand now that wars waged by this country have nothing to do with freedom or democracy or human rights. What they have to do with is the domination of power to yield profits. I understand now that the purpose of the U.S. military complex is to expand imperialism to dominate those who have less money and less technology.

Now I also understand where the money comes from to expand imperialism and who gains and who loses from the expansion. The money comes from workers: the everyday workers who pay their hard-earned tax dollars are the ones who pay for the billions of dollars invested in the military, and the billions of dollars that go into research of advanced technology.

Instead of building a society that houses the homeless, educates the illiterate, and cares for the sick, these imperialists rely on poverty and crime to fatten their pockets, while blaming us for our destitution; and what makes their strategy so effective is that they make us believe that if we'd just pull ourselves up by the bootstraps, get off welfare and stop doing drugs, we too could enter the imperialist class, as they proliferate the destruction of our families and our own self-respect.

Since most of us have to sell our labor to survive, we're at the mercy of rich imperialists whose only objective is to make profits. At any time, companies can fold up at the drop of a hat and move to another city or even, what's more profitable, to a Third World country to exploit the labor of those people who believe that earning four dollars an hour is a blessing. Now that sanctions have been lifted against South Africa, we can expect to see our brothers and sisters further exploited by American companies as well as South African ones.

The rich companies are allowed to make larger profits while leaving the unemployed to compete for jobs. When no other jobs can be found, workers join the military, or sell drugs and even their bodies to survive. We all know that survival is the first law of nature, and so does the government and the rich companies that bank on it and profit from our dependency.

This imperialist system wages racism and sexism and whatever other "isms" they need against the people to divide them in order to exploit them for profits. It's an economic strategy that works exquisitely. These imperialists have developed class and race discrimination to aid with exploitation and domination.

In order for rich people to rule and continue to be rich, they need poor people to rule over. And at the very bottom of this hierarchy are people of color. We are the objects of the racist attacks waged by imperialism. We are the largest consumers in society, who are selectively exploited the most. This government would like us to believe it's because we have broken families and we don't want to work, but would rather receive welfare and do drugs.

The truth of the matter is the imperialists have waged a war against our people for the purpose of profit-making. Our people are so busy trying to survive in this oppressive society that they don't understand a war is being waged against them by the oppressors.

The oppressors, the land and property owners in our society, will do anything, and I mean anything, in their power to maintain domination. They own the mainstream media and, to a great extent, are able to manipulate the thoughts of the oppressed. There is nothing they will not do to maintain domination. And right now they have the power.

And the imperialists want us to feel grateful that we live in a country that is free to exploit the working class by any means necessary. As a matter of fact, they've spent millions of dollars on red, white and blue you-name-it, to bolster pride in a nation that was built on slavery and continues to survive on the exploitation of workers all over the world. The only people who are free in this country are the rich people who run it. So, knowing all this makes it a little difficult for me to attend monthly drills.

I'm very proud of the peace movement here in the Bay Area. I know that the movement has done wonderful things to aid Farcia and myself when we chose to speak out against oppression. And I can't thank them enough. I understand that it is, and is going to continue to be, a bitter struggle for workers and especially people of color to win this camouflaged war against us, but we must.

People of color in this country have to liberate themselves. We cannot criticize others for not allowing us to be involved in the forefront of the struggle. We have to come out against our oppression in record-breaking numbers and take charge of our own liberation. And I know that we will.

We have to begin to unite and confront all the racist attacks against us. We are constantly being attacked because we are people of color. Desert Storm was an attack against people of color in this country because we have such high percentages of brothers and sisters in the military due to economic deprivation. And it's true that we face greater danger than our white counterparts when we try to rise up because we're at the bottom. And we know when anyone emerges who can unite our people, they will kill them right away.

Still, we cannot allow them to harness our progression. We have to fight them 'til the day we die anyway, so we might as well unite and do it together.

DONALD PAYNE
(1934–)

Donald M. Payne was elected to represent the 10th Congressional District of New Jersey in 1988. As New Jersey's first African American congressman, Payne has served as a member of the International Relations Committee and its Subcommittee on the Western Hemisphere and Subcommittee on Africa. Congressman Payne has been at the forefront of efforts to restore democracy and human rights in nations throughout the globe, including South Africa, Namibia, Haiti, Zaire, Nigeria, China, Eastern Europe and Northern Ireland. He was one of five members of Congress chosen to accompany President Clinton and Hillary Rodham Clinton on their historic six-nation tour of Africa. In 2003, President Bush appointed Payne as one of two members of Congress to serve as a congressional delegate to the United Nations. Congressman Payne comments on the U.S. efforts to rebuild Kuwait, but reminds his government that rebuilding African American communities should not be forgotten in the process.

The Reconstruction of Kuwait
March 12, 1991

. . . . Mr. Speaker . . . from Crispus Attucks, the first African-American to shed his blood on the earth of this country back in April of 1770, to many other African-Americans, they served very well in times of War. We saw Peter Salem at the Battle of Bunker Hill who fired the shot that killed Major Pitcairn who led the Boston Massacre at that Battle of Bunker Hill when they said, "Don't fire until you see the whites of their eyes." It was an African-American who was the hero of that particular war.

Mr. Speaker, we can go on. The Rough Riders were well known because they were led by Teddy Roosevelt, a person who became our President, but little is it known that at one point Teddy Roosevelt's Rough Riders were about to be annihilated at San Juan Hill, and it was the Buffalo Soldiers, an African-American group of soldiers, who led the way and reached the top of San Juan Hill to save the Rough Riders. In World War I we saw Nihim Roberts and Private Robinson who single-handedly, two persons, captured a whole brigade of Germans in the trench warfare where both of them, being wounded, continued to hurl grenades, and Mr. Nihim Roberts was a neighbor of mine and was a World War I hero who was captured.

So, we can go on and on about the many outstanding contributions made by African-Americans during times of wars, however, Mr. Speaker, I would hope that we would now think to the future, and I would like to indicate that I have put in a resolution, and I urge my colleagues here in the House of Representatives to support this very important resolution, that the gentleman from Ohio [Mr. Stokes] and the gentleman from Maryland [Mr. Mfume] and the gentlewoman from Maryland [Mrs. Morella] and I have introduced. Our plan will give women and minorities, who played such a vital role in the success of Operation Desert Storm, the opportunity to participate in a meaningful way in the rebuilding of Kuwait.

Throughout history, African-Americans have courageously answered the call to military service to our country. A recent production at Ford's Theater centered around the heroic actions during World War II of the Tuskegee airmen, black fighter pilots who flew over 1,500 combat missions and shot down more than 400 enemy aircraft. In the segregated era in which they served, these war heroes were not able to enjoy the full rights accorded other citizens when they returned home. We can't change history, we can't change the indignities suffered by veterans of past wars, but we can seize the present moment to ensure that in 1991, the doors of opportunity are open to every American.

The war in the Persian Gulf took a painful toll on my neighborhood in Newark, NJ, as one of our fine young men became the youngest casualty of Operation Desert Storm. Pvt. Robert Talley, 18 years of age, who attended the same high school that I did, lost his life in the desert before he had a chance to fulfill his hopes and dreams.

This morning's Washington Post carried a very moving photograph taken at Arlington National Cemetery at the funeral of Army Maj. Marie T. Rossi, a female pilot from Oradell, NJ, who was killed in a helicopter crash in Saudi Arabia.

Mr. Speaker, as we mourn the loss of these promising young people, it is fitting that we honor their memory by working for a better America where everyone has a chance to succeed.

We know from the Department of Labor statistics that we still have a long way to go. African-Americans, who serve in disproportionate numbers in the military, are vastly overrepresented in our national jobless rate. In 1989, the black unemployment rate was 11.4 percent compared to 4.5 percent for whites.

Despite progress, women have not attained economic equality in the American work force. On the average, a woman with a college degree still earns less than a man with a high school diploma. Statistics indicate that women working full-time, year-round, earn only 65 percent of what men make.

As the rebuilding of Kuwait gets underway, contracts will be awarded and jobs will become available. The Government of Kuwait has stated that it will be their policy to give favorable treatment to American companies for the 5-year rebuilding program. The resolution I have introduced along with my colleagues encourages the Government of Kuwait to award a significant number of contracts to women and minority-owned businesses as well as to small and disadvantaged firms. We are also asking the help of President Bush, Secretary of Defense Cheney, the Secretary of the Army, and the heads of several U.S. Government agencies involved in the reconstruction process.

Mr. Speaker, there are many ways to show patriotism and to honor those who have served our country. I believe that one of the best ways is to shape a future that gives all citizens the opportunity to fulfill the American dream. I urge my colleagues in Congress to support our resolution as we move forward to rebuild Kuwait and to reaffirm our own sense of purpose and resolve.

Notes

1. William P. O'Hare, "Wealth and Economic Status," *Crisis* 91 (December 1984): 6–7.

2. For a detailed discussion of the devastating social and economic conditions suffered by African Americans at the end of the 1970s, see Manning Marable, *Race, Reform and Rebellion: The Second Reconstruction in Black America, 1945–1990* (Jackson: University Press of Mississippi, 1991), 153–57.

3. Ronald Walters, *Black Presidential Politics in America* (Albany: State University of New York Press, 1988), 76.

4. Robert C. Smith, "Black Appointed Officials: A Neglected Area of Research in Black Political Participation," *Journal of Black Studies* 14.3 (March 1984): 373.

5. Kai Wright, *Soldiers of Freedom: An Illustrated History of African Americans in the Armed Forces* (New York: Black Dog & Leventhal, 2002), 261.

6. Marable, *Race, Reform and Rebellion*, 171.

7. Hanes Walton Jr., *Invisible Politics: Black Political Behavior* (Albany: State University of New York Press, 1985), 95.

8. Adam Clymer, "President Carter Rejects Jordan's Criticism," *New York Times*, July 26, 1977.

9. Katherine Tate, *From Protest to Politics: The New Black Voters in American Elections* (Cambridge, Mass.: Harvard University Press, 1993), 60.

10. Burton I. Kaufman and Scott Kaufman, *The Presidency of James Earl Carter Jr.* (Lawrence: University Press of Kansas, 1993), 206–7.

11. *Public Papers of the Presidents of the United States: Jimmy Carter, 1977*, vol. 2 (Washington, D.C.: U.S. Government Printing Office, 1978), 956.

12. Further information on Carter's foreign policy initiatives can be found in John Dumbrell, *American Foreign Policy: Carter to Clinton* (New York: St. Martin's, 1997), 11–52.

13. Dumbrell, *American Foreign Policy*, 35.

14. Robert G. Weisbord and Richard Kazarian Jr., *Israel in the Black American Perspective* (Westport, Conn.: Greenwood Press, 1984), 122.

15. See Weisbord and Kazarian, *Israel*, 122–30, for a reaction to Andrew Young's resignation. Also see Eddie Stone, *Andrew Young: Biography of a Realist* (Los Angeles: Holloway House, 1980), 136–42.

16. Lucius J. Barker, Mack H. Jones and Katherine Tate, *African Americans and the American Political System* (Upper Saddle River, N.J.: Prentice Hall, 1999), 187, 282.

17. Anita Hill, *Speaking Truth to Power* (New York: Anchor Books, 1977), 77.

18. *In Opposition to Clarence Thomas: Where We Must Stand and Why* (Washington, D.C.: Congressional Black Caucus Foundation, 1991); Ronald W. Walters, *White Nationalism/Black Interests* (Detroit, Mich.: Wayne State University Press, 2003), 238.

19. "Jesse Jackson's Philosophy," campaign position paper, 1984.

20. Frank Clemente and Frank Watkins, *Keep Hope Alive: Jesse Jackson's 1988 Presidential Campaign* (Boston: South End Press, 1989), 9.

21. Karin L. Stanford, *Beyond the Boundaries: Jesse Jackson in International Affairs* (Albany: State University of New York Press, 1997), 89.

22. Walters, *Black Presidential Politics*, 182.

23. For additional information on the apartheid system, see James Barber, *South Africa in the Twentieth Century* (Oxford: Blackwell, 1999).

24. Ronald W. Walters, *Freedom Is Not Enough* (Lanham, Md.: Rowman & Littlefield, 2005), 182.

25. Augusta J. Jones Jr., "Kinder, Gentler? George Bush and Civil Rights," in *Leadership and the Bush Presidency*, ed. Ryan J. Barilleaux and Mary E. Stuckey (Westport, Conn.: Praeger, 1992), 181.

26. Jones, "Kindler, Gentler?" 184.

27. Donna Britt, "Robinson, a Voice for Africa: The Lobbyist and His Power of Persuasion," *Washington Post*, March 13, 1990.

28. William Minter, "The U.S. and the War in Angola," *Review of African Political Economy*, March 1991, 50, 135–44.

29. U.S. Department of State Dispatch, "Fact Sheet: U.S. Initiatives for Demining and Landmine Control," May 30, 1994.

30. James A. Baker with Thomas M. DeFrank, *The Politics of Diplomacy: Revolution, War and Peace, 1989–1992* (New York: Putnam, 1995), 104; Steven Hurst, *The Foreign Policy of the Bush Administration* (London: Cassell, 1999), 40.

31. See Hurst, *Foreign Policy*, 29, for a critical examination of the "New World Order."

32. Colin Powell with Joseph E. Persico, *My American Journey* (New York: Random House, 1995), 303; see page 149 for Powell's thoughts on Vietnam.

33. Powell with Persico, *American Journey*, 434.

34. Hurst, *Foreign Policy*, 49; Kevin Buckley, *Panama: The Whole Story* (New York: Simon & Schuster, 1991), 230.

35. David Mervin, *George Bush and the Guardianship Presidency* (New York: Macmillan, 1996), 168.

36. Billy Montgomery, "Congressmen Call for Invasion Investigation," *Michigan Citizen* 12.8 (January 20, 1990): 1.

37. Christina Jacqueline Johns and P. Ward Johnson, *State Crime, the Media, and the Invasion of Panama* (Westport, Conn.: Praegar, 1994), 88–89; the authors detail the debate about the number of estimated casualties. The Department of Defense Southern Command's estimates ranged from 50 to 300, while Panamanian human rights estimates ranged as high as 2,000.

38. Clayton R. Newell, *Historical Dictionary of the Persian Gulf War 1990–1991* (Lanham, Md.: Scarecrow Press, 1998).

39. Newell, *Historical Dictionary*, 112.

40. Newell, *Historical Dictionary*, 96.

41. *Washington Post*, August 6, 1990.

42. Newell, *Historical Dictionary*, 66–67.

43. Richard Hatcher, "Guns vs. Butter: Many Blacks Oppose American Role in War, Citing Domestic Needs," *Wall Street Journal*, January 25, 1991.

44. Ronald V. Dellums, "Voices: Why Do You Think the USA Is in the Persian Gulf?" *USA Today*, November 30, 1990.

45. *Dellums v. Bush*, 752 F. Supp. 1141 (Washington, D.C.: 1990).

46. Azania Howse, "The War against Us All," *The Anti-Warrior*, January 3, 1992.

47. Hatcher, "Guns vs. Butter."

48. Juan Williams, "Race and War in the Persian Gulf: Why Are Black Leaders Trying to Divide Blacks from the American Mainstream?" *The Washington Post*, January 20, 1991.

49. "Iraqi Invasion Decried by Jackson in Iowa: Send U.N. Troops to Liberia," *Omaha World*, August 6, 1990.

50. Hatcher, "Guns vs. Butter."

51. Sonya Ross, "Coretta King Tells Churchgoers to Oppose War but Support Troops," *Seattle Times*, January 20, 1991.

52. William E. Schulz, "Coretta Scott King Calls for Education, Not War," *Austin American Statesman*, January 21, 1991; Les Hausner, "In King's Honor, Chorus Swells against Gulf War," *Chicago Sun-Times*, January 22, 1991.

53. Hausner, "In King's Honor."

54. Jesse Jackson, "Ignore Bush's Ploys: Vote for Change," *Newsday*, November 5, 1990.

55. Powell with Persico, *American Journey*, 400.

56. Wright, *Soldiers of Freedom*, 273.

57. Office of the Under Secretary of Defense Personnel and Readiness, *Career Progression of Minority and Women Officers*, Department of Defense, November 23, 1999.

58. Pentagon numbers quoted in Hatcher, "Guns vs. Butter."

59. Williams, "Race and War."

60. Hatcher, "Guns vs. Butter."

61. Steven Holmes, "Military Moves to Aid Racial Harmony," *New York Times*, April 5, 1995.

62. Hatcher, "Guns vs. Butter."

63. Williams, "Race and War."

64. Williams, "Race and War."

65. Williams, "Race and War."

66. Williams, "Race and War."

67. Yvonne Latty, *We Were There: Voices of African American Veterans from World War II to the War in Iraq* (New York: Amistad, 2005), 155.

68. William J. Simmons, "Operation Desert Shield/Storm through the Eyes of a Black Lieutenant: Saga 1," title 407 at www.greatunpublished.com (accessed 2001).

69. Newell, *Historical Dictionary*, 101.

70. "Iraqi Invasion Decried by Jackson in Iowa: Send U.N. Troops to Liberia," *Omaha World*, August 6, 1990.

71. Joseph B. Treaster, "Confrontation in the Gulf; 700 Women and Children Freed; Thousands of Westerners Remain," *New York Times*, September 2, 1990; Greg McDonald, "Jesse Jackson on a 'Journalistic Mission,'" *Houston Chronicle*, August 29, 1990.

⁓

CHAPTER TEN

Iraq War:
Patriot Games

2 0 0 3 – P R E S E N T

The domestic climate that spawned the U.S. invasion of Iraq on March 20, 2003, was arguably different from the one of thirteen years earlier, when the U.S. was embattled in the Persian Gulf War. William Jefferson Clinton had just completed two terms as the U.S. president, serving from 1993–2001, after defeating George H. W. Bush in his reelection bid. Bill Clinton became the first Democratic president since the one-term presidency of Jimmy Carter. Although presenting himself as a moderate during the campaign, supporting such policies as the death penalty and welfare reform, Clinton was able to capture more than 80 percent of the African American vote.[1] During Clinton's tenure, African Americans continued to support his administration even though he advocated for the Personal Responsibility and Work Opportunity Reconciliation Act, a version of welfare reform that instilled harsh work requirements. The Violent Crime Control and Law Enforcement Act (1994), which expanded the federal death penalty, added a variety of new and federal offenses and invoked mandatory sentences, was also supported by the Clinton administration, despite the opposition from most African American leaders.

President Clinton, however, did not totally ignore the interests of his African American constituency. During his two terms, Clinton appointed the most African Americans in history to high-level cabinet positions. Before Clinton, African Americans had been "given one cabinet position, frequently at HUD or HEW (now HHS). But, Clinton placed four Blacks in his cabinet—at Energy, Agriculture, Veterans Affairs and Commerce, and named numerous African Americans to subcabinet positions."[2] Overall, 13 percent of Clinton's administration and more than 19 percent of his judicial appointments to the federal courts were African American.[3] Clinton also appointed Reverend Jesse Jackson as special envoy for the Promotion of Democracy in Africa, a role that made him an adviser to the president on African policy. Recognizing the need to improve race relations, especially in the wake of the Million-Man March, the brutalization of Haitian immigrant Abner Louima by the New York City police and the African American reaction to the O. J. Simpson verdict, President Clinton instituted a "National Conversation on Race." The eminent scholar John Hope Franklin was appointed by the president to lead that discussion. President Clinton went even further to demonstrate his support by refusing to submit to Republican pressure to end affirmative action. Instead, Clinton engendered a new policy, "Mend it, don't end it," which supported an end to quotas and reform, but not elimination of affirmative action. Clinton also initiated economic growth opportunities for American inner cities through a program called the New Markets Initiative, a brainchild of Reverend Jesse Jackson, which gave tax breaks to companies investing in those areas. Other more mainstream initiatives of Clinton also benefited the African American community, including the Family and Medical Leave Act (1993), which allowed family members to take a leave of absence from work for three months for catastrophic events and illnesses, without fear of being fired.

In addition to the foregoing symbolic and policy indicators of support for their community, African Americans were impressed with Clinton's relative ease around them, his long-standing relationship with their leaders in Arkansas, his comfort in African American churches and knowledge of African American culture. Proof of Clinton's respect for African American culture was signaled when he played the saxophone on a television show hosted by Arsenio Hall during the campaign and then later invited Maya Angelou, the noted Black poet, to speak at his inauguration. Donna Brazile, Democratic party strategist, said that Bill Clinton "not only understood our language and our songs, he understood our dreams and aspirations."[4] The fact that his wife, Hillary Clinton, had previously worked as a civil rights attorney, was considered a bonus for African Americans. During Clinton's reelection bid, he received 84 percent of the African American vote.[5]

African American support for the president paid off. By the time Clinton left office, African American unemployment was down to its lowest point in history, hovering around 7 percent.[6] A Census Bureau report showed that the poverty rate for African Americans had fallen to an all-time low of 24 percent by the year 2000 from 33 percent in 1993.[7] On the international front,

African Americans were impressed with Clinton's efforts to prevent nuclear proliferation and his mediation attempts in the Israeli-Palestinian conflict. Clinton also authorized military intervention to end the Bosnian and the Kosovo War and engaged in air attacks on Saddam Hussein's Iraq. As commander-in-chief, Clinton was most noted for his "Don't ask, don't tell" policy, which allowed homosexual men and women to serve in the military as long as their sexuality remained secret.[8] Also as commander-in-chief, Clinton recognized the valor and bravery of African American soldiers. "On January 16, 2001, President Bill Clinton presented Corporal Andrew Jackson Smith's family members with the Medal of Honor he earned during the Battle of Honey Hill during the Civil War in November 1864."[9] The battle was fought to cut off the Savannah-Charleston railroad link and keep Confederate forces from interfering with General William Sherman's "March to the Sea," in which 60,000 men marched from Atlanta to the Atlantic Ocean, destroying the South's economic resources. During the bloody battle of Honey Hill, 5,000 Union troops advanced through the 300 yards of swamp to get to the road, but ended up walking into a slaughter. During the furious fight, the color-bearer was shot and killed, but Corporal Andrew Jackson Smith retrieved both the state and federal flags. Corporal Smith continued to lead his troops into battle, while exposing himself as the target. He had been nominated for the Medal of Honor in 1916, but "the Army claimed, erroneously, that there were no official records to prove his story and his extraordinary acts of courage."[10] Bill Clinton honored his heroism 137 years later, when he presented his 93-year-old granddaughter and seven other family members with the Medal of Honor "for conspicuous gallantry and intrepidity at the risk of his life above and beyond the call of duty."[11] In 1999, President Clinton also issued a presidential pardon to Lt. Henry Ossian Flipper, West Point's first Black graduate. Flipper had been falsely charged with embezzlement, court martialed and convicted and then dishonorably discharged in 1881. Claiming that the charges were based on prejudice, Flipper spent the rest of his life trying to clear his name. However, it wasn't until President Clinton's pardon that the path was cleared for Flipper to receive an honorable discharge.[12]

President Clinton broke new ground on the relationship between the U.S. and Africa as well. He became the first U.S. president to make state visits to several African countries, including Uganda, Ghana, Senagal and South Africa. The purpose of the trip in 1998 was to establish a new partnership with Africa and demonstrate U.S. respect for African culture. Although the mission did not produce any groundbreaking new proposals, upon his return Clinton helped to push through Congress a few new bills for aid to African countries and provided momentum for the passage of the African Growth and Opportunity Act on May 18, 2000. The trade bill was designed to lower tariffs and quotas on products from sub-Saharan Africa.[13] Clinton's most significant foreign policy failure was also related to the continent of Africa. From April through July 1994, an estimated 800,000 to 1,000,000 Tutsis and moderate Hutus were slaughtered in Rwanda. Despite the pleas of African and African American leaders, President Clinton refused to intervene militarily to end the bloodshed. Later, Clinton even admitted that he regarded his inaction duirng the Rwandan genocide as a "personal failure."[14] Clinton did, however, deploy American troops to Somalia, with the intent of protecting and aiding humanitarian assistance efforts for civilians. Even though Operation Restore Hope ended in disaster, which was signaled by the dragging of a U.S. soldier's body through the streets of the Somalian capital, and the brutal clashes between the U.S. soldiers and rival Somalia chiefans, African Americans applauded Clinton for his willingness to use U.S. resources to aid an African nation. The Clinton administration withdrew U.S. troops after they suffered 17 deaths and 77 were wounded at the hands of Somalia militiamen.[15]

On Haiti, after a hunger strike by TransAfrica's executive director Randall Robinson, Clinton changed his restrictive immigration policy toward Haitian refugees. In 1994, Clinton sent U.S. troops into Haiti to restore Jean-Bertrand Aristide as president, ending a period of intense violence. Aristide, who had been elected, had been ousted in a coup just seven months into his term in 1991.

Hoping to garner similar support from a Democratic president, African Americans gave Clinton's vice president, Al Gore, 90 percent of their vote during the presidential election campaign of 2000.[16] Gore's challenger was George W. Bush, the former governor of Texas and son of the previous President George H. W. Bush. It was easy for African Americans to deny Bush their support. Although he ran for the presidency as a compassionate conservative, Governor Bush was well known for supporting the death penalty, which was disproportionately applied to African Americans in comparison to whites. Governor Bush presided over 131 executions within five years, more than in any other state.[17] In addition, Bush was opposed to affirmative action and refused to support a federal hate crimes law. Bush had also offended African Americans when he appeared at Bob Jones University, an educational institution based in South Carolina that overtly prohibited interracial dating. African Americans were additionally opposed to Bush's running mate, Dick Cheney, the former secretary of defense for the George H. W. Bush administration and chief of staff to President Gerald Ford.

The relationship between African Americans and George W. Bush became further strained at the end of the hotly contested election that landed Bush in the White House. African American voters argued that they had been disenfranchised and charged the Republican-led state government in Florida with voter tampering, harassment at the polls and fraud. Florida, whose governor at the time of the elections was Jeb Bush, the younger brother of George W. Bush, was the swing state of the election. The election was close. The polls closed "with a statewide difference of 1,800 votes between the candidates."[18] On election night, Florida's 25 electoral votes were originally called for former vice president Albert Gore but then retracted and given to George W. Bush, making him the president-elect. Then allegations of vote tampering and fraud were levied against the Bush-led Republican Party the next day and brought to national attention by organizations such as the NAACP, Rainbow Push Coalition and the National Action Network. Former vice president Albert Gore, who won the popular vote, challenged the decision in court and requested the courts allow for a ballot recount in several counties. The Florida Supreme Court allowed a hand-count of the ballots in the four predominately African American counties of Miami-Dade, Broward, Volusia and Palm Beach.

The recount efforts showed Bush's lead over Gore closing, so Governor George Bush and his supporters took their case to end the recount to the Supreme Court. Despite the continuing recount and probes into the possible civil rights violations, the conservative-leaning Supreme Court handed down a decision in *Bush v. Gore* to end the counting, thereby handing the election over to George Bush.[19] African Americans saw the Supreme Court as a partner who aided and abetted Bush's "stealing" of the election.[20] Vice President Al Gore eventually conceded the presidential race and President-Elect George Bush was victorious.

As president, Bush's domestic agenda centered on lowering taxes, promoting educational vouchers, a balanced budget, advocating for the right of religious organizations to receive federal funding for charitable programs, ending abortions and advocating for oil drilling in the Arctic National Wildlife Refuge. Bush's foreign policy platform supported strengthening ties to Latin America, especially Mexico, and reduced involvement in "nation-building" and other minor military engagements indirectly related to the U.S.

Specifically on the question of race, President Bush "attempted to reach out to the black community with appointments, symbolic gestures, and substantive policies."[21] Substantive policies included prohibiting racial profiling by federal law enforcement agencies, proposals to increase low-income and minority home ownership and implementing policies to raise the performance

302 ~ Chapter Ten

of low-income and minority students through the "No Child Left Behind Act." On foreign policy, Bush proposed substantial increases in funds to combat AIDS in Africa, authorized a special envoy to mediate the Sudanese civil war and sent a small peace-keeping force to Liberia. Symbolic support included hanging a portrait of Martin Luther King Jr. in the White House, laying a wreath at King's tomb, hosting Thomas Jefferson's Black relatives at the White House and condemning the statement of Senator Trent Lott, who talked positively of the segregationist views of Senator Strom Thurmond.[22] On appointments to his administration, Bush selected General Colin Powell as the first African American secretary of state and Professor Condoleezza Rice as his national security advisor. Approximately 7.5 percent of Bush political appointments were African American.[23] As did President Clinton, the new president visited several African countries. Bush also hosted African leaders at a Washington summit and held a state dinner for the president of Uganda.

President Bush, however, received strong criticism for attempting to overrule the affirmative action program at the University of Michigan, which allowed the school to take race into account in admission decisions. African Americans also criticized the integrity of the No Child Left Behind program, which emphasized testing but did not address issues of cultural bias within the testing instrument. In addition, inadequate funding for the program prevented schools in their communities from adhering to the program's strict guidelines. The Bush administration's proposed changes to the Social Security program did not bode well for the African American community, either. The new rules would allow individuals to invest a portion of their Social Security taxes into secured investments. African Americans saw this proposal as an opportunity for investment firms, but not for them. In particular, African Americans were infuriated with Bush for refusing to address the age requirements to receive Social Security, which essentially required African American men to pay into the system, but who on average died before the age of 65, and therefore could not collect any benefits.[24] But perhaps most importantly, African American leaders objected to Bush's tax cuts, which they saw as disproportionately benefiting predominately rich, white Americans.

On international relations, African Americans opposed the Bush administration's forced removal of Haitian president Jean-Bertrand Aristide from office into exile in 2004. African Americans were even more incensed in August 2001, when President Bush's delegation walked out of the World Conference against Racism, Xenophobia, and Related Intolerance held in Durban, South Africa. U.S. officials objected to several issues on the conference agenda, especially reparations for African Americans and the Palestinian/

Israeli conflict. Instead of addressing those issues directly, the Bush administration representatives left the conference. It seems, however, that the African American community's most vehement and long-lasting objection has been President Bush's declared war against Iraq. On September 11, 2001, terrorists affiliated with Al-Qaeda, a Muslim extremist group, hijacked four planes and flew them into the World Trade Center in New York City and the Pentagon in Washington, D.C. The fourth plane crashed into a remote field in Somerset, Pennsylvania. Overall, the acts of terrorism claimed nearly 2,800 lives.

Almost immediately Osama bin Laden, head of an international network of Muslim terrorist camps, was declared the main suspect responsible for the attacks. Al-Qaeda, a group devoted to the jihad, or Islamic holy war, against secular governments of the Muslim Middle East and Western powers, consists of thousands of trained militants in multiple locations all over the world who are determined to bring all Muslims under fundamentalist Islamic law. Bin Laden, considered one of the most significant financial sponsors of Islamic extremist activities, used his wealth to finance jihads around the world.[25] Osama bin Laden was also suspected of being the mastermind behind the World Trade Center attack in 1993 that resulted in the death of six people and injury to another 1,000.

As early as September 14, 2001, Congress passed the Post 9-11 Use of Force Act, which authorized President Bush "to use all necessary and appropriate force against those nations, organizations, or persons he determines planned, authorized, committed, or aided the terrorist attacks that occurred on September 11, 2001, or harbored such organizations or persons, in order to prevent any future acts of international terrorism against the United States by such nations, organizations or persons."[26] After Congress rendered its decision, the president quickly sent U.S. troops into Afghanistan to hunt down Osama bin Laden and associates of Al-Qaeda, declaring that he wanted them dead or alive. The majority of the nation supported President Bush's response to the terrorist attacks. Several CNN/USA Today/Gallup polls conducted in September 2001 indicated that 90 percent of Americans approved of President Bush's plan to wage war on Al-Qaeda. Even though the Bush administration demonstrated no indication of changing its policies to address the domestic crisis in the African American community, after the terrorist attacks African Americans rallied behind the president. A Zogby International poll that same month indicated that 94 percent of African Americans rated Bush's handling of the attacks as excellent, good or fair. Patriotism was at its height among all races and the American flag was flown in most communities, Black and white. Cheryl Poinsette Brown commented on patriotism and flying her flag as a way to "show our commitment and solidarity with other Americans and to demonstrate our staunch resolve to prevent further such attacks on our soil."[27] Even Bishop T. D. Jakes, one of the most popular African American ministers, who hosts more than 28,000 members, urged his congregation to pray in support of President Bush. Jakes said to his congregation:

> You've got to put your King James English up and start praying up to date. We're not fighting no two-thousand-year-old demon. This is a 2001 contemporary, twenty-first century devil who is hacking into our computer systems. We have to pray against hackers. You gotta start praying in tongues and praying in the Holy Ghost, and watch and pray and believe God. And God said, "In the time of harvest." Tell Osama bin Laden, "It's harvest time." Tell the demonic forces behind him, "It's harvest time." Tell every country that's harboring these enemies, "It's harvest time." God said, "In the time of harvest, I will bind the tares into bundles to burn them."[28]

Shortly after the terrorist attacks on 9/11, President Bush turned his focus to Iraq. Declaring that the Middle East nation possessed weapons of mass destruction and was harboring terrorists, President Bush connected the 9/11 attacks to Iraq and argued that the U.S. was in imminent danger from Saddam Hussein. Bush also asserted that Hussein was partly responsible for the continued destabilization in the Middle East because the Arab leader financed terrorists and aggravated the Israeli-Palestinian conflict. The solution, according to Bush, was to make the world safer by removing the Hussein regime from power. Furthermore, once Hussein was ousted from office, the United States would aid in setting up a democratic government. Surely, the Iraqi people would be very grateful for U.S. intervention to liberate them from such a cruel dictator.

On March 30, 2003, President Bush issued a spirited call to patriotic arms and led U.S. troops in a preemptive strike against Iraq. U.S. citizens, such as African American columnist Larry Elder, gave tremendous support to the president. Elder also criticized antiwar demonstrators, who he argued ignored the vast number of crimes that Saddam Hussein committed against humanity. According to Elder, those protestors were demonstrating "support for the torturers and total contempt for the victim."[29] Another respected African American columnist, Earl Ofari Hutchinson, understood African American support for the war. He asserted that "Many Blacks do revile Bush for his attack on affirmative action, his conservative judicial appointments, his refusal to expand hate crimes legislation, support for school vouchers, meat-axe tax cuts, and the slash and burn of social programs . . . But they, as most Americans, are scared stiff of terrorist attacks."[30]

But soon after the war in Iraq began, Black and white Americans began to question the real motives of the president. Bush had seemingly lost interest in capturing Osama bin Laden, but instead put an inordinate amount of U.S. resources into capturing Saddam Hussein. What was most troubling to many Americans was the administration's failure to find any weapons of mass destruction (WMD), which was the Bush administration's primary reason for the strike against Iraq and which Colin Powell adroitly argued before the United Nations that Iraq possessed. However, the Iraq Survey Group, a multinational force spearheaded by the U.S., Britain and Australia to find the WMDs, concluded that Iraq no longer had any. The Iraq Survey Group worked in concert with the UN inspectors Hans Blix and Mohamed Elbaradei.[31] Still U.S. citizens, out of patriotism, supported the president, even after the passage of the USA PATRIOT Act—Uniting and Strengthening America by Providing Appropriate Tools Required to Intercept and Obstruct Terrorism (October 2001)—which gave the government the right to ignore civil rights and civil liberties if one was suspected of affiliation with terrorism.

More intense scrutiny of the administration began to occur after the capture of Hussein on December 13, 2003. The failure of the U.S. to secure peace in the country raised even more eyebrows, especially when the Bush administration continued to assert that eventually the Iraqi people would express support for their liberators from tyranny. Instead, Iraqi militants and international terrorists began to wage war in order to take over the country. Foreign visitors, reporters and workers in Iraq were taken hostage and sometimes beheaded while being videoed and then shown on live television. Thousands of bombings, which included suicide bombings, car and bus bombings, claimed the lives of hundreds of innocent civilians.

Declining support for the president was reflected in the results of his reelection bid for a second term. Although the Bush-Cheney ticket defeated the Democratic team of Senator John Kerry of Massachusetts for president and Senator John Edwards of North Carolina for vice president, they did so only by scant margins. African Americans overwhelmingly supported the Democratic team, giving Kerry 88 percent of its vote.[32]

During his second term, questions about Bush's true motivations for invading Iraq began to escalate. Eventually, antiwar sentiment began to spread globally. Critics maintained that the real goal of the Bush administration was to control Iraqi oil. The fact that the oil and energy multinational corporation Halliburton, formerly chaired by Vice President Cheney, received a "no-bid" multi-billion-dollar contract for oil-well fire fighting in Iraq, made questions about the president's motives appear even more legitimate. One of the most effective antiwar protests was an investigative documentary entitled

Fahrenheit 9/11, produced by Michael Moore and released on June 25, 2004. In *Fahrenheit 9/11*, Moore outlined the Bush family connection to the bin Laden family and other companies who were profiting tremendously from the war. It was those connections, along with a few others presented in the documentary, that Moore believed exposed the real reason for the invasion. African American Captain Delon R. Powell, who served in Iraq and voted for President Bush twice, echoed Moore's sentiments when he said, "It's not just oil. It's not just liberation. It's a by-product of Iraq being a strategic post for the United States, between Iran and Syria . . . The cost of operating in Germany is getting too expensive."[33] By December 2005, an ABC News/*Washington Post* poll indicated that only 46 percent of Americans approved of Bush's handling of Iraq.

Surprisingly, one of the earliest challenges to the Bush policy came from inside the administration. General Colin Powell had repeatedly questioned the need for a preemptive strike against Iraq.[34] In a meeting with President Bush on August 5, Secretary Powell set forth his concerns about the potential war. Not only could war destabilize friendly regimes in the Middle East, but it might also divert attention from other important issues domestically and internationally. He further explained to Bush that if he pursued the war, the U.S. would be responsible for the country, including its rebuilding. Powell told Bush, "You are going to be the proud owner of 25 million people . . . You will own their hopes, aspirations and problems. You'll own it all."[35] To the chagrin of Vice President Dick Cheney and Secretary of Defense Donald Rumsfeld, both considered hawkish on the war, Powell persuaded the president to seek authority from the U.S. Congress and the UN before going to war. Later Powell testified before the UN to offer proof of Iraq's possession of WMDs.[36]

In the halls of Congress, while most members were concerned that their failure to support the policy of President Bush might appear unpatriotic, one lone African American member of Congress, Barbara Lee, became the voice of dissent. Congresswoman Lee, a Democrat from California and also a member of the Congressional Black Caucus (CBC), cast the only vote against the Post 9-11 Use of Force Act. In her remarks on September 16, 2001, Rep. Lee pointed out that "military action will not prevent further acts of international terrorism against the United States." She explained that she did not want America to repeat the same mistakes made in the past by embarking on "an open-ended war with neither an exit strategy nor a focused target," much like it did during the Vietnam War. Moreover, attacking so soon would "inflame prejudice against all Arab Americans, Muslims, Southeast Asians, or any other people because of their race, religion, or ethnicity."³⁷ Michael Eric Dyson, an African American minister and professor, applauded Congresswoman Lee for her stance. In an article written soon after the vote, Dyson questioned why Congresswoman Lee was the only person in Congress to stand up to the "machinery of war."³⁸ In his argument against the war, Dyson reminded African Americans that they too have experienced terrorism, but have not responded violently against their country. According to Dyson, "This is the same government that refuses to acknowledge your pain and the domestic terrorism that we confront on a daily basis in Watts, Oakland, Harlem, and Detroit. The same government that refuses to stop racial profiling and police brutality—that's terrorism, too. And now we, as people of color, are being seduced into believing that the only alternative is to do to them what has been done to us, to bomb them as they have bombed us."³⁹

In addition to the dissent earlier voiced by General Powell and Congresswoman Barbara Lee, an African American serviceman turned against his own military unit. On March 23, 2003, just two days after the U.S. invasion of Iraq, an African American army sergeant, Hasan Akbar, attacked the 101st Airborne Division, also known as the "Screaming Eagles," as they were preparing to move from central Kuwait to Iraq. At 1:00 a.m., Akbar launched grenades into several tents and returned fire to soldiers who fled from the exploding tents. The attack took the lives of two soldiers and wounded 14 more, many of whom were senior command staff of the brigade. The incident stirred up memories of fragging—the killing of an American soldier by another with the use of a fragmentation grenade. Approximately 600 American soldiers were killed from fragging incidents during Vietnam.⁴⁰

Hasan Akbar, born Mark Fidel Kools, grew up in the rough neighborhood of Watts in Los Angeles and found the Muslim faith at a young age. He excelled through school and earned aeronautical and mechanical engineering degrees at the University of California, Davis.⁴¹ Through adulthood and up until the attack, there were conflicting accounts about his character. Some would describe him as a typical bachelor, while others would say he was a strict Muslim and closely followed the guidelines of his faith. But his fellow battalion members in Iraq described him as an insubordinate who possessed the kind of attitude that resulted in disciplinary actions. But no one predicted the forthcoming violence.

Lawyers for Akbar pleaded not guilty by reason of insanity, stating that he was deeply conflicted by his religious beliefs because he suspected that the pending invasion would cause the deaths of many fellow Muslims. His lawyers also claimed that he was suffering from "the blues" at the time of the attack because of the constant ridicule he experienced as the only African

American and Muslim in his battalion. Claims were presented in the case that some soldiers antagonized Akbar by joking that they might mistake him for one of the Iraqis and shoot him one day. Akbar claims that because of those kinds of comments, he suffered from paranoia, and on the night of the attack he felt like he was defending his life. Despite all attempts by the defense to prove Akbar was mentally ill, a military jury found him guilty of all counts, and sentenced him to death.[42]

Younger African Americans who embraced hip-hop culture became involved in the antiwar effort. Russell Simmons, a member of Musicians United to Win without War, sent a message to the troops overseas. Simmons stated that "They're playing you like a bunch of suckers right now. I hate to sound mean, but they're sending you to war. Blacks and browns are gonna die on the frontline . . . We're fighting and we're not protecting ourselves. While we're at home, we should vote. We should exert our power. We should not be moved around like sheep. Speak up. It's alright to speak up."[43]

Aside from the individual acts of dissent and opposition to the Iraq War, African Americans en masse questioned the Patriot Act, which they believed would unfairly target their community. Certainly, African Americans have long complained of being subjected to racial profiling, especially while driving. Commonly referred to as "Driving While Black (DWB)" the discriminatory practice was beginning to gain national attention when September 11 occurred. DWB is based on the assumption that certain minorities were most likely to be engaged in criminal activity and therefore commonly sought out by law enforcement, pulled over, searched and even held in custody with no evidence that the person was a legitimate suspect in a crime. But once the 9/11 attacks occurred, the attention to racial profiling dwindled. Reflecting memories of the FBI's Counterintelligence Program of the 1960s, which sought to destroy Black leadership and organizations, African Americans were concerned that they might be subjected to further mistreatment on the streets and in their homes.[44]

African Americans also expressed concern that the war would result in long-term economic instability and might siphon away government resources that could be used to uplift their community. Hugh Price, head of the National Urban League, argued that the safety net for the poor would be harmed by the billions of dollars that would be spent on the war.[45] Ronald Walters, professor at University of Maryland, College Park, and director of the African American Leadership Institute, stated in his article "Collateral Damage" that the U.S. government has not considered the sacrifices of the war by "Americans who need such things as prescription drugs, a Social Security safety net, college loans, Medicaid and Medicare, election reform funded, sufficient affordable housing and strategic support for the budget of those states whose economies have gone into the tank." Walters further criticized Bush's suggestions that the U.S. should slow down spending to save money for war, instead of speeding up spending to bail out the economy.[46] As of 2005, Congress has appropriated $261 billion to Operation Iraqi Freedom. By the end of 2006, Congressional estimates skyrocket to more than $320 billion.[47]

For other African Americans, the war in Iraq served as confirmation of the racist nature of U.S. foreign policy. The facts that the U.S. delegation walked out of the World Conference on Racism just days before the attack, had refused to negotiate with the PLO and had previously labeled Nelson Mandela of South Africa a terrorist did little to persuade African Americans otherwise. What confirmed the view for many African Americans that U.S. policy was still rooted in racism was the Bush administration's slow response to help African Americans who were stranded in New Orleans after the most damaging hurricane ever to hit that city. For many African Americans, the administration's lackluster response to Hurricane Katrina was tinged with racism and reflected the lack of concern for African Americans. It was easy for anti-Bush leaders to point to the vast amount of money that was being spent on Iraq, compared to the lack of attention given to New Orleans.[48]

The longstanding concerns about inequality and disparate treatment of African Americans inside the U.S. armed forces have also surfaced. One case that received a fair amount of attention occurred after the capture of the 507th Ordnance Maintenance Company on March 23, 2003, by Iraqi troops after a wrong turn off their path. While eleven of the company's soldiers were killed in the ambush, six were captured. In the company were Jessica Lynch, a white, 19-year-old private from West Virginia, and Shoshanna Johnson, an African American single mother who became the first Black female POW in American history. Held captive for days, Johnson, Lynch and the rest of their company were eventually rescued. When the prisoners of war returned home, they encountered a media frenzy, but most of it surrounded Jessica Lynch, who was credited for her courage and patriotism. Songs were written about Lynch and the governor of West Virginia greeted her at a parade held in her honor.[49] TV and news reports alleged that despite her life-threatening injuries, which included a head laceration, injury to her spine and fractures to her arms and legs, Lynch heroically emptied her rifle as she fired on her attackers. As Lynch became America's Sweetheart, Johnson faded into the background. Even though Johnson had been held captive for 22 days, subjected to demeaning conditions, beaten relentlessly and shot through both legs, Lynch went on to receive multimillion-dollar book and movie deals regarding her ordeal. Lynch even received more compensation for her injuries from the army. Lynch received 80 percent of her disability benefit compared to Johnson, who only received 30 percent of her disability benefit.[50]

African American civil rights leaders expressed outrage at the shabby treatment of Johnson. Jesse Jackson exclaimed that both Lynch and Johnson had the same commitment to the country, but their treatment was far from the same. Even Jessica Lynch contended that instead of firing her rifle repeatedly, it had jammed. According to Lynch, "I didn't kill anybody . . . We left a lot of men behind."[51] The U.S. Army denied any claims of racism toward Johnson, claiming Lynch suffered far more injuries than Johnson, therefore needing more assistance, even though Lynch had not been shot.[52]

Patricia Roberts, mother of Jamaal Addison, an African American, who was the first soldier from Georgia to be killed in Iraq, spoke out against the war and President Bush. As in the case of Cindy Sheehan, a white female resident of Berkeley, California, who became a prominent anti-Iraq War activist after the death of her son, Casey Sheehan, Roberts wanted to meet with Bush to discuss the war. Sheehan had attracted international attention for her demonstration outside of President George W. Bush's Texas ranch in August 2005 after his refusal to meet with her. Although Sheehan had previously met with the president with other families in June 2004 at Fort Lewis Washington, three months after her son's death, she still did not understand the purpose and the handling of the war. After Bush refused to meet with her again, she staged a protest and has since organized peace camps throughout the country.

Jamaal Addison's mother also felt slighted by the president. He had refused a meeting with her to offer his apologies as he did with other parents of slain soldiers, claiming he was "picking and choosing" which parents he would offer his condolences to. In an interview with Amy Goodman on National Public Radio, Patricia Roberts questioned the manner and process by which the president determined which families he would meet with. Roberts stated, "I haven't gotten the opportunity to talk to him. So I would like to know how he goes about it. Is it the ones that support the war? And that's the ones that he's talking to, those soldiers that survived? Is he talking to the families that once their child is gone, that they still support him? Are those the families he's talking to? I don't know who he is talking to. All I know is that he is not talking to me."[53]

African American mistrust of the commander-in-chief was reflected in the decline of their enlistment into the army. The number of Black recruits fell from 41 percent in fiscal year 2000 to 13.9 percent in 2005.[54] Certainly, fear of being killed or injured was the number one reason among all young people to avoid military service, according to the U.S. Military Image Study, who interviewed 3,236 youth ages 16 to 24.[55] This fear, however, for African Americans has proven to be valid. Twenty-eight percent of the 130,000 troops dispatched to Iraq were African American and as of September 2004, Blacks were 13 percent of the 980 killed.[56]

Congressman Charles Rangel of New York, a Purple Heart and Bronze Star African American veteran of the Korean War, launched an effort to close the racial and class enlistment disparity in the armed forces. Rangel proposed a reinstatement of the draft in January 2003 and then again in May 2005. Justification for the initiative included the concern that poor people and minorities were more likely to sign up for the military because they lacked access to other viable opportunities; that few if any of the members of Congress and the Bush administration who advocated war had close family members in service; and that the military had suffered a decline in recruitment, as a result of the unpopular war. Although Rangel's proposals have not passed, he vows to continue the fight for class sensitivity in the military.

The voices of African Americans in this section reflect the changes in society since the end of the civil rights movement. Prior to the civil rights movement, only a few African Americans served in Congress, while today more than 40 are members. For the first time in history African Americans have held two of the most important positions in the U.S. foreign policy apparatus. Suffice it to say that while the majority of African Americans have reduced their support for Bush policies, former Secretary of State Colin Powell and now the current Secretary of State Condoleezza Rice have been responsible for the implementation of that policy. For some African Americans these appointments signal respect for their talent and experience in the arena of foreign policy. For others, however, the policies that have been promoted by the Bush administration are antithetical to the interests of African American people.

In this contemporary age, African Americans and others rely heavily on the Internet, which has developed into a full global communication network, to promote their perspective. The World Wide Web has magnified the depth, breadth and speed with which information can be shared. This new connectedness has facilitated the ability to galvanize and mobilize enormous networks of people, as would be evidenced again and again in very large scale anti-globalization and antiwar demonstrations around the world. Many of the presentations here are a reflection of the availability of communications online.

This book's final section includes commentary that sets forth the perspectives of African American government officials, journalists and scholars including secretaries of state Colin Powell and Condoleezza Rice, Farai

Chideya, Gail Buckley and Maulana Karenga. Presidential candidate, Reverend Al Sharpton, also presents the African American view on the war within the context of his presidential bid. And finally, elected officials reflect the position of African Americans within the context of their official duties. The Congressional Black Caucus has released several statements challenging the legitimacy of the war, one of which is represented here. In addition, Congresspersons Charles Rangel (New York) and Barbara Lee (California) also used their official position within the House of Representatives to make statements on the Iraq War.

COLIN L. POWELL
(1937–)

Born in New York City, Powell grew up in Harlem and the South Bronx. He graduated from the City College of New York and subsequently served two tours of duty in Vietnam. Then, Powell became a White House Fellow, chief military assistant under Secretary of Defense Weinberger and assistant to the president for National Security Affairs under Ronald Reagan. Powell became a four-star general in April of 1989 and in August of that same year was appointed the chairman of the Joint Chiefs of Staff under President George H. W. Bush. In 2001, Powell was named the first African American secretary of state by President George W. Bush. In the following editorial, Powell sets forth the Bush administration's rationale for engaging in a preemptive strike against Iraq, specifically emphasizing the belief that Hussein was harboring weapons of mass destruction (WMD). The commentary originally appeared in the Wall Street Journal *as an opinion-editorial in 2003.*

We Will Not Shrink from War
February 3, 2003

President Bush warned in his State of the Union address that "the gravest danger facing America and the world is outlaw regimes that seek and possess nuclear, chemical and biological weapons." Exhibit A is Saddam Hussein's Iraq. As the president said, we need only look at how Saddam has terrorized, oppressed, and murdered his own people to understand his methods. And, perhaps most critically, the President confirmed that Iraq has open channels and ties to terrorist organizations, including al Qaeda.

Last November, the UN Security Council unanimously passed Resolution 1441, giving Iraq one last chance to disarm peacefully or "face serious consequences." However, instead of disarming, Iraq has responded to Resolution 1441 with empty claims, empty declarations, and empty gestures. Just a week ago, UN chief weapons inspector Hans Blix told the Security Council that "Iraq appears not to have come to a genuine acceptance, not even today, of the disarmament that was demanded of it." Indeed, the Iraqi regime is going to great lengths to conceal its weapons of mass destruction. It has removed material from sites it knew were likely to be inspected. The regime also has an active program of coaching scientists before they talk to inspectors and only permits interviews when minders are present. On top of that, thousands of pages of sensitive weapons-related documents have been found in private homes.

Resolution 1441 established two key tests: a full and accurate disclosure of Iraq's weaponry and a requirement to cooperate immediately, unconditionally, and actively with the inspectors. Iraq has failed both tests. Iraq's declaration of its weapons holdings is incomplete and inaccurate and provides no substantive information on the disposition of its weapons of mass destruction. Not surprisingly, the UN inspectors have found it woefully deficient. In his report to the Security Council, Mr. Blix noted that Iraq has failed to account for its production of the deadly nerve agent VX, some 6,500 chemical bombs, and about 1,000 metric tons of chemical agent. Iraq also previously acquired the materials to make much more anthrax than it declared.

In their inspections, Mr. Blix's team discovered a number of chemical warheads not previously acknowledged by Iraq. Iraq also continues to acquire banned equipment, with proscribed imports arriving as recently as last month. The inspectors also reported that Iraqi activity is severely hampering their work. For example, Iraq has refused the inspectors' request to use a U-2 reconnaissance aircraft, a critical tool for inspections. Inspectors are accompanied everywhere by Iraqi minders, are slandered by Iraqi officials as spies, and face harassment and disturbing protests that would be unlikely to occur without the encouragement of the authorities.

On Wednesday, I will present to the Security Council U.S. intelligence showing further evidence of Iraq's pattern of deception. Our evidence will reinforce what the inspectors told the Security Council last week—that they are not getting the cooperation they need, that their requests are being blocked, and that their questions are going unanswered. While there will be no "smoking gun," we will provide evidence concerning the weapons programs that Iraq is working so hard to hide. We will, in sum, offer a straightforward, sober and compelling demonstration that Saddam is concealing the evidence of his weapons of mass destruction, while preserving the weapons themselves. The world must now recognize that Iraq has not complied with the will of the international community as expressed in Resolution 1441. Iraq has failed the resolution's two tests—to disclose and to cooperate—in a manner that constitutes a further material breach of the resolution.

In response, the U.S. will begin a new round of full and open consultation with our allies about next steps. Much has been made of the friction between the U.S. and some of its traditional partners over how to proceed with Iraq. We will work to bridge our differences, building on the bedrock of our shared values and long history of acting together to meet common challenges. The fruits of our partnership are evident all around the globe, from Western Europe to Japan, Korea, Bosnia, and Afghanistan.

Together we must face the facts brought to us by the UN inspectors and reputable intelligence sources. Iraq continues to conceal deadly weapons and their components, and to use denial, deception and subterfuge in order to retain them. Iraq has ties to and has supported terrorist groups. Iraq has had no compunction about using weapons of mass destruction against its own people and against its neighbors.

President Bush's message has been clear from the beginning. The President eloquently and persuasively set forth the U.S. position at the UN on Sept. 12: A peaceful outcome to this situation is possible if Iraq cooperates with the UN and disarms. Unfortunately, Saddam seems to be leading his nation down another path. The U.S. seeks Iraq's peaceful disarmament. But we will not shrink from war if that is the only way to rid Iraq of its weapons of mass destruction.

CONDOLEEZZA RICE
(1954–)

Born in Birmingham, Alabama, Secretary of State Condoleezza Rice is noted for her lifelong record of stellar achievement. Trained as a classical pianist in her younger years, she attended college at the University of Denver. Upon receiving her doctorate in 1981, she joined the faculty of Stanford University, where she eventually became the provost. From 1989 to 1991, Rice served in the Bush administration as director and then senior director of Soviet and East European Affairs in the National Security Council, and as special assistant to the president for National Security Affairs. Rice became the assistant to the president for National Security Affairs, commonly referred to as the national security advisor, in 2001. Considered more hawkish than her predecessor, Rice was appointed secretary of state during George W. Bush's second term, replacing Colin Powell. This editorial provides further justification for the war against Iraq and describes the reasons why the U.S. had to act immediately. Rice's editorial originally appeared in the Wall Street Journal *in 2003.*

Why We Know Iraq Is Lying
March 26, 2003

Eleven weeks after the United Nations Security Council unanimously passed a resolution demanding—yet again—that Iraq disclose and disarm all its nuclear, chemical and biological weapons programs, it is appropriate to ask, "Has Saddam Hussein finally decided to voluntarily disarm?" Unfortunately, the answer is a clear and resounding no.

There is no mystery to voluntary disarmament. Countries that decide to disarm lead inspectors to weapons and production sites, answer questions before they are asked, state publicly and often the intention to disarm and urge their citizens to cooperate. The world knows from examples set by South Africa, Ukraine and Kazakhstan what it looks like when a government decides that it will cooperatively give up its weapons of mass destruction. The critical common elements of these efforts include a high-level political commitment to disarm, national initiatives to dismantle weapons programs, and full cooperation and transparency.

In 1989 South Africa made the strategic decision to dismantle its covert nuclear weapons program. It destroyed its arsenal of seven weapons and later submitted to rigorous verification by the International Atomic Energy Agency. Inspectors were given complete access to all nuclear facilities (operating and defunct) and the people who worked there. They were also presented with thousands of documents detailing, for example, the daily operation of uranium enrichment facilities as well as the construction and dismantling of specific weapons.

Ukraine and Kazakhstan demonstrated a similar pattern of cooperation when they decided to rid themselves of the nuclear weapons, intercontinental ballistic missiles and heavy bombers inherited from the Soviet Union. With significant assistance from the United States—warmly accepted by both countries—disarmament was orderly, open and fast. Nuclear warheads were returned to Russia. Missile silos and heavy bombers were destroyed or dismantled—once in a ceremony attended by the American and Russian defense chiefs. In one instance, Kazakhstan revealed the existence of a ton of highly enriched uranium and asked the United States to remove it, lest it fall into the wrong hands.

Iraq's behavior could not offer a starker contrast. Instead of a commitment to disarm, Iraq has a high-level political commitment to maintain and conceal its weapons, led by Saddam Hussein and his son Qusay, who controls the Special Security Organization, which runs Iraq's concealment activities. Instead of implementing national initiatives to disarm, Iraq maintains institutions whose sole purpose is to thwart the work of the inspectors. And instead of full cooperation and transparency, Iraq has filed a false declaration to the United Nations that amounts to a 12,200-page lie.

For example, the declaration fails to account for or explain Iraq's efforts to get uranium from abroad, its manufacture of specific fuel for ballistic missiles it claims not to have, and the gaps previously identified by the United Nations in Iraq's accounting for more than two tons of the raw materials needed to produce thousands of gallons of anthrax and other biological weapons.

Iraq's declaration even resorted to unabashed plagiarism, with lengthy passages of United Nations reports copied word-for-word (or edited to remove any criticism of Iraq) and presented as original text. Far from informing, the declaration is intended to cloud and confuse the true picture of Iraq's arsenal. It is a reflection of the regime's well-earned reputation for dishonesty and constitutes a material breach of United Nations Security Council Resolution 1441, which set up the current inspections program.

Unlike other nations that have voluntarily disarmed—and in defiance of Resolution 1441—Iraq is not allowing inspectors "immediate, unimpeded, unrestricted access" to facilities and people involved in its weapons program. As a recent inspection at the home of an Iraqi nuclear scientist demonstrated, and other sources confirm, material and documents are still being moved around in farcical shell games. The regime has blocked free and unrestricted use of aerial reconnaissance.

The list of people involved with weapons of mass destruction programs, which the United Nations required Iraq to provide, ends with those who worked in 1991—even though the United Nations had previously established that the programs continued after that date. Interviews with scientists and weapons officials identified by inspectors have taken place only in the watchful presence of the regime's agents. Given the duplicitous record of the regime, its recent promises to do better can only be seen as an attempt to stall for time.

Last week's finding by inspectors of 12 chemical warheads not included in Iraq's declaration was particularly troubling. In the past, Iraq has filled this type of warhead with sarin—a deadly nerve agent used by Japanese terrorists in 1995 to kill 12 Tokyo subway passengers and sicken thousands of others. Richard Butler, the former chief United Nations arms inspector, estimates that if a larger type of warhead that Iraq has made and used in the past were filled with VX (an even deadlier nerve agent) and launched at a major city, it could kill up to one million people. Iraq has also failed to provide United Nations inspectors with documentation of its claim to have destroyed its VX stockpiles.

Many questions remain about Iraq's nuclear, chemical and biological weapons programs and arsenal—and it is Iraq's obligation to provide answers. It is failing in spectacular fashion. By both its actions and its inactions, Iraq is proving not that it is a nation bent on disarmament, but that it is a nation with something to hide. Iraq is still treating inspections as a game. It should know that time is running out.

CONGRESSIONAL BLACK CAUCUS

The Congressional Black Caucus (CBC) was founded in January 1969 by a group of African American members of the House of Representatives. The CBC's primary goal is to support legislation that will promote equality for African Americans and others of similar experience. The CBC emphasizes educational achievement, adequate employment, social justice and quality health care. CBC Chair Elijah E. Cummings (D-Maryland) set forth the following statement on the Iraq War on behalf of the CBC. Ultimately, the CBC argues that there was no convincing evidence that Iraq posed an imminent threat and therefore rejected the idea of a unilateral first strike. The organization of African American Congressmen also declared that the Bush administration failed to answer serious questions about its plans for the political and economic stability of Iraq at the end of hostilities and the potential impact of the war on the domestic economy.

Statement on Possible Military Action in Iraq
March 18, 2003

Mr. Speaker— I would like to insert into the record the Congressional Black Caucus' principles on U.S. military action in Iraq. They are as follows:

1. We oppose a unilateral first-strike action by the United States without a clearly demonstrated and imminent threat of attack on the United States.

2. Only Congress has the authority to declare war.

3. Every diplomatic option must be exhausted.

4. A unilateral first-strike would undermine the moral authority of the United States, result in substantial loss of life, destabilize the Mid East region and undermine the ability of our nation to address unmet domestic priorities.

5. Further, any post-strike plan for maintaining stability in the region would be costly and would require a long-term commitment.

Mr. Speaker—I rise at a moment when America stands at the brink of war.

Our actions in Iraq will define our moral standing in the world—for this generation and for generations yet unborn.

I have given my oath to do everything within my power to support our men and women in uniform.

We have a great American tradition that when we engage in combat we support our troops.

I will fulfill that solemn obligation.

However, I also have pledged my commitment to ensure that their sacrifice is warranted and just.

That obligation does not allow me to remain silent tonight.

Mr. Speaker, the President has declared that he will allow no more time for a negotiated disarmament of Iraq.

We all know the terrible consequences of that decision.

The stakes are enormous.

Many human beings will be harmed and others will be killed.

And, the course of American foreign policy could be seriously changed.

So, before a single shot has been fired, I must again raise what I consider to be the fundamental question about this 'preemptive war.'

By what authority—by what right does this nation justify the taking of life in Iraq?

Mr. Speaker—the American people have created the strongest military force in history.

We, in this Congress, will continue to support our troops—we will continue to assure that they are the best trained and equipped in the world.

Yet, as a people, Americans have never subscribed to the proposition that our might makes us right.

America has never led by military power alone—but by our devotion to principle, and the legitimacy of our mission.

And, now, that principled foundation of our national security has been placed in jeopardy and the legitimacy of our mission and therefore the credibility of our nation is challenged by a significant part of the global community and our own citizens.

The Administration has failed to achieve the U.N. approval and broad-based international support that are critical to achieving our objectives and protecting our men and women in uniform in the Middle East.

We have an obligation to ask why the Administration has failed to make its case.

If the President's rationale for war were self-evident, a broad-based, multinational "coalition of the willing" would indeed have materialized.

At the heart of the Administration's failure, I am convinced, is the absence of clear and convincing evidence that Iraq poses an imminent threat—either to the United States or to other nations of the world.

Moreover, the Administration has yet to adequately explain the consequences of going to war to the American people.

Have we received clear and convincing evidence that the President's decision:

—will not destabilize the Middle East,

—will not make our defense against terrorism more difficult, and

—will not undermine our ability to meet the compelling domestic needs of Americans here at home?

Where is the Administration's comprehensive plan for the political and economic stability of Iraq once hostilities have ended?

Where is the President's evaluation of the cost of military conflict and reconstruction?

Where is the President's analysis of the impact upon our economy?

Will both affluent and working class Americans share fairly in that sacrifice?

The answers to these questions raise the classic conflict between whether we pursue questionable international missions or spend the resources for urgent domestic priorities.

Mr. Speaker, that is why we have not yet received the Administration's answers to any of these critical questions.

Fundamentally, however, the issue of war remains one of morality.

Following President Bush's ultimatum last night, the Vatican offered this response:

Whoever decides that all peaceful means that international law has put at our disposition have been exhausted assumes serious responsibility before God, his conscience and history.

I submit, Mr. Speaker, that the heavy weight of this responsibility is shared by the President and every member of this House and that realization should give us pause, that we have pursued the right course and that we are doing the right thing by this military action.

So, tonight, as I speak, tens of thousands of religious congregations throughout the world—women and men of every faith tradition—are praying that peace will prevail, for the good of our country and the enlightened progress of humanity.

May God protect our men and women in uniform—and all of the innocents who now stand in harm's way, and bring them home safely.

And, may God guide America during these dangerous times.

AL SHARPTON
(1954–)

Reverend Alfred Sharpton was born in Brooklyn, New York. He demonstrated a passion for direct action and civil disobedience at an early age. He became an ordained preacher by the age of 10. Sharpton founded the National Youth Movement in 1971 to register young people to vote, provide them with job opportunities and fight against drug abuse. He has pursued other interests outside of civic justice, including making a record with James Brown in the 1970s and organizing youth with Don King in the 1980s. However, his primary focus has always been bringing attention to injustices. Sharpton founded the National Action Network in 1991 to increase voter education, provide aid to the poor and support disadvantaged businesses. The National Action Network is also well known for its high-profile marches against racism and human rights abuses. In 2004, Sharpton was one of two African Americans who ran for the Democratic nomination for president. All of the declared presidential candidates were invited to deliver a speech on public policy issues and policy alternatives at the Take Back America conference sponsored by the Campaign for America's Future. In Sharpton's address he explains why he ran for the nation's highest office and his reasons for speaking out against the war in Iraq.

Take America Back
June 6, 2003

Thank you. I'm very happy and honored to be here this morning and I'm very happy to join people that are not afraid to stand up and call themselves progressives at a time like this in American history. I think that the first problem we have facing the election in 2004 is that too many of us have been intimidated into apologizing for being right. There are those who say that as a Democratic party we've had to go to the right to win. The results are that today we do not control the Senate, the House, the White House or the Supreme Court. The sellout of progressive politics has been a total disaster for the Democratic party. Not only is it morally wrong and politically cheap, it doesn't even work! The folks that brought us into this disaster should not be the advisors on how to get us out of the mess they brought us in.

We're coming out of a war that we still don't know why we went in. I was the first candidate to speak out against the war. I made it to all the marches— some candidates came late, left early. I opposed the war because I said it was wrong and there were not any weapons of mass destruction. They're still looking for the weapons. We want to know, where are the weapons that the Secretary of State brought evidence of before the UN? Where are the weapons that they had the video and the audio tapes of? If you could find the weapons before the war, how come you can't reveal the weapons now?

The other night, I was here in a Washington bar, and someone ran over to me and said, "Do you have a comment?" I said, "A comment about what?" They said, "They just indicted Martha Stewart." I said, "For what?" They said, "For lying." I said, "I didn't know you could get indicted for lying in this country!" We have come out of a war with weapons we can't find. God, our President told us a year and a half ago that we were going to go and get bin Laden! He can't find him. We had to go to Iraq to get Hussein. We don't know if he's living or dead, he can't find him. Everything Bush has gone after, he can't find! I shouldn't be surprised because I can't find the votes in Florida that made him the President in the first place!

Why am I running? First of all, in the year 2000, the principles of American democracy were undermined. There are those who say, "We should just get over it." This is the next national election since 2000. What they did in Florida must be answered at the polls in 2004. We don't have 5 votes on the Supreme Court, but we have millions of votes in the 50 states if we go and organize and mobilize and quit imitating the folks that we should be getting rid of! Every declared Presidential candidate was invited to deliver a speech on public policy issues and policy alternatives at the Take Back America conference. The Campaign for America's Future and the Institute for America's Future do not endorse candidates.

The Sharpton platform includes that we must make it a Constitutional right to vote. The argument before the Supreme Court in Gore v. Bush was basically that "states control voting." It was a states' rights argument. The Supreme Court went with that, kicked it back to the state of Florida, where Katherine Harris certified the election. The only way to avoid, or prevent that from happening again, is to propose a Constitutional amendment to give us the right to vote, therefore empowering the Federal Government over states. House Joint Resolution 28, House Joint Resolution 29 guaranteeing quality health care for all Americans and quality education. We cannot just keep arguing with the Republicans about program, without changing the premise. If we made it a Constitutional right to healthcare, we wouldn't be cutting bills in the midnight hours over prescription drugs when our grandma should have the right to drugs in America!

Our problem is, that we have too many leaders of the party who have been elephants running around with donkey jackets on, thinking that we don't recognize who they really are. You cannot be on both sides of the aisle. You cannot stand up for war in Iraq and occupation in Iraq and spending billions in Iraq, when we have 50 states with record state deficits. They say to us, "Well, you've got to understand, Reverend, we've got to deal with occupying Iraq." What about the 50 states you already occupy? Then Bush proposes a tax cut. What is really a tax shift. By cutting as he has, it has caused state budget deficits to increase. Then they tax working class people with higher property tax, higher sales tax, higher mass transit. It's a working class tax. They shifted the burden over to us. We need to fight back. We don't need to fight back with a lower tax cut, we need to fight back with no tax cut. Put the money back! Use that money for the fundamental aims of this country to give children education. Not some children. Not privatization schemes. Not giving one a voucher, another child a school. Give them all a quality education. We can afford it if we wanted to!

I'm the only candidate that is unilaterally against the death penalty. It is embarrassing that a Republican governor in Illinois showed more moral courage than members of my own party. We need to deal with this! We must have real progressives that are real because they believe it, not just trying a campaign strategy. There are some that are running that have become progressive to distinguish themselves. Then there are others of us that have always been progressive to define ourselves. Many candidates support the civil rights movement. I was on the front line. Many support fighting for labor. I've gone to jail fighting for the right to work. Many supported stopping the bombing in Vieques. I did 90 days. I'm not a liberal support in progress, I'm a progressive born and bred fighting back and I'm not asking for your help now, I've always been there!

I met my campaign manager, Frank Watkins, 27 years ago when I was the New York Youth Director of Reverend Jackson's organization. As I keep meeting these new progressives, I said, "Frank, was he in Rev. Jackson's campaign?" He said, "Nope, just met him." "Were they there?" "Nope, just met them." It's strange to me how people can come to us that scorned us, never walked with us, never supported us, and want to make some last minute road to Damascus convergence and expect us to support them. Every declared Presidential candidate was invited to deliver a speech on public policy issues and policy alternatives at the Take Back America conference. The Campaign for America's Future and the Institute for America's Future do not endorse candidates. when we don't even know where they will be in 2005. I urge you, let's not play games with people that have never stood with us before. We can't win unless we build a movement! This can't be a clubhouse race with a nice, pretty resume. We've got to go to the streets, we've got to go door to door, we've got to get the disaffected, the disinherited. We've got to get America back so we can Take America Back!

I grew up in New York, but my parents are from the South. I had a grandmother who had a little farm in Alabama and I remember I used to ask her about different animals because coming out of the urban center, I didn't know that much about it. We didn't have a donkey, but I remember reading about a donkey and I asked her, "How do you handle a donkey?" She said, "Well, donkeys are stubborn. Donkeys sometime don't obey the will of those around them. But if you slap the donkey, you can make the donkey respond." There are those that say, "Reverend, don't raise progressive points! Don't say different things of accountability, that's divisive!" I'm not being divisive, I'm trying to slap this donkey! I'm not trying to hurt another candidate, I'm trying to slap this donkey! I'm trying to wake it up. I'm trying to get it up 'cause if I can slap this donkey, I can make it kick George Bush out the White House! We got to slap this donkey 'til we Take America Back!

BARBARA LEE (D-CA)
(1946–)

Born in El Paso, Texas, Lee moved with her family to California in 1960. She later graduated from Mills College in Oakland, California, and earned a master's degree in social welfare from the University of California, Berkeley, in 1975. Representative Lee began her political career by working as an intern in the office of Congressman Ron Dellums and later became his chief of staff. In 1998, in a special election upon Dellums's retirement, she succeeded him as the 9th District of California representative to the U.S. Congress. Barbara Lee has the distinction of being the only member of Congress who voted against H.J. Res. 64, a bill that reduced congressional oversight over President Bush's war conduct in Iraq.

Regarding War with Iraq
September 12, 2003

The American people are being told by President Bush and other members of the Administration that we have to attack Iraq because our nation is in imminent danger from Saddam Hussein. However, neither Congress nor the American public have been shown evidence linking Hussein to September 11th. We have received no proof that Iraq has the means or intent to use weapons of mass destruction against us. We have not been told why the danger is greater today than it was a year or two ago or why we must rush to war rather than pursuing other options.

We do know that virtually all our allies in the Islamic world and in Canada, Europe, Asia, and Africa are strongly opposed to this proposed assault. Statesmen such as Kofi Annan and Nelson Mandela have beseeched us to turn away from this disastrous course. Many Middle Eastern countries that supported the United States in the Gulf War will not support this attack.

The doctrine of preemption being promulgated by the Bush Administration would set an extremely dangerous precedent: we would be attacking a nation not out of self-defense or even imminent danger but out of anxiety. This violates international law, United Nations principles, and our own long-term security interests.

War with Iraq poses enormous risks, including the dangers for American servicemen and women and for Iraqi civilians; the deployment of hundreds of thousands of U.S. troops; and the potential destabilization of the Middle East. War would likely derail any chance at a Palestinian-Israeli agreement and undermine our efforts to forge a secure peace in Afghanistan and elsewhere. And, it would divert billions of dollars from our own profound domestic needs, including healthcare, prescription drugs, education, and homeland security.

This is a price we do not have to pay. There are viable alternatives: they begin by working with the U.N. Security Council and our friends and allies in the world to renew U.N. weapons inspections in Iraq. Renewing inspections will require diplomacy and cooperation, including the willingness of the United States to consider reducing and eventually eliminating nonmilitary sanctions on Iraq after inspections have resumed.

CHARLES B. RANGEL
(1930–)

Charles B. Rangel is a Democratic member of Congress from the state of New York. As a congressman, Rangel is well known for promoting legislation and programs to assist the disadvantaged communities. Rangel was the principal author of the Federal Empowerment Zone project, the Low Income Housing Tax Credit and the Work Opportunity Tax Credit. His efforts have provided thousands of jobs for underprivileged young people, veterans and ex-offenders. In the late 1980s Rangel joined the fight against apartheid, leading the effort to pass one of the most effective anti-apartheid measures resulting in several Fortune 500 companies leaving South Africa. He also served in the Korean War and was awarded the Purple Heart and Bronze Star. In this press release, Congressman Rangel explains why he introduced legislation to reinstitute the military draft in the wake of the Iraq War.

War's Burden Must Be Shared
January 7, 2003

Some people have questioned my motives for introducing legislation to reinstitute the military draft and requiring alternative national service by young people who cannot serve.

In brief, my bill would replace the existing Selective Service law to establish a system in which all American men and women, as well as legal permanent residents, aged 18 to 26, would be subject to compulsory military service or alternative civilian service. The President would determine the numbers needed and the means of selection. Deferments would be limited to those completing high school, up to the age of 20, with no exemptions for college or graduate school.

There are some who believe my proposal is really meant to show my opposition to a unilateral preemptive attack against Iraq by the U.S. Others believe that I want to make it clear that, if there is a war, there should be a more equitable representation of all classes of Americans making the sacrifice for this great country.

The fact is, both of these objectives are mine. I truly believe that decision-makers who support war would more readily feel the pain of conflict and appreciate the sacrifice of those on the front lines if their children were there, too. I don't make too much of the fact that only four members of the 107th Congress, which voted overwhelmingly in favor of war with Iraq, had children in the military. That is only a symptom of a larger problem, in which it is assumed that the defense of our country is the sole responsibility of paid volunteers.

But what if I am wrong in my desire for peace and in my doubts that Iraq is an imminent threat? If President Bush, the Congress and other supporters of an invasion are right and war is inevitable, then everyone who loves this country is bound by patriotic duty to defend it, or to share in the sacrifice of those placed in harm's way.

The disproportionately high representation of the poor and minorities in the enlisted ranks is well documented. Minorities comprise 35 percent of the military and Blacks 20 percent, well above their proportion of the general population. They, along with poor and rural Whites do more than their fair share of service in our ground forces. Yet the value of our foot soldiers is demeaned by those who promote the unproven notion that high-tech warfare will bring a quick and easy victory in Iraq.

I fear that the Bush administration's apparent determination to invade Iraq could thrust us into all-out war, perhaps a religious war, in the Middle East. I do not share Defense Secretary Rumsfeld's certainty that the U.S. has the capacity to defeat Iraq and North Korea in quick succession. Most dismaying is the absence of any discussion of the potential loss of life and the principle of shared sacrifice—in both the military and economic spheres.

In fact, the administration is using the rhetoric of war while engaging in politics as usual. While deploying thousands of troops to the Middle East, the President is promoting $600 billion in additional tax cuts which will primarily benefit the most affluent Americans, those whose sons and daughters are least likely to set foot on the sands of Iraq.

If objections to his economic proposal are "class warfare," as the President has said, then President Bush himself has started the war.

GAIL BUCKLEY
(1952–)

Gail Buckley is a graduate of Radcliffe College. She is an author, intellectual and scholar of African American history. Her first book, The Hornes: An American Family, *is a history of Buckley's mother, musical legend Lena Horne, and her family.* The Hornes *became an American Masters documentary. Buckley's latest book, fifteen years in the making, is* American Patriots: The Story of Blacks in the Military from the Revolution to Desert Storm. *The book chronicles the Black American military experience. In this editorial, Buckley draws attention to President Bush's attempts to end the University of Michigan's affirmative action program. She argues that diversity does not occur by accident, but is the result of motivation and planning. Minorities are overrepresented in the military because they are actively recruited into the all-volunteer army. These same minorities are admitted to the military, but cannot enroll in institutions of higher learning.*

Black Soldiers OK, Why Not Students?
April 26, 2003

The young victors of Iraq II are, like all ages and ranks in the military, a picture of American diversity. But the Bush administration seems to believe that diversity on the battlefield is fairer than diversity in higher education.

In some ways, the all-volunteer military still looks like the old unfair draft. According to military figures for 2000, blacks were 12% of the population and 22% of the military; Hispanics were 13% of the population and 9% of the military, and whites were 70% of the population and 63% of the military. The military may be all-volunteer, but the deferments are still economic; thus, poorer whites and minorities enlist. Why should those who can't afford college be the only young people who have to go to war? Some young people know they have the opportunity only to sacrifice, not to aspire.

While military diversity represents the American ideal, this diversity is relatively new. Iraq II is only the fourth war in American history in which blacks and whites, from the beginning of conflict, have fought as equals. The first was the Revolution, the second was Vietnam and the third was the 1991 Gulf War. Today's diversity didn't happen by accident. It's the result of a series of initiatives by three Presidents: Harry Truman, John F. Kennedy and Jimmy Carter. All three were veterans who tried to redress racial unfairness in the military. And no one can deny that both America and the military are better off. Their decisions didn't constitute affirmative action as the term is currently understood, but they affirmed the best of American patriotic values: All sacrifice is equal.

Truman desegregated the military in 1948. Kennedy swept the last vestiges of official racism away in 1961. But by the late 1960s and early '70s, severe racial tensions contributed to what the military called the breakdown of the Army. Post-Vietnam, "Be All You Can Be" became the motto for male and female volunteers, and the only recognized color was Army green.

When Carter appointed Clifford Alexander secretary of the Army in 1977, diversity came to higher ranks. Alexander, the first black secretary, rejected his first general officers list (a roster of colonels to be promoted to one-star general) because no blacks were on it. The revised Pentagon list included, among others, Col. Colin Powell.

Now, on another battlefield where fairness and traditional American values are at stake, President Bush has entered the fray in a way that might disappoint Truman, Kennedy and Carter—to say nothing of the diverse and courageous 20-year-olds of Iraq II. In opposition to a long list of retired generals and admirals, all the service academies, 70 Fortune 500 companies and almost every accredited college and university in the country, Bush came out, uninvited, against the University of Michigan on affirmative action. In the face of budget cuts in veterans' benefits and a closed door on higher education, Bush seems to be saying that all sacrifice isn't equal to the diverse young soldiers of Iraq.

If he can't see the fairness in affirmative action for higher education, maybe he should reinstate the draft.

FARAI CHIDEYA
(1970–)

Farai Chideya, a native of Baltimore, Maryland, is a journalist, with work featured in some of the premier publications across the nation. She is a frequent guest on radio and television talk shows and provides commentary for television news. Chideya covers a variety of issues in her work, including youth, politics, gender and race. Chideya is also the author of several books, including Don't Believe the Hype: Fighting Cultural Misinformation about African Americans *(2005);* The Color of Our Future *(1999) and her latest publication,* Trust: Reaching the 100 Million Missing Voters *(2004). In this editorial Chideya expresses African American sentiments on the treatment of Shoshana Johnson, the first African American female prisoner of war (POW). She compares the treatment of the white female soldier Jessica Lynch to Johnson, by the media and institutions of government. Also included in this excerpt is a poem written by Nuyorican Poetry Slam winner Kahlil Almustafa on Shoshana Johnson.*

A Double Standard for Heroes?
November 14, 2003

What do you call a black war hero? A nigger.

In the crudest of senses, this twist on the old joke about black PhDs sums up the political backdrop of Calvin Baker's lyrical novel "Once Two Heroes." Set in the European battlefields of World War II, in black Los Angeles and in the white South, the book ranges masterfully across geography, race and point of view. The novel follows the struggles and glories of two war heroes, one black, one white, and their divergent and fatally convergent life paths. Although it is a period piece, its echoes are very much present day.

Take the case of Shoshana Johnson.

Johnson is a single mother of a young daughter. She enlisted in the Army in hopes it would help her become a chef. Instead, the Army specialist was deployed to Iraq, shot through both legs and held prisoner for 22 days. (She was captured in the same ambush as Jessica Lynch, but remained in captivity longer.) Her slow and painful recovery was not charted by the media with the same zeal as her friend Lynch. In fact, there was hardly any coverage of her journey at all.

Today Johnson remains partially disabled, unable to stand for long periods (which clearly impacts her desired career), and haunted by flashbacks to her ordeal. But the U.S. Army, so buoyed by the publicity around the Lynch case, has now dealt Johnson and her family a severe blow. While Jessica Lynch is being discharged from the army with an 80-percent disability benefit, Johnson is being discharged on only 30-percent disability. The difference will mean a loss of nearly $700 per month for Johnson and her child.

Reluctantly, the Johnson family began to turn to the media that had spurned them, speaking out about her plight. Her father, Claude Johnson, told reporter Lee Hockstader of the *Washington Post* that there was a double standard.

"I don't know for sure that it was the Pentagon," he said. "All I know for sure is that the news media paid a lot of attention to Jessica."

The family has enlisted the help of Rev. Jesse Jackson. Although his help is bound to be effective, it is necessary only because of the tiresome dance of race in America, where whites are seen as the default models for society, and black achievements are looked at with puzzlement.

Jessica Lynch's face graces the cover of *Time* magazine; her interviews and excerpts of her book have been scattered across national television. Now, only because of a small but growing outcry, Shoshana Johnson may get her due as well.

Nuyorican Poetry Slam winner Kahlil Almustafa has even written a poem about Johnson. It begins:

> There are no lack of
> affirmative action programs on the front lines
> of the U.S. military, there is full equality
> in killing and in death

It ends thus:

> Yr coming home
> has been covert, quiet
> sneaking back into the country
> beneath media radar. Yr life as a single, Blk mother
> will not make any front page news.
> Perhaps there is a codicil: Yr life as a single, Blk mother
> will not make any front page news
> until people wake up, and raise hell.

MAULANA KARENGA
(1941–)

Dr. Maulana Karenga is professor and former chair of Black Studies at California State University–Long Beach. An activist-scholar of national and international recognition, Dr. Karenga is one of the most important figures in recent African American history, having played a major role in Black political and intellectual culture since the 1960s. He has, along with his organization United Slaves (US), played a major role in such movements as Black Power, Black Arts, Black Studies, the Independent Schools, Afrocentricity, Ancient Egyptian Studies, the Million Person marches and currently the Reparations Movement. In addition, he has lectured on the life and struggle of African peoples on the major campuses of the United States and in Africa, the People's Republic of China, Cuba, Trinidad, Britain and Canada and is the chair of the organization US and the National Association of Kawaida Organizations. He holds two Ph.D.'s, one in political science (United States International University) and another in social ethics (University of Southern California), as well as an honorary doctorate from the University of Durban, South Africa. Dr. Karenga is also the author of numerous scholarly articles and books including Introduction to Black Studies; Odu Ifa: The Ethical Teachings; and Maat, the Moral Ideal in Ancient Egypt: A Study of Classical African Ethics. Moreover, Dr. Karenga is the creator of the pan-African cultural holiday Kwanzaa and the Nguzo Saba (the Seven Principles) and author of the authoritative book on Kwanzaa, Kwanzaa: A Celebration of Family, Community and Culture. Below is Dr. Karenga's commentary on U.S. aggression in Iraq. Within the commentary, the scholar sets forth the tenets of a just war theory from an African-centered perspective and argues that they must be met in order for any war to receive African American support.

Statement on Peace, Justice and Resistance to War
February 28, 2003

We live in difficult and dangerous times and now stand, bracing ourselves, on the brink of an almost certain war which could engulf the world in ways no one can perceive or predict. And yet we must be clear on where we stand and stand there resolutely. We stand with the oppressed who struggle for freedom, the wronged and injured who struggle for justice, the masses of people who struggle for power over their destiny and daily lives, and the peoples of the world who struggle for peace in their own time and place. Surely, it is the teachings of the ancestors in the *Husia* that say we are morally obligated "to bear witness to truth and to set the scales of justice in their proper place among those who have no voice." Thus, we stand in active solidarity with the actual and intended victims of aggression, occupation, neocolonialism, racism, sexism, classism and all other forms of oppression and constraints on human freedom and human flourishing.

We issue this statement, then, in resistance and opposition to the proposed war against Iraq which by definition is a war against the Iraqi people without justification and thus unjust, immoral and illegal. This position evolves from the ancient and ongoing tradition of our ancestors which teaches us to respect life, to love justice, to cherish freedom, to treasure peace, and to constantly struggle to bring good in the world and not let any good be lost. It is the ethical tradition of the *Husia* and the *Odu Ifa*, of Harriet Tubman, Frederick Douglass, Sojourner Truth, Henry McNeal Turner, Fannie Lou Hamer, Malcolm X, Ella Baker, Martin Luther King and others who taught us a rightful way to walk in the world. It is a tradition which rejects the policy of peace for the powerful and war for the vulnerable, dominance and security for the rich and right race and oppression and insecurity for all others in the world. We stand resolutely among the peoples of the world who reject and resist this unjust war as we struggle for freedom for the oppressed, justice for the injured and wronged, power for all people over their destiny and daily lives, and peace for the world. And for us *peace is the practice of justice which ends oppression and hostilities and provides security and well-being for all.*

We call on African peoples everywhere to stand in active solidarity with the peoples of the world who have overwhelmingly rejected and resist this proposed war which is without moral and legal limits, and without due respect for collective considered judgment at home or abroad. In taking this stand, we also reject the willful misreading of the meaning of the tragic events of 9/11 and the manipulation of the resultant fear and sense of insecurity in order to wage a self-defined preemptive and limitless war of aggression, curtail and violate human and civil rights and establish a racial and cultural imperium in the world.

For the proposed war against Iraq is not an isolated initiative. Rather, it is part of a post-9/11 imperial offensive which carries with it racist and colonial conversations and commitments of "crusades" to protect "the civilized world" against "dark and evil nations" in "dark corners of the world." And if it is not checked, it will have a profoundly negative effect on the struggles for freedom, justice and peace in the world. Our position against war with Iraq is informed by the ancient African moral understanding that we are to *pursue peace always, conscientiously avoid war, and engage even in just war reluctantly and with considered moral restraint.* The aim here is to cultivate a predisposition for peace and a presumption against war and where war cannot be avoided, to provide guidelines to restrict its conduct and reduce its devastating consequences. Within this framework, our ethical tradition requires several conditions for a just war which the proposed war against the Iraqi people by the Bush administration does not meet. These criteria are: 1) just cause; 2) collective considered judgment; 3) just means; 4) consequences of common good; and 5) last resort.

Just Cause.

There is no just cause for a war against Iraq. A just cause or just war cannot be aggressive or preemptive. It must always be defensive and it can be defensive in three possible ways, i.e., as: (a) an act of self-defense against immediate attack or imminent grave danger in the process of unfolding; (b) a liberation struggle against foreign occupation or severe internal oppression; and (c) a humanitarian intervention to prevent or halt genocide, ethnic cleansing or any other massive killing of a whole population. The U.S. attempt to use the first justification is false on its face. There is no evidence of attack, involvement in an attack or an imminent attack on the U.S. by Iraq. Nor is there any evidence of Iraq's having the ability to seriously attack or harm the U.S. or its allies, given the devastation it has suffered in the U.S.-led invasion of 1991 and the sustained brutal bombing by the U.S. and Britain ever since then. Moreover, there is no provision in the U.N. Charter for wars of preemptive aggression, or for overthrowing governments, assassinating leaders of other countries or conquering and colonizing other countries for national, corporate or family interests. Indeed such aggression is called "a crime against peace" and international law.

Therefore, the Bush Administration is rushing to wage a war not of *self-defense* but rather a war of *self-aggrandizement*—in a word, a war of vigilante aggression, outlaw resource acquisition and imperial expansion against a vulnerable and long-suffering people. More precisely, it is a war: (a) to seize and control the oilfields, water and strategic position of Iraq; (b) to expand and consolidate U.S. dominance of the Middle East and in the process strengthen its ally Israel, in its occupation of Palestine and in its status as the dominant power in the region; (c) to enhance the US' and Israel's capacity to dictate limitations on the inevitable Palestinian state; (d) to terrorize and cower other states and people who oppose its policies; and (e) to reaffirm and insure white hegemony in the region and the world, militarily, politically, economically and culturally. In a word, it is racialized globalization in its rawest and most ruthless form—i.e., white supremacy expanding and consolidating its presence and power in the world, camouflaging its quest to empire with claims of concern for national security and masking its racial aspects with culturally-coded references to saving the "civilized world."

Collective Considered Judgment.

War as a life-and-death matter should not be decided or declared without adequate discussion and debate. Nor should it be declared in the name of a people without their counsel and consent or be waged on behalf of a world that has overwhelmingly rejected it as unjust, illegitimate and immoral. The gravity of war requires a vigorous and varied public discussion that works its way through the customary mix of fact, fiction and manipulated fear and meaningfully addresses issues of morality, law, politics and horrific consequences of such a grave decision and act. The Bush administration has not explained in an honest and open way the horrible consequences and costs of war for Iraq, the U.S., the region and the world, nor offered space for public discussion, debate and dissent. And Congress, except for a courageous few, has conceded in submissive silence. Indeed, the Bush regime and its media allies have worked to discourage and divert public debate from the issue. In the wake of the tragic events of 9/11, they have cultivated a culture of fear and false alarm to suppress and cast suspicion on dissent from the official line, even suggesting that those who dissent are treading on treasonous ground and "should watch what they say and do." Also, they have created an endless enemies list and given the country daily doses of possible dangerous discoveries which range from missing vials of viruses to suspicious Muslim charities. And they have created a daily regimen of elementary school color-coded alerts to inspire different levels of alarm, fear and uncertainty.

Moreover, they have refused to discuss the occupation and liberation of Palestine, even though it is at the heart of the Middle East crisis and has unavoidable implications for peace, freedom and justice in the region and the world. Also, the Bush administration has framed its discourse and policies in fundamentalist religious ideas of the evil in the world and the evil of the world. In such a context, the president transforms into a preacher who demonizes countries and their leaders, prays for guidance to war and sermonizes on the need for an endless war and crusade to "rid the world of evil."

Moreover, with characteristic religious certainty, Bush has tried to devalue and discredit the unprecedented international opposition to the war which has emerged so quickly and extensively. In defiance of world opinion, international law, and the will of the American people, Bush has declared he will wage war with or without UN consent or cooperation. Seeking support only as a desirable cover for his conduct, he shows disdain for diplomacy and contempt even for his allies and rules persons, nations and the UN irrelevant unless they accept the rightness of his irrational and reckless rush to war. Furthermore, he has bullied, bribed and promised punishment to states to coerce them into compliance and silence. He thus has tried to stifle and discredit dissent, invoked peace while demanding war, and argued against dictatorship while dismissing the democratic dissent and will of the country, the UN and the world.

Just Means.
Even in the case of a justified use of force, a just war by definition is a limited war, a war with moral and legal limits. The principle of just means, thus, requires a conscientious effort to restrict and reduce the deaths, damage and devastation of war, especially in relation to innocent civilians. This demands discriminate and proportionate use of force, a condition not met by the Bush administration's plans for the largest and most devastating bombing raids on Iraq since WW II and Hiroshima and Nagasaki. Indeed, the Bush administration boasts of its bombing intentions as if they were invoking a divine appearance, one which they say will cause "shock and awe."

The estimated deaths for an attack on Baghdad are extremely high and the resultant refugee population will also create additional burdens and pain for a long-suffering people. Already the U.S. and British incessant bombing and use of degraded uranium shells and the cruel and unjust sanctions against the Iraqi people have caused approximately a million deaths and injuries, increased cancer and birth defects and widespread malnutrition, as well as greatly damaged the country's infrastructure. An intensified war with weapons of catastrophic consequences can only cause even more undeserved casualties and suffering to the Iraqi people.

The planned use of so-called "overwhelming force" and *weapons of catastrophic consequences* in Iraq insures massive civilian deaths and injures and extreme devastation of civilian infrastructure and the environment must be condemned and resisted. Such massive attacks, especially on cities and population centers are clear crimes against humanity and must be condemned and resisted. For they do not restrict weapons use nor the targets attacked. On the contrary, the bombing of Baghdad and other cities would make targets out of innocent civilians caught up in circumstances not of their making and not in their control.

Calling the mass killing of civilians collateral damage does not eliminate or ease the moral imperative to avoid the targeting and injuring of innocents. Nor does it hide the horrific nature of the use of disproportionate violence from high-tech *catastrophic weapons* which creates a greater evil than the supposed evil to be overcome. Indeed, for all the talk about the evil of weapons of catastrophic destruction, the catastrophic weapons which the U.S. boasts about will have similar devastating consequences. The U.S. has promised to use most of them in the planned war and has threatened to use even nuclear ones. In fact, the glorification of these high tech weapons of mass destruction and talk of their "precision" and "smartness" help to desensitize the American public to the planned deaths of the distant, demonized and degraded people now called enemy. They cultivate a callousness born of physical and emotional distance from the actual killing fields and the desire for a quick and devastating victory over the so-called evil enemy. Thus, delivery of the crushing blow is turned over to high-flying piloted and pilotless planes and distant computers which are not concerned with ground zero collateral damage. But we are morally compelled to be concerned, for this so-called collateral damage is dead and injured people and their devastated homes, hospitals, schools, factories, food and water supply and places of worship as well as other civilian infrastructures essential to the life and well-being of the people.

Consequences of Common Good.

There are no consequences of common good for such an unprovoked, unjustifiable and unjust war. It is grossly wrong and does not benefit the world or the American people to kill and wound thousands and thousands of innocent Iraqi civilians, half of whom are children; to conquer and occupy their country; to seize their oil, water and other resources; to damage and destroy irreplaceable treasures from one of humanity's oldest civilizations, paralleling ancient Egypt in its age and importance to human history; to contaminate, degrade and devastate the environment of Iraq and neighboring areas; to violate international law and weaken international institutions; to trample on the right of self-determination of peoples; to destabilize the region and the world; to cause unnecessary casualties among U.S. and Iraqi soldiers in an unjust war; to encourage and provoke inevitable retaliatory attacks against the U.S. and its people in this country and around the world and to squander needed resources for social and human good on a needless and unjust war.

Clearly the human, environmental, economic and political costs outweigh the weak, transparent and self-serving arguments put forth for a preemptive war of aggression. The human costs to the Iraqi people are incalculable, especially for the vulnerable, children, women, the ill and aged who always suffer most in wars. People of color and the poor of the U.S. who are represented in the U.S. army in disproportionate numbers will pay a great price with lives lost in greater numbers and through the diversion of needed resources to a war the whole world condemns. In a word, domestic needs for housing, food, health care, education, employment and other vital requirements for social well-being will be sacrificed on the altar of racialist reasoning and imperialist assertion of power in the world.

Last Resort.
The principle of last resort grows out of a predisposition for peace and a presumption against war. It assumes, as the *Odu Ifa* teaches, that "war ruins the world" and is a great evil which should be avoided. Moreover, it assumes a rational and moral preference for peace over war and is always reluctant to wreak the havoc of death and devastation on the world that comes with war, even a defensive one. By definition a preemptive war is not a last resort, but the first even *prior* resort. For *to preempt* is *to act prior to*—prior to discussion, negotiation and the pursuit of alternatives to war. Preemptive war, then, is by definition, *preemptive aggression*. And in spite of the Bush administration's raising the issue of self-defense, there is no issue of threat or attack. Even his intelligence agencies, before being coerced into compliance with the thrust for war, reported Iraq offered no real threat to the U.S.

Having failed to kill or capture its targeted prey in a war of retribution for 9/11, the Bush administration has turned our attention to a new demon and a war of manifest destiny and colonial "democracy" in a quixotic attempt to remake the Arab and Islamic world in its own image and interest. Having failed in its policies at home, it turns our attention to the quest for a quick, destructive and diversionary victory abroad. Bush proposes to achieve peace by waging an unjust and illegal war and to protect the world from a fantasized threat by violating international law and weakening international institutions in a series of actions resembling a rogue state. He proposes to teach the Iraqi people democracy by conquering them and imposing a U.S. military dictatorship over them until they are "mature" according to his measure. And he promises to protect this country from group terrorism by practicing a state terrorism against an already devastated country and long-suffering people.

It is a project that reeks with "chosen race" and messianic notions of U.S. power and place in the world. It assumes the U.S. has the might and thus the right to impose a pax Americana on the world and secure its safety through unilateral preemptive aggressive actions against any suspected and vulnerable threats. But peace and the security it cultivates cannot be built on or depend on the whims and weapons of a superpower acting unilaterally and against the opinion and interests of the world. Peace is a self-conscious and cooperative task, a shared good achieved through justice, reaffirmed in freedom and reinforced in mutual respect for the rights and needs of all.

To act coercively and unilaterally outside international law and international institutions is not only to set a dangerous precedent of international vigilantism and further erode both international law and institutions. It also reinforces the evolving conception in the world that the U.S. is a superpower rogue state which dismisses international opinion, violates international norms and has no constraints or checks except what it wishes to impose on itself and is thus a real threat to the world. In such a context, the imperative of defense becomes one of arming like North Korea and not finding oneself vulnerable like Iraq.

A real concern for peace and security in the world must cultivate and sustain a comprehensive approach. It must realize there is no security without peace, no peace without justice, no justice without freedom and no freedom without the power of people over their destiny and daily lives everywhere whether in the U.S., Afghanistan, Iraq or Palestine. Thus, it must avoid the selective morality and hypocrisy of war on a weak Iraq and negotiation for a nuclear-armed North Korea, of approving Israel's possession of weapons of mass destruction and prohibiting other states in the region from having them with threats of attack, of waging war to free an occupied Kuwait, and vetoing and dismissing initiatives to end the Israeli occupation of Palestine. Likewise, peace for the Middle East and the world must include the liberation and statehood of Palestine, self-determination or autonomy for the Kurds, freedom for other oppressed peoples, justice for all and the elimination of weapons of mass destruction in the region and the world.

The long and difficult task to eliminate WMD's in the region and the world requires: 1) rejection of the double standard which permits WMD's for racially and politically favored countries and prohibits them for others; 2) strict observance of conventions against them for all countries, large and small; 3) continuing negotiation for reduction and elimination of them; 4) reinforced systems of safeguard for existing ones; 5) eliminating export of them and related technologies; and 6) an earnest and ongoing struggle to ultimately eliminate armed force as a means of settling conflict among the nations and people of the world. This protracted struggle, the ancestors assure us in the *Husia,* requires a morality of self-discipline, hard work, patience and peaceful practices that "transforms our enemies into allies and our foes into friends." And at the heart of these practices must be an *ethics of sharing,* a genuine commitment to and equitable sharing of all the goods of the world. This includes: *shared status* with no superior or inferior people or person and respect for all as equal bearers of dignity and divinity; *shared knowledge* in its most profound and useful forms as a human right; *shared space* of neighborhood, country, environment and the world; *shared wealth* and resources of the world; *shared power* in self-determination and democracy; *shared interests* which are life-affirming and life-enhancing; and *shared responsibility* for building the good and sustainable world we all want and deserve to live in.

BARACK H. OBAMA
(1961–)

Barack Obama is currently the junior senator from the state of Illinois and a leading Democratic candidate for president in 2008. Obama was born in Hawaii, August 4, 1961. A product of mixed-race heritage, Obama's mother was white from a small town in Kansas and his father was Kenyan. They met at the University of Hawaii as students. Although Obama spent most of his early life in Hawaii, from ages six to ten he lived in Indonesia with his mother and stepfather. As a young adult, Obama moved to New York and graduated from Columbia University in 1983. He then earned a law degree from Harvard University, where he became distinguished as the first African American president of the *Harvard Law Review*. Because of his concern for disadvantaged people, Obama chose to put his corporate law career on hold to become a community organizer and later a civil rights lawyer in Chicago. He eventually ran for office and served in the Illinois Senate for eight years. During his tenure as a state legislator, Obama was selected to deliver the keynote address at the Democratic National Convention in 2004. That same year he was elected to the United States Senate, becoming the third African American since Reconstruction to serve in the prestigious legislative body. As a member of the Senate Obama has championed the Earned Income Tax Credit, early childhood education, and ethics reform. As a presidential candidate, Obama has spoken out against the war in Iraq and has called for a gradual withdrawal of troops. Below is his floor statement on the Iraq War.

Floor Statement of Senator Barack Obama on Iraq Debate
Wednesday, June 21, 2006

Mr. President, in October of 2002, I delivered a speech opposing the War in Iraq.

I said that Saddam Hussein was a ruthless man, but that he posed no imminent and direct threat to the United States.

I said that a war in Iraq would take our focus away from our efforts to defeat al-Qaeda.

And, with a volatile mix of ethnic groups and a complicated history, I said that the invasion and occupation of Iraq would require a U.S. occupation of undetermined length, at undetermined cost, with undetermined consequences.

In short, I felt the decision unfolding then to invade Iraq was being made without a clear rationale, based more on ideology and politics than fact and reason.

It is with no great pleasure that I recall this now. Too many young men and women have died. Too many have been maimed. Too many hearts have been broken. I fervently wish I had been wrong about this war; that my concerns had been unfounded.

America and the American people have paid a high price for the decision to invade Iraq and myriad mistakes that followed. I believe that history will not judge the authors of this war kindly.

For all these reasons, I would like nothing more than to support the Kerry Amendment; to bring our brave troops home on a date certain, and spare the American people more pain, suffering and sorrow.

But having visited Iraq, I'm also acutely aware that a precipitous withdrawal of our troops, driven by Congressional edict rather than the realities on the ground, will not undo the mistakes made by this Administration. It could compound them.

It could compound them by plunging Iraq into an even deeper and, perhaps, irreparable crisis.

We must exit Iraq, but not in a way that leaves behind a security vacuum filled with terrorism, chaos, ethnic cleansing and genocide that could engulf large swaths of the Middle East and endanger America. We have both moral and national security reasons to manage our exit in a responsible way.

I share many of the goals set forth in the Kerry Amendment. We should send a clear message to the Iraqis that we won't be there forever, and that by next year our primary role should be to conduct counter-insurgency actions, train Iraqi security forces, and provide needed logistical support.

Moreover, I share the frustration with an Administration whose policies with respect to Iraq seem to simply repeat the simple-minded refrains of "we know best" and "stay the course." It's not acceptable to conduct a war where our goals and strategies drift aimlessly regardless of the cost in lives or dollars spent, and where we end up with arbitrary, poll-driven troop reductions by the Administration—the worst of all possible outcomes.

As one who strongly opposed the decision to go to war and who has met with servicemen and women injured in this conflict and seen the pain of the parents and loved ones of those who have died in Iraq, I would like nothing more than for our military involvement to end.

But I do not believe that setting a date certain for the total withdrawal of U.S. troops is the best approach to achieving, in a methodical and responsible way, the three basic goals that should drive our Iraq policy: that is, (1) stabilizing Iraq and giving the factions within Iraq the space they need to forge a political settlement; (2) containing and ultimately defeating the insurgency in Iraq; and (3) bringing our troops safely home.

What is needed is a blueprint for an expeditious yet responsible exit from Iraq. A hard and fast, arbitrary deadline for withdrawal offers our commanders in the field, and our diplomats in the region, insufficient flexibility to implement that strategy.

For example, let's say that a phased withdrawal results in fifty thousand troops in Iraq by July 19, 2007. If, at that point, our generals and the Iraqi government tell us that having those troops in Iraq for an additional three or six months would enhance stability and security in the region, this amendment would potentially prevent us from pursuing the optimal policy.

It is for this reason that I cannot support the Kerry Amendment. Instead, I am a cosponsor of the Levin Amendment, which gives us the best opportunity to find this balance between our need to begin a phase-down and our need to help stabilize Iraq. It tells the Iraqis that we won't be there forever so that they need to move forward on uniting and securing their country. I agree with Senator Warner that the message should be "we really mean business, Iraqis, get on with it." At the same time, the amendment also provides the Iraqis the time and the opportunity to accomplish this critical goal.

Essential to a successful policy is the Administration listening to its generals and diplomats and members of Congress—especially those who disagree with their policies and believe it is time to start bringing our troops home.

The overwhelming majority of the Senate is already on record voting for an amendment stating that calendar year 2006 should be a period of significant transition to full Iraqi sovereignty, with Iraqi security forces taking the lead for the security, creating the conditions for the phased redeployment of United States forces from Iraq. The Levin Amendment builds on this approach.

The White House should follow this principle as well. Visiting Iraq for a few hours cannot resuscitate or justify a failed policy. No amount of spin or photo opportunities can change the bottom line: this war has been poorly conceived and poorly managed by the White House, and that is why it has been so poorly received by the American people..

And it's troubling to already see Karl Rove in New Hampshire, treating this as a political attack opportunity instead of a major national challenge around which to rally the country.

There are no easy answers to this war. I understand that many Americans want to see our troops come home. The chaos, violence, and horrors in Iraq are gut-wrenching reminders of what our men and women in uniform, some just months out of high school, must confront on a daily basis. They are doing this heroically, they are doing this selflessly, and more than 2,500 of them have now made the ultimate sacrifice for our country.

Not one of us wants to see our servicemen and women in harm's way a day longer than they have to be. And that's why we must find the most responsible way to bring them home as quickly as possible, while still leaving the foundation of a secure Iraq that will not endanger the free world.

Notes

1. Ronald W. Walters, *Freedom Is Not Enough: Black Voters, Black Candidates, and American Presidential Politics* (Lanham, Md.: Rowman & Littlefield, 2005), 57.

2. Hanes Walton Jr. and Robert C. Smith, *American Politics and the African American Quest for Universal Freedom* (New York: Pearson/Longman, 2006), 237.

3. Walton and Smith, *American Politics*, 211.

4. Dewayne Wickham, *Bill Clinton and Black America* (New York: Ballantine, 2002), 49–50.

5. Wickham, *Bill Clinton*, 60.

6. Walters, *Freedom*, 160.

7. U.S. Bureau of the Census, *Income, Poverty, and Valuation of Noncash Benefits*, Current Population Reports Series P60-188, 1993. U.S. Bureau of the Census, Housing and Economic Household Statistics Division, Poverty and Health and Statistics Branch, *Historical Poverty Tables: Current Population Survey, Annual Social and Economic Supplements*, 2006.

8. "President Seeks Better Implementation of Don't Ask, Don't Tell," *CNN News*, December 11, 1999.

9. Kai Wright, *Soldiers of Freedom: An Illustrated History of African Americans in the Armed Forces* (New York: Black Dog & Leventhal, 2002), 72; "President Clinton Awards Medals of Honor to Corporal Andrew Jackson Smith and President Teddy Roosevelt," aired January 16, 2001, 11:45 a.m.

10. Wright, *Soldiers of Freedom*.

11. Wright, *Soldiers of Freedom*.

12. Wright, *Soldiers of Freedom*, 108.

13. R. W. Apple Jr. "Analysis: Africa Faces Hurdles, Despite Clinton's Optimism," April 3, 1998, at www.nytimes.com; James Bennett, "On the African Stage, the Clintons Share Top Billing," April 3, 1998, at www.nytimes.com.

14. William Jefferson Clinton, *My Life* (New York: Knopf, 2004), 593.

15. Vin Weber, "A Crisis of Competence: Failure of Clinton Administration's Foreign Policies," *National Review*, November 15, 1993.

16. Walters, *Freedom*, 95.

17. Anthony Lewis, "Texas Executions: G. W. Bush Has Defined Himself, Unforgettably, as Shallow and Callous," *New York Times*, June 17, 2000.

18. Walters, *Freedom*, 97.

19. See Douglas Kellner, *Grand Theft 2000: Media Spectacle and a Stolen Election* (Lanham, Md.: Rowman & Littlefield, 2001).

20. Walters, *Freedom*, 103–5.

21. Walton and Smith, *American Politics*, 203.

22. Walton and Smith, *American Politics*, 204.

23. Walton and Smith, *American Politics*, 211.

24. Dean Baker, "Empty Promise: The Benefit to African American Men of Private Accounts under President Bush's Social Security Plan," at www.cepr.net.

25. Frontline, "Hunting Osama Bin Laden: Who Is Osama Bin Laden and What Does He Want?" at www.pbs.org/wgbh/pages/frontline.

26. Richard F. Grimmett, *Authorization for the Use of Military Force in Response to the 9/11 Attacks* (P.L. 107-40), Legislative History, CRS Report for Congress, January 4, 2006, Order Code RS 22357.

27. Cheryl Poinsette Brown, "Patriotism Comes in Black," in *The Paradox of Loyalty: An African American Response to the War on Terrorism*, ed. Julianne Malveaux and Reginna Green (Chicago: Third World Press, 2002), 30.

28. Bishop T. D. Jakes, "The Gathering of America," in *9.11.01: African American Leaders Respond to an American Tragedy*, ed. Martha Simmons and Frank A. Thomas (Valley Forge, Pa.: Judson Press, 2001), 21–25.

29. Larry Elder, "Anti-War Demonstrators Ignore Iraqi Terror," *World Net Daily*, March 13, 2003.

30. Earl Ofari Hutchinson, "Not All Blacks Say 'No' to Iraq War," *Namibian*, April 14, 2003.

31. David L. Phillips, *Losing Iraq* (Boulder, Colo.: Westview Press, 2005), 222; Central Intelligence Agency, *Comprehensive Report of the Special Advisor to the DCI on Iraq's WMD*, September 30, 2004.

32. Walters, *Freedom*, 195. Also see CNN election results for a tally of Bush's support; "CNN American Votes 2004," www.cnn.com.

33. Quoted in Eugene Kane, *Milwaukee Journal Sentinel*, August 27, 2005, at www.jsonline.com.

34. Bob Woodward, *Plan of Attack* (New York: Simon & Schuster, 2004), 148–53.

35. Woodward, *Plan*, 150.

36. Woodward, *Plan*, 156–57.

37. Press release, Congresswoman Barbara Lee, "Regarding War with Iraq," Barbara Lee Official Home Page, September 12, 2002.

38. Michael Eric Dyson, "What Have I Left?" in *9.11.01: African American Leaders Respond to an American Tragedy*, ed. Martha Simmons and Frank A. Thomas (Valley Forge, Pa.: Judson Press, 2001), 67–78.

39. Dyson, "What Have I Left?"

40. Jessica Wehrman, "Fragging Stirs Memories of Vietnam," *America at War*, March 24, 2003, at www.capitolhillblue.com.

41. Manual Franzia, "Army Soldier Is Convicted in Attack on Fellow Troops," *Washington Post*, April 22, 2005.

42. Eric Ruder, "Muslim Soldier Gets the Death Penalty, While Politicians Forgive Murder in Iraq," *Socialist Worker*, May 6, 2005, 1–2.

43. Evette Porter, "Speaking Out: Black Americans Talk about the War," March 22, 2004, at www.africana.com.

44. Thulani Davis, "Post–9-11 Civil Rights: If You're Black, Who's Got Your Back?" *Village Voice*, December 18–24, 2002, at www.villagevoice.com.

45. Hugh B. Price and Kim Gandy, "Don't Sacrifice the Poor," *Washington Post*, October 15, 2001.

46. Ronald W. Walters, "Collateral Damage and the Iraq War," December 8, 2003, at www.blackpressusa.com.

47. Amy Belasco, *The Cost of Iraq, Afghanistan and Other Global War on Terror Operations since 9/11*, CRS Report for Congress, April 24, 2006, 7–8.

48. Michael Dyson, *Come Hell or High Water: Hurricane Katrina and the Color of Disaster* (New York: Basic Civitas, 2006).

49. Rick Bragg, *I Am a Soldier, Too: The Jessica Lynch Story* (New York: Knopf, 2003), 193.

50. Lee Hockstader, "Insult to Injury: Raw Deal for Jessica Lynch's Black Comrade-in-Arms," *Sydney Morning Herald*, October 25, 2003.

51. Bragg, *I Am a Soldier*, 71.

52. "Are African-American Soldiers and War Veterans Being Treated Differently?" *New York Beacon*, November 3, 2003; Nicholas D. Kristof, "Saving Private Jessica," *New York Times*, June 20, 2003.

53. Amy Goodman, "Mother of First Soldier from Georgia Killed in Iraq Also Demands to Speak with Bush," August 22, 2005, at www.democracynow.org.

54. Tom Philpott, "Analysis: Study Shows 41 Percent Drop in Number of Black Army Recruits since 2000," *Stars and Stripes*, March 4, 2005.

55. Philpott, "Analysis"; Tom Regan, "Blacks, Women Avoiding US Army," *Christian Science Monitor*, March 9, 2005.

56. Greg Zoroya, "A Portrait of the Dead," *USA Today*, September 8, 2004.

~

Source Acknowledgments

1. Revolutionary War

Banneker, Benjamin, "Letter to the Secretary of State. A Plan of Peace-Officer for the United States," published as *Copy of a Letter from Benjamin Banneker to the Secretary of State, with his Answer*, Philadelphia, 1792. It originally appeared in the almanac in 1793, and was made accessible by P. Lee Phillips, "The Negro Benjamin Banneker: Astronomer and Mathematician," *Records of the Columbia Historical Society* 20 (1917): 114–20.

Griffin, Ned. "Petition to the General Assembly of the State of North Carolina." Reprinted in *A Documentary History of the Negro People in the US*, vol. 1, *From the Colonial Times through the Civil War*, edited by Herbert Aptheker, 13–14. New York: Carol, 1951.

Hill, Lancaster, et al. "Massachusetts Slaves Petition for Freedom." In *Colored Patriots of the American Revolution*, edited by William C. Nell, 47. New York: Arno Press and the *New York Times*, 1968.

King, Boston. "Memoirs of the Life of Boston King: A Black Preacher. Written by Himself, during his Residence at Kingswood-School." *The Methodist Magazine (London)*, March 1798.

Wheatley, Phillis. "To His Excellency General Washington." *Pennsylvania Magazine*, April 1776.

2. War of 1812

"Confessions of a Virginia Rebel." In *Calendar of Virginia State Papers*, edited by H. W. Flournoy, vol. 10, 120–23. Richmond, Virginia: 1892.

Cuffe, Paul. "Letter to William Allen." In *Paul Cuffe: Black America and the African Return*, edited by Sheldon H. Harris, 181–82. 1812; New York: Simon & Schuster, 1972.

Delany, Martin Robinson. *The Condition, Elevation, Emigration and Destiny of the Colored People of the United States*. Amherst, N.Y.: Humanity, 2004. "Politically Considered" was originally privately printed in Philadelphia in 1852.

Roberts, James. *The Narrative of James Roberts, Soldier in the Revolutionary War and at the Battle of New Orleans*, 13–17. Chicago: printed for/by the author, 1858.

3. Civil War

Brown, William Wells. "A Demand for the Black Man." *Liberator*, May 16, 1862.

Delany, Martin. "Recruiting Black Troops for the Civil War." Reprint from ms. in War Records Office, National Archives, Washington, D.C.

Douglass, Frederick. "Men of Color, To Arms!" In *A Documentary History of the Negro People in the US*, vol. 1, *From the Colonial Times through the Civil War*, edited by Herbert Aptheker, 477–80. New York: Carol, 1951.

Gooding, James Henry. "Letter to the Editors." *Mercury*, August 21, 1863.

Truth, Sojourner. "The Valiant Soldier." In *Narrative of Sojourner Truth; A Bondswoman of Olden Time, With a History of Her Labors and Correspondence Drawn from Her "Book of Life."* 1881. Electronic reprint, edited by Olive Gilbert and Frances W. Titus. Reprinted with the permission of UNC Chapel Hill, "Documenting the American South."

Tubman, Harriet. "Letter to Franklin Sanborn." *Boston Commonwealth*, July 17, 1863.

4. Spanish-American and Philippines-American Wars

Du Bois, W. E. B. "The Philippine Mulatto." In *An ABC of Color*, 148–49. New York: International Publishers, 1925. Reprinted with permission of International Publishers Co., Inc., New York.

Fortune, Thomas T. "The Filipino: Some Incidents of a Trip through the Island of Luzon." *Voice of the Negro* 1 (June 1904): 240–46.

Saddler, Sergeant M. W. "The Patriotism of the Sons of Ham." *Freeman*, July 30, 1898, and August 27, 1898.

Turner, Henry McNeal. "The Quarrel with Spain." *Voice of Missions*, July 1898.

———. "The Negro and the Army." *Voice of Missions*, May 1899.

Washington, Booker T. "An Address in the National Peace Jubilee." In *The Booker T. Washington Papers*, edited by Louis R. Harlan and Raymond W. Smock, vol. 4, 490–92. Urbana: University of Illinois Press, 1975.

5. World War I

Du Bois, W. E. B. "Close Ranks." *Crisis*, July 16, 1918.

———. "Returning Soldiers." *Crisis*, May 18, 1919.

Garvey, Marcus. *Philosophy and Opinions of Marcus Garvey*, edited by Amy Jacques-Garvey, 93–94, 96. New York: Atheneum, 1980. Reprinted with permission of Scribner, an imprint of Simon & Schuster Adult Publishing Group.

Johnson, Jack, and Dick Schnaap. *Jack Johnson Is a Dandy; An Autobiography*, 108–9, 240–41, 242. New York: Chelsea House, 1969.

McKay, Claude. "If We Must Die." *Liberator* 2 (July 1919).

N.A.A.C.P., Washington, D.C. branch. "What the N.A.A.C.P. Has Done for the Colored Soldier: 1918." Four-page leaflet. Reprinted in *A Documentary History of the Negro People in the US 1910-1932*, vol. 3, *From the N.A.A.C.P. to the New Deal*, edited by Herbert Aptheker, 207–8. New York: Carol, 1973.

Randolph, A. Philip, and Chandler Owen. "Who Shall Pay for the War?" *Messenger*, November 1917.

———. "Negroes to Be at Peace Conference in Europe." *Messenger*, January 1918.

———. "Pro-Germanism among Negroes." *Messenger*, July 1918, 13.

Scott, Emmett Jay. "The Negro and the War Department." *Crisis* 15 (December 1917), 76. Reprinted in *A Documentary History of the Negro People in the US 1910-1932*, vol. 3, *From the N.A.A.C.P. to the New Deal*, edited by Herbert Aptheker, 194–95. New York: Carol, 1973.

Wells, Ida B. *Crusade for Justice: The Autobiography of Ida B. Wells*, 367–70. Chicago: University of Chicago Press, 1970. Reprinted with permission of University of Chicago Press.

6. World War II

Hughes, Langston. "My America." In *What the Negro Wants*, edited by Rayford W. Logan. Chapel Hill: University of North Carolina Press, 1944. Reprinted with permission of University of North Carolina Press.

Powell, Adam Clayton, Jr. "Is This a White Man's War?" *Common Sense* 11.4 (April 1942): 111–13.

Randolph, A. Philip. "A Call to the Negro American to March on Washington." *The Black Worker*, May 1941.

Rustin, Bayard. "Letter to the Draft Board." In *Time on Two Crosses: The Collected Writings of Bayard Rustin*, edited by Devon W. Carbado and Donald Weise, 11–13. San Francisco: Cleis Press, 2003. Reprinted with permission of Cleis Press.

White, Walter. "White Supremacy and World War I." Speech given at the NAACP War Emergency Conference (July 12–16). Reprinted in *A Documentary History of the Negro People in the United States*, vol. 4, *From the New Deal to the End of World War II*, edited by Herbert Aptheker, 474. New York: Carol, 1992.

William, Hastie H. "Why I Resigned." *Chicago Defender*, February 6, 1943. Reprinted in *The Negro American: A Documentary History*, edited by Leslie H. Fishel and Benjamin Quarles, 473–76. Glenview, Ill.: Scott Foresman, 1967. Reprinted with permission of the *Chicago Defender*.

Yergan, Max. "Relation of Negros to War." Reprinted with permission of the Moorland Spingarn Collection, Howard University, Max Yergan Vertical File, n.d.

7. Korean War

Bethune, Mary McLeod. "Warns Those on Home Front of Their Debt to Boys in Korea." *Chicago Defender*, September 16, 1950, 6. Reprinted with permission of the *Chicago Defender*.

———. "The Huge Job of Civil Defense Is Protection of All People." *Chicago Defender*, May 19, 1951, 6. Reprinted with permission of the *Chicago Defender*.

Marshall, Thurgood. "The Reminiscences of Thurgood Marshall." Reprinted with permission from the Oral History Collection of Columbia University.

Robeson, Paul. "Denouncing the Korean Intervention." Speech given at rally sponsored by the Civil Rights Congress, Madison Square Garden, New York City, June 28, 1950. Press release, Council on African Affairs, June 29, 1950. Reprinted in *Paul Robeson Speaks: Writings, Speeches, and Interviews 1918–1974*, 252–53. New York: Brunner/Mazel, 1978. Reprinted with permission of Paul Robeson Jr.

Scott, Beverly. "One Man's War." In *No Bugles, No Drums: An Oral History of the Korean War*, edited by Rudy Tomedi, 175–83. New York: Wiley, 1993. Reprinted with permission of John Wiley & Sons, Inc.

8. Vietnam War

Ali, Muhammad. "The Champ." In *We Won't Go: Personal Accounts of War Objectors*, edited by Alice Lynd, 226–34. Boston: Beacon, 1968. Reprinted with permission of Beacon Press, Boston.

Bunche, Ralph. "Race and Vietnam." In *Ralph Bunche: The Man and His Time*, edited by Benjamin Rivlin, 259. New York: Holmes & Meyer, 1990. Reprinted with permission of Ms. Joan Bunche and Dr. Benjamin Rivlin.

Keyes, Alan L. "The Blessings of Liberty, the Blessings of Life." The American Legion, San Antonio, Texas (1967). Reprinted with permission of the American Legion.

King, Martin Luther, Jr. "A Time to Break the Silence." Speech delivered April 4, 1967, at Riverside Church in New York City. In *Freedomways Readers: Prophets in Their Own Country*, no. 2, edited by Esther Cooper Jackson, 167–75. Boulder, Colo.: Westview Press, 1967.

Newton, Huey P. *To Die for the People: The Writings of Huey P. Newton*, 178–85, 182–85. New York: Random House, 1972. Reprinted with the permission of Random House Inc.

Rowan, Carl Thomas. "Martin Luther King's Tragic Decision." *Reader's Digest* 91, no. 545 (September 1967): 37–42. Reprinted with permission of *Reader's Digest*.

X, Malcolm. "Two Minutes on Vietnam." Answer to question, Militant Labor Forum, January 7, 1965, which appeared in *Malcolm X Speaks*. Grove/Atlantic, 1965. Reprinted with permission of Clyde Taylor.

9. Persian Gulf War

Dellums, Ronald. "Shedding the Mentality of War Brinkmanship Got Us into This, but We Could Still Step Back from the Edge of Ground Fighting." *Los Angeles Times*, February 14, 1991.

Howse, Azania. "The War against Us All." *Anti-Warrior*, published by the GI Refusnix, ed., January 3, 1992. Reprinted with permission of Jeff Patterson, *Anti-Warrior Newspaper*.

Jackson, Jesse, Sr. "Ignore Bush's Ploys: Vote for Change." *Newsday*, November 5, 1990.

Jackson, Jesse, Sr. "An Ironic Deadline for the Gulf Crisis." *Newsday*, December 10, 1990. Reprinted with permission of Reverend Jesse Jackson.

Payne, Donald. "The Reconstruction of Kuwait." Statement before Senate, March 12, 1991. 102nd Cong., 2nd sess., *Congressional Record*, H1653.

Young, Andrea, and Stanley Knighton. "Race and War in the Persian Gulf." *Washington Post*, February 2, 1991. Reprinted with permission of A. Knighton-Stanley.

10. Iraq War

Buckley, Gail. "Black Soldiers OK, Why Not Students?" At www.globalblacknews .com (April 26, 2003).

Chideya, Farai. "A Double Standard for Heroes?" At www.alternet.org (November 14, 2003). Reprinted with permission of Farai Chideya.

Congressional Black Caucus. "Statement on War with Iraq." March 18, 2003.

Karenga, Maulana. "A Statement on Peace, Justice and Resistance to War." *Harambee Notes* 3, nos. 1 and 2, 3–5, 7. Reprinted with permission of Maulana Karenga.

Lee, Barbara. "Regarding War with Iraq: Press Release." Barbara Lee Official Home Page. Ninth Congressional District of California. September 12, 2002.

Obama, Barack. "Floor Statement of Senator Barack Obama on Iraq Debate." www .obama.senate.gov, accessed June 21, 2006.

Powell, Colin L. "We Will Not Shrink from War." *Wall Street Journal*, February 2003. Reprinted at www.usinfo.state.gov.

Rangel, Charles. "War's Burden Must Be Shared: Press Release." Congressman Charles Rangel Official Site. At www.house.gov (January 7, 2003).

Rice, Condoleezza. "Why We Know Iraq Is Lying." *Wall Street Journal*, March 2003. Reprinted at www.usinfo.state.gov (February 12, 2004).

Sharpton, Al. "Presidential Campaign Speech." Take Back America Conference Campaign for America's Future, June 6, 2003.

Index

Edgerton, Robert, 107
Edwards, Alonzo, 112
Edwards, John, 305
Eighth New York Cavalry, 57
Eisenhower, Dwight D., 188, 189, 214, 215
Elbaradei, Mohamed, 305
El Caney, Battle of, 82
Elder, Larry, 304
11th U.S. Colored Troops, 58–59
emancipation: John Fremont's proclamation, 55–56; Lincoln and, 56, 57–58
Emancipation Proclamation, 57
Emergency War Conference, 169
Emerson, John, 52
emigration, proposals involving the Philippines, 86
emigration to Africa: Henry Turner and, 78; Martin Delany and, 32, 67; revolutionary era Black loyalists and, 14; War of 1812 and, 32–33, 36–37
entertainment industry, accused of un-American activities, 182
Equal Employment Opportunity Commission (EEOC), 261, 264
Equiano, Olaudah, 11
Espionage Act, 109
Ethiopia, 140, 142
"Ethiopian" brigade, 11
Europe, James Reese, 111
Executive Orders: No. 8802, 146, 151; No. 9066, 147; No. 9981, 151, 187
executive orders, establishing the Civil Rights Section, 144
expansionism, 4, 79

Fagan, David, 86
Fahrenheit 9/11 (documentary), 306
Fair Employment Practices Committee, 146, 151
Family and Medical Leave Act of 1993, 298

Farmer, James, 219
Farrakhan, Louis, 138
fascism, 140
Faubus, Orval, 185, 222
Federal Bureau of Investigation (FBI), 129, 145
Federal Deposit Insurance Corporation (FDIC), 139
Federal Employee Loyalty Program, 181
Fellowship for Reconciliation (FOR), 218
Ferdinand, Franz, 103
54th Massachusetts Infantry Regiment, 58, 70
Fletcher, Arthur, 264
Flipper, Henry Ossian, 299
Ford, Gerald, 224, 258
foreign policy: Bill Clinton, 299–300; Black nationalism on, 4; George H. W. Bush, 265–66; Jimmy Carter, 259–60
Forrest, Bedford, 58, 59
Forten, James, 32, 33, 39–40, 49, 50
Fort Huachuca, 112
Fort Pillow Massacre, 58–59
Fort Sumter, 54
Fortune, T. Thomas, 86, 87, 97–98
fragging, 223, 307
France: Black culture and, 111; honoring of Black soldiers, 110; Indochina and, 212, 213; Josephine Baker and, 185
Franco, Francisco, 140
Franklin, Benjamin, 11
Franklin, John Hope, 49, 298
Frasier, E. Franklin, 186
free Blacks: during the Revolutionary War, 11–13, 14; 1790 population, 14
Freedmen's Bureau, 67, 92
Freeman, Elizabeth (Mum Bett), 14
Free Soil Party, 50
Freetown, Sierra Leone, 14
Fremont, John C., 55–56

Minh, Ho Chi, 212–13, 214, 215, 217, 221
Missouri Compromise, 52
Mitchell, John, Jr., 81
Mondale, Walter, 262
Monroe, James, 79
Monroe Doctrine, 79
Montgomery bus boycotts, 210
Montgomery Improvement Association (MIA), 210
Moore, Michael, 306
Moscow Olympics, 260
Muhammad, Elijah, 138, 145
Muhammad, Wallace Fard, 138
mulattos, Filipino, 85–86, 99–100
Musicians United to Win without War, 308
Mussolini, Benito, 140

Nagasaki, 148
Namibia, 259
napalm, 217
Napoleon Bonaparte, 31
The Narrative of Sojourner Truth (Truth), 72
A Narrative of the Proceedings of the Black People During the Late Calamity in Philadelphia (Allen and Jones), 31
National Action Network, 322
National Advisory Commission on Civic Disorder, 211–12
National Association for the Advancement of Colored People (NAACP): activities during World War I, 105; Camp Logan crisis and, 112; civil rights movement and, 210; courts-martial of African American soldiers and, 188; Du Bois and, 99, 132, 185–86; formation of, 132; Ida B. Wells and, 106; lobbying for junior officers' training, 108; opposition to Clarence Thomas, 264; reaction to King's antiwar stance, 220; Thurgood

Marshall and, 194; Walter White and, 169; work done for African American soldiers in World War I, 132–33
"National Conversation on Race," 298
National Labor Relations Act, 146
National Liberation Front (NLF), 215
National Negro Congress (NNC), 183
National Organization for Women, 264
National Peace Jubilee, 87, 89–91
National Recovery Administration (NRA), 139
National Socialist German Workers Party (Nazi Party), 140
National Union for the Total Independence of Angola (UNITA), 265
National Urban League (NUL), 105, 210, 264
Nation of Islam, 138, 225, 229
Native Guards, 59
Navy Cross, 147
Nazi Germany, 140–41
Nazi Party, 140
The Negro World (newspaper), 129
Newby, Dangerfield, 52
New Deal, 139
"New Frontier" program, 215
New Jewel Movement, 262
New Markets Initiative, 298
New Orleans, Battle of, 32, 33, 38–39, 41–46
Newton, Huey P., 225, 250–52
Ngo Dinh Diem. *See* Diem, Ngo Dinh
Niagara Movement, 78, 99
Nixon, Richard M., 215, 220, 221, 224, 258
Nobel Peace Prize, 210, 236, 248
Non-Aligned Movement, 5
Noriega, Manuel, 267
North American Air Defense Command, 188
North Atlantic Treaty Organization (NATO), 214

~

About the Editor

Karin L. Stanford is assistant professor of Pan African studies and African American politics at California State University, Northridge. She has written numerous articles on African American politics and African Americans in the international arena. She is the author of several books and articles, including *Beyond the Boundaries: Rev. Jesse Jackson and International Affairs*. Dr. Stanford is also coeditor of *Black Political Organizations in the Post–Civil Rights Era* (New Brunswick, N.J.: Rutgers University Press, 2003). Her teaching interests are African American politics, African American social movements and the politics of hip-hop.